Cambridgeshire
2007-2(

Louise Bacon   Alison Cooper   Hugh Venables

Additional contributing authors

Peter Bircham   Derek Langslow
Roger Buisson   Vince Lea
Andy Cotton   Gavin Paterson
Mike Everett   Rob Pople
Peter Herkenrath   Doug Radford
Michael Holdsworth   Andrew Tongue
Charlie Kitchin

Cambridgeshire Bird Club 2013
ISBN: 978 0 902038 27 1

Cambridgeshire Bird Club 2013

Bacon, Cooper & Venables: Cambridgeshire Bird Atlas 2007-2011, Cambridge, 2013
is published under Creative Commons Licence CC BY-NC-ND 3.0

You are free to share, copy, distribute or transmit any of the text and maps; but rights in any illustrations remain with the artists, from whom specific permission should be sought. Ordnance Survey mapping data remains Crown Copyright. If sharing or copying any text or maps, you must attribute the atlas correctly, as above. You may not use the text or maps for commercial purposes. You may not alter, transform, or build upon the text or maps.

To purchase a copy, or for any other enquiries, see http://www.cambridgebirdclub.org.uk/

INTRODUCTION

This book is not a complete avifauna, or a site guide. It summarises four years of fieldwork (2007–11), in winter and in the breeding season, surveying the distribution and abundance of birds across Cambridgeshire. At a county level this has not been done before; whilst there were breeding-season surveys in 1979–83 (Hunts Atlas 1988) and 1988–92 (Cambs Atlas 1994), these concentrated on distribution and breeding status but not abundance. A winter survey at county scale has not been attempted previously, although data were collected to contribute to the national Wintering Atlas (Lack, 1986). The present survey was part of the British Trust for Ornithology (BTO) Bird Atlas project; many other counties have taken advantage of the BTO's online system to embark on county atlases. It represents a comprehensive snapshot of how birds use the diverse landscape of Cambridgeshire at the present time. Maps show both distribution and abundance taken from structured timed counts. In national terms, the BTO's Bird Atlas 2007–11 is the third breeding-season survey (these have been carried out at 20-year intervals) and the second wintering one. These surveys have become increasingly useful for determining changes in population size and geographic distribution – an invaluable information source for conservation and land-use planning.

Cambridgeshire geography

The modern county of Cambridgeshire covers 1,310 square miles (338,900 hectares). It is an amalgamation of the pre-1974 counties of Cambridgeshire, Huntingdonshire, and the area known as the Soke of Peterborough, which has been shunted variously through Huntingdonshire and Northamptonshire. It equates to the current (2012) administrative county of Cambridgeshire, and the Unitary Authority area of the City of Peterborough. The northernmost part (north-east corner) is only approximately 10 km from the coast (the Wash west of King's Lynn) whereas the most southerly point is only 40 km north of the M25.

Cambridgeshire weather and climate

Cambridgeshire has a drier, sunnier climate than average for England, with slightly warmer summers and colder winters, being sheltered from the prevailing westerly weather. The annual mean temperature in Cambridge is 10 °C, ranging from a mean low in January of 4.2 °C to a mean high in August of 17 °C. Between 1971 and 2000, there was an average of 42 days of air frost per year, concentrated in December to February; in the same period average rainfall was 554 mm, and annual mean sunshine 1,501 h. For comparison, the UK figures are: 8.6 °C mean temperature, 56 frost days, 1,126 mm rain and 1,355 h sunshine. During this atlas period (2007–11), we experienced two mild winters and two much harder ones; the winter of 2009/10 included the coldest December–February period since 1965. The four summers had temperatures above average, two damper and the last two drier – the summer of 2011 was the second driest for Eastern England on record (Met Ofice website).

Cambridgeshire landscape and geology

Cambridgeshire is essentially an agricultural landscape, with two main soil types: the clays and the flat, peaty fens. There are significant other geologies, with chalk in the south of the county, limestone between Peterborough and the Midlands, and similar conditions to the Brecks from north of Newmarket out to the Suffolk border, although the latter never reaches the prime biodiversity habitat of the true Brecks over the border in Norfolk and Suffolk. Much of the county is below the 5 m contour, and parts are even below sea-level, but the south and west are much higher and even could be described as gently hilly, rising to the heady heights of 146 m near Great Chishill, close to the Essex border.

Most of the agriculture is intensive arable; a landscape of wheat and oil-seed rape dominates much of the county both on the clay and fen soils. The latter are also notable for vegetable production; both fen soils and the southern chalk produce a wider variety of crops, including sugar beet, peas, and potatoes, than the two standard crops of the clay lands. The intensive arable nature of the farming means that much of the county is somewhat monocultural but still surprisingly important for birds, including nationally important numbers of some of our declining farmland birds. The fenland peaty or silty soils are often characterised by very large fields with ditches and tracks forming the only divisions; clay and chalk areas more frequently have hedges dividing fields, adding a three-dimensional aspect to the landscape.

Cambridgeshire is the least wooded county in England; approximately 3% of the county can be classified as woodland – mostly this is ancient woodland, or plantations on an ancient site, but there are also modern plantations and small areas of wet woodland. The English average woodland coverage is 8.4% and the British average 11%. Our largest woodlands are ancient woodlands, of which Bedford Purlieus, Monks Wood and Brampton Wood are the three largest at 211, 155 and 137 ha. These have a distinctive population of birds and often have a wider importance to the surrounding area due to connectivity supplied by hedgerows.

Probably our most important non-arable landscape is the range of wetland habitats which form so many of our key birdwatching sites. The remnant fens, whilst rich in biodiversity, are not necessarily as critical for birds as some other sites, such as the network of gravel pits along river valleys, and the washlands of several of our rivers. Two very large washlands, the Ouse and the Nene, were designed primarily to remove floodwater from large catchments in order to spare the surrounding fens from flooding. Regular flooding within the Washes has prevented arable farming there, and traditional grassland and water-management practices have ensured the survival of this wetland habitat. Consequently, these areas have become very significant bird sites year-round, although they face challenges in the 21st century as a result of changed rainfall patterns: flooding during the breeding season and insufficient rains in some winters. Smaller washlands can be found on other rivers – the Cam, the Lark and the Little Ouse are all embanked, with seasonally flooded grasslands alongside providing valuable habitat. Gravel pits are probably some of our most-watched sites, and proliferate along the Ouse valley and a little more widely in the Peterborough area as a result of gravel extraction and brick-making. This tendency to allow abandoned gravel-extraction sites to fill with water has provided areas of rich habitat, which have increased in extent during the past 20 years. The other significant water body in Cambridgeshire is Grafham Water, a 6.28 km² Anglian Water reservoir in central Huntingdonshire. In addition, there are two projects now underway to create extensive areas of fen and other wetland habitats on former arable land adjacent to existing fens. Other habitat-creation projects include reedbed creation on gravel or arable sites, and small private wetlands. However, together these wetlands and water bodies of all kinds comprise no more than 3% of the county. Whilst the draining of the fens is now a matter of history, and the amount of wetland has increased compared to 20 years ago, it is worth noting that Grafham Water is only approximately a quarter of the size of the ancient Whittlesey Mere, the largest of several meres which dominated the fens until 200 years ago when drainage commenced in earnest.

Our more minor habitats include important parts of the cultural and landscape history of the county. Orchards, whilst far less common than 20 years ago, still feature strongly in some parts of the county, and those managed on more traditional, less intensive, lines can provide very good habitat. In particular, orchards occur in the Wisbech area, the villages along the Ouse corridor such as Somersham, Bluntisham and across to Over, Willingham and Cottenham towards Cambridge, and they remain a local feature of south-west Cambridgeshire. Parkland is rarely considered by many birdwatchers, but west of Peterborough and in south-west Cambridgeshire there are several well-connected parkland areas containing a mix of woodland, tree-belts, grassland (often still grazed by livestock), and often a formal area next to the house.

Grassland is probably one of our scarcest habitats, especially away from rivers, amounting to less than 1% of the county; wet grasslands such as river washes are one of our most vital habitats for some of our scarcest or most declined breeding birds.

The Cambridgeshire Land-use Survey (unfortunately excluding Peterborough) provides useful information about land use and how it varies across different districts; it can be downloaded from the County Council website.

Cambridgeshire sites

Within this chequered landscape is a network of designated and protected sites, some of great significance for our bird populations, and as a consequence popular with birdwatchers. Several national or local charities own and manage nature reserves for the benefit of birds and other wildlife. There is a network of Sites of Special Scientific Interest (SSSIs), mostly designated for plants and invertebrates, of which many are privately owned but include footpaths for access. Many of our ancient woodlands are privately owned SSSIs; these can provide vital habitats for woodland birds. There is a network of County Wildlife Sites, a county-based designation with no absolute protection in law; none of these was chosen for their bird life, but they include many gravel pits that are undoubtedly key sites for waterbirds.

The RSPB owns several key reserves within the county, as well as managing an arable farm (Hope Farm, at Knapwell) which uses conventional techniques while pioneering simple environmentally beneficial measures which other farmers can adopt through environmental stewardship schemes. The RSPB reserves are some of the county's top sites for birds: the Ouse and Nene Washes, Fowlmere in the south, and the pioneering partnership with the aggregate industry in the Ouse valley which is creating the Ouse Fen wetlands. Additionally the RSPB now manages the former gravel workings at Fen Drayton Lakes, which lie to the east of St. Ives and extend almost to Swavesey. This complex of gravel pits, scrapes and grassland has a good network of trails and viewing hides and screens.

Fowlmere, once a commercial watercress bed, is now a complex of reedbed, wet woodland and an area of drier grassland. It is one of the few significant wetlands in the south of the county, and hosts large roosts of buntings, corvids and other birds, as well as a year-round array of wetland birds such as Water Rails, Little Grebes and Kingfishers.

The Ouse Fen complex, whilst relatively new, and with active gravel extraction still underway, is developing into a large reedbed and open-water complex along both sides of the River Ouse. It now reaches as far as Berry Fen, a wet grassland SSSI close to the Ouse Washes. The 2,400 ha Ouse Washes is one of the largest and most important freshwater wetlands in the UK; it is internationally important for wintering waterfowl and nationally important for breeding waterfowl. Habitat management primarily involves grazing to maintain a short sward. The Ouse Washes have been severely affected by the increasing frequency of flooding; spring flooding in particular has led to a decline in both the numbers and success of breeding birds, notably Black-tailed Godwits. Since 2000 wet grassland has been successfully created on land outside and adjacent to the Washes, to provide flood-free habitat for breeding waders. The Ouse Washes are split between Norfolk and Cambridgeshire: 58% is in Cambridgeshire and of this, 855 ha are owned by the RSPB, and 186 ha by the Wildlife Trust for Bedfordshire, Cambridgeshire and Northamptonshire.

In the north of the county, the floodplain meadows of the Nene Washes extend over 1,350 ha. While not so flood-prone as the Ouse Washes, they are also internationally important for wintering waterfowl and nationally important for breeding waterfowl. The RSPB manages 800 ha for a number of key breeding birds including Black-tailed Godwits, Snipe, Spotted Crakes and Cranes. The Washes are also the location for the RSPB re-introduction programme for Corncrakes.

Wildlife Trust nature reserves in Cambridgeshire

Since buying its first reserve in 1962 at Hayley Wood the Wildlife Trust for Bedfordshire, Cambridgeshire and Northamptonshire has gone on to protect all manner of wildlife habitats across 48 nature reserves in Cambridgeshire – from wetlands to chalk pits, and from hay meadows to ancient woodlands. Trust nature reserves are extremely varied and most are not primarily managed for birds. The Trust's aim is to improve, enlarge and connect them wherever possible. This way it is hoped to increase the variety and numbers of birds and other wildlife that they support – and also make them more resilient to climate change.

Trust reserves stretch from the black peat of the fens to the rolling white chalk of the Gog Magogs, from the limestone grassland and brick pits of Peterborough to the ancient woodlands, chalk streams and hay meadows of Huntingdonshire and South and East Cambridgeshire. Together they add up to a vital refuge for a wide array of the county's wildlife – shaped by both the soil and human use.

Some of the Trust's most important sites for birds are unimproved wet grasslands that are permanently grazed rather than cut for hay. Largest and most important of these is the Ouse Washes in Cambridgeshire where the Trust owns land alongside the RSPB. Lesser-known Mare Fen near Swavesey is a smaller but important reserve for overwintering waders and wildfowl, and provides a valuable refuge for waterfowl when water on the Washes is too deep. At the time of writing the Trust had just acquired the lease on another important site along the Ouse valley at Cow Lane gravel pits near Godmanchester, better known to the Bird Club as Godmanchester tip and pits.

Grafham Water is one of the prime birdwatching spots in the county. With nine miles of shoreline, and around 170 bird species recorded each year, there is always something to see. In partnership with Anglian Water, the Trust manages the nature reserve encircling the western side of the reservoir. Nationally important numbers of wintering wildfowl have earned the reservoir its SSSI status – including Coot, Tufted Ducks and Great Crested Grebes. Other winter visitors include Pochard, Goosander, Goldeneye and Wigeon. Grafham Water is a major draw for birders year-round, with deep water vital in winter, and during spring and autumn migration; it is one of Eastern England's few reliable sites for wintering Great Northern Divers. The lagoons, not part of the Trust reserve but part of the Anglian Water management, are valuable breeding areas for waders and wetland passerines. Additionally, the woodlands here have Nightingales and other declining woodland residents.

Dogsthorpe Star Pit in Peterborough is worthy of special mention. This former brickpit on the edge of Peterborough is a mixture of shallow pools, reedbed and hawthorn scrub where Bitterns, Marsh Harriers, Snipe and Tawny Owls can be seen or heard in season. The adjacent tip also has its attractions, mostly for those birders keen on gulls.

Moving to drier land, many of Cambridgeshire's surviving semi-natural ancient woodlands are protected by the Trust. Famous for their carpets of bluebells in late spring, places such as Hayley, Waresley and Lady's Wood are also home to Treecreepers, woodpeckers and Marsh Tits. Ancient hay meadows fringed with old hedgerows such as those at Houghton, Chettisham, Soham and Upwood Meadows provide a flower-rich setting where Turtle Doves, Bullfinches and a variety of warblers may be seen. By contrast, newly created grasslands managed by the Trust at Cambourne have become one of the most highly productive breeding areas for Skylarks locally as well as providing for a wide variety of suburban and other grassland birds. Cambourne's lakes also provide an occasional migration stopover and breeding and wintering habitat for several waterfowl.

Most Wildlife Trust reserves are freely open to the public at all times; for a full list see the map opposite or visit www.wildlifebcn.org

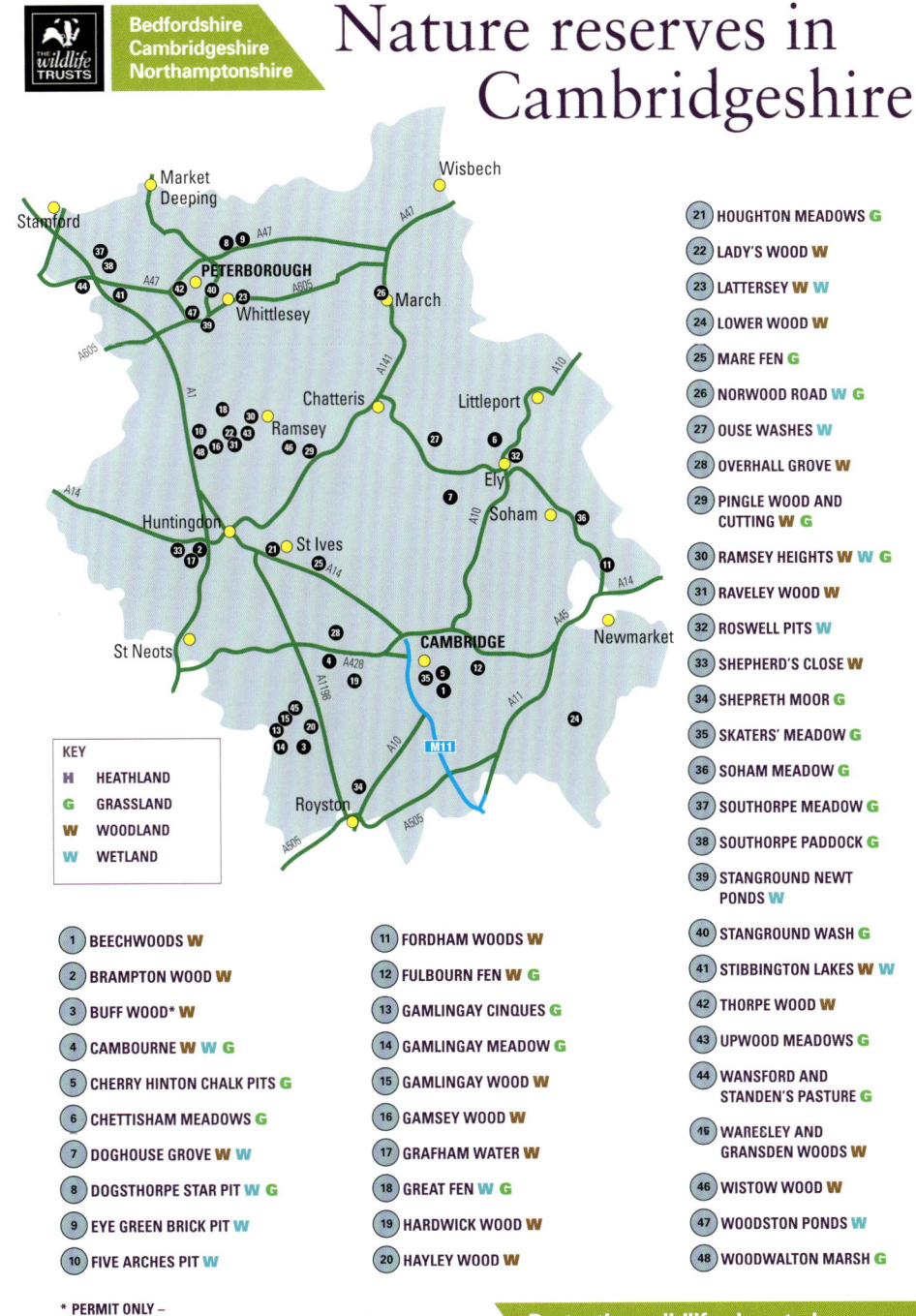

Nature reserves in Cambridgeshire

Bedfordshire Cambridgeshire Northamptonshire — The Wildlife Trusts

KEY
- **H** HEATHLAND
- **G** GRASSLAND
- **W** WOODLAND
- **W** WETLAND

#	Reserve	Type
1	BEECHWOODS	W
2	BRAMPTON WOOD	W
3	BUFF WOOD*	W
4	CAMBOURNE	W G
5	CHERRY HINTON CHALK PITS	G
6	CHETTISHAM MEADOWS	G
7	DOGHOUSE GROVE	W W
8	DOGSTHORPE STAR PIT	W G
9	EYE GREEN BRICK PIT	W
10	FIVE ARCHES PIT	W
11	FORDHAM WOODS	W
12	FULBOURN FEN	W G
13	GAMLINGAY CINQUES	G
14	GAMLINGAY MEADOW	G
15	GAMLINGAY WOOD	W
16	GAMSEY WOOD	W
17	GRAFHAM WATER	W
18	GREAT FEN	W G
19	HARDWICK WOOD	W
20	HAYLEY WOOD	W
21	HOUGHTON MEADOWS	G
22	LADY'S WOOD	W
23	LATTERSEY	W W
24	LOWER WOOD	W
25	MARE FEN	G
26	NORWOOD ROAD	W G
27	OUSE WASHES	W
28	OVERHALL GROVE	W
29	PINGLE WOOD AND CUTTING	W G
30	RAMSEY HEIGHTS	W W G
31	RAVELEY WOOD	W
32	ROSWELL PITS	W
33	SHEPHERD'S CLOSE	W
34	SHEPRETH MOOR	G
35	SKATERS' MEADOW	G
36	SOHAM MEADOW	G
37	SOUTHORPE MEADOW	G
38	SOUTHORPE PADDOCK	G
39	STANGROUND NEWT PONDS	W
40	STANGROUND WASH	G
41	STIBBINGTON LAKES	W W
42	THORPE WOOD	W
43	UPWOOD MEADOWS	G
44	WANSFORD AND STANDEN'S PASTURE	G
45	WARESLEY AND GRANSDEN WOODS	W
46	WISTOW WOOD	W
47	WOODSTON PONDS	W
48	WOODWALTON MARSH	G

* **PERMIT ONLY** – please obtain permission from the Trust before visiting this site

Protecting wildlife close to home

Although the RSPB and the Wildlife Trust clearly play a vital role in managing key birdwatching sites in the county, there are also several National Nature Reserves (NNRs) managed by Natural England. Woodwalton Fen and Holme Fen, both among the last remnants of true fenland and the latter one of lowland England's largest damp birch woodlands, are both good sites for birds such as wintering finches like redpolls and also for wetland species. Additionally, a partnership with the Wildlife Trust and others, the Great Fen Project is a landscape project connecting these two reserves and re-creating significant areas of wet grassland, fen, etc.; this will become a major bird site as the habitats increase and improve from their arable starting point a decade ago. There are other key NNRs for birds – Castor Hanglands and Monks Wood, both large areas of ancient woodland and scrub, providing vital areas for some of our most declining woodland birds such as Lesser Spotted Woodpeckers and Nightingales. Chippenham Fen is also an NNR; despite restricted access away from a single footpath it is still a good site to listen for wetland warblers, breeding Woodcock and other fenland birds.

The other large remnant of fen at Wicken, managed by the National Trust, is also the focal point of a large wetland restoration project. The core of the Wicken complex, the old Wicken Fen reserve, is a wonderful place, but arguably equally good for birds are the newer habitats to the south and east: Adventurer's Fen (now well established) and the newer, wet grassland, pools and fen creation at Baker's Fen and Tubney Fen out towards the villages of Burwell and Reach. These are proving extremely valuable for species such as breeding waders, hunting raptors, Barn Owls, etc. The Wicken Vision is to increase this wetland still further over the next decades, down along the Cam towards Cambridge.

The National Trust also owns Wimpole Hall in the south-west of the county, and the parkland is proving to be a good spot for woodland species, with regular Raven sightings, and the pools seem to be a county stronghold of Mandarins. It is increasingly on the radar of county birdwatchers, and this area also supports a range of farmland birds as well as the woodland and parkland specialists, especially those restricted to the south-west of the county.

Returning to the Ouse valley, Paxton Pits is probably the other significant site worthy of mention. Managed by Huntingdonshire District Council away from the area still officially an active gravel working, the site is important for its wintering wildfowl, passage waders, and Nightingale population, which, along with that of Castor Hanglands, is one of the largest in the county.

There are many other sites in the county – this summary seeks to highlight just a few of the best. The Cambridgeshire Bird Club and the Peterborough Bird Club websites both list their more important sites in a gazetteer, and provide short articles on these. The map on the back cover of this book highlights some of the significant sites for birders in the county.

Atlas methods

The standard mapping units of a county atlas are the tetrad and the 10 km square, the latter becoming more important when mapping at a national scale. A tetrad is a 2 km x 2 km square inside the 10 km squares of the UK national coordinate grid system, i.e. an area of 4 km², and is a handy land parcel for a survey. Tetrads are lettered A–Z (omitting O) in columns from the bottom left corner of a 10 km square. Thus, TL57H is the four 1 km squares TL5274, 5374, 5275, and 5375. The figure opposite illustrates this system.

At the planning stage of the national atlas, the BTO approached county bird clubs to determine whether they were planning to carry out a county atlas as part of the national atlas period. This allowed us to tie our fieldwork and data collection into the BTO system, cutting out issues of design and planning and leaving the simple task of how to cover 969 tetrads effectively over four years. The minimum target for the national atlas was to have timed visits from eight tetrads in each 10 km square; ideally for our county atlas we wanted to cover as many as possible of the 25 tetrads in each 10 km square. Previous national atlases had focused on distribution and to some extent abundance but this time the use of timed visits of either one or two hours, twice in summer and twice in winter, to a chosen tetrad with counts of each species seen or heard were expected to provide both distribution and abundance data. The summer surveys also included an assessment of breeding activity, which is vital for mapping breeding-season distributions effectively. Experimental fieldwork showed that a visit of 1–2 h was sufficient to record about 80% of the expected birds in a square; the species list and breeding observations could be augmented using roving records, taken from random observations, targeted walks or other surveys but not of a timed nature (meaning that they could be used for distribution but not abundance data).

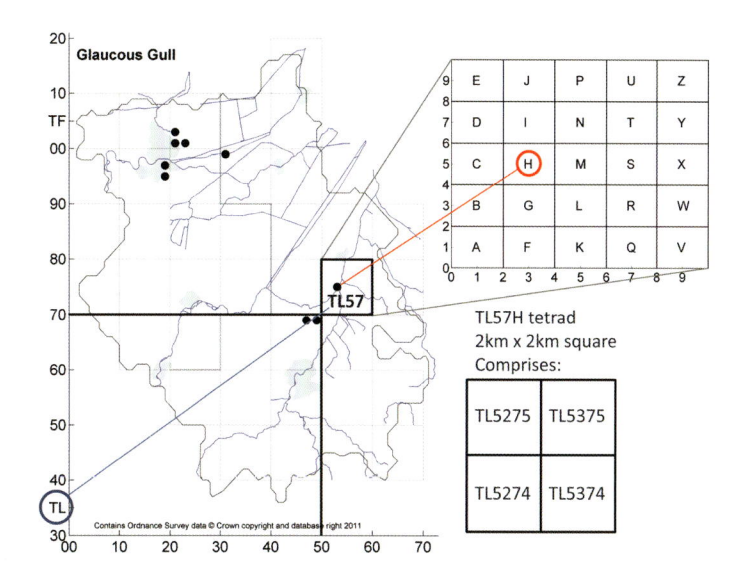

The winter survey period was from the beginning of November to the end of February, and the summer period from the beginning of April to the end of July. These were split into two halves (early and late) for timed tetrad visits (TTVs throughout this publication). The four years included the winters 2007/8, 2008/9, 2009/10 and 2010/11, and the summers of 2008, 2009, 2010 and 2011. Breeding evidence was also allowed from February, March and August, although general records from these months were outside the valid recording period.

Publicity through the BTO membership, Cambridgeshire Bird Club and the wider community encouraged people to sign up for TTVs and also to contribute roving records for squares. The gathering of breeding evidence involved the use of field signs that fell into four basic categories: confirmed, probable, possible and non-breeding.

The field signs for the breeding categories include:
Confirmed breeding – a nest with eggs or young, calls of young in a nest, an adult bird gathering food or carrying a faecal sac, recently fledged young, a recently used nest, distraction display such as that utilised by game birds or an adult seen entering or leaving a nest hole
Probable breeding – gathering nest material, breeding-display flights, singing males over a period of longer than a week, multiple males showing territoriality, a pair seen together or breeding-season alarm calls
Possible breeding – a singing male or other observations of the species in a likely breeding habitat
Non-breeders including summering non-breeders and migrants.
Records could be submitted with no indication of the breeding category, defined here as 'No evidence'.

For the TTVs, the choice of route was down to the observer, but they were advised to try to ensure that representative habitats were covered in the one- or two-hour visit, if possible, and the use of publicly accessible areas was promoted. Arranging access to private land was often not necessary if suitable public paths and roads were available. Each hour was logged separately. There was no requirement to keep to the same route for all four visits, especially if coverage of more diverse habitats was enabled by varying the route.

Additional records were gained through the use of data from core BTO surveys such as the Breeding Bird Survey (BBS), Ringing and Nest Recording schemes, and from targeted RSPB and similar surveys. The former were used as species records only, and BBS participants were asked to submit records of breeding evidence separately; data from the latter two schemes were used to inform both distribution and breeding evidence. Additionally, data from BTO BirdTrack and services such as Birdguides were incorporated, and volunteers such as those from the Cambridgeshire Bird Club trawled their datasets to check whether gaps in the atlas dataset could be filled from the county data. The number of volunteer hours contributing to the production of this atlas is much larger than any of us thought possible and it is a great testament to the dedication of birdwatchers across Cambridgeshire and beyond. It is also fair to say that the publicity, especially by the BTO, for this atlas, brought in many observers new to formalised survey techniques and making something more significant of their birdwatching. The dataset was validated and all records of county rarities and significant species were checked with county records committees and annual reports; any left unvalidated were not included.

One of the priorities for later seasons was to ensure that as many tetrads as possible across the county were covered sufficiently to generate a short species list – a target of 20 species seemed ideal. The Cambridgeshire Bird Club organised several roving days, mobilising teams of two to four to rove widely in poorly covered parts of the county, with the aim of adding species to tetrad lists. This proved extremely valuable in covering those parts of the county with no resident birdwatchers, away from obvious reserves and centres of population. However, those parts of the county still received the poorest coverage, and the few uncovered tetrads are mostly away from significant centres of population or perceived interest.

One of the main hurdles to overcome was persuading birdwatchers to venture into the perceived 'deserts' – areas of farmland and possibly small villages away from their known landscape – but the dedication of the few who did so often led to the reward of an unexpected sighting. The other main priority as the survey progressed was to obtain the highest breeding status of as many species and as many tetrads as possible; this was achieved partly by roving birdwatchers and partly by encouraging TTV surveyors and others actively to seek out breeding evidence.

For the owls, data from the Cambridgeshire Bird Club Breeding Owl Survey 2004–06 are included here, truncated from their original published form, to augment the data from the atlas work, which, given the nocturnal habit of owls, was inevitably incomplete. The Breeding Owl Survey tried to map the breeding distribution of owls in the county through specialised field surveys in advance of the atlas fieldwork period, and good coverage of the county was achieved, although with gaps in Huntingdonshire, areas west of Peterborough, and the far south-eastern parts of the county.

Our achievements
This work was only possible through the efforts of a significant number of volunteers and organisations – 908 different registered users contributed directly to the atlas, either through a single roving record, BirdTrack lists, participation in TTVs, or through other BTO surveys such as Ringing, Nest Recording or the BBS. It should be noted that for both Ringing and Nest Recording, data were only available for the first three winter and summer seasons.

The total number of tetrads in the county, including peripheral tetrads where only fragments were in the county, was 969. The number of tetrads covered by TTVs in summer was 723 (75%), and in winter 774 (80%). The southern half of the county had nearly 100% coverage, while coverage in the north was sparser. The number of tetrads with no records was remarkably small – five in summer and nine in winter.

The top two maps below show the species richness in winter and summer. Most squares recorded between 20 and 60 species in summer and between 10 and 40 in winter; the highest species richness in both seasons was along the four main river valleys, most noticeably in the Ouse valley gravel pits complex and the Ouse and Nene Washes. Additional summer and winter maps (bottom row) show those tetrads with a species list of fewer than 25 species (coloured), and 25 or greater (dark red-brown). This highlights tetrads with either poor species diversity or poor recording effort.

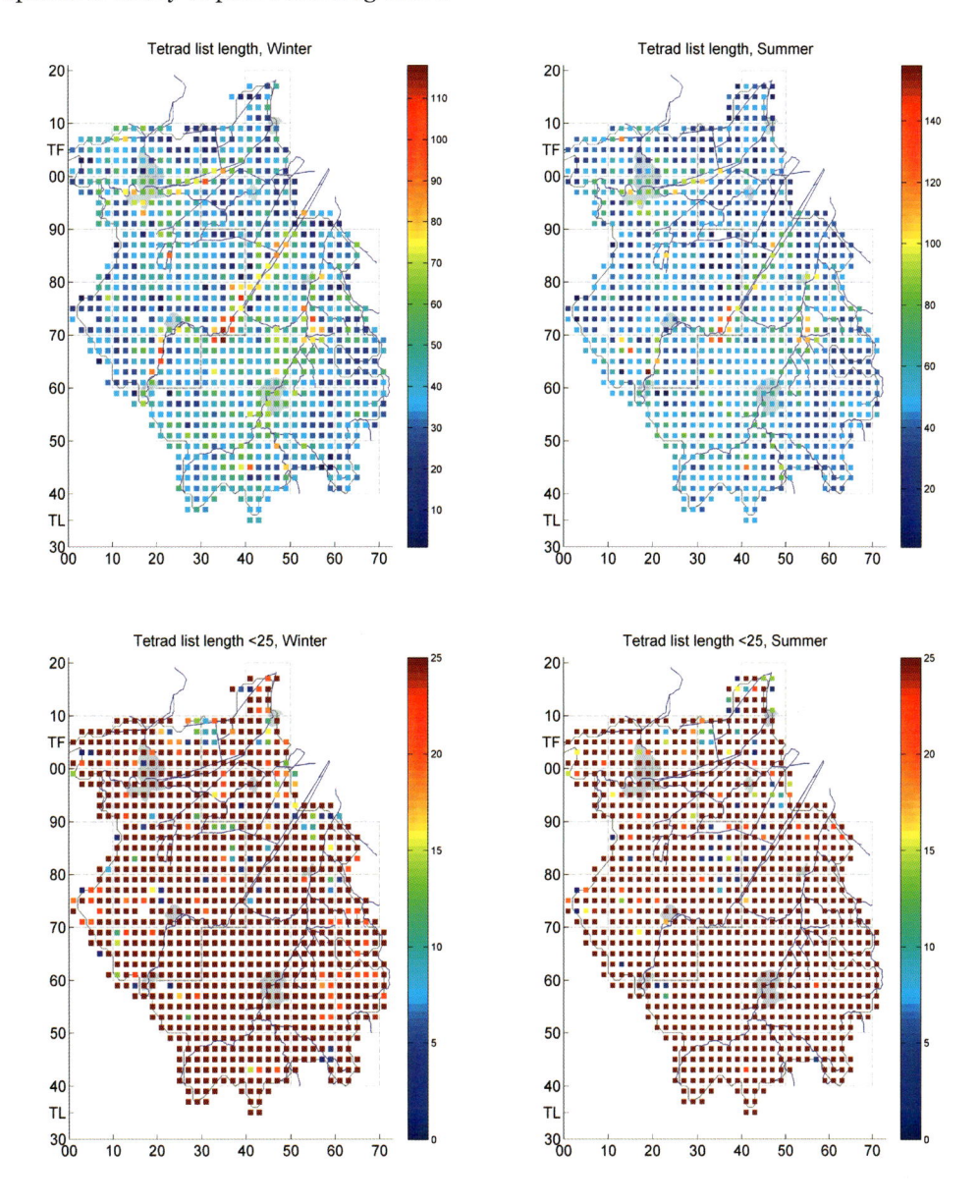

Recording effort is shown in the next set of maps (top two maps below), which show the number of separate visits to any tetrad. Most squares received 10 or fewer visits in either winter or summer. To examine the poorly recorded tetrads better, additional maps highlighting tetrads with five or fewer visits also are shown (bottom two maps), against a background of dark red squares for tetrads receiving more than five visits. Once again, it is apparent that the main river valley sites and urban centres logged more visits per tetrad than the wider farmed landscape.

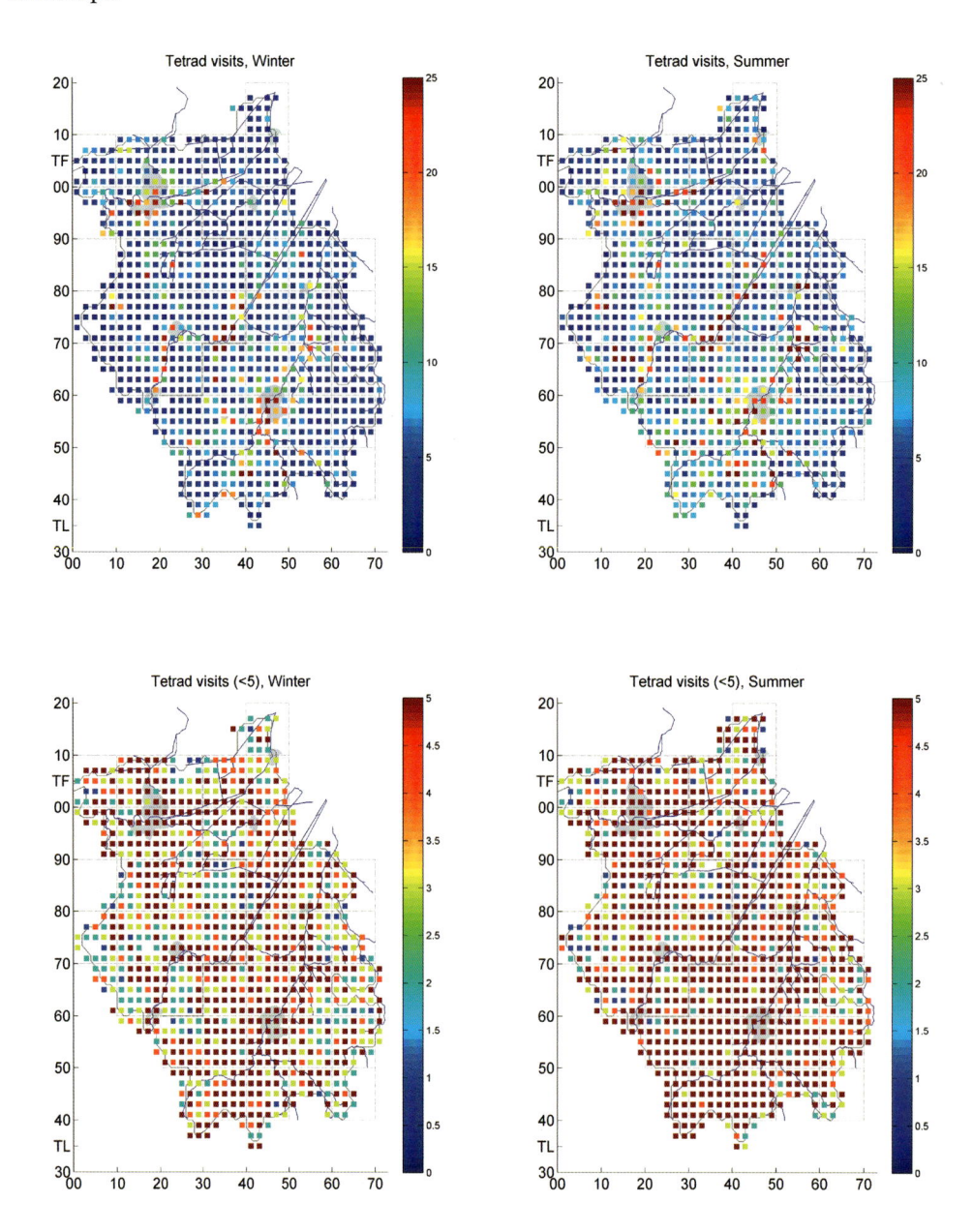

Changes in the avifauna of Cambridgeshire

National declines in some of our bird populations are becoming more widely publicised with the advent of the Red List and Amber List (Eaton *et al.*, 2009). These lists are based on an assessment of population declines in terms of numbers and, to a lesser extent, distribution, in a UK and European context.

There is no similarly structured assessment for counties; without previous population or distribution estimates this is not a simple task. However, we have been able to compare our breeding-season maps and percentages of tetrads occupied with those determined in the previous two breeding-season atlases. We have provided these comparisons in the species texts. We have also been able to produce current population estimates based on proportions of the new UK population estimates (Musgrove *et al.*, 2013) supplied to us by the BTO.

There are several species which stand out for their population changes. First, we have lost several breeding species which featured in the past atlases. Golden Oriole and Willow Tit have not been recorded breeding in the county for around a decade. The former still occurs occasionally on migration, but its status as a UK breeder is now looking highly tenuous. Willow Tit appears to be retreating northwards; this species possibly bred on our Northamptonshire border, but breeding was not proved within the county. The pitfalls of separating this species from Marsh Tit will no doubt increase as fewer birdwatchers connect with it in the lowlands of England. Lesser Redpoll was confirmed as breeding in around 20% of the county in the previous atlases – very few records within the breeding season were obtained this time, and most of these were likely to be wintering birds lingering before their northern migration. A similar pattern was also seen for several scarcer birds in the previous atlases. Tree Pipit, Whinchat, Wheatear and Common Redstart were all recorded then as scarce breeders; we see these species purely as passage migrants today. Black-tailed Godwit is now a very scarce breeder, and Ruff have not bred in the county for some time. Stone-curlews retain a tenuous foothold, occasionally breeding in parts of the arable chalk of the south or east. As this is such a sensitive species no maps are shown, and no species account is provided. Similarly, Montagu's Harrier, as well as being a passage migrant, is also an occasional breeder; whilst a species account is provided, no maps are shown for the breeding season.

There are other significant declines – most noticeable amongst birds of ancient woodlands, such as Hawfinch, Lesser Spotted Woodpecker, Nightingale and Woodcock, and in the numbers of farmland birds. The latter have received widespread attention. In Cambridgeshire, typical farmland birds such as Corn Bunting and Grey Partridge are still found in numbers of national significance but most have declined. Our migrants also have fluctuating fortunes, partly due to problems they face on migration or at their wintering quarters, but also for some, such as the Turtle Dove, within our changing arable landscape.

It is not all a picture of declines and local extinctions, however; there is a remarkable group of species which have either recolonised the county of their own accord, or have formed part of re-introduction programmes.

The fact that persecution of raptors has diminished, and that the use of seriously detrimental pesticides is less common, has meant that we now have several breeding raptors which did not feature in previous atlases; Peregrine, Marsh Harrier and Hobby are now expanding into several suitable areas of the county. The two most striking raptor gains are Buzzard and Red Kite, which previously were birds of seriously restricted range in the UK far to the west. Our maps this time show that the Buzzard is probably our most widespread raptor – as a result of a rapid expansion during the last 15 years. Red Kites were the subject of a re-introduction programme in Northamptonshire and the Chilterns around two decades ago; both of these populations have done so well that they have naturally expanded their range, and we have birds which originated from both of these sites. Red Kites have not yet colonised the east of the county, but are now familiar birds of the western half, and doubtless their spread will continue in the coming years.

Wetland birds too have increased in some cases as a result of more extensive, better-connected habitat and improved water quality. Little Egrets now breed in the county and winter in higher numbers. At the time of the previous atlases they were rare wintering birds in southern England; now we expect them to become a more widespread feature of our heronries in summer, and of our wetlands and even farmland and grasslands close to waterways out of the breeding season. Bitterns have returned to the county, both in winter and within the last six years or so as a very scarce breeder; the first birds to breed at Kingfishers Bridge made it into the local media. Now they breed at several sites, and hopefully this small population will have a secure future. Cranes similarly have changed from winterers and wanderers to the establishment of a small breeding population; we can hope for stability of this population, but expansion into further potential habitat is not out of the question. Another addition has been assisted; the Corncrake was unlikely to re-establish itself on its own, but a re-introduction programme into suitable habitat has established a small population at the Nene Washes. They are breeding, but this remains a very tenuous population.

Avocet is yet another wetland species which has arrived of its own accord; breeding now takes place at several sites, mostly on gravel pits or other artificially created wetland sites with islands, scrapes, etc. One privately owned wetland has been extremely successful at providing habitat for this wader.

Far fewer passerines have arrived as additions to the county avifauna in recent years; breeding of Stonechat and Black Redstart has occurred on an ad hoc basis for many years. The most striking addition is Raven, which whilst not yet confirmed as a breeder, is probably at least holding territories in both the north-west and far south-west of the county. This species has rapidly increased in population and range across England during the last decade and, although still a scarce bird, sightings are sufficiently regular in a few locations as to make breeding inevitable soon.

Both Cetti's Warbler and Bearded Tit were recorded as breeders in the early 1980s, but the hard winters mid-decade seemed to have removed both as breeding birds. Our warming climate in recent years has led to recolonisation, with breeding reported at several suitable sites. Bearded Tit, in particular, seems to be increasing; Cetti's Warbler population trends are a little less clear. The two hard winters of the atlas period may have had some effect, but their small populations seem to be well established.

Two further colonist passerines are woodland birds: Firecrest and Siskin. Neither is yet particularly widespread, but it is possible that numbers will increase. There seems to be enough habitat; maybe it is our milder climate which is helping the Firecrest. Its expansion in the neighbouring Brecks is very marked, and our birds are likely colonists from there. The Siskin is an irruptive winter visitor in the main, but it would seem that we have a very small summering population in woods in the south of the county.

One species not included in this atlas is the Ruddy Duck (*Oxyura jamaicensis*). This North American species is currently the focus of a nationwide population cull. Although it was recorded during the atlas, it is not appropriate to map these data. The cull, carried out by Defra, will protect populations of the globally threatened White-headed Duck (*Oxyura leucocephala*) in mainland Europe (particularly Spain). Our Ruddy Duck population has spread into Europe and risks hybridising with the White-headed Duck, further endangering this species. The Ruddy Duck is being removed from Spain, and this British cull is intended to preclude recolonisation from the UK.

This book – structure

Following this Introduction are species accounts for those species which we consider to be part of our regular wintering or breeding avifauna. The criterion for inclusion was a minimum of five tetrads in the distribution category for either season. Several migrant species, such as Wheatear, Whinchat, Redstart, Ring Ouzel and a range of others might also have qualified, with maps for the summer season containing more than five dots. It is clear from the data, however, that these were migrants – either moving through the county in April–May or during the post-breeding season in July. These species are excluded as they cannot currently be considered to be part of our breeding avifauna. Where possible, each account compares the current population to the information available in previous atlases, and summarises the current distribution and abundance. Any potential biases in the data are considered, such as difficulty of detecting breeding evidence, under-recording of nocturnal species and, for some species, whether key years influenced the maps presented, for example specific influxes of an irruptive winter migrant. Spotted Crake and Corncrake were also included, although not quite meeting the mapping criteria. The Spotted Crake is possibly under-recorded and is an important breeding species. The Corncrake is also shown, partly as a reference for future publications documenting its changed population, and partly in acknowledgement of the widely publicised reintroduction programme.

Most species accounts, especially those for breeding species, contain a table giving the absolute number of tetrads in which the species was recorded, and additionally the numbers of tetrads with the different categories of breeding. A percentage figure is also provided for total winter and summer tetrads, out of the 969 tetrads comprising the county. Note that some of these tetrads contain only a tiny fragment of the county and hence the bird *may* have been seen over the border. As not all squares were covered for TTVs, the percentages recorded in TTVs, if given in a species account, may vary from the numbers in the table.

Maps are provided for most species, and in most cases two maps are given for each season. The left-hand map provides a representation of abundance, taken from TTV visits, plotted as a count per hour (hence it is possible to record 0.5 birds if only one individual was recorded during a two-hour TTV). Open circles in abundance maps indicate TTVs on which this species was not recorded, and gaps represent tetrads where no TTV was carried out in that season. The right-hand map shows distribution – all tetrads where the species was recorded. In winter, distribution is shown as black dots, but for summer different colour/shape symbols are used representing categories of breeding evidence. Occasionally, abundance (TTV) maps are omitted where so few birds were logged on TTVs that these maps were uninformative. One or two species deserve special treatment due to their sensitivity to disturbance; no summer maps are shown for these species.

An attempt has been made to estimate populations for each species. For some, it was relatively straightforward – usually the scarcer species or those with well-documented wintering populations such as wildfowl. For other species, estimates of breeding and wintering numbers were provided by a subgroup of the authors, based on the survey data and local knowledge.

As the species accounts were written by a range of writers – birdwatchers with different outlooks, often writing about groups of birds in which they have a strong interest – there is variation in the style and, to a lesser extent, content. There has been no attempt to remove these differences in style, and we are very grateful to all the writers, proofreaders and artists who have been involved in this project, and to the BTO for data provision.

We are also grateful to the individuals and companies who have provided financial sponsorship, without whom this project would have been much more difficult to bring to publication: Cambridge BotanicS Ltd., Cambridgeshire & Peterborough Biodiversity Partnership, Sir Charles Chadwyck-Healey, Bob Jarman, Trumpington Farm Company and David White of White Bros, Hawk Mill Farm.

Abbreviations

BBS	Breeding Bird Survey
BTO	British Trust for Ornithology
CBC	Cambridgeshire Bird Club
CBR	Cambridgeshire Bird Report
NNR	National Nature Reserve
RBBP	Rare Birds Breeding Panel
RSPB	The Royal Society for the Protection of Birds
TTV	Timed tetrad visit
WBBS	Waterways Breeding Bird Survey
WeBS	Wetlands Bird Survey

Species Accounts

Louise Bacon (pp. 22–27, 30–31, 34–35, 50, 71, 110–112, 158–166, 187–189, 221, 226–247)
Peter Bircham (pp. 82–89, 92–97, 126–129, 132–141, 144–147, 260)
Roger Buisson (pp. 200–201, 248–251, 262–285)
Andy Cotton (pp. 52–59)
Mike Everett (pp. 116–119, 130)
Peter Herkenrath (pp. 148–157, 176–186)
Michael Holdsworth (pp. 202–205, 252–259)
Charlie Kitchin (pp. 18–21, 28–29, 32–33, 36–49)
Derek Langslow (pp. 206–207, 210–220)
Vince Lea (pp. 60–67, 98–107, 120–125, 190–199, 208–209, 222–225)
Gavin Paterson (pp. 108–109, 113–115)
Rob Pople (pp. 167–175)
Doug Radford (pp. 90–91)
Andrew Tongue (pp. 142–143)
Hugh Venables (pp. 68–70, 72–80)

Artists

Richard Fowling [pp. 26, 108, 131, 140 (mixed gull flock), 162, 236, 265 (Brambling and Chaffinches)]
Ben Green [pp. 1 (Lapwing), 24, 51, 72, 81, 85, 86, 104, 107, 150, 176, 184, 203 (mixed hirundines), 239, 244, 253, 261, 270, 272, 282, 288]
James Hanlon (p. 65)
Richard Johnson [pp. 17 (Snipe), 36, 47, 48, 54, 82, 88, 92, 97, 102, 117, 121, 126, 188, 226, 234, 246, 279, 280, 294]
Steph' Thorpe [pp. 230 (mixed thrushes), 284]

Cover Cranes by James Hanlon

Proofreaders Robin Cox, Mike Everett, Vicki Harley, Michael Holdsworth, Richard Thomas and Hugh Venables

Mapping Hugh Venables

Production editor Alison Cooper

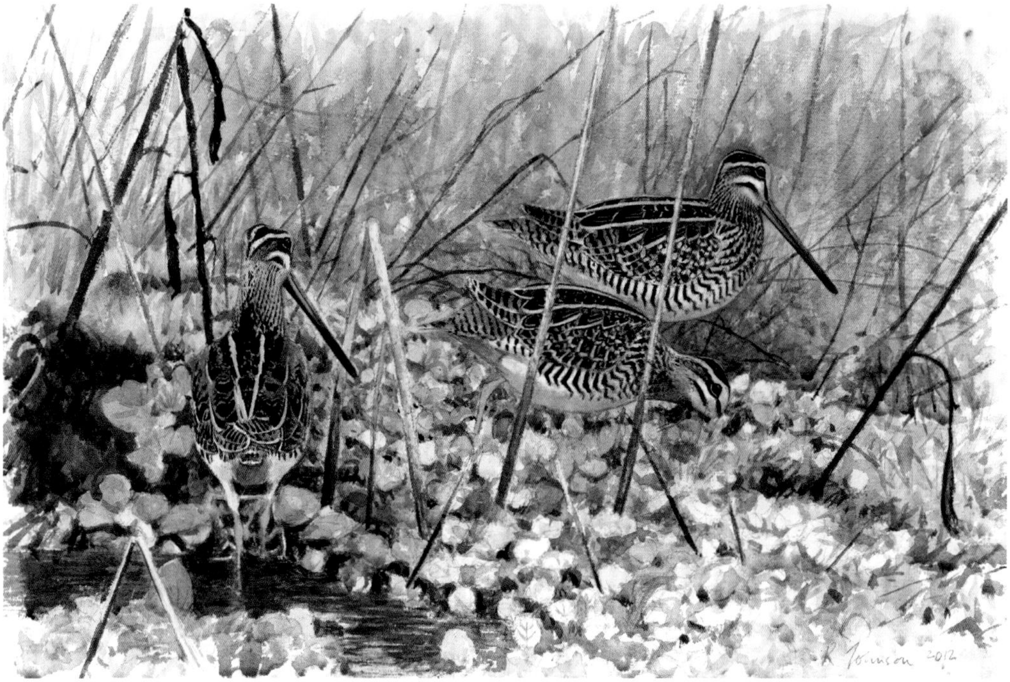

MUTE SWAN *Cygnus olor*
Green List. Fairly common resident; large non-breeding population

Breeding population estimate: 200-500 pairs, many non-breeding birds
Wintering population estimate: 2,000-5,000 individuals

Mute Swans are primarily a species of lowland eutrophic waters so it is no surprise that Cambridgeshire has a large and nationally significant breeding and wintering population. Mute Swans are found in a variety of wetland habitats from the water-filled ditches of the washlands to natural rivers, mineral workings, farm and village ponds and fenland drains. They are highly territorial and spacing of nests and pairs is related to the carrying capacity of the wetland and their hostility to each other. The Mute Swans of Cambridgeshire are descended from naturalised stock and have lost much of their fear of humans; they can be found in close proximity to humans in small wetlands where their diet of aquatic plants is supplemented by artificial feeding. Despite their being large and obvious, it is likely that the true distribution and numbers of Mute Swans have been under-represented in the fens where many smaller drains and reservoirs remained unsurveyed; genuine gaps in distribution occur in the largely waterless uplands in the south and west of the county.

The first recorded census in 1955 found 59 pairs in old Cambridgeshire; since then the UK and Cambridgeshire population has increased dramatically, partly as a result of the banning of anglers' lead weights in 1987 and partly because of the increase in available habitat through mineral extraction. Mute Swans are long-lived birds that have few natural predators and we can expect to see the population continue to grow; BBS trends for Eastern England show a 19% increase between 1995 and 2010 (Risely *et al.*, 2012). The maps show a high density of breeding birds along the main rivers and washlands, and a less-dense population throughout the fens, with more isolated breeding occurring elsewhere. Confirmed and probable breeding occurred in 248 tetrads; taking into account multiple occupancy and unsurveyed tetrads, the breeding population is is probably between 200 and 500 pairs. The TTVs recorded 2,498 birds, presumably including large numbers of non-breeding birds.

The wintering and breeding distributions are very similar, although Mute Swans are not entirely sedentary: Cambridgeshire birds move short distances between breeding, moulting and wintering areas. The top winter site in the county is the Ouse Washes. This site is the fourth most important in the UK for wintering Mute Swans and the only fenland site of international importance; the average peak in the four atlas years was 806. The Cambridgeshire section alone had an average peak of 606. For the other main sites the average peak was: Ouse Fen 158, Nene Washes 138, Paxton Pits 134, Fen Drayton 131, Grafham Water 88 and Barleycraft gravel pits 40 (data from CBRs). Winter TTVs recorded twice the number of individuals as summer TTVs, with a similar distribution.

Large flocks of non-breeding immature Mute Swans are a feature of the Cambridgeshire countryside, particularly around water bodies. In winter they feed on arable crops such as wheat and rape, causing some economic damage; this is more significant than that caused by the "wild" swans because they do not leave in the spring but remain until driven away by farmers or by the height of the crop preventing take off and landing.

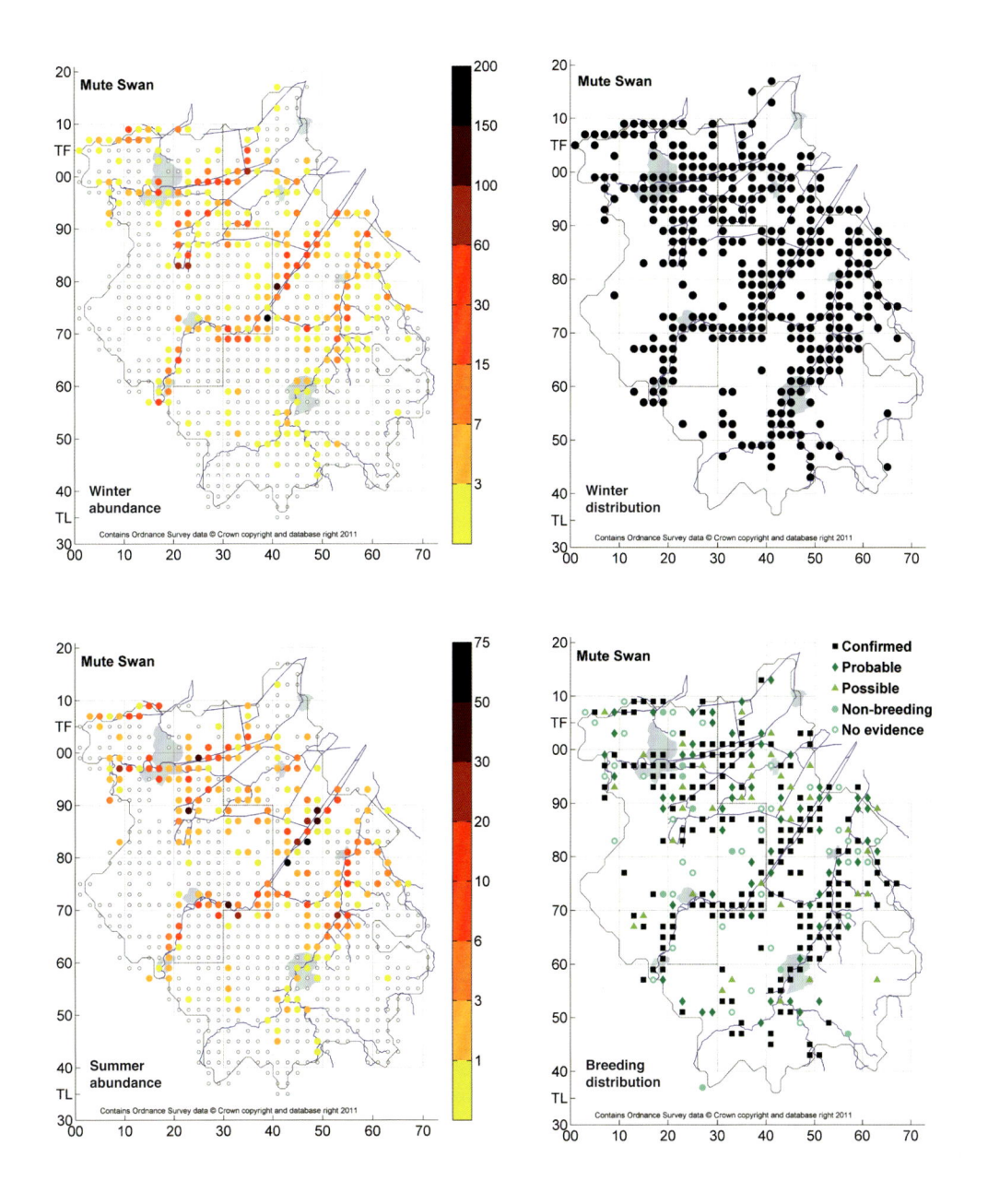

	Confirmed	Probable	Possible	Non-breeding	No evidence	Total summer (% county)	Total winter (% county)
Total tetrads	185	63	37	9	38	332 (34%)	366 (38%)

BEWICK'S SWAN *Cygnus columbianus bewickii*
Amber List. Locally common winter visitor, some passage migrants. Chiefly on the main washes

Not a breeding species
Wintering population estimate: 2,000-4,000 individuals

The Cambridgeshire fens are internationally important for Bewick's Swan. In the four winters of the atlas the Nene Washes supported an average peak of 851 (CBR 85) and the Cambs Ouse Washes 1,466 (CBR 85). The combined Norfolk and Cambs Ouse Washes supported 5,024. Many birds are drawn to Welney; it is easy to forget that this was a rare species in the fens until the 1950s. The species is now amber-listed because the UK population has fluctuated downwards during the last two decades. The atlas period saw the lowest indices since the mid-1970s; the UK population was estimated to be 7,000 in 2009/10 (Eaton *et al.*, 2012). During this decline the fenland population has remained relatively stable; smaller sites in the west of the country have suffered the greatest reductions. Bewick's Swans were recorded in 89 tetrads, a little over 9% of the county, and TTVs recorded 3,196 birds, all in the fens. The Cambridgeshire population of Bewick's Swans generally ranges from 2,000 to 4,000 birds.

Ringing and collar records provide a vivid picture of the vast movements that these long-lived birds make between their breeding grounds in Arctic Russia, stop-over sites in the Baltic states and their wintering grounds. The English fens represent an extension to the Dutch and German wintering grounds, and cold weather on the continent drives more birds across. The Washes offer safe roosting sites and the finer grasses of the Nene Washes are also a good food source but Bewick's Swans spend much of the daylight hours feeding away from the washlands on arable crops, principally sugar beet, potatoes, wheat and rape. Tradition and energetics mean that they are usually found in fields near to the washlands, as demonstrated by the roving records map, but they will venture further afield and small numbers are recorded elsewhere, although they are rare outside the fens. The recent increase in farm reservoirs and other water bodies in the fens has provided alternative roost sites that makes complete and accurate surveying difficult.

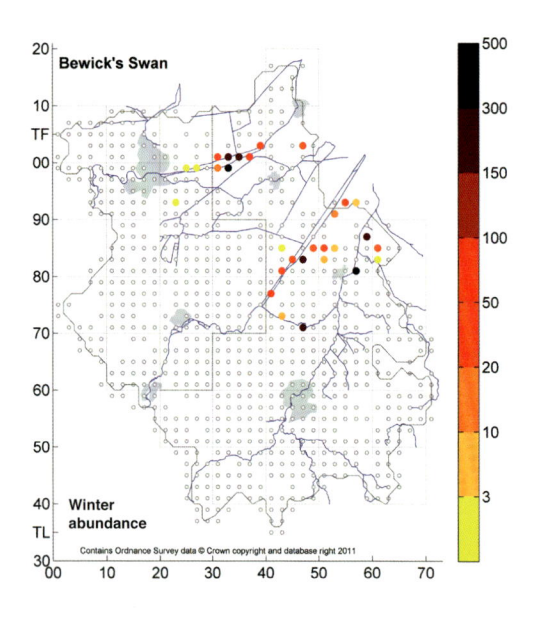

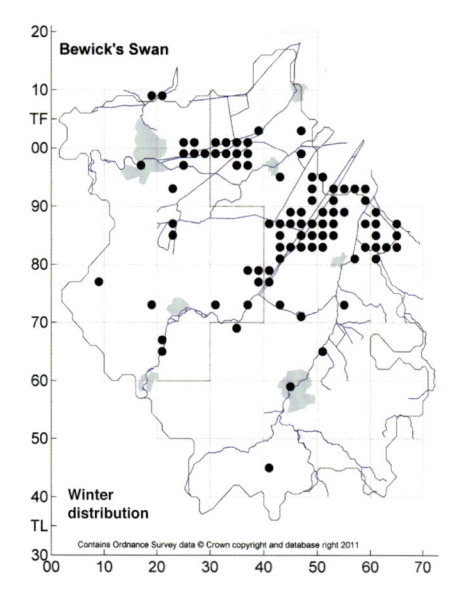

WHOOPER SWAN *Cygnus cygnus*
Amber List. Locally common winter visitor, some passage migrants. Chiefly on the main washes

Not a breeding species
Wintering population estimate: 4,000-6,000 individuals

The Ouse Washes are by some margin the most important site in the UK for wintering Whooper Swans; the February 2011 roost count was 7,271, a new record. The four-year average for the site is 5,706, and for the Cambridgeshire section it is 3,922. The Nene Washes is also a site of international importance with a four-year average of 540. The UK, and in particular the fenland, Whooper Swan population is growing rapidly; as recently as 1983 the peak count on the Ouse Washes was 223. In 2009/10 the UK population was estimated to be 16,502 birds, an increase of 9.6% on the previous estimate from 2004/05. During the current atlas survey period the fenland population of over 6,000 represents more than a third of the UK population.

The 105 tetrads in which Whooper Swans were recorded are almost entirely in the fens and clustered around the Ouse and Nene Washes. The washlands provide safe roosts, and Whooper Swans spend much of the day feeding on sugar beet tops and other arable crops within easy reach of the Washes. Other wetlands such as the Great Fen/Woodwalton area and Ely Beet Pits attract flocks, and birds are being drawn away from the Washes by the availability of safe roosts on farm reservoirs and gravel pits. This may be particularly so when the shallow flooded washlands freeze over.

Most UK and fenland Whooper Swans are of Icelandic origin but a small proportion are from Fennoscandia; the fens will receive a slightly larger proportion of these birds than sites in the north of the country. The first birds usually arrive in early October with numbers peaking in December or January; the main departure is in March although the last birds linger well into April. Injured birds occasionally summer in the fens. The peak Nene Washes count is frequently in March when flocks can be seen departing to the north-west.

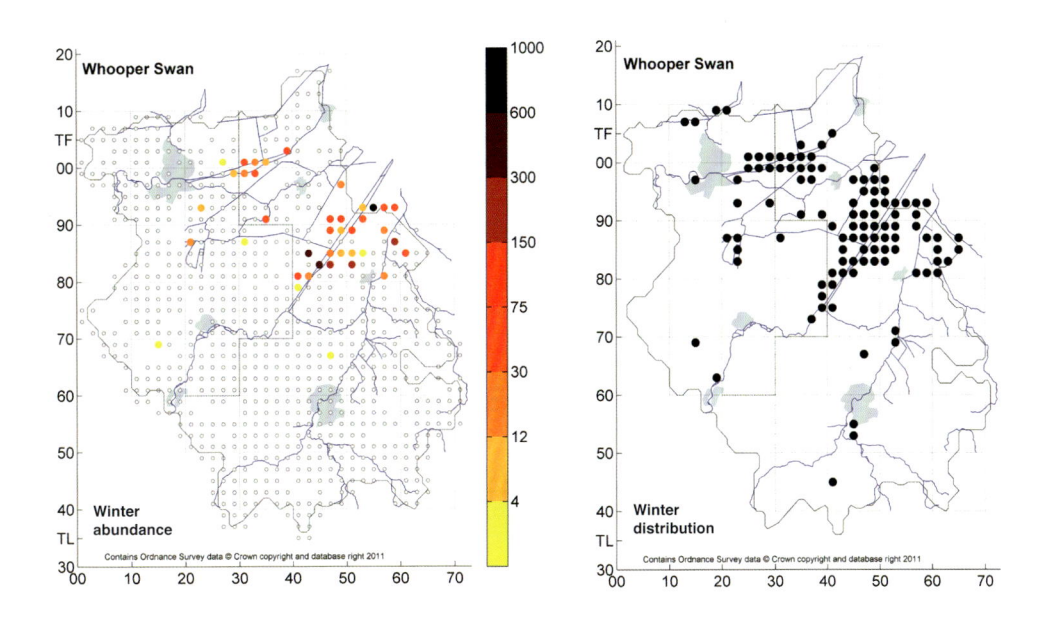

TUNDRA BEAN GOOSE *Anser fabalis rossicus*
Amber List. Scarce winter visitor; some escapees. Nearly all county records refer to this race

Not a breeding species

TAIGA BEAN GOOSE *Anser fabalis fabalis*
Amber List. Very rare winter visitor; some escapees

Not a breeding species

PINK-FOOTED GOOSE *Anser brachyrhynchus*
Amber List. Uncommon winter visitor and passage migrant; escaped birds regular

Not a breeding species
Wintering population estimate: 5-50 individuals

WHITE-FRONTED GOOSE (Greater White-fronted Goose)
Anser albifrons
Green List. Uncommon winter visitor; escaped birds regular

Not a breeding species
Wintering population estimate: 20-40 individuals, may be escapees or wild birds

Four winter-visitor grey geese are present in the UK, and they are occasionally found in Cambridgeshire. Small groups often appear on wetlands or fen arable or, particularly for the Bean Goose, as a singleton in a flock of resident Greylag Geese, temporarily taking the opportunity to feed with local birds. Pink-footed Geese seem to have been turning up more regularly, especially in the northern part of the county, as the population wintering on the Norfolk coast has increased. This species is found in larger groups than the others, appearing in flocks of up to 30–40. Tundra and Taiga Bean Geese are scarce winter visitors to the UK, so to have records from several tetrads for each of these subspecies during the atlas period is noteworthy. These species were not found every winter, and the mobile nature of wintering geese means that a single group could be recorded in several neighbouring tetrads over a period of a couple of months.

A single group of three Taiga Bean Geese was recorded in five tetrads, in early 2010, on the Nene and close to the Ouse Washes. Tundra Bean Geese were noted from eight tetrads, in three clusters, two similar to the Taiga Bean Geese and the third representing a set of records in the Cam-Ouse valley around Wicken and Kingfishers Bridge. Pink-footed Geese were recorded from 25 tetrads, mostly along the Ouse valley but also along the Nene valley and Washes, including the tidal Nene near Wisbech.

Occasional escapes of both White-fronted and Pink-footed Geese occur, and records of such individuals will not have been ruled out in this atlas; they can be difficult to discriminate in the field from their truly wild counterparts. The large wetland complexes with suitable arable nearby are the most likely areas for grey geese, and the distribution maps reflect this, with many of the records for all four species coming from the Ouse and Nene Washes, nearby arable land and the Ouse valley wetlands. The latter site choice seems especially true for White-fronted Goose, which was recorded from eight tetrads.

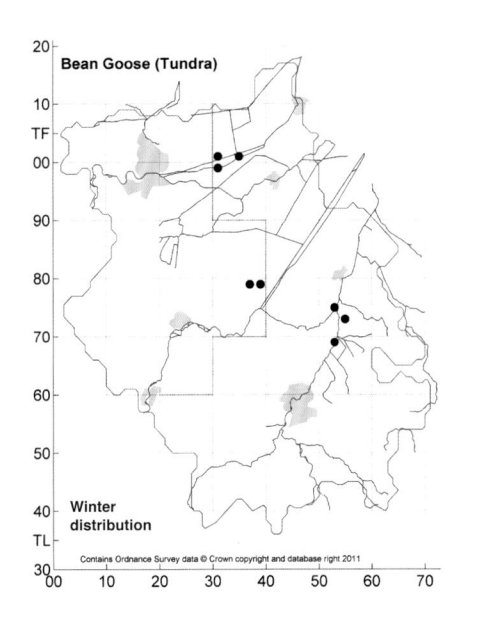

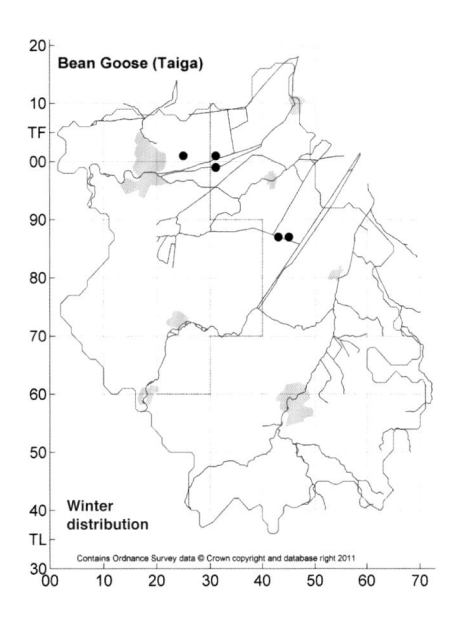

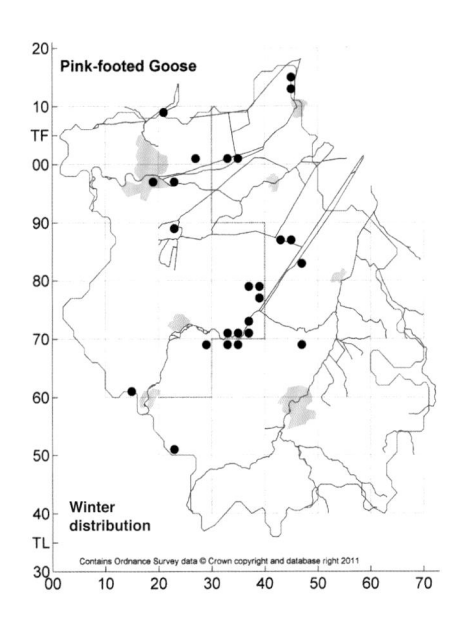

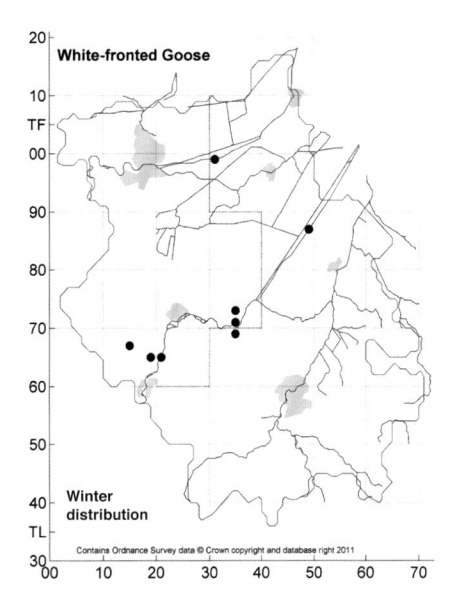

GREYLAG GOOSE *Anser anser*
Amber list. Fairly common resident. Many feral

Breeding population estimate: 50-250 pairs, many non-breeding birds
Wintering population estimate: 2,500-7,500 individuals

The Greylag Goose is one of the most common geese in Cambridgeshire, with records from 23% and 15% of TTVs in winter and summer, respectively, approximately the same proportion of the county from which Canada Geese were recorded. The distribution maps show a similar pattern, with a concentration along the main rivers and gravel-pit complexes. The greater number of tetrads occupied in the summer indicates some dispersal to smaller waterbodies for breeding. Those records not directly on a watercourse will inevitably be on smaller lakes elsewhere; this species is tolerant of humans, although perhaps to a lesser extent than Canada Geese.

The BBS trend shows a 15-year (1995–2010) increase of 168% in the UK and an 85% increase in Eastern England (Risely *et al.*, 2012). Whilst it is correct that our southern Greylag Geese derive from escaped or released stock, recent studies have shown that there is little genetic difference between these and Greylags breeding and wintering in the northern UK that are more generally considered truly wild. Hence they should no longer be considered separate populations (Mitchell *et al.*, 2012).

The Greylag Goose has increased in breeding-season distribution and density since the previous Cambs and Hunts atlases. It was found then in around 7% of county tetrads during the breeding season, compared with 27% of tetrads recording this species in the present atlas, with a peak TTV count of 120. The largest flocks recorded during the atlas period were 879 in winter and 653 in summer. The Greylag Goose is a prolific breeder and is a regular sight at many of our gravel pits, country park lakes and rivers in sizeable flocks including young birds. It is relatively easy to confirm breeding for this species – large groups of fluffy grey goslings are rarely unobtrusive. Its propensity to hybridise with other geese also means that Greylag–Canada Goose crosses are seen with increasing frequency, and presumably Greylag–Barnacle Goose crosses will be recorded in tandem with the expanding feral Barnacle Goose population.

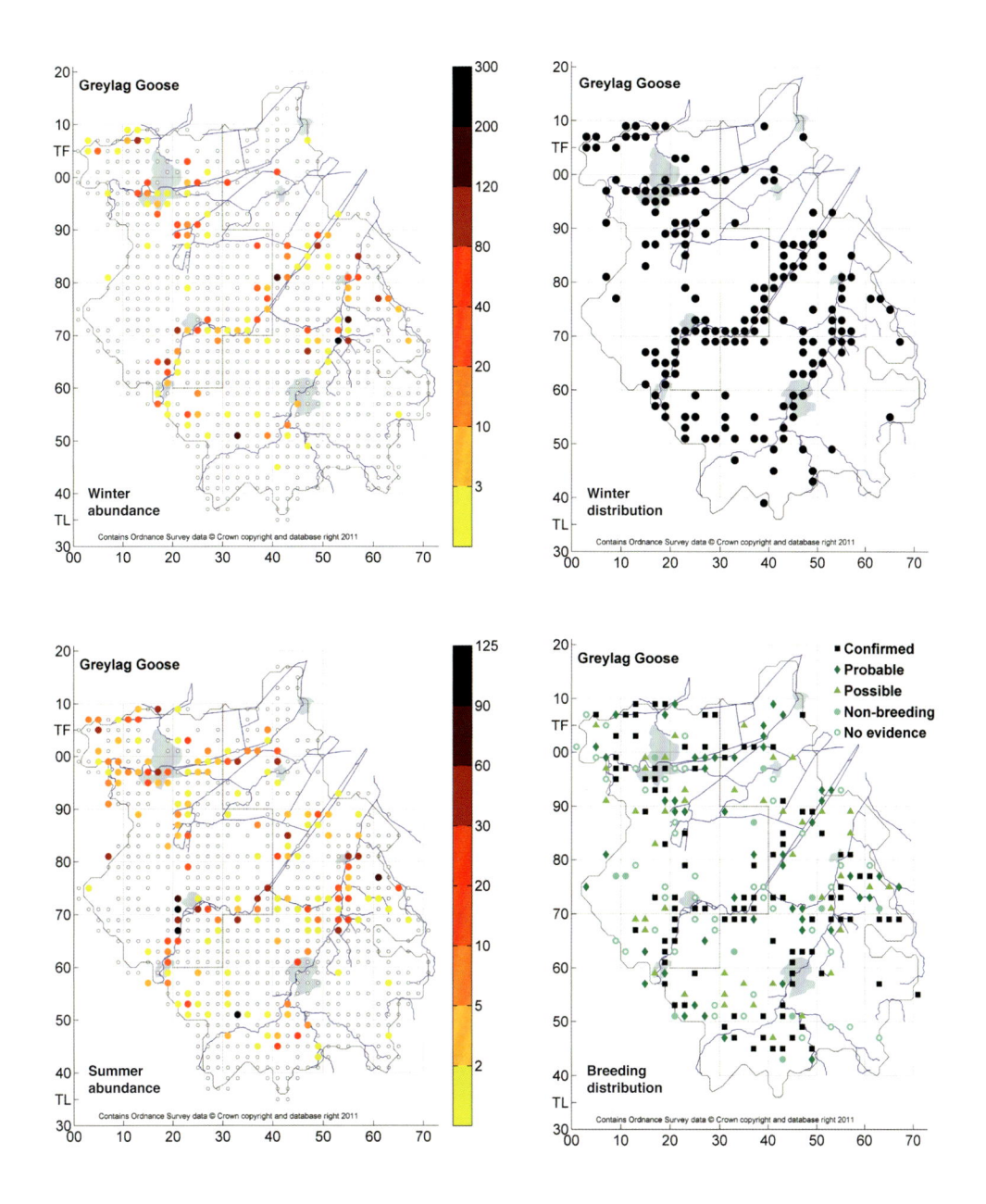

	Confirmed	Probable	Possible	Non-breeding	No evidence	Total summer (% county)	Total winter (% county)
Total tetrads	104	51	44	12	46	257 (27%)	182 (19%)

CANADA GOOSE (Greater Canada Goose) *Branta canadensis*
Fairly common naturalised resident

Breeding population estimate: 100-300 pairs, many non-breeding birds
Wintering population estimate: 2,000-7,000 individuals

Probably our most familiar goose as a resident in suburban parks, on gravel pits and on large wetland reserves. Its distribution and abundance are very similar to the Greylag Goose; it was recorded in 21% of summer and 15% of winter TTVs. In the previous Cambs and Hunts atlases, it was present in approximately 11% of tetrads during the summer. The peak counts recorded during the atlas period were 158 in summer at Barleycraft gravel pits and 1,378 in winter on the Ouse Washes (Cambridgeshire only). Despite its tolerance of waterbodies close to humans, its distribution still indicates a strong affinity for the major river valleys.

The current BBS trend shows a 15-year increase, both across the UK and in Eastern England (Risely *et al.*, 2012).

Canada Goose is an essentially sedentary species in the county and movements locally within river-valley complexes are likely to reflect variation in food resources. The greater number of tetrads occupied in summer indicates some movement to smaller waterbodies for breeding. There is no evidence of movements over any significant distance.

Breeding is relatively easy to confirm, as for Greylag Geese, and it can be a semi-colonial breeder; large groups of fluffy goslings are usually quite obvious, and post-breeding groups can reach large numbers. Breeding was recorded throughout the county, in nearly all tetrads containing areas of water of sufficient size to hold this species.

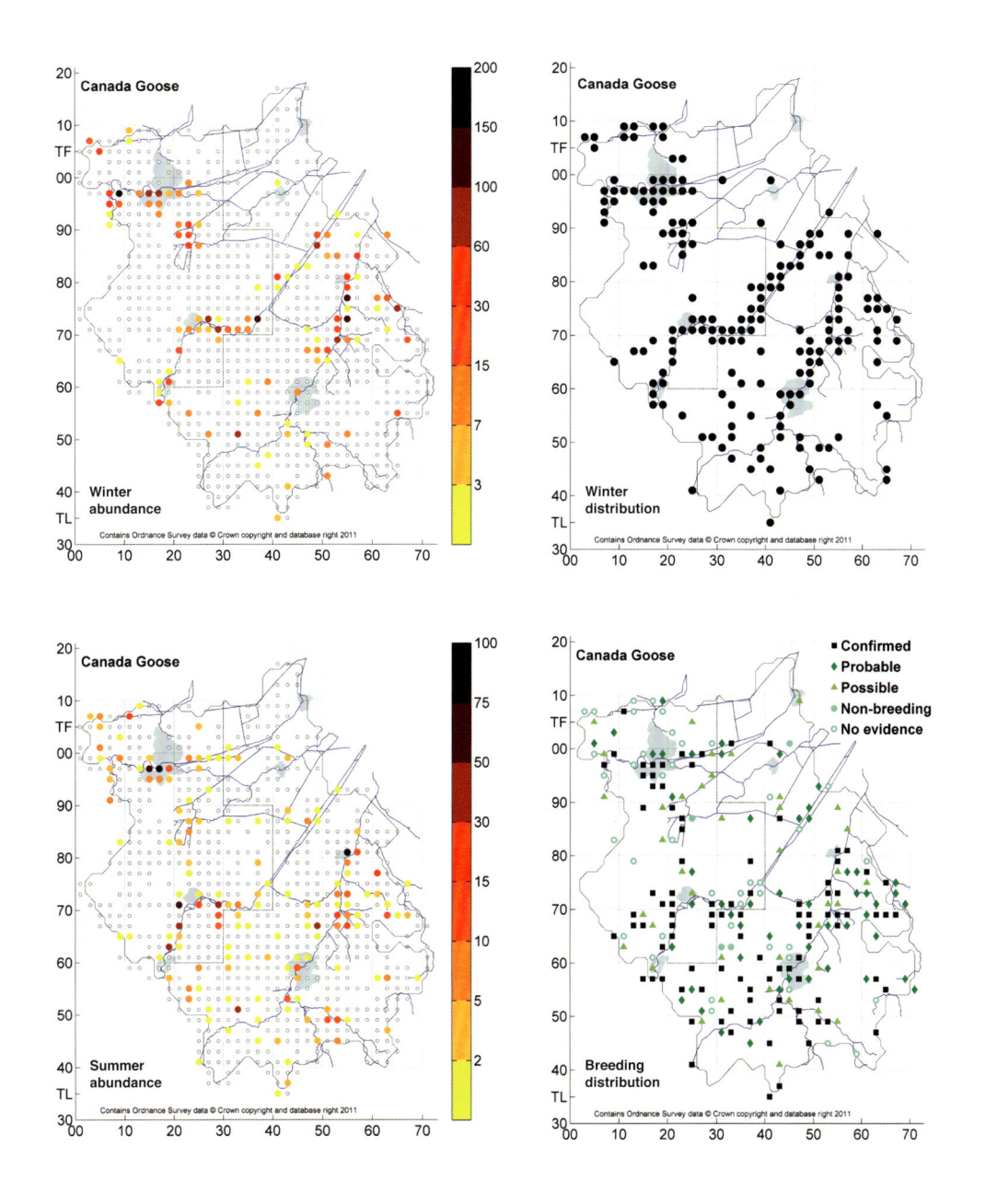

	Confirmed	Probable	Possible	Non-breeding	No evidence	Total summer (% county)	Total winter (% county)
Total tetrads	98	53	39	4	41	235 (24%)	178 (18%)

BARNACLE GOOSE *Branta leucopsis*
Amber List. Wild birds are rare winter visitors; the great majority are escapes

Breeding population estimate: 1-2 pairs, some non-breeding birds
Wintering population estimate: 10-100 individuals

Few if any of the Barnacle Geese recorded during the atlas period are truly wild birds; the most likely exceptions being 15 at Pymoor on 22nd February 2009 and 12 on the Ouse Washes from 15th to 21st December 2009. The Greenland and Svalbard populations winter well to the north in Scotland and Lindisfarne, respectively, so these records may also refer to naturalised birds, although possibly of Dutch origin. In the past wild birds were occasionally recorded in the fens; there is a record of 15 on the Nene Washes in January 1951, so a wild origin cannot be entirely ruled out.

The UK naturalised population is increasing rapidly and there is now a well-established and expanding population in Bedfordshire; this is the likely source of most of the Cambridgeshire records. Colour-ring sightings confirm this, although birds recorded to the north-west of Peterborough may be from a separate population. Feral Barnacle Geese have been recorded annually since 1973, but even into the 1980s records were still only of single birds (Bircham, 1989). Most winter records remain in single figures, although there are occasional larger influxes of Bedfordshire birds including a recent count of 78 at Paxton Pits on 5th December 2010. Most records are from flooded and abandoned gravel pits, and mostly in the Ouse valley. It is likely that this species will become an increasingly common sight in Cambridgeshire, as it has in parts of the Netherlands where the feral population is overgrazing wet meadows to the detriment of breeding waders.

Small numbers, in single figures, are summering, notably at Ouse Fen and Colne Fen and in other gravel pit sites in the Ouse valley. A small population is establishing in the Cam and Granta valleys near Sawston, with up to 10 birds year-round at Hinxton's Genome Park. In 2010 a pair bred at the nearby Whittlesford gravel pits, rearing five young.

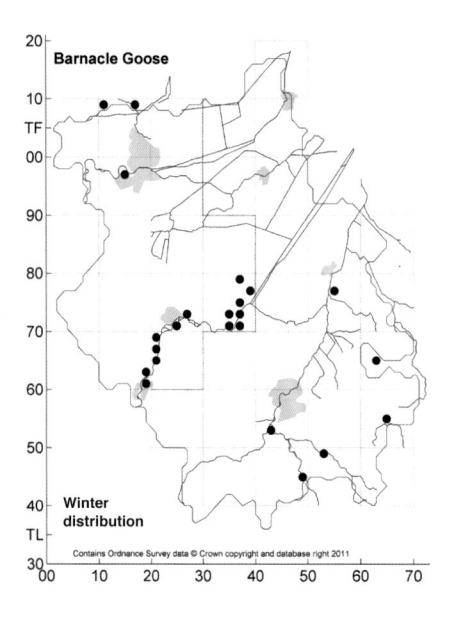

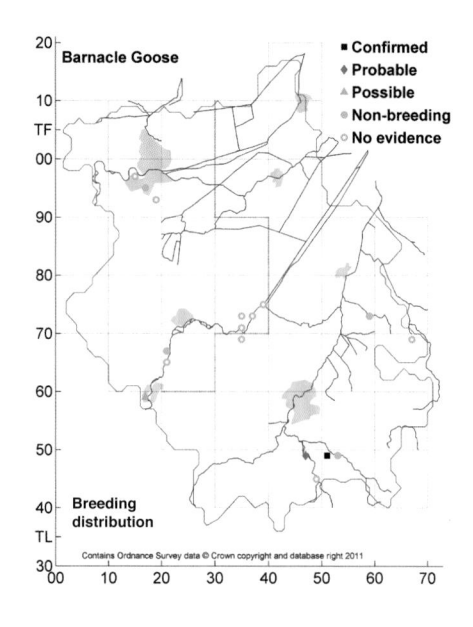

BRENT GOOSE (Brant Goose) *Branta bernicla*
Amber List. Scarce annual winter visitor and passage migrant. All records are for the nominate dark-bellied race

Not a breeding species
Wintering population estimate: 1-10 records annually

The main UK site for wintering Brent Geese is at the Wash, where there was an average peak of 16,660 birds during the atlas survey period, although they are found at many southern and eastern estuaries. That so few birds are recorded in Cambridgeshire shows their strong preference for coastal habitats. The handful of records in the county come mostly from well-watched wetlands and during periods of movement, when small numbers of birds are driven inland by poor weather or choose to take the shortest overland route to or from the Thames Estuary or south coast.

Any Brent Geese that do visit the county rarely stay for long – a quick feeding session prior to continuing their journey. This situation is unlikely to change; wintering patterns in Brent Geese are relatively stable. Dark-bellied Brent Goose is red-listed; the UK has internationally important populations in winter which have undergone a long-term (30-year) decline of 6% and a 10-year decline of 15% (Eaton *et al.*, 2012).

Brent Geese were recorded in 12 tetrads, either to subspecies or species level; all will be records of the dark-bellied nominate race.

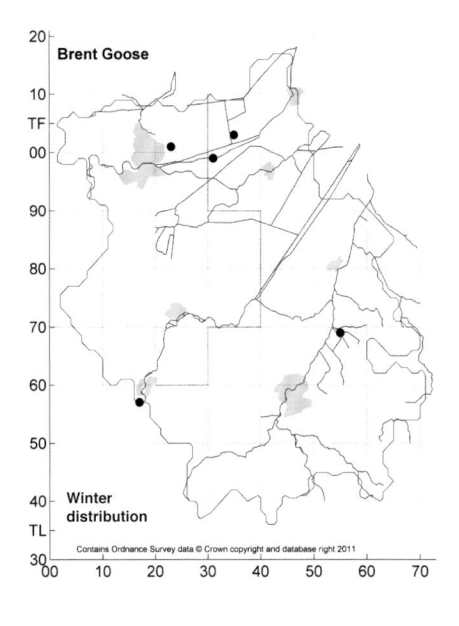

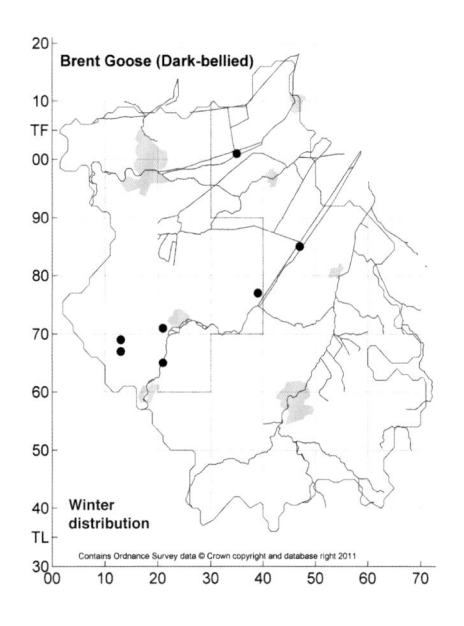

EGYPTIAN GOOSE *Alopochen aegyptiaca*
Uncommon wanderers from naturalised populations and escapees, now breeding

Breeding population estimate: 1-10 pairs
Wintering population estimate: 20-100 individuals

Egyptian Geese first became naturalised in Norfolk, where most still reside, but they are slowly expanding in range.

They first bred in the county in 1988 and then in 1991 at Fen Drayton; no further breeding was recorded until 2008 since when breeding has been annual.

The Ouse valley gravel pits, especially those between St. Ives and the base of the Ouse Washes, and, increasingly, the Ouse Washes themselves are the county stronghold. There is little difference between the winter and summer distribution maps; very few were recorded during summer TTVs. Breeding was confirmed in four tetrads, probable in five others, and possible in a further eight. One of the confirmed breeding sites was at the far eastern edge of the county, in parkland. This goose is likely to continue its expansion, and will become a more regular sight across our wetlands. Breeding is not easy to confirm as it nests in holes in trees or rabbit holes within wetlands, presumably on islands or isolated parts of sites away from people and predators. The broods of hatched goslings, however, are easier to locate and formed the majority of confirmed breeding records.

The flock size outside of the breeding season increases each year, but this species remains confined to the river-valley wetlands complexes.

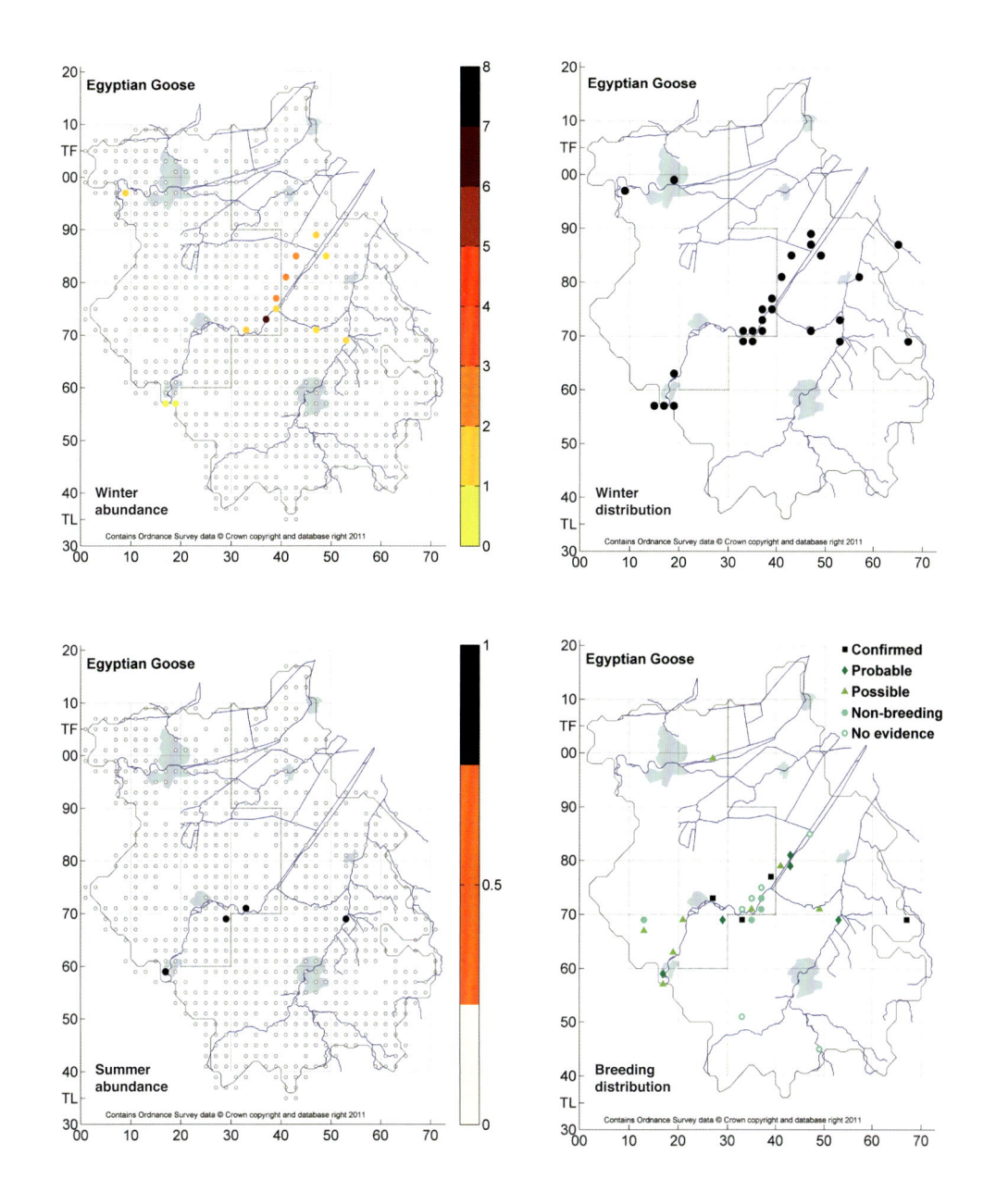

	Confirmed	Probable	Possible	Non-breeding	No evidence	Total summer (% county)	Total winter (% county)
Total tetrads	4	5	8	4	6	27 (3%)	26 (3%)

SHELDUCK (Common Shelduck) *Tadorna tadorna*
Amber List. Uncommon passage migrant and local breeder

Breeding population estimate: 50-100 pairs
Wintering population estimate: 50-250 individuals

This coastal species has made its way up the tidal rivers of land-locked Cambridgeshire and was first recorded breeding at the Nene Washes in 1936 (Nisbet & Vine, 1955). An increase in inland breeding was a national phenomenon between the 1968–72 and 1988–92 national atlases and this has continued in Cambridgeshire on the newly created wetlands along the main river valleys and at Grafham Water. The conspicuous plumage of the Shelduck and its presence on open water makes it a relatively easy species to survey; the maps are likely to represent an accurate picture of their distribution. The main breeding sites during this atlas period are the Nene Washes with an average breeding population of 25 pairs and the Ouse Washes with 15. Numbers have decreased at the latter site in recent years, probably as a result of excessive spring flooding. Other sites are mostly along the fenland rivers, notably near Foul Anchor on the River Nene, Maxey on the River Welland, the Lark and the Cam. Further south, Shelducks are regular breeders in the gravel pits of the Ouse valley, and at Grafham Water. It seems to have retreated from the Cam valley and no longer breeds in Cherry Hinton (Cambs Atlas 1994). Shelducks can also be found breeding in suitable tree cavities in old orchards in the north-east of the county.

Compared to the previous Cambs and Hunts atlases the percentage of tetrads with confirmed and probable breeding has decreased slightly from 5% and 6%, respectively, to 4%. This probably reflects a difference in survey techniques rather than a decline in breeding numbers as the percentage of tetrads in summer in which Shelducks were present increased from 7.5% and 6.5%, respectively, to 10%. BBS trends for Eastern England between 1995 and 2010 also show a large (33%) increase (Risely *et al.*, 2012). The breeding-season TTVs recorded 226 birds but this is thought to include a number of non-breeding birds.

Since the 1980s the wintering population on the nearby Wash has dropped from over 15,000 to the present 6,000, although this appears to have had little effect on wintering and breeding numbers in Cambridgeshire. Cambridgeshire birds join most other birds from north-west Europe in the Heligoland Bight for their post-breeding moult; only a handful remain in the late summer and autumn – a few females stay behind with their broods and some fully grown independent juveniles. They start to return to the county in January with numbers reaching a peak in February and March. The late-winter increase is a prelude to the breeding season and the distributions are therefore very similar in winter and summer; the main sites are the Ouse and Nene Washes. The Nene Washes average peak counts for the years 2007–2011 were 61 in February and 91 in March; on the Cambs Ouse Washes these were 49 and 54. The highest ever count for the county was 282 at the Ouse Washes in February 1997.

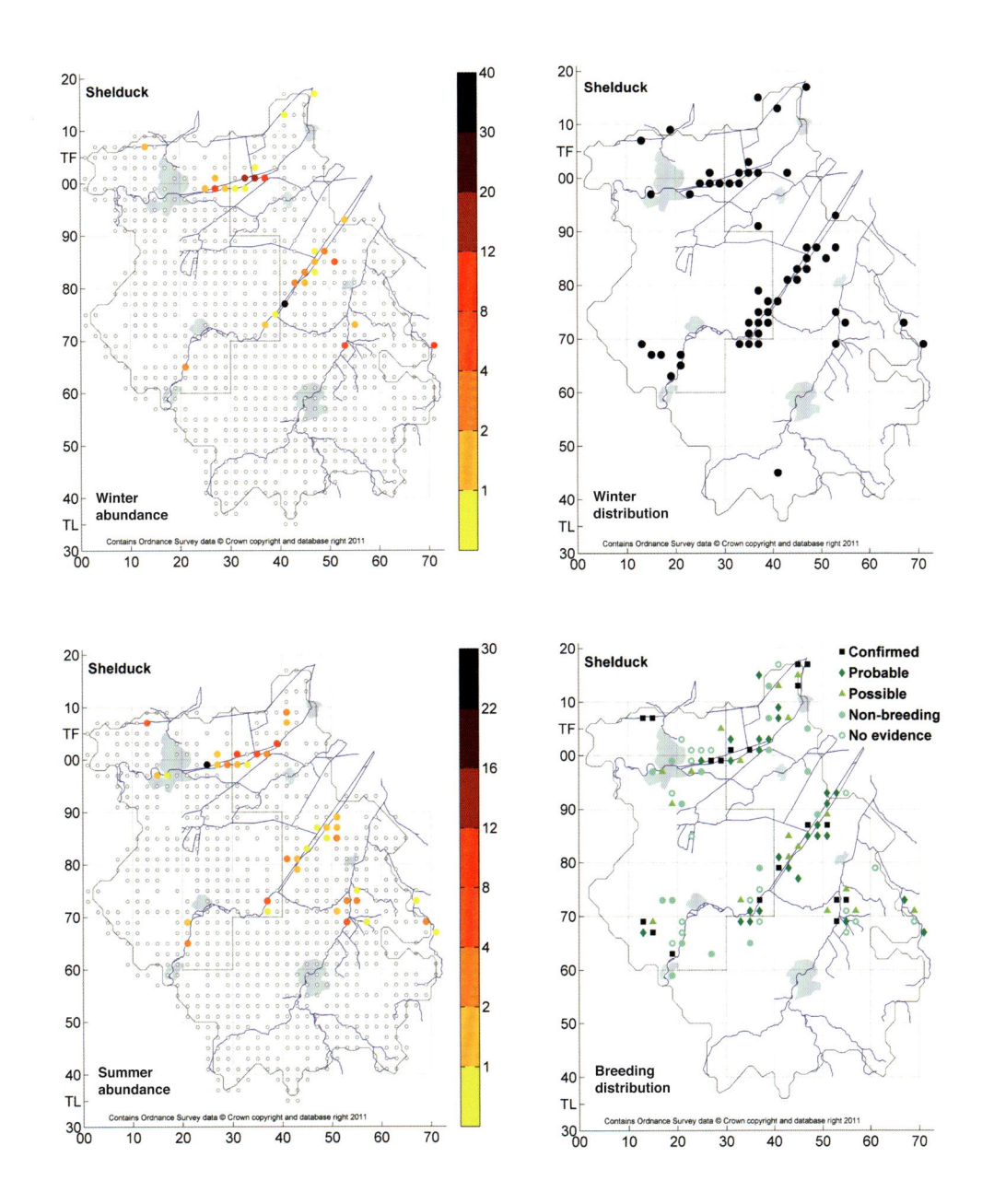

	Confirmed	Probable	Possible	Non-breeding	No evidence	Total summer (% county)	Total winter (% county)
Total tetrads	19	27	18	17	20	101 (10%)	54 (6%)

MANDARIN DUCK *Aix galericulata*
Uncommon naturalised resident and escapee

Breeding population estimate: 5-20 pairs
Wintering population estimate: 40-150 individuals

The Mandarin has a very restricted range in the county with most records coming from the south-west. Despite its plumage, it is not the easiest bird to spot, especially females or young birds. The use of holes for nesting also means that it is unobtrusive in the breeding season, not often seen in places where other waterfowl are found. Records seem to come from the upper reaches of the Cam, and from some areas of parkland where lakes surrounded by trees provide ideal habitat. These places are not necessarily areas with regular public access.

In the previous Cambs Atlas the first breeding date was given as approximately 1990, with records from only three tetrads. As old Cambridgeshire is now their stronghold with most of the submitted records, its population has clearly increased in this part of the county. The previous Hunts Atlas, however, had 10 tetrads with Mandarins, mostly in the parkland zone west of Peterborough. They have become far less common in that area, with reports from only two tetrads on the upper Nene and none from other likely areas such as Burghley or Milton estates.

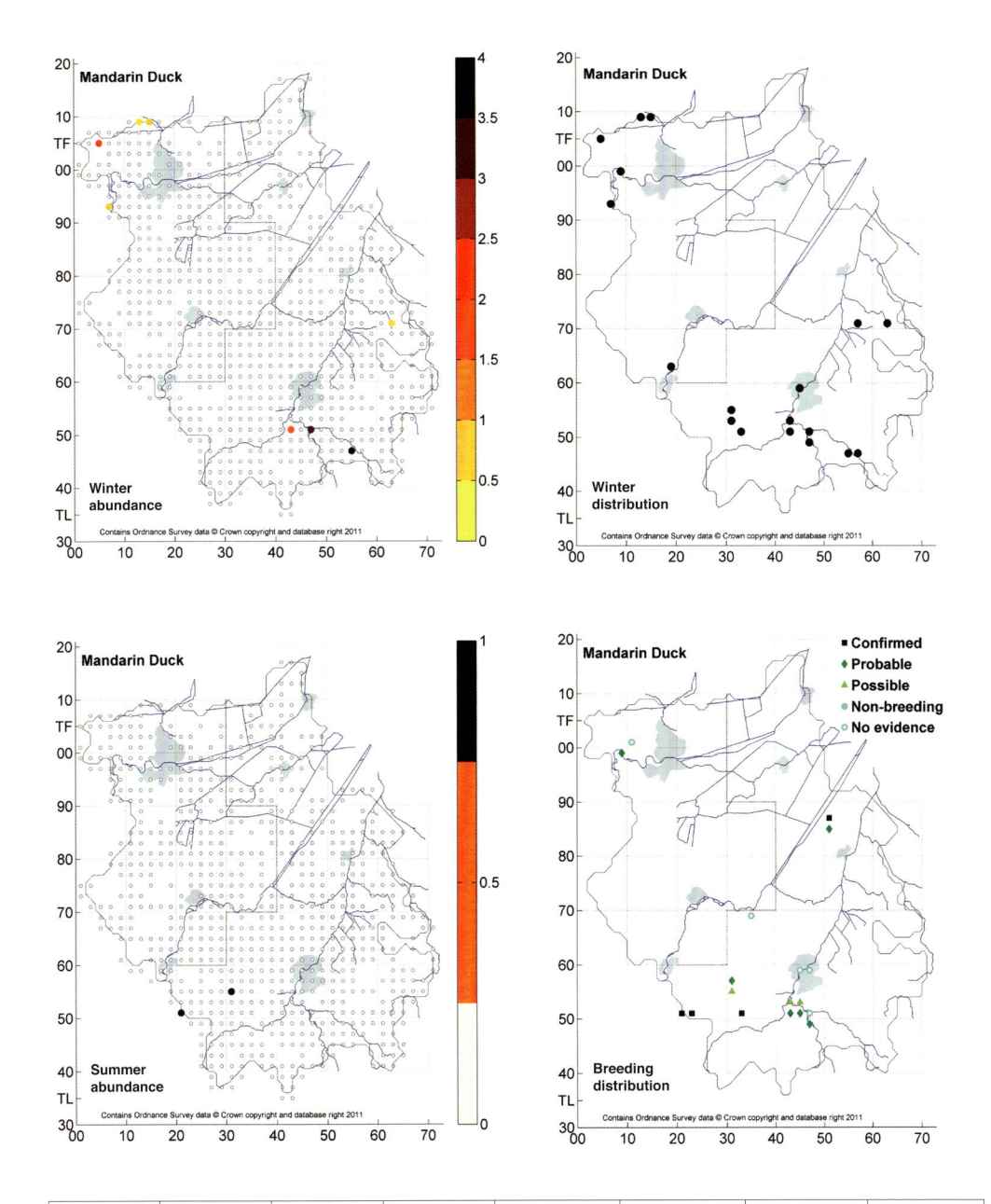

	Confirmed	Probable	Possible	Non-breeding	No evidence	Total summer (% county)	Total winter (% county)
Total tetrads	4	6	3	0	5	18 (2%)	18 (2%)

WOOD DUCK *Aix sponsa*

This species is not considered to be on the British or county lists. However, breeding was confirmed in a nest box in a woodland site during two summers of the atlas, a pair was present at another site and a possible breeder at a third, all in the southern parts of the county. The nest-box breeder was in a Tawny Owl box and reared a brood in 2010, and possibly again in 2011. This is one of the few accurately documented nesting attempts nationally for this species. Wood Duck was recorded from five tetrads in winter.

WIGEON (Eurasian Wigeon) *Anas penelope*
Amber List. Abundant winter visitor and passage migrant: regularly summers/ occasionally breeds

Breeding population estimate: 0-4 pairs
Wintering population estimate: 50,000-75,000 individuals

Wigeon is the most abundant duck wintering in Cambridgeshire and the greatest concentrations of this highly gregarious bird are on the Ouse and Nene washlands. In the four winter survey periods the average peak counts for the main Cambridgeshire sites were: Ouse Washes 19,475, Nene Washes 15,656, Fen Drayton 2,395, Barleycraft gravel pits 1,950, Ouse Fen 1,290, Kingfishers Bridge 1,135, Paxton Pits and Wicken Fen both 834 (data from CBRs). The winter TTVs recorded a total of 32,823 birds. Cold weather across north-west Europe in January 2011 produced one of the highest WeBS counts for many years; the whole Ouse Washes had a total of 43,010 Wigeon. In the Cambs section there were 26,780, while there were 20,460 on the Nene Washes, and from other sites in excess of 10,000, giving a total of over 57,000 birds.

The flocks can be highly mobile, responding to disturbance, freezing and flooding. Excessively deep winter flooding on the Ouse Washes has reduced numbers and pushed birds to other sites like the Nene Washes, where the creation of further disturbance-free habitat has also helped to increase numbers. In cold snaps birds that do not leave for the coast find that the tidal rivers generally remain ice-free as does the deeper water of mineral pits and reservoirs. Wigeon are almost entirely vegetarian and primarily grazing birds; the shallowly flooded washes and the grassy surrounds to gravel pits provide ideal feeding. Much of the feeding takes place at night, particularly in disturbed areas; this part of their distribution goes largely unrecorded but is usually close to safe daytime roosts.

The breeding grounds of most of our wintering Wigeon lie between the Baltic and the River Ob just east of the Urals. Birds generally depart in March and early April although a handful of pairs usually stay, mostly on the Ouse and Nene Washes, and may attempt to breed. In 2011 breeding was confirmed at Kingfishers Bridge when a female was seen with two young in June.

Wigeon

Winter abundance

Winter distribution

Summer abundance

Breeding distribution

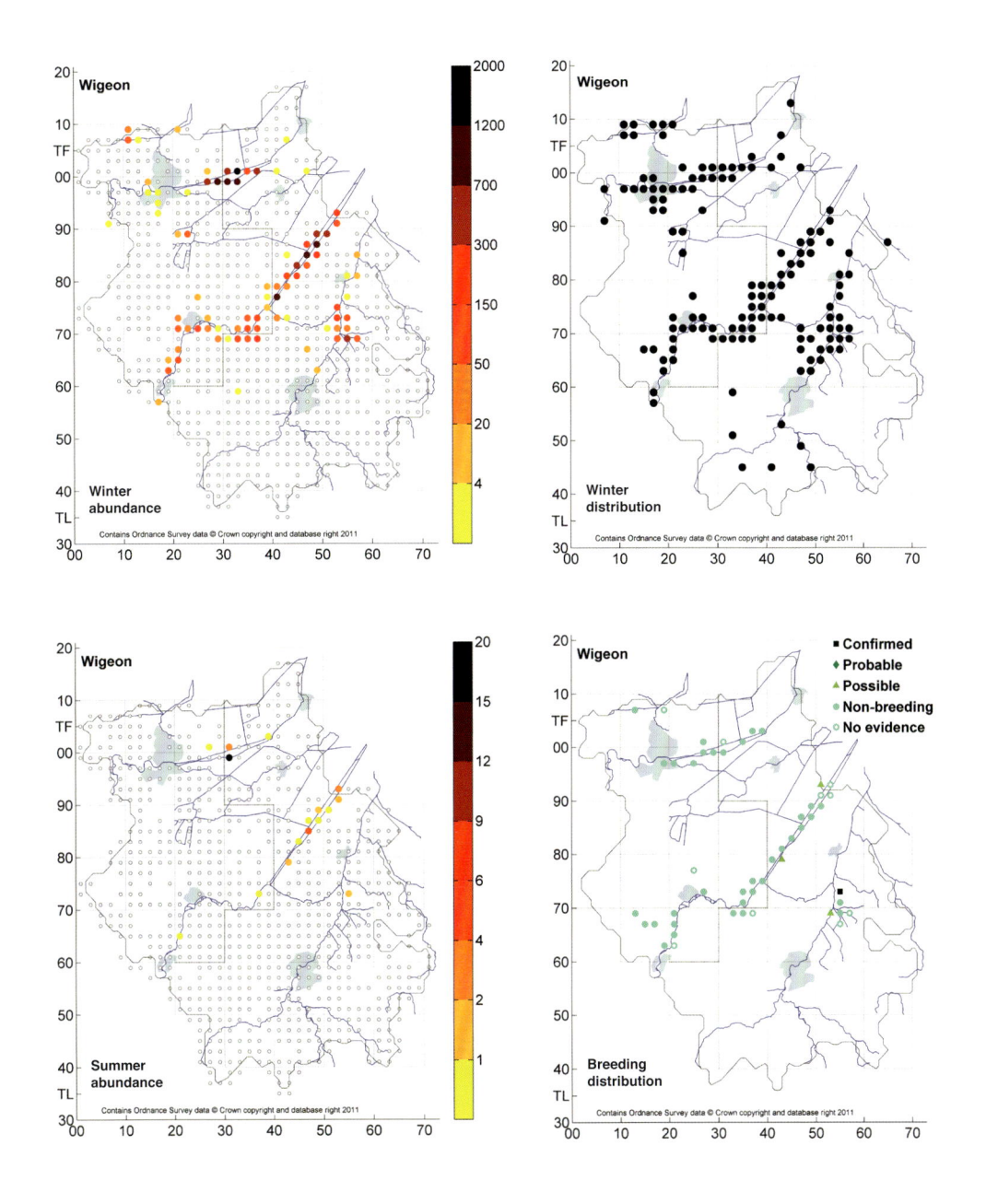

	Confirmed	Probable	Possible	Non-breeding	No evidence	Total summer (% county)	Total winter (% county)
Total tetrads	1	0	3	36	10	50 (5%)	134 (14%)

GADWALL *Anas strepera*
Amber List. Scarce local naturalised resident and fairly common winter visitor: slowly increasing

Breeding population estimate: 200-300 pairs
Wintering population estimate: 2,500-5,000 individuals

The naturalised Gadwall has now been established in the county for decades and the population continues to grow steadily, partly in response to the creation of new habitat in the form of flooded mineral workings along the main river valleys. The previous Cambs Atlas describes how birds were first recorded summering on the Nene Washes in the 1950s; although breeding had been proved on Burwell Fen in 1938, the first record of the recent expansion was on the Ouse Washes in 1964.

In this atlas period, confirmed and probable breeding occurred in 8% of tetrads, considerably more than the 3% and 2% in the previous Cambs and Hunts atlases, respectively. This mirrors the BBS trends showing a significant increase of 79% for Gadwall in England between 1995 and 2010 (Risely *et al.*, 2012).

In the breeding season Gadwall are found along the washes and the main rivers, and are absent from large tracts of the county, even in the fens where many drains, large and small, do not attract them. They thrive in eutrophic, lowland, open-water bodies where they and their ducklings feed almost exclusively on submerged aquatic plants. The main breeding sites with four-year averages for numbers of breeding pairs are the Ouse Washes (110) and Nene Washes (55). Other sites that regularly have breeding pairs in double figures include Kingfishers Bridge, Ely Beet Pits and the River Ouse pits at Fen Drayton and Barleycraft. Gadwall were recorded in 107 tetrads in the breeding season; TTVs recorded 561 birds.

Ringing recoveries show that the UK breeding population is not entirely sedentary, and some post-breeding Gadwall use the Ijsselmeer (Netherlands) and winter in France; a dispersal that increases in cold winters (Wernham *et al.*, 2002). Numbers in the fens tend to peak in February and March. The UK winter population is increased by continental birds from as far as the Baltic states; however, most wintering birds are of naturalised origin. The distribution of suitable habitat leads to broadly similar breeding and winter distributions. The four-year average peak counts for the main wintering sites are: Ouse Washes (Cambs only) 600, Fen Drayton 473, Paxton Pits 296, Nene Washes 294, Ouse Fen 258, Buckden and Stirtloe Pits 229. The 2010–2011 figure for national importance is 250. Wintering Gadwall were recorded in 14% of tetrads and the TTVs recorded 2,958 birds; the winter population is estimated to be around 3,000 birds. Apart from the Nene Washes, these sites are all concentrated in a relatively short stretch of the River Ouse and Washes. Gravel pits offer consistently good habitat compared with the Washes where flood conditions dictate wintering numbers; the Nene Washes are often not flooded while the Ouse Washes are frequently too deep, both leading to reduced numbers.

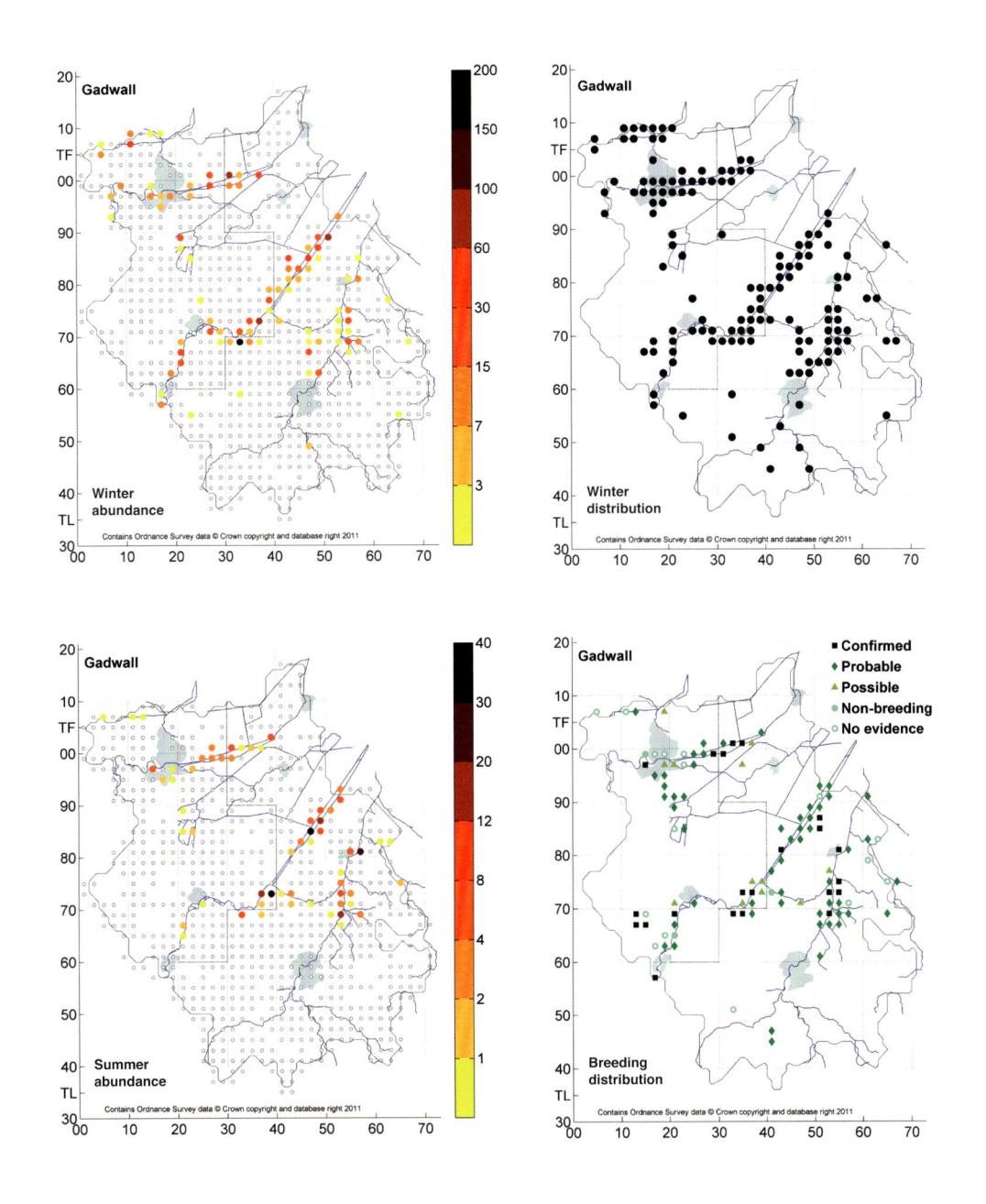

	Confirmed	Probable	Possible	Non-breeding	No evidence	Total summer (% county)	Total winter (% county)
Total tetrads	22	54	12	3	16	107 (11%)	140 (14%)

TEAL (Eurasian Teal) *Anas crecca*
Amber List. Scarce annual breeder; very common passage migrant and winter visitor

Breeding population estimate: 20-30 pairs
Wintering population estimate: 7,000-10,000 individuals

Teal are found primarily in the fens and on the wetlands of the Ouse Valley. However the atlas shows that they are widely distributed and it may well be that they are under-represented by the data. Many of these small and relatively inconspicuous ducks are found in small groups in fen drains and farm reservoirs where they could have gone unrecorded. They are also not the easiest birds to count in large mixed flocks dominated by other species. The Nene and Ouse Washes are the main sites for Teal and are of national importance; the four-year average peak winter counts were 3,319 and 2,875 (Cambrigeshire only), respectively. These are considerably larger than counts for the other main sites: Wicken Fen 349, Fen Drayton 299 and Grafham Water 186. Other wetland sites frequently record numbers in the low hundreds, but many Teal are found in small numbers scattered throughout the county. In February 2010, 9,012 were counted on the Nene Washes, twice the previous highest count for the site and a new county record. The winter TTVs found 6,210 Teal; it is estimated from WeBS counts that the normal winter population is between 7,000 and 10,000 birds.

Wintering Teal from the UK and Cambridgeshire breed mainly in Finland and western Russia; they return to the fens in substantial numbers in September and numbers peak in January and February, after which they emigrate very quickly. The spring TTVs and roving records include the breeding population and passage and non-breeding summering birds. Breeding Teal prefer the oligotrophic wetlands typical of the northern UK to the eutrophic ones of lowland Cambridgeshire. However, Teal have bred for many years in the main wetlands of the fens and despite a national decline in recent years they continue to do so: confirmed breeding was recorded on the Ouse Washes in 2008 and 2010, Nene Washes in 2010 (RSPB records, record not mapped) and Ely BF in 2011. However, the proportion of tetrads with confirmed breeding has declined since earlier county atlases, even though the total number of occupied summer tetrads is around 50% higher. In the previous atlases, 11 tetrads held confirmed breeding, 19 probable and 15 possible, amounting to 4.6% of the county. Because of the secretive nature of Teal it is likely that in most years successful pairs and failed breeding attempts remained undetected. Changes in county boundaries and survey methodology make direct comparisons with earlier atlases difficult but there appears to have been little change in the distribution of breeding birds. The breeding population is probably 20–30 pairs.

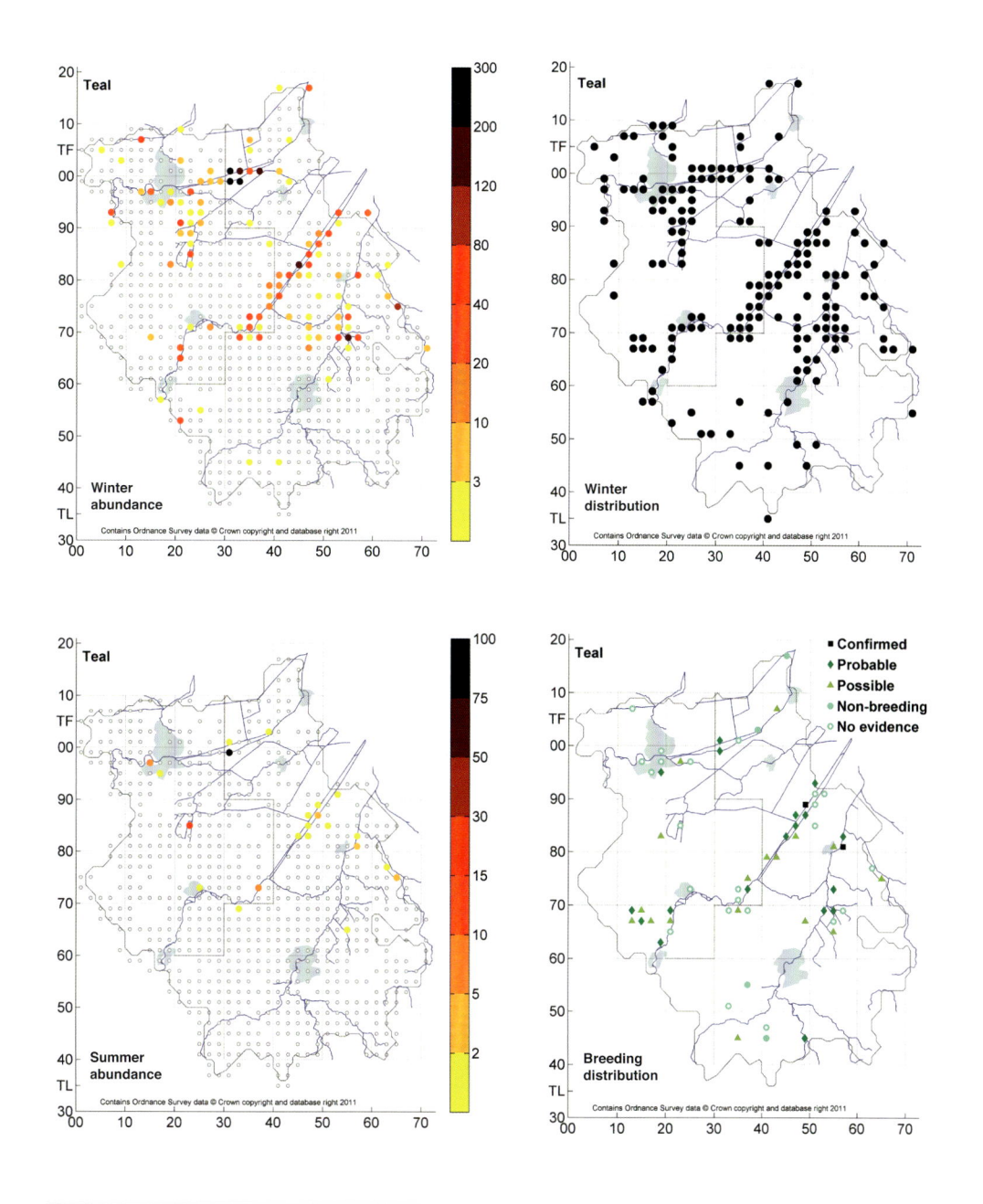

	Confirmed	Probable	Possible	Non-breeding	No evidence	Total summer (% county)	Total winter (% county)
Total tetrads	2	18	17	4	23	64 (7%)	178 (18%)

There were seven records of the Teal's cousin, **Green-winged Teal (*Anas carolinensis*)**, a rare vagrant from North America, during the atlas period, but we do not include a map here. Records were from Grafham Water (July 2007 and July 2010), Woodwalton Fen (January 2008 and June–July 2008), Maxey Pits and Nene Washes (February 2009), Maxey Pits (April 2010) and Crown Lakes (March 2011).

MALLARD *Anas platyrhynchos*
Amber List. Very common resident and winter visitor. Partially feral population and released birds/escapees

Breeding population estimate: 2,500-6,000 pairs
Wintering population estimate: 5,000-15,000 individuals

The Mallard is the most widespread of all wildfowl in the county, and is found in all types and sizes of wetlands. However there are large gaps in their distribution in the upland south and west of the county. There are also marked concentrations of both breeding and wintering birds on the main washes and the river valleys, where the species has benefited from the increasing amount of open water available in the form of gravel pits. There is a distinct concentration in the drained arable fens, where numerous man-made watercourses from small farm ditches to broad and sometimes tidal channels will support breeding Mallard. Since the 1990s there has been a dramatic increase in the number of small farm reservoirs. The gaps in distribution in the fens that appeared in earlier atlases have been reduced by better coverage but the problem of surveying fenland ditches and reservoirs still persists; these gaps are unlikely to represent an absence of breeding or wintering Mallard.

The Mallard is one of the few duck species to be covered effectively by the BBS; results show that between 1995 and 2010 the population has grown significantly by 30% in England and 15% in Eastern England (Risely *et al.*, 2012). In Cambridgeshire the proportion of tetrads with confirmed and probable breeding actually decreased from 72% and 52% in the previous Hunts and Cambs atlases, respectively, to 49% in the present atlas. However, this is likely to reflect changes in survey techniques and effort rather than a reduction in distribution. Mallard were found in 67% of TTVs and were present in 70% of all tetrads in summer, very similar to or higher than the previous atlases. Large numbers are known to breed on well-surveyed wetlands; four-year averages were: Ouse Washes 433 pairs, Nene Washes 225 and Fen Drayton 120.

There has been a steady national decline in wintering numbers since the 1990s that appears to have stabilised during the atlas survey period. The breeding population is sedentary or locally dispersed and in winter probably outnumbered by continental immigrants. Greater numbers are recorded in cold winters when more continental birds arrive but also because birds are forced out of the smaller ditches and wetlands into the larger ones, where they are recorded more easily in surveys. With a British population likely to be in excess of 500,000 neither of the main washlands are of national importance, although the Ouse Washes is one of the main sites in the country with an average in the four-year survey period of 3,115. The Cambridgeshire section average is 2,133, that for the Nene Washes 975 and Grafham Water 482.

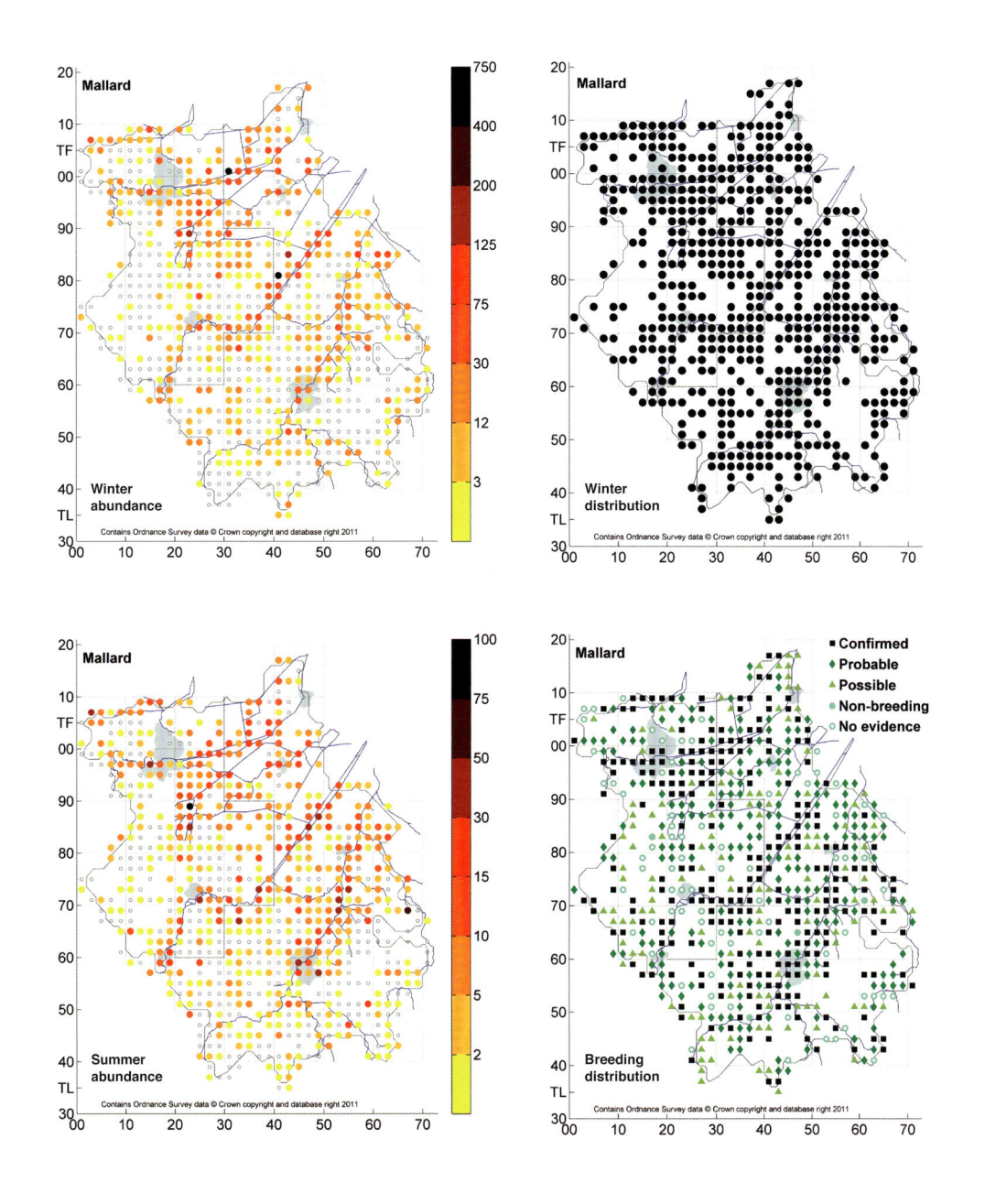

	Confirmed	Probable	Possible	Non-breeding	No evidence	Total summer (% county)	Total winter (% county)
Total tetrads	251	219	128	4	76	678 (70%)	570 (59%)

PINTAIL (Northern Pintail) *Anas acuta*
Amber List. Locally common winter visitor/passage migrant; has bred sporadically

Breeding population estimate: 2-10 pairs
Wintering population estimate: 2,500-5,000 individuals

The handsome and elegant Pintail is a species for which Cambridgeshire is particularly important, principally as a wintering species but also as an occasional breeder. It has probably bred in the county since the 1920s although this was not proved until 1947 and is still irregular. The small numbers of breeders are likely to be stragglers from the winter; most Pintail leave in March but they are opportunistic breeders and a delayed departure leads to high spring counts and increased chances of breeding. There are regular spring records, particularly from the Ouse and Nene Washes, of birds that show no indication of breeding, but when conditions and timing are right, the birds will do so. Typical Pintail breeding grounds are lowland, eutrophic wetlands, and the right conditions are most frequently found on the floodplain grasslands of the Ouse Washes, which is by some margin the principal site, although numbers have declined since the early 1970s when there were as many as 20 pairs. The Nene Washes has also declined as a breeding site (there were four tetrads with confirmed breeding in the previous Hunts Atlas), while the gravel-pit complexes and wetlands to the south of the Ouse Washes are of increasing importance. Birds were recorded from only 15 tetrads during summer and confirmed breeding records were from the Ouse Washes in 2009 and 2010 and Berry Fen in 2011.

The wintering population of Pintail in north-west Europe increased dramatically in the 1970s and this was reflected in the numbers using the Cambridgeshire washlands, but there are signs of a recent decline in both the UK and Cambridgeshire that was noticeable during the atlas survey period. Eaton *et al.* (2012) cite a 17% decline as a long-term (30-year) trend and a 10-year trend of -15%. Most wintering Pintail in the UK are found on sheltered estuaries, and Cambridgeshire is exceptional in having two freshwater sites of international importance for this species. The four-year averages for the Nene and Cambridgeshire Ouse Washes are 1,714 and 984, respectively.

Wintering Pintail originate mostly from Finland and western Russia, and start arriving in the fens at the end of October; numbers peak in January and February. In the winters of the atlas period the maximum count was 2,400 on the Nene Washes in January 2010. Much smaller numbers, usually in single figures, are to be found on other wetlands, mainly in the fens and the Ouse valley; this clumping with a few large concentrations and scattered individuals elsewhere is a feature of wintering Pintail in north-west Europe (Wernham *et al.*, 2002). Wintering Pintail were recorded from 51 tetrads, a little over 5% of the county. On the freshwater washlands numbers fluctuate widely, depending on flood conditions and ice. The two winters 2009/10 and 2010/11 were exceptionally cold and Pintail will leave, probably for the south coast and France, when the washlands are frozen; the deep floods that are increasingly frequent on the Ouse Washes may also suppress numbers of this dabbling duck.

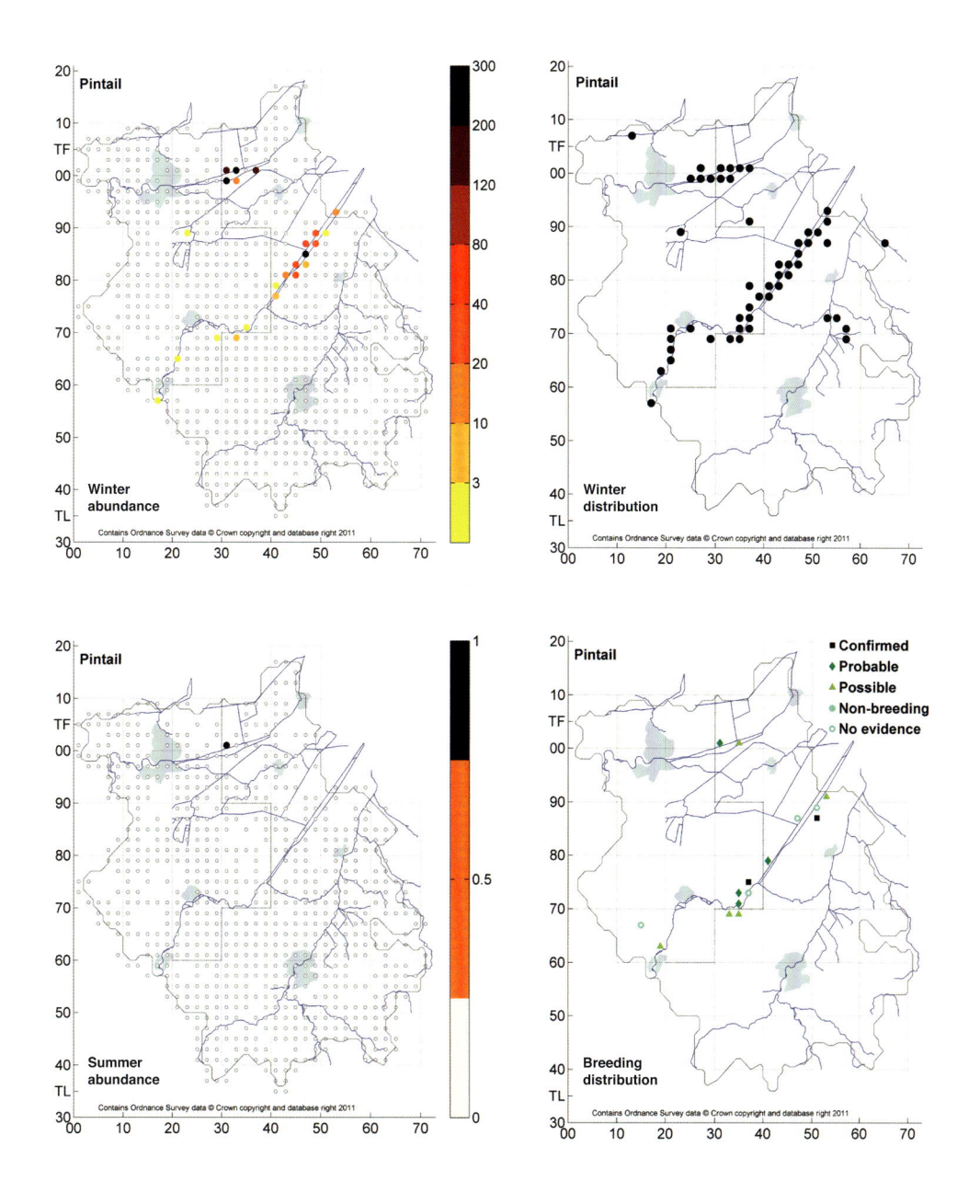

	Confirmed	Probable	Possible	Non-breeding	No evidence	Total summer (% county)	Total winter (% county)
Total tetrads	2	4	5	0	4	15 (2%)	51 (5%)

GARGANEY *Anas querquedula*
Amber List. **Scarce migratory breeder and passage migrant**

Breeding population estimate: 10-20 pairs
Not a wintering species

Cambridgeshire is the most important county and the Ouse Washes the most important site in the UK for this scarce breeding bird. The first appearance of Garganey in the spring is one of the great pleasures of birdwatching on the washes, where they are one of the earliest and most attractive of the spring migrants. The splendid eye-catching plumage of the drake and the dry rattling call is unmistakable but the birds can be hard to detect once the breeding season is underway. Their preferred breeding habitat is lowland floodplain meadow with eutrophic water bodies in the form of shallow seasonal pools and well-vegetated, water-filled ditches. This habitat is found primarily on the washlands of the fens, and the map highlights four distinct concentrations: the Nene Washes, Ouse Washes, Cam Washes/Wicken Fen area and the multiple and varied wetlands on the River Ouse where it reaches the fens.

Garganey are opportunistic breeders and the population fluctuates from year to year, partly depending on the numbers arriving in the UK and also on the suitability of the habitat they find available. Floodplains are a naturally volatile habitat that are not always in ideal condition; the Ouse Washes in particular has suffered from prolonged spring flooding which limits nesting opportunities. During the atlas period the Cambridgeshire Ouse Washes average was eight pairs and the Nene Washes 3.5; no other sites had confirmed breeding. However, 34 tetrads recorded confirmed, probable and possible breeding, considerably more than in previous county atlases which implies that the range and perhaps the population has expanded slightly since the 1980s. This may be a result of the increasing quantity and quality of habitat on new and expanding nature reserves such as Wicken Fen and Kingfishers Bridge. The Cambridgeshire breeding population is in the range of 10–20 pairs.

In the previous Cambs Atlas, breeding was confirmed in six, probable in five and possible in five tetrads and in the Hunts Atlas was probable in four and possible in two tetrads, amounting to around 2% of the county; the present results represent an increase on these values.

Outside the atlas survey dates, there is a late-summer/autumn increase in numbers, particularly on the Ouse Washes; in August–September 2012 128 Garganey were present. This is the largest count of Garganey for the UK and took place at the end of a very wet summer when the Ouse Washes were draining after extensive flooding, leaving large shallow pools.

Most of Europe's Garganey winter in huge flocks in the Sahel region of West Africa, with a few in the Mediterranean; there are occasional wintering records in England. A bird was present at Paxton Pits from 7th to 10th January 2007 (just prior to the atlas period), and although birds usually return in March and April the earliest birds can be in February. Two tetrads recorded Garganey during the winter period (both in February).

Garganey

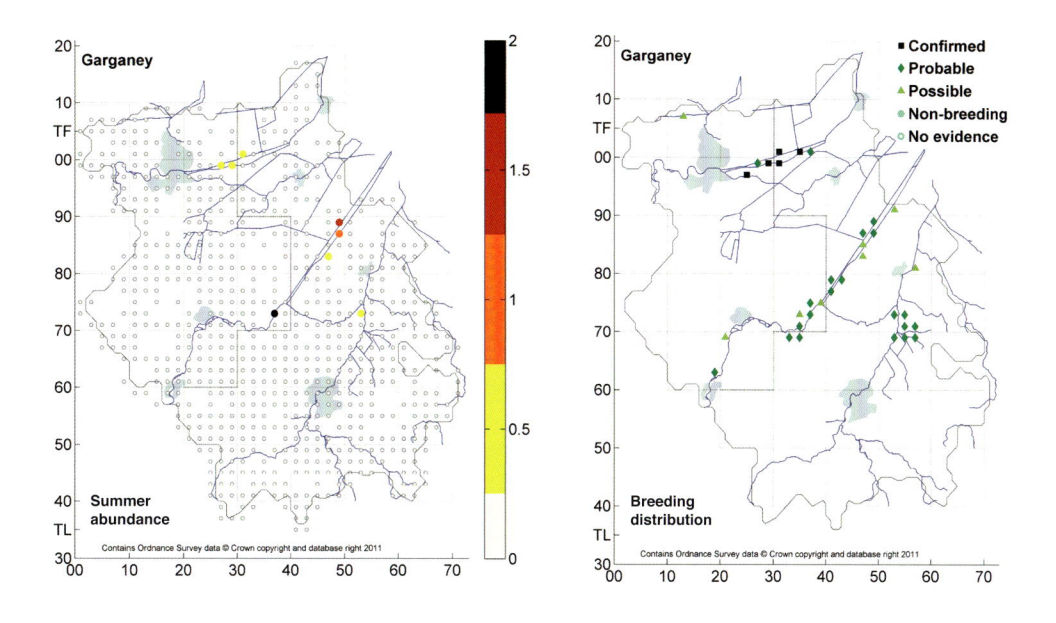

Summer abundance

Garganey

Breeding distribution

- ■ Confirmed
- ◆ Probable
- ▲ Possible
- ● Non-breeding
- ○ No evidence

	Confirmed	Probable	Possible	Non-breeding	No evidence	Total summer (% county)	Total winter (% county)
Total tetrads	5	21	8	0	0	34 (4%)	2 (0.2%)

47

SHOVELER (Northern Shoveler) *Anas clypeata*
Amber list. Uncommon resident; fairly common winter visitor and passage migrant

Breeding population estimate: 250-400 pairs
Wintering population estimate: 1,000-1,500 individuals

The Ouse Washes is the most important site in the UK for wintering Shoveler, a good proportion of which occur in the Cambridgeshire section. The average peak winter counts at the four main sites are: Ouse Washes (Cambridgeshire only) 859, Nene Washes 226, Grafham Water 168 and Colne Fen GP 73. Numbers peak in the county in March (outside the atlas survey period) and are likely to include wintering and passage birds as well as local breeding birds returning from their wintering grounds. The wintering birds were recorded in 98 tetrads, 10% of the total, and 1,310 birds were counted in TTVs. The wintering population ranges from 1,000 to 1,500 birds.

The winter population is found on the main washlands and in the valleys and gravel pits of the four main rivers: Welland, Nene, Ouse and Cam, with an almost complete absence from the uplands in the west and south of the county. Wintering numbers nationally have shown a steady long-term increase (70% over 30 years; Eaton *et al.*, 2012), thought to be a response to milder winters, although the national index dipped during the period of the atlas probably in response to freezing conditions in two cold winters. Shoveler are highly sensitive to freezing conditions and numbers can fluctuate widely among years.

Research on the Ouse Washes found Shoveler to be the most carnivorous of the dabbling ducks, using their large bills to filter small invertebrates as well as seeds. The drakes are unusually territorial for dabbling duck, which combined with their bold and distinctive appearance makes detection relatively easy. The females are less easy to detect during breeding; the presence of large young is the easiest way to confirm breeding but they are often not visible until late in the season. They are a species of lowland eutrophic wetlands, particularly marshes and grazing marshes. The Cambridgeshire fens are one of the UK breeding strongholds with concentrations of birds on wetlands managed as nature reserves where seasonal pools and water-filled ditches are present. The Ouse Washes (Cambridgeshire) average for the four atlas years was 156 pairs, the Nene Washes 55 pairs; other sites, mostly gravel pits, are usually in single figures. Their distribution has changed little since the previous Cambs and Hunts atlases, with the exception of a greater number of records in the Fen Drayton–Ouse Fen area. Breeding numbers have increased, and although they vary widely, there are regularly over 250, and sometimes as many as 400 pairs. In the previous atlases there were 18 tetrads with confirmed/probable breeding in each half of the county, a further 14 possible in Cambs and six possible in Hunts.

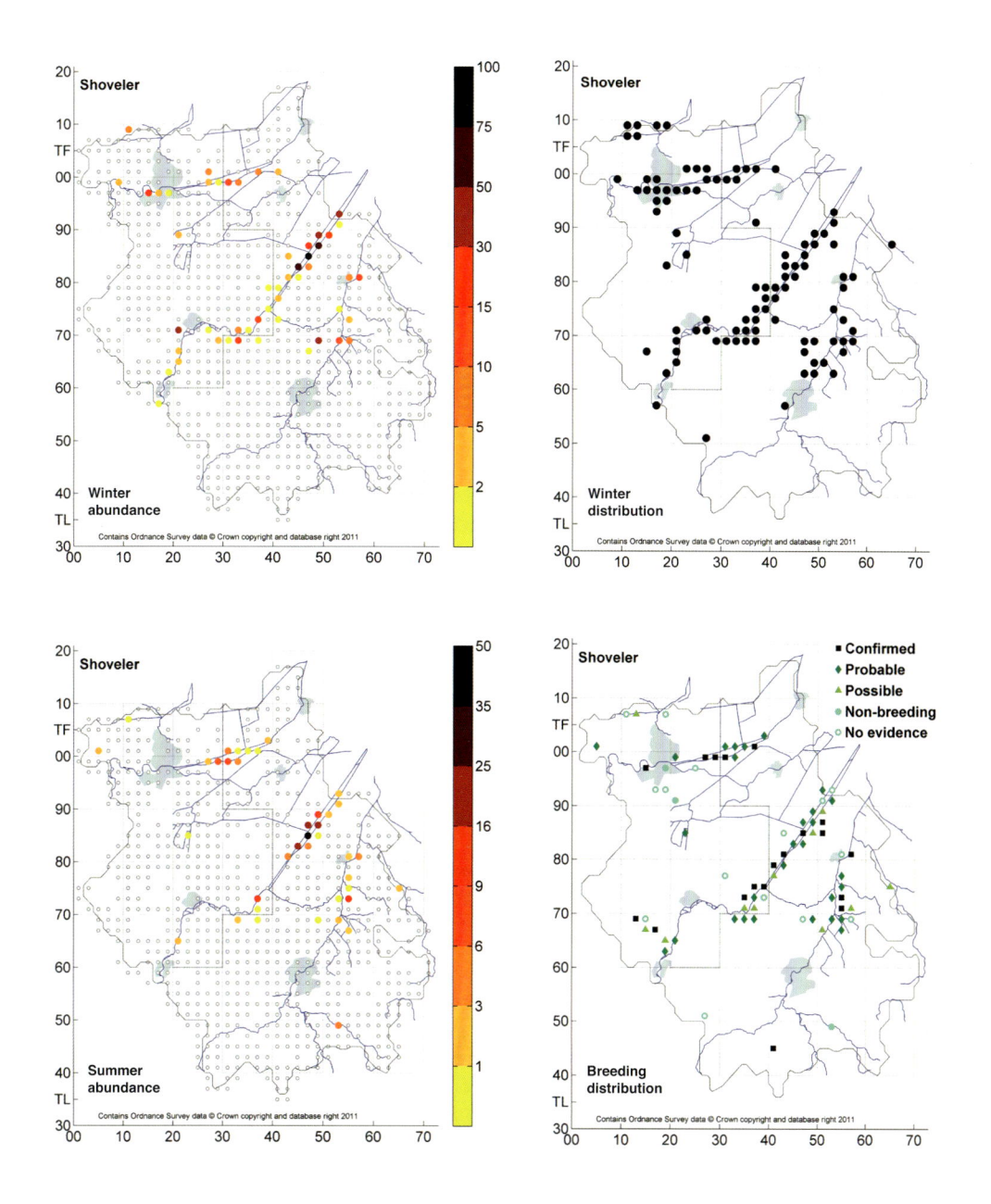

	Confirmed	Probable	Possible	Non-breeding	No evidence	Total summer (% county)	Total winter (% county)
Total tetrads	19	29	11	3	15	77 (8%)	98 (10%)

RED-CRESTED POCHARD *Netta rufina*
Uncommon visitor; some are escapees or released birds

Breeding population estimate: 1-5 pairs
Wintering population estimate: 2-10 individuals

Yet another non-native wildfowl, the Red-crested Pochard has long been present in the county where the population is considered to have originated from accidental releases or escapes. Its true breeding status is unclear, with only one confirmed breeding attempt recorded in the Welland valley west of Peterborough. Ferry Meadows, Paxton Pits and Fen Drayton Lakes all had probable breeders; the Paxton-Buckden stretch of the Ouse had a wide scatter of records deemed to be of non-breeders, as did Grafham Water.

The winter distribution covered the same area, but additionally birds were recorded from sites in the Ouse-Cam confluence area, such as Kingfishers Bridge.

It is unclear how many birds there are moving around the county to constitute this set of tetrads. No data to examine this have been collected, but it seems likely that a few small populations may exist, and breeding may become established in any of these colonies in time.

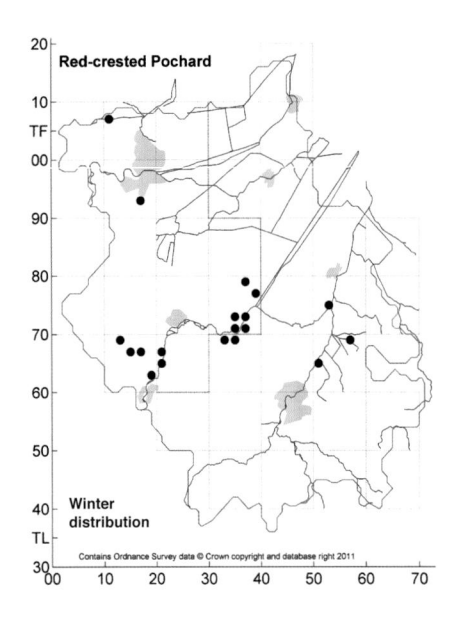

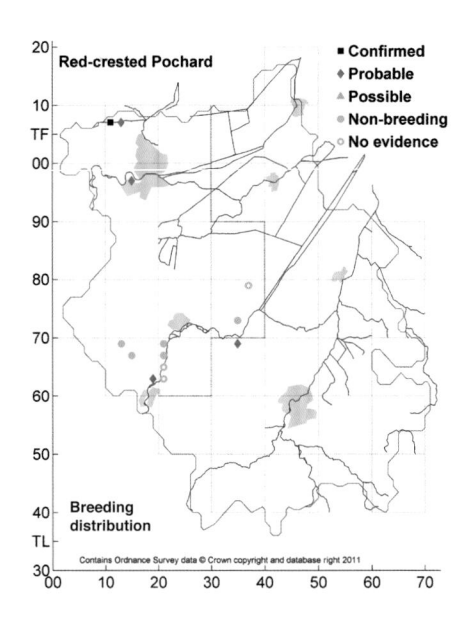

	Confirmed	Probable	Possible	Non-breeding	No evidence	Total summer (% county)	Total winter (% county)
Total tetrads	1	4	0	5	3	13 (1%)	19 (2%)

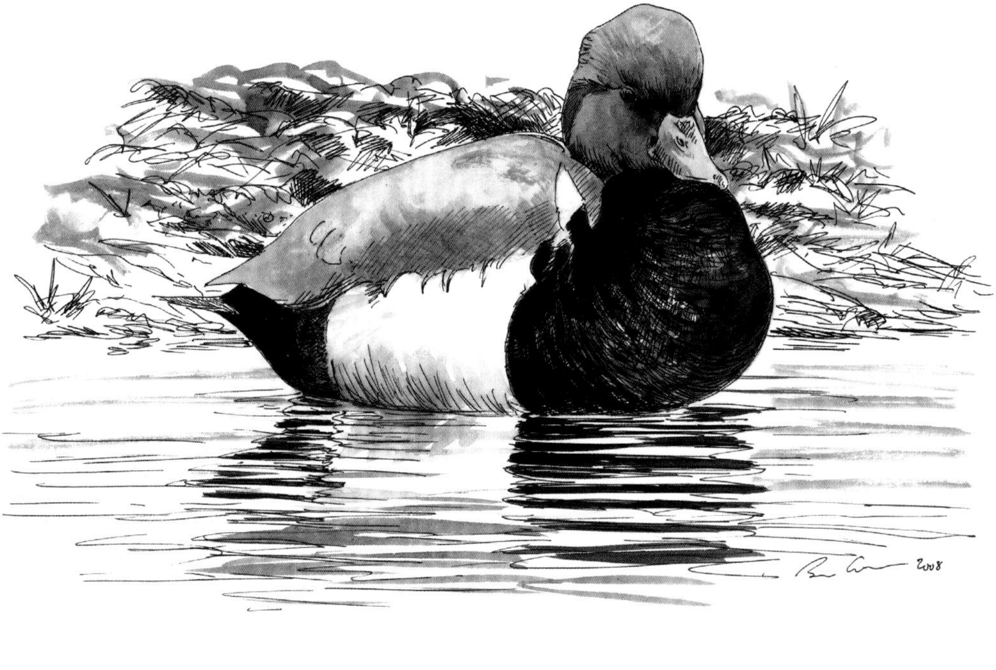

POCHARD (Common Pochard) *Aythya ferina*
Amber List. Scarce resident; common winter visitor and passage migrant

Breeding population estimate: 30-40 pairs
Wintering population estimate: 2,500-3,000 individuals

During winter, the Pochard is a relatively widespread visitor. Two areas stand out: along the valley of the River Great Ouse and the Ouse Washes, and the Nene valley. The highest TTV counts were along the Ouse Washes and to a lesser extent on other Ouse valley pits and Welland pits. Lower concentrations of birds are found along the valley of the River Cam; away from main rivers most birds were only recorded by roving records rather than on TTVs, highlighting the somewhat scattered nature of a proportion of this species which utilises sites away from the large pits. Average peak winter counts at key sites were: Ouse Washes (Cambs) 1,491, Paxton Pits 264, Grafham Water 252, Nene Washes 215 and Fen Drayton 186. The national long-term trend is a 50% decline for wintering populations.

During the breeding season, the Pochard is a much scarcer bird, recorded from only 55 tetrads. In the previous Cambs Atlas breeding was confirmed in four tetrads, probable in six and possible in a further four. The equivalent breeding figures for the previous Hunts Atlas were four, six and eight tetrads. Confirmed breeding was thus in eight tetrads across the county and this species was recorded in a total of 32 tetrads; this is far fewer than in the current atlas although confirmation of breeding was similar. The number of birds present in the breeding season with no breeding evidence explains the higher tetrad count.

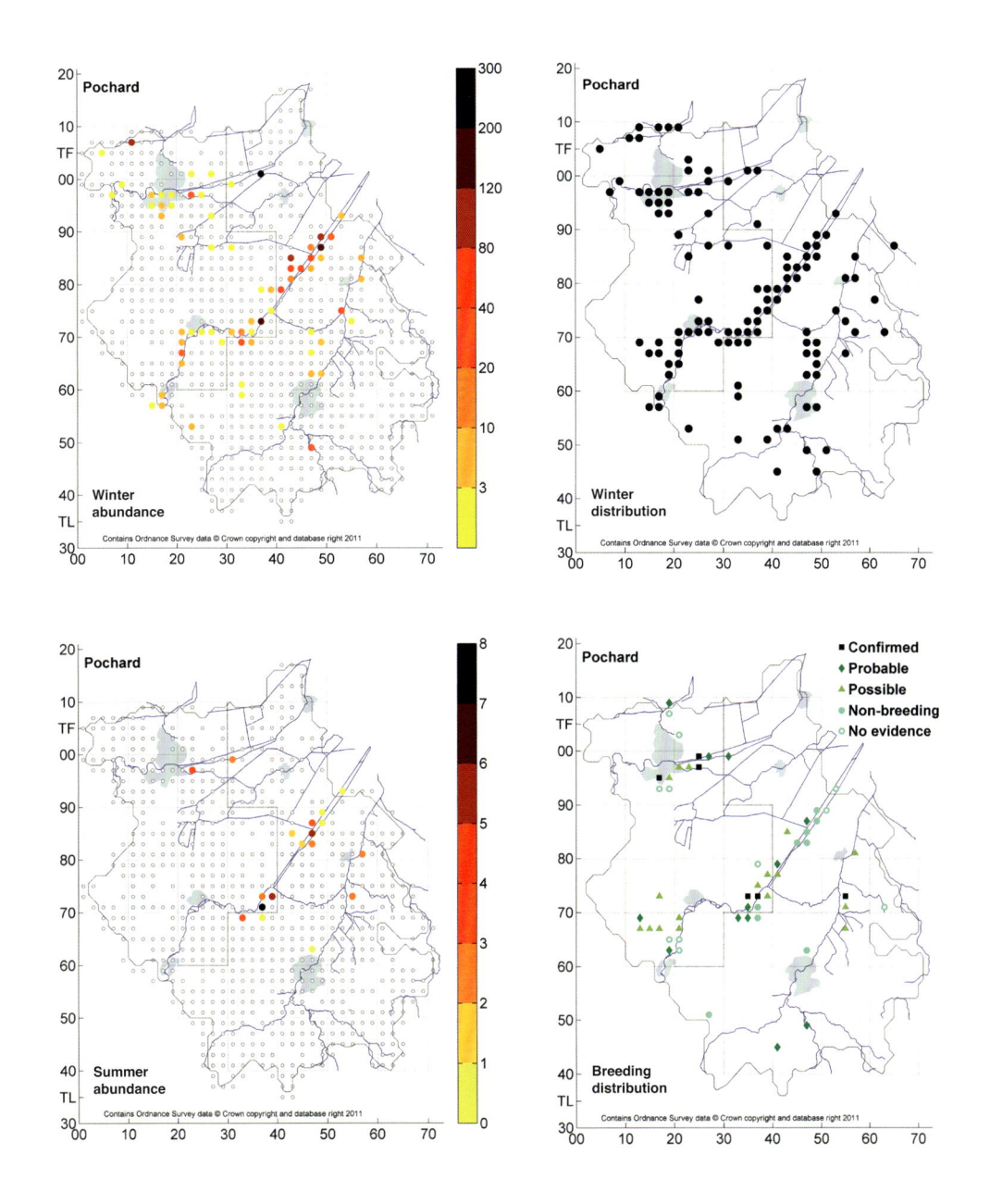

	Confirmed	Probable	Possible	Non-breeding	No evidence	Total summer (% county)	Total winter (% county)
Total tetrads	6	12	17	9	11	55 (6%)	115 (12%)

TUFTED DUCK *Aythya fuligula*
Amber List. **Fairly common resident; common winter visitor and passage migrant**

Breeding population estimate: 200-500 pairs
Wintering population estimate: 2,500-6,000 individuals

The winter populations of Tufted Ducks in the four years of the atlas were: 4,665 in 2007/08, 2,629 in 2008/09, 3,264 in 2009/10 and 4,410 in 2010/11, giving an average of 3,742. The greatest concentrations were found along the valley of the River Great Ouse. It is the most widespread of all the diving ducks, and large numbers are also found on and around the Ouse Washes and in the valleys of the River Cam and River Nene. Tufted Ducks also appear in numbers in the brick pits to the north of Peterborough. Average peak winter counts at key sites were: Ouse Washes 1,813, Grafham Water 1,710, Paxton Pits 757 and Fen Drayton 521.

During the breeding season significant numbers breed in gravel pits and other large lake complexes and small numbers also breed in small water bodies such as farm reservoirs and lakes in business parks. For instance, Tufted Ducks now breed regularly on several of the lakes created in the new settlement of Cambourne. Their ability to utilise these kinds of breeding sites may be a contributing factor to their increasing population. BBS 15-year trends for the UK imply a 46% increase (Risely *et al.*, 2012). Wintering trends (Eaton *et al.*, 2012) show a 30-year increase (19%) but a 10-year decline of 11%. The higher number of occupied tetrads in summer compared to winter suggests dispersal to smaller waterbodies for breeding.

Tufted Ducks are unobtrusive during the breeding season, and do not nest until quite late in the summer; the most likely clue to successful breeding is the appearance of ducklings in July, hence the low proportion of confirmed-breeding tetrads. In the previous Cambs Atlas 80 tetrads had probable/confirmed breeding with presence in 27 other tetrads; in the Hunts Atlas breeding was confirmed in 64 tetrads, probable in 26 and possible in seven others. Together this represented 21% of the county. A slightly higher number of tetrads was recorded in the present atlas in which the summer total was 212 tetrads (22%).

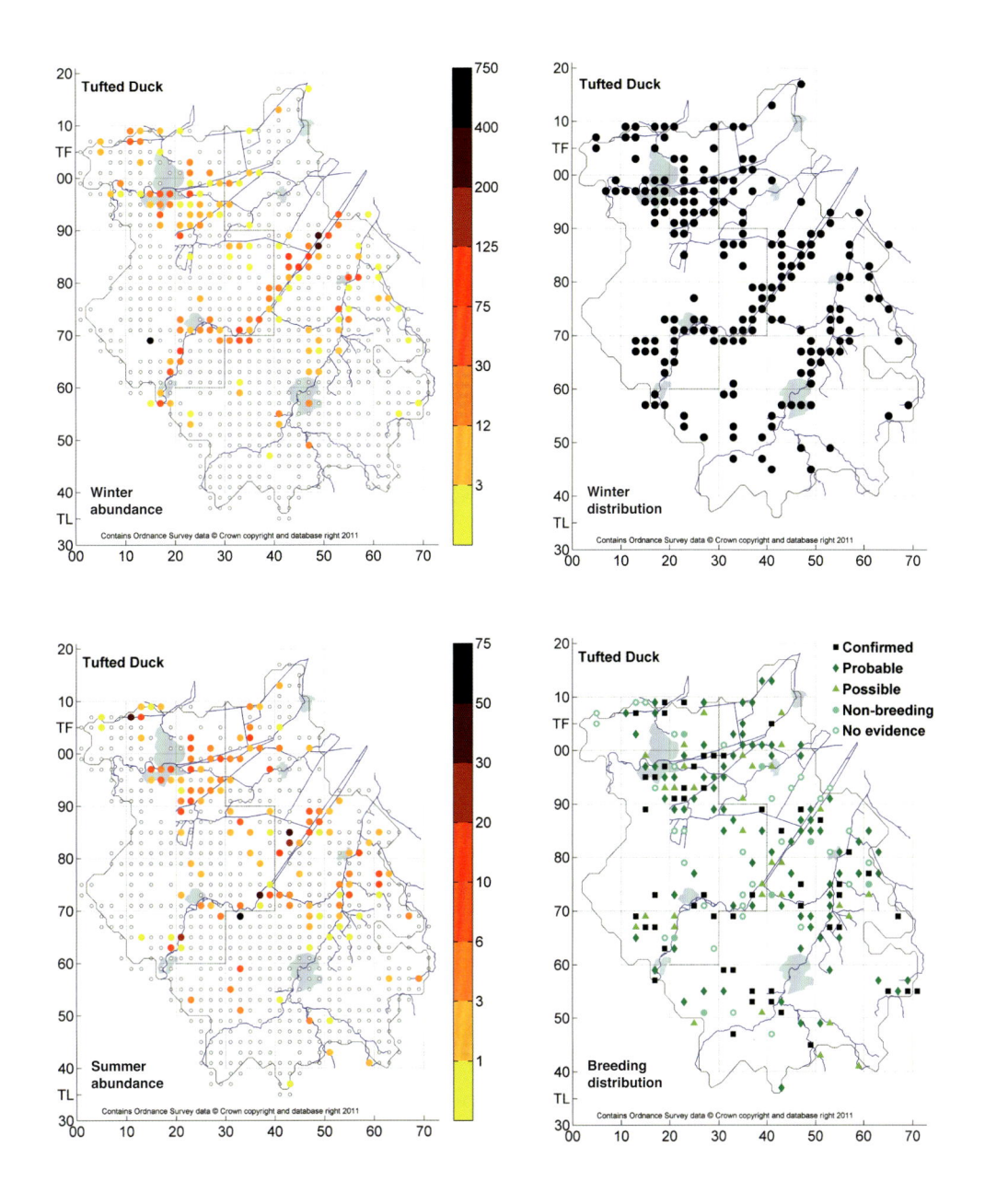

	Confirmed	Probable	Possible	Non-breeding	No evidence	Total summer (% county)	Total winter (% county)
Total tetrads	53	88	32	7	32	212 (22%)	195 (20%)

SCAUP (Greater Scaup) *Aythya marila*
Red List. Scarce annual passage migrant and winter visitor

Not a breeding species
Wintering population estimate: 5-15 records annually

The winter populations of Scaup in the four years of the atlas were: ten in 2007/08, 14 in 2008/09, ten in 2009/10, and eight in 2010/11, giving an average of 11.

A scarce winter visitor, often within flocks of Tufted Ducks, usually only one or two birds are found at a site. Grafham Water often has three or four birds present through the winter, and four were recorded in the winter of 2008/9 on the lakes at Cambourne. Away from Grafham Water, there are few regular sites for this erratic visitor – any of the wetland complexes suitable for diving ducks could host a wintering Scaup.

Scaup often spend a substantial part of a winter at a site, rather than fleetingly passing through, and often linger through into April (the summer recording season), although these birds are preparing for their journey northwards. No summer data are shown here.

Scaup were recorded in 24 tetrads through the four winters of the atlas.

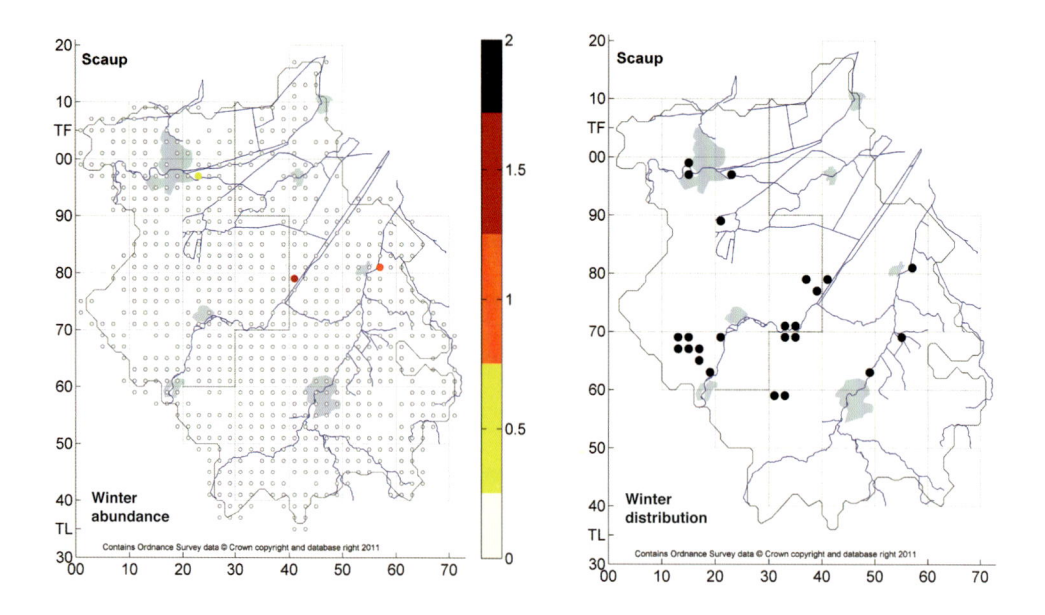

GOLDENEYE (Common Goldeneye) *Bucephala clangula*
Amber List. Fairly common winter visitor and passage migrant; occasionally summers

Not a breeding species
Wintering population estimate: 200-400 individuals

The winter populations of Goldeneye in the four years of the atlas were: 345 in 2007/08, 213 in 2008/09, 163 in 2009/10, and 311 in 2010/11, giving an average of 258.

The Goldeneye is a winter visitor to our larger, deeper-water sites: Grafham Water and the Ouse valley gravel pits hold significant populations. The largest concentrations are found along the valley of the River Great Ouse, on and around the Ouse Washes and in the brick pits around Peterborough. Further groupings follow the valleys of the River Cam and River Nene. Average peak winter counts at key sites during the atlas period were: Grafham Water 114, Paxton Pits 105 and Fen Drayton 101.

Nationally, the long-term (30-year) trend is a 28% decline, and the 10-year trend shows a 43% decline (Eaton *et al.*, 2012). It was recorded in 54 tetrads (6%), 29 on TTVs. Whilst the peak count on TTVs was 16, this was much lower than the largest counts derived from roving records or other surveys such as WeBS counts.

A few summer records were collected during the atlas period, from 18 tetrads, but these are all considered to be non-breeding individuals remaining in wintering locations in the Nene and Ouse valleys. No maps are shown for the summer season.

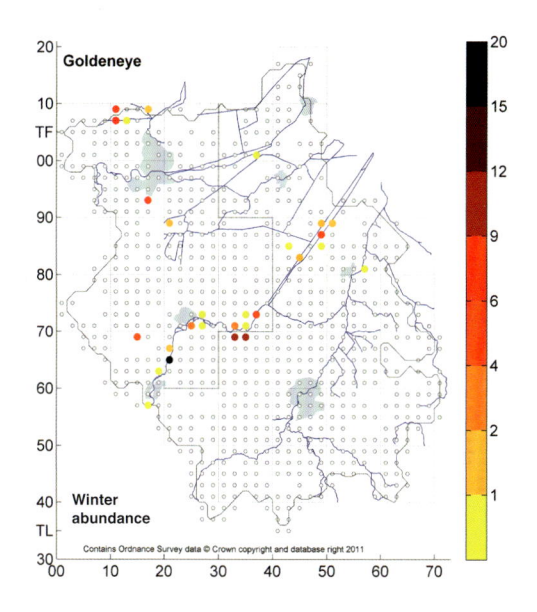

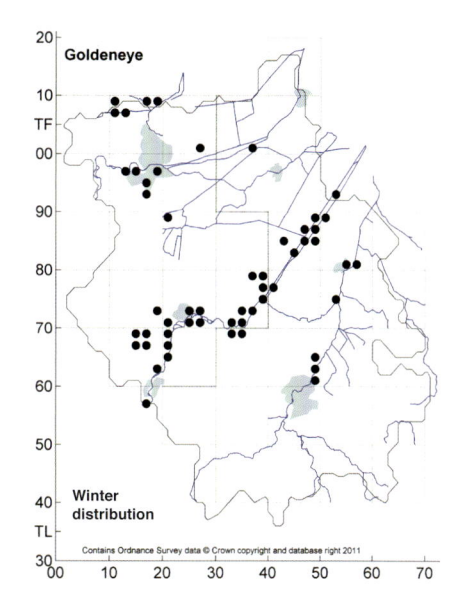

SMEW *Mergellus albellus*
Amber List. Uncommon, annual winter visitor

Not a breeding species
Wintering population estimate: 30-100 individuals

Possibly the most prized of our winter-visitor ducks, the sight of a Smew flock always lifts a winter day's birdwatching. They have traditionally been most frequent visitors to the Ouse valley at sites such as Paxton Pits or Fen Drayton Lakes. The availability of suitable habitat is increasing as a number of wetland projects are creating suitable waterbodies in this area. Smew also turn up irregularly in other spots, on the pits of the Welland and the reserves along the Cam valley. The large washlands reserves are not favoured.

Average peak winter counts at key sites were: Barleycraft 22 and Paxton Pits 13. Flocks of more than 10 were also recorded during the atlas period at Grafham Water and Fen Drayton, the latter including birds now mostly residing at Barleycraft. All other sites logged these birds purely on roving visits; it was recorded from 20 tetrads in total.

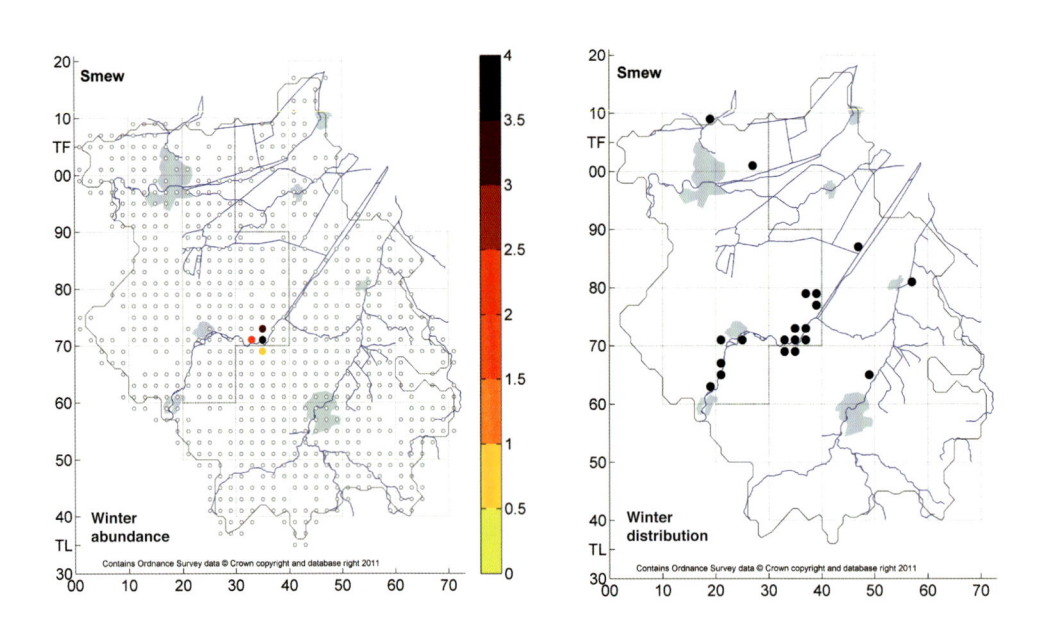

GOOSANDER (Common Merganser) *Mergus merganser*
Green List. Fairly common winter visitor; has summered

Not a breeding species
Wintering population estimate: 20-50 individuals

In southern England Goosanders have a preference for significant areas of water, hence most of the 47 winter tetrads where this bird was recorded are sites such as Grafham Water and the Ouse valley pits. The Nene valley pits also occasionally have birds. The other notable area where Goosanders are regularly recorded is in the Welland valley, on the border with Lincolnshire. Peak counts at some key sites were: Maxey gravel pits 22, Deeping High Bank 20, and Grafham Water 17.

On the Nene Washes they are presumably found on the deeper, tidal northern river (the Nene channel), as this would provide the most suitable habitat. In colder winters, Goosanders occasionally move to other rivers, and several observations of birds on the Cam north of Cambridge and downstream towards Swaffham and Bottisham were typical of this, observed in the colder winters of the second half of the atlas period.

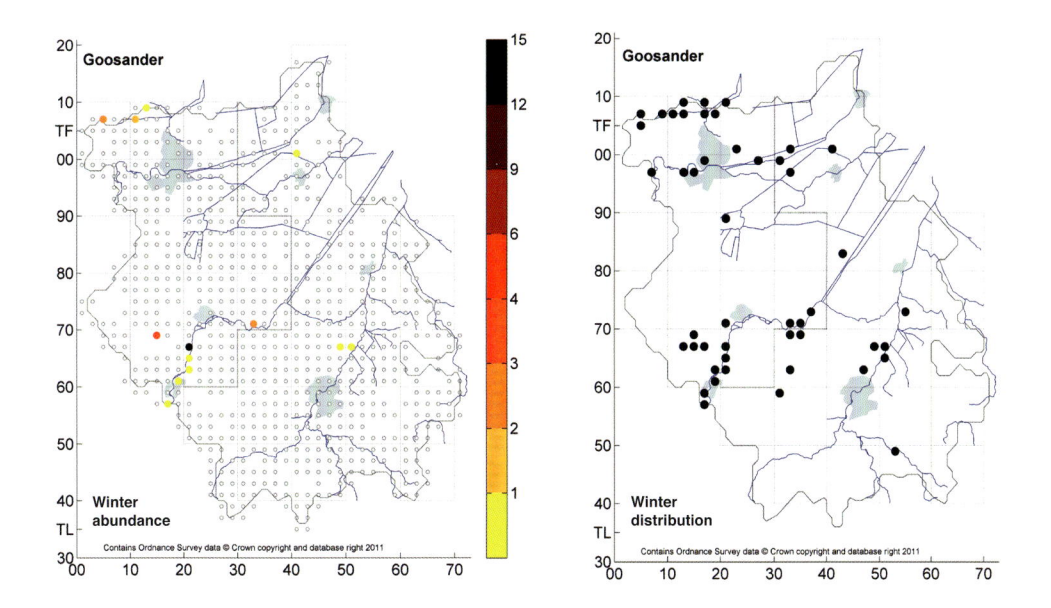

There were four tetrads where **Red-breasted Merganser (*Mergus serrator*)** were found during the atlas period, which narrowly misses inclusion. This species can be found on our deeper rivers and reservoirs during hard winter weather. The two fairly cold winters during the atlas period account for these records.

RED-LEGGED PARTRIDGE *Alectoris rufa*
Very common naturalised resident (with frequent releases)

Breeding population estimate: 3,000-5,000 pairs
Wintering population estimate: 7,500-15,000 individuals

This species, first introduced in the 18th century, is widely distributed across the county with high similarity between the winter and summer maps, as expected for a sedentary resident. Red-legged Partridges are found in every 10 km square in the county. It was confirmed to be breeding in 34 of these 10 km squares, with probable breeding in every other 10 km square except TL08, which contains a tiny part of the county (possible breeding was noted in a tetrad adjacent to the county boundary even here). Being associated with open arable land, the commonest land use in the county, it is hardly surprising that it is so widespread.

The abundance of this species is relatively even across much of the county, but there are centres of higher population density in the fenland area south and east of Peterborough, and, even more so, in the south-east of the county; both these centres of high density had relatively few TTV visits, so the areas of white space can be interpreted as probably holding numerous birds as well. Note that the scale on the winter density map reaches a frequency of 50 birds per hour. It is notable that the fenland areas have a high density of Red-legged Partridges in summer and winter whereas the density in the south-east of the county is much higher in winter than in summer; intensive game-keeping activities here are associated with winter-released birds, artificially increasing the population. The south-west and northern parts of the county have moderate, patchy, populations, while all urban centres show a markedly low density, with records coming only from Cambridge city out of the major conurbations, where it occurs on allotment and common land.

As an abundant non-native species, Red-legged Partridges are not high on most birdwatchers' agenda. Furthermore, they inhabit farmland areas not particularly visited by birdwatchers. In arable, they can be relatively difficult to count accurately, spending much time walking among crops taller than the birds. This is particularly so when there are young birds, making proof of breeding – sightings of family parties – difficult to obtain. Of the almost 2,000 records submitted during the breeding season, only 89 were of confirmed breeding status, which is an obvious underestimate. Pairs spend a lot of time in close proximity in the breeding season, a habit that was widely used to provide probable breeding status.

Nationally, Red-legged Partridges are most abundant in Eastern England, and Cambridgeshire reflects this, the density being almost double that of the UK average. Monitoring data suggest a shallow decline over time since the Common Bird Census began in 1966, but there was a period in the late 1970s when this species peaked, coinciding with the period of the Hunts Atlas. Locally, BBS data show moderate declines in both occupancy of squares and density since 1995.

The highest summer counts came from TTVs, with 31 in one hour at TL27N and 22 in an hour at TL55B. In the winter, larger counts were obtained from roving data, with 88 in TL55 around Six Mile Bottom, whereas 69 was the peak hourly count from a TTV at TL45M.

In the winter, Red-legged Partridge was recorded in 49 out of the 51 10 km squares (not recorded in two peripheral squares). At the tetrad level, it was recorded in 564 out of the 969 county tetrads (58%).

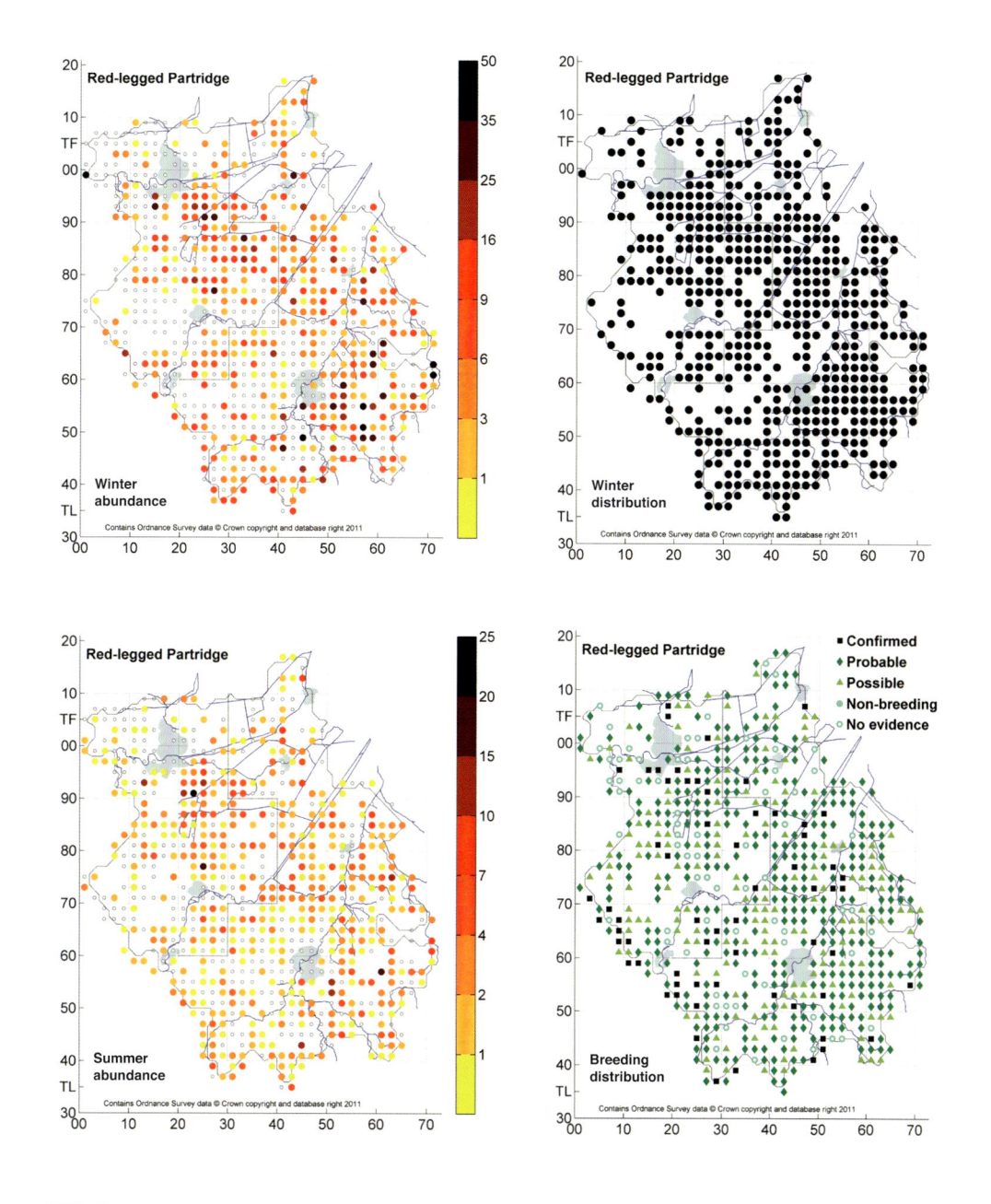

	Confirmed	Probable	Possible	Non-breeding	No evidence	Total summer (% county)	Total winter (% county)
Total tetrads	63	374	170	0	70	677 (70%)	564 (58%)

GREY PARTRIDGE *Perdix perdix*
Red List. Scarce resident; population much declined and fairly local (some releases)

Breeding population estimate: 500-2,000 pairs
Wintering population estimate: 1,000-5,000 individuals

Grey Partridge is a resident, sedentary species; the four maps show similar distribution and abundance patterns. The major concentration is in the southern chalk areas, in and around TL24, 34 and 44. Secondary centres of importance are similar to the Red-legged Partridge strongholds, the fens south of Peterborough and south-east Cambridgeshire between Cambridge and Newmarket. All these areas are characterised by free-draining soils, either chalk (in the south) or peat (in the north), and arable cultivation. Grey Partridges are widely distributed, with only TF00 in the north-west lacking any 10 km records in both seasons. The number of Grey Partridges seen per hour was about eight times lower than Red-legged Partridge. Grey Partridge was confirmed as a breeding species in only 18 of the 10 km squares mapped, with 30 other 10 km squares having no confirmed breeding, although most of these recorded probable breeding. Confirmed breeding was far higher in the southern stronghold, and the area to the west of Cambridge.

Grey Partridges require thick herbage for nesting and abundant insect food for chick development; the winter diet is largely plants and seeds. Modern agriculture has removed many of the features that formerly made this an abundant farmland bird. In the areas of clay soils, autumn-sown wheat crops mean that there is little winter food due to the loss of stubble; the crop develops too early for the chicks to forage for insect food in it, and herbicide and insecticide use deplete the amount of food available. On the peat and chalk soils, a greater variety of crops tends to be grown, including spring-sown barley and sugar beet, which has helped this species to persist in these areas.

The difficulties of detecting breeding activity, as for Red-legged Partridge, combined with the rarity of Grey Partridge, means that confirmed breeding was probably underestimated in the atlas fieldwork, while probable breeding, thanks to this species' high pair-bonding characteristics, was regularly recorded. Areas managed specifically for game shoots, with predator control and winter food supplies may have above-average densities, but many such estates are difficult to access. It is, therefore, likely that the counts underestimated the total present.

The distribution has changed little since the previous two atlases, although it was recorded in most tetrads in the Hunts Atlas. Confirmed breeding was recorded far more regularly then, with just six 10 km squares not having this level of evidence.

Nationally, Grey Partridges are most abundant in eastern regions, benefiting from the drier climate. They appear to be declining more in intensively farmed East Anglia, however, so the Cambridgeshire density lies close to the average for the UK as a whole. Monitoring data show that the species has been in decline since the 1970s: a 90% decline since 1970, and a 55% decline since BBS surveys began in 1995. On Cambridgeshire BBS squares the density has not changed over this period (remaining at 0.5 per square) but occupancy has declined from 29% to 17%.

In the summer period, a count of 29 was made in TL55 around Six Mile Bottom, while 117 were counted there on one winter visit, logged at 10 km resolution rather than tetrad. The highest counts recorded from a single tetrad were of 17 in TL24Z, Croydon (summer) and 51 in TL44D, Fowlmere (winter). In the winter, Grey Partridge was recorded in 47 out of the 51 10 km squares (not recorded in four peripheral squares). At the tetrad level, it was recorded in 212 out of the 969 county tetrads (22%).

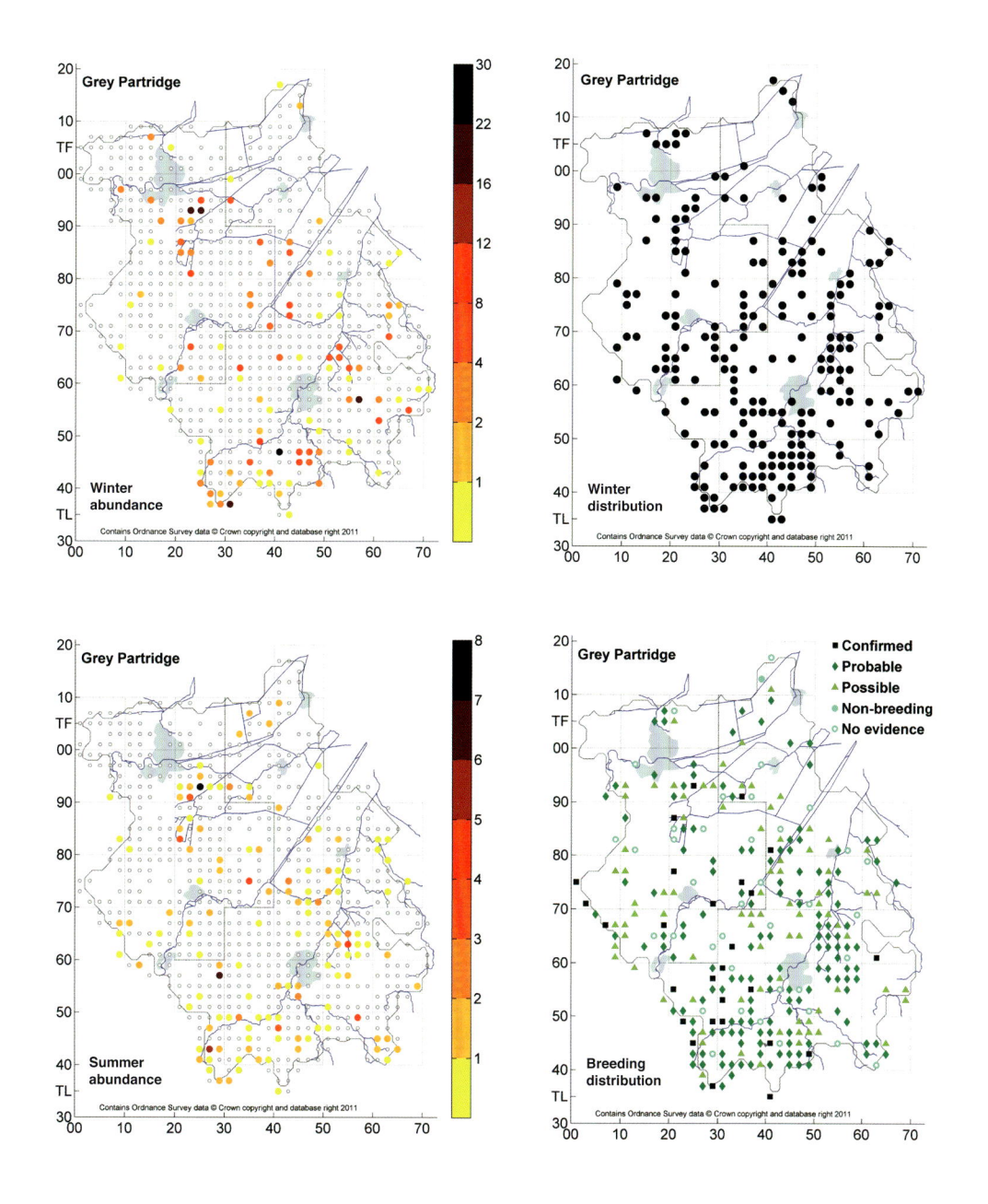

	Confirmed	Probable	Possible	Non-breeding	No evidence	Total summer (% county)	Total winter (% county)
Total tetrads	27	148	82	1	38	296 (31%)	212 (22%)

QUAIL (Common Quail) *Coturnix coturnix*
Amber List. Scarce summer visitor in variable numbers; breeding rarely confirmed

Breeding population estimate: 0-50 calling males
Not a wintering species

Quails can turn up almost anywhere with suitable habitat – expanses of dry grassland or arable crops with an open structure. They are rare, and are monitored by the RBBP (Holling *et al.*, 2012). Pooling records over the four atlas years shows a distinct cluster in the southernmost chalk regions – TL44 contained half of the probable breeding tetrads. The fens probably hold a strong Quail population, but due to the lack of observers in this area many remain undetected; the main clusters here are close to the human population centres of Ely, March and Peterborough, reflecting higher observer effort. The clay soils in the west of the county are sparsely occupied.

Proof of breeding for a rare, tiny, cryptic and skulking species like this is difficult to obtain, and no confirmed breeding was recorded during the atlas period. Singing males, however, are easily heard. The most reliable means of establishing probable breeding was therefore two encounters of calling males – either two calling to each other or one calling over a period of time to confirm a territory. The majority of records were of single singing males, leading to the possible breeding category being most widely used.

The UK lies at the western edge of the Quail's European range so our population fluctuates considerably according to irruption behaviour further south. The number of tetrad records per year was: 12 in 2008, 23 in 2009, 13 in 2010 and 18 in 2011.

No Quails were recorded in the Hunts Atlas, but in the Cambs Atlas, they were found in 23 tetrads, including two confirmed cases of breeding and 14 probable breeding records. The most important areas in the UK are the grasslands of Salisbury Plain, but they can occur right up to the Northern Isles. We have slightly below-average density for this species.

Two tetrads shared the honours of highest counts: TL23Y and TL29D both had three in the summer of 2011.

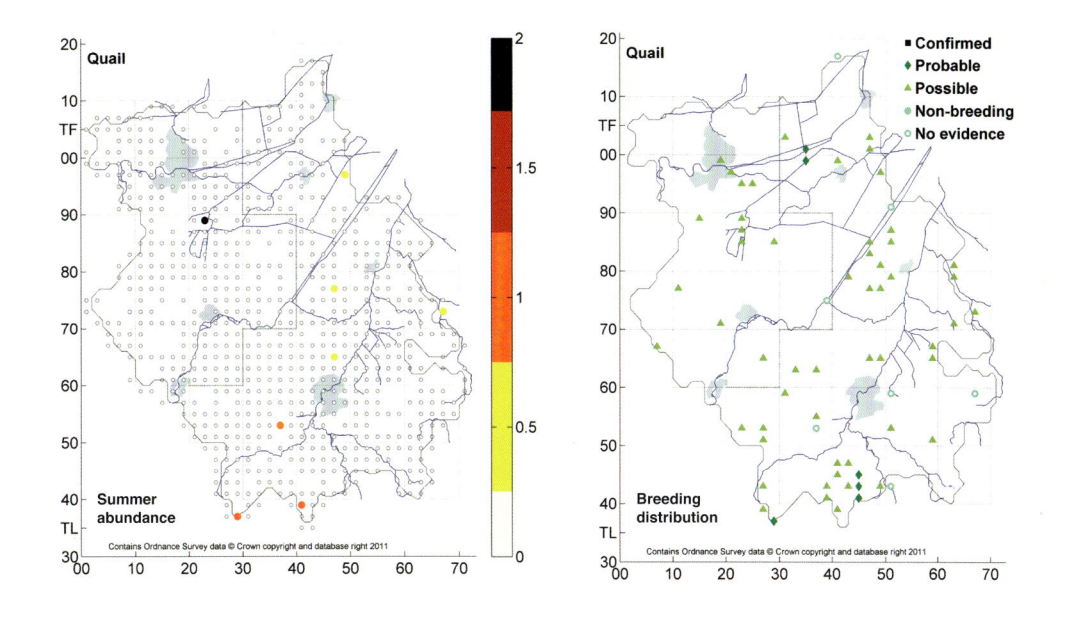

	Confirmed	Probable	Possible	Non-breeding	No evidence	Total summer (% county)
Total tetrads	0	6	54	0	7	67 (7%)

PHEASANT (Common Pheasant) *Phasianus colchicus*
Very common naturalised resident (with frequent releases)

Breeding population estimate: 40,000-50,000 pairs
Wintering population estimate: 100,000-200,000 individuals

Away from our towns and cities, Pheasants are ubiquitous in Cambridgeshire, occurring most frequently in farmland but not averse to venturing into more semi-natural habitats, such as woodland and reedbeds. Summer and especially winter TTVs show higher densities in the fenland area south of Peterborough as seen for the other gamebirds, but there are other densely populated areas such as south of Cambridge, east of Cambridge (but not south-east of Cambridge) and south-west Hunts. The main area of the fens averages the greatest density. TTVs also showed a wide range of densities, with some recording no Pheasants, but others achieving over 50 per hour, especially in the winter when recently released birds boost the population before the shooting season depletes them again. There seems to have been a greater degree of confirmed breeding in south-west Huntingdonshire, but otherwise breeding was confirmed across the county, although not particularly thoroughly.

The Pheasant is an easy species to see and hear, and females with broods of young are relatively easy to find, so we can expect these maps to be an accurate reflection of their status. If nest-failure rates are high, it is likely that breeding attempts would go unnoticed as the nests are well concealed and adults do not bring food to the nests.

Previous county atlases showed presence in summer in 95% (Hunts Atlas) and 74% (Cambs Atlas) of tetrads; the current occupancy of 87% falls within these previous figures implying that distribution has not changed. Confirmed breeding status came from a much greater proportion of tetrads in the past, with 257 tetrads in the Hunts Atlas having confirmed breeding, for example. This is nearly three times the number of tetrads with confirmed breeding recorded in this atlas for the whole of modern Cambridgeshire.

Nationally, Pheasants are widely distributed, although absent from north-west Scotland and rather sparse in Wales; East Anglia and southern England are the strongholds. We host a fairly average density during the summer, but are considerably below average in the winter based on atlas data for Cambridgeshire populations as a proportion of the UK totals; presumably other regions have more active release programmes. Nationally they are increasing, according to BBS figures by 35% since 1995; locally abundance on Cambridgeshire BBS squares declined by almost 50% during this period. A slight decline was reported for Eastern England in the BBS report for 2011 (Risely *et al.*, 2012).

A summer TTV count of 55 in one hour was made in TL25A, whereas the three highest winter counts came from roving visits, with the peak being 220 in TF00Z. Winter TTVs also had higher counts than summer, with 78 in an hour at TL65Z being the maximum. In the winter period, Pheasants were recorded in 792 tetrads (82%) and 50 10 km squares.

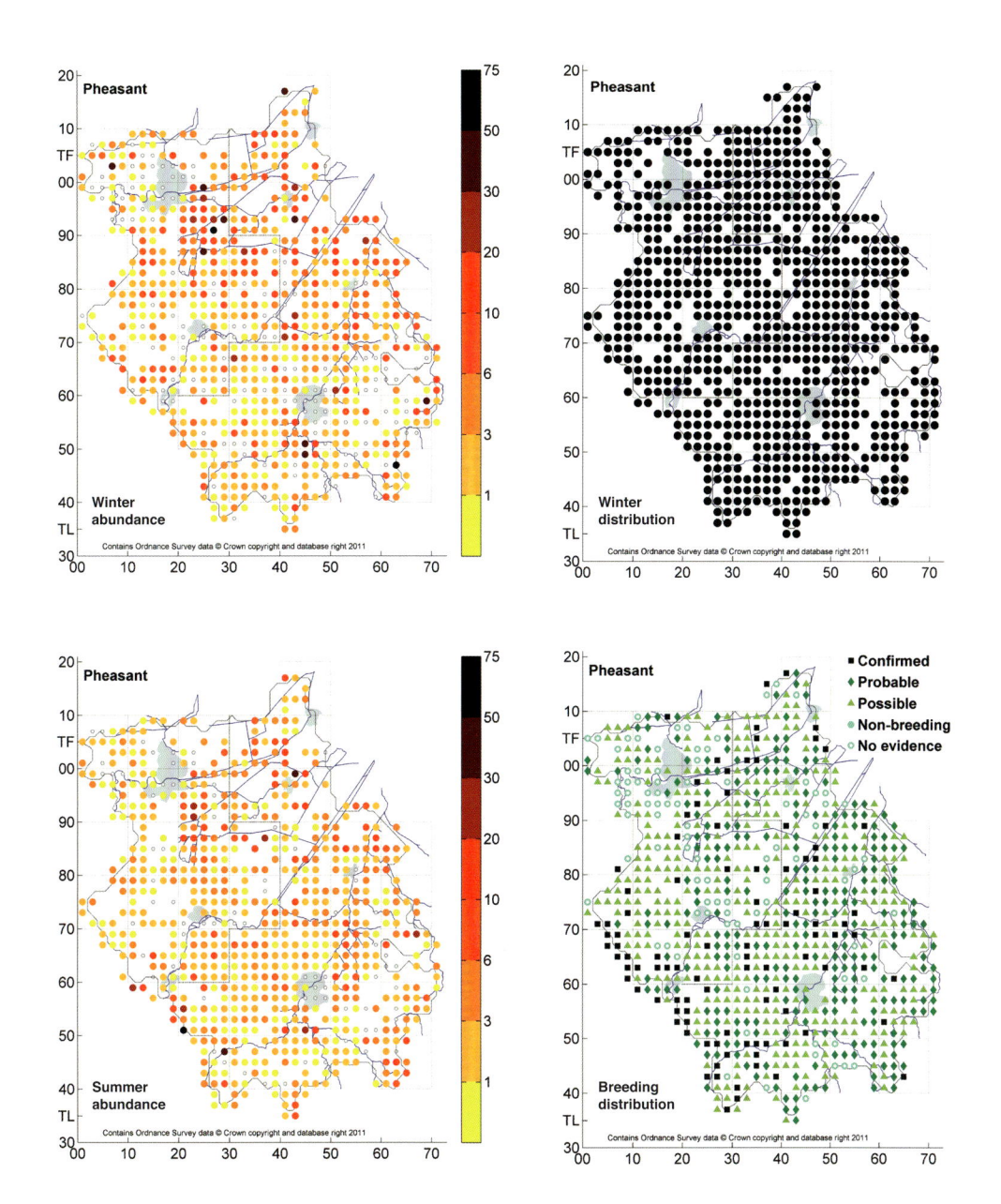

	Confirmed	Probable	Possible	Non-breeding	No evidence	Total summer (% county)	Total winter (% county)
Total tetrads	102	271	380	0	90	843 (87%)	792 (82%)

CORMORANT (Great Cormorant) *Phalacrocorax carbo*
Green List. Resident breeder; greatly increased migrant and winter visitor

Breeding population estimate: 150-200 pairs
Wintering population estimate: 750-1,500 individuals

The Cormorant is now a familiar inland bird, although this represents a recent shift in distribution. In the UK the species breeds on rocky coastlines and increasingly in trees inland. It can disperse widely from breeding and roost sites and is found on large and small areas of standing water and along rivers and large fenland drains – anywhere with sufficient water for fishing.

Breeding was confirmed at Paxton Pits, the Ouse Washes and the Nene Washes, recording 70, 85 and 23 pairs, respectively, in 2011 (CBR 85). In addition, the maps show widely dispersed non-breeding birds across the county. This contrasts with records in only seven tetrads in the previous Cambs Atlas. Individuals first breed at three years of age, hence there is a large non-breeding population. Cormorants have become a familiar sight at large lakes, along rivers and large fenland drains and even on smaller drains and farm ponds. During TTV counts Cormorants were recorded in a quarter of all surveyed tetrads, indicative of the wide network of rivers and drainage channels and the number of gravel pits in the county. They are largely absent from drier areas. The increase in numbers and spread of the Cormorant has brought it into conflict with fishing interests where lakes are stocked at unnaturally high fish densities.

Cormorant was described as a non-breeder in the previous Cambs Atlas, becoming a more frequent visitor to the county after first breeding at the Ouse Washes in 1983 and Fen Drayton in 1985. Colonisation began in Huntingdonshire at Little Paxton Pits in 1983, when fieldwork for the Hunts Atlas finished, hence it was not included in that publication.

Nationally the species is green-listed, although each race (*carbo* and *sinensis*) is individually amber-listed due to the UK having a significant and localised population, respectively (Eaton *et al.*, 2012). The nominate race *carbo* breeds mostly by the coast, with *sinensis* breeding predominantly inland. The shift to an inland distribution is mirrored across other parts of the country.

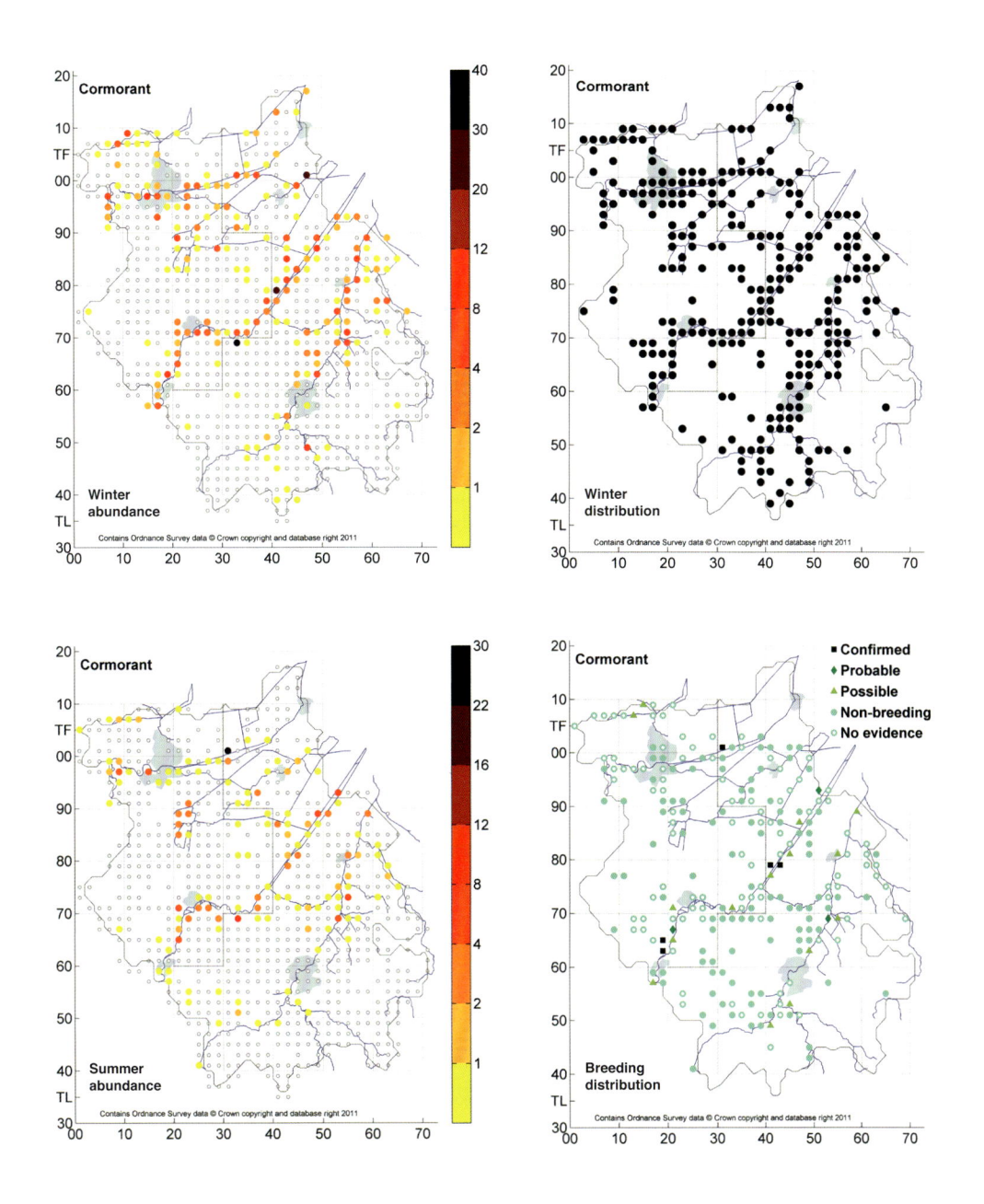

	Confirmed	Probable	Possible	Non-breeding	No evidence	Total summer (% county)	Total winter (% county)
Total tetrads	5	3	15	107	101	231 (24%)	273 (28%)

BITTERN (Eurasian Bittern) *Botaurus stellaris*
Red List. Very rare resident; uncommon visitor, mainly in winter; increasing numbers now summer

Breeding population estimate: 1-6 booming males
Wintering population estimate: 5-30 individuals

The recovery of the Bittern is a national and local success story. From a low point of 11 males nationally in 1997, none in Cambridgeshire, there has been a concerted effort at habitat creation and improvement. Some of this has occurred in Cambridgeshire and just over the border at Lakenheath in Suffolk. A shift to inland breeding will hopefully make the species more secure against the risk of coastal flooding damaging low-lying reserves (as happened at Cley in 1996 and 2007). Habitat improvement has centred around an increased understanding of the requirements of Bitterns for deep wet reedbeds with a sufficient edge between cover and open water. At newly created sites such as Ouse Fen these requirements can be incorporated into land profiling and water-level control. At sites without water-level control, prospects of breeding will be determined largely by the winter and spring weather. Significant amounts of work are required to prevent succession from reedbed to wet woodland.

The far-carrying boom of the male Bittern is an obvious sign of this species and is therefore used widely as a measure of population. The species is otherwise largely unobtrusive and rarely seen. Mitigating against this is the fact that it occurs for prolonged periods in well-watched wetland areas. This means that the distribution maps from roving records are much more complete than any of the abundance maps from TTVs. Only one winter and four summer TTVs recorded Bittern, so these maps are not shown here. Good fortune would be required to record the species in the given time period. The winter population is swelled by immigrants from Scandinavia and the Baltic states and is estimated at 600 nationally. During winter the species occurs at a number of wetland sites away from breeding locations. Maturing vegetation around new gravel pits will initially provide good habitat for wintering birds but without management this will lose its value through serial succession to wet woodland. Conversely, at new sites, significant management is useful in speeding up the colonisation of wetland by phragmites.

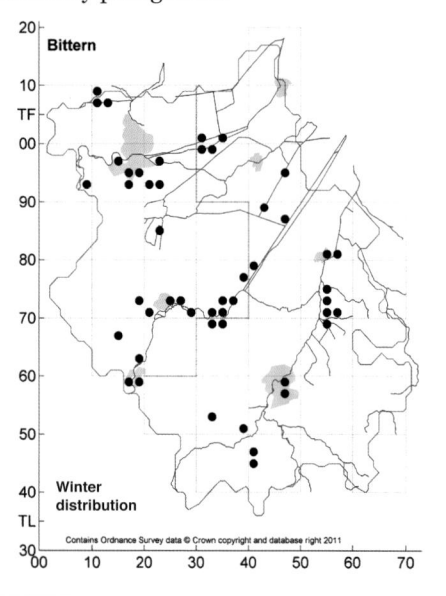

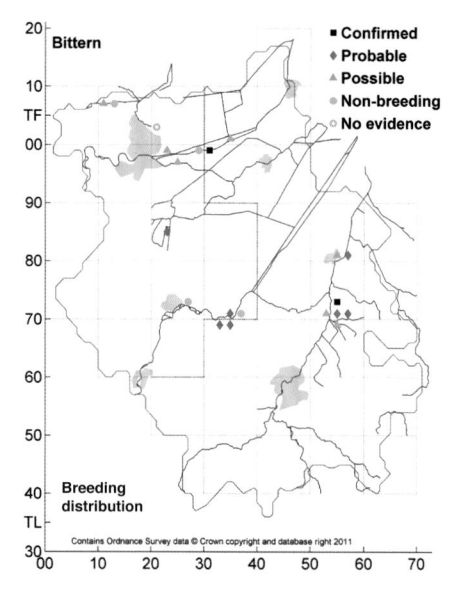

	Confirmed	Probable	Possible	Non-breeding	No evidence	Total summer (% county)	Total winter (% county)
Total tetrads	2	7	7	4	1	21 (2%)	49 (5%)

GREAT WHITE EGRET (Great Egret) *Ardea alba*
Scarce visitor from the continent

Not a breeding species
Wintering population estimate: 1-7 records annually

Like Little Egret, this species was a real rarity nationwide during the last atlas period 20 years ago. These days, whilst much less numerous than Little Egret, it is no longer considered a national rarity. It winters in significant but low numbers, and was recorded breeding in the UK for the first time in 2012.

During the winters of the atlas, Great White Egret was recorded from 11 tetrads. Winter birds tend to be singletons, and adopt an area of fenland drains or river banks, remaining within this chosen range for several weeks. Increasingly recorded in late summer, Great White Egrets will inevitably become a more familiar sight, although its colonisation of the UK is 15 years behind Little Egret. Colour-ringing has shown that birds are dispersing northwards from France and the Netherlands, with several records of UK birds ringed as nestlings across the Channel.

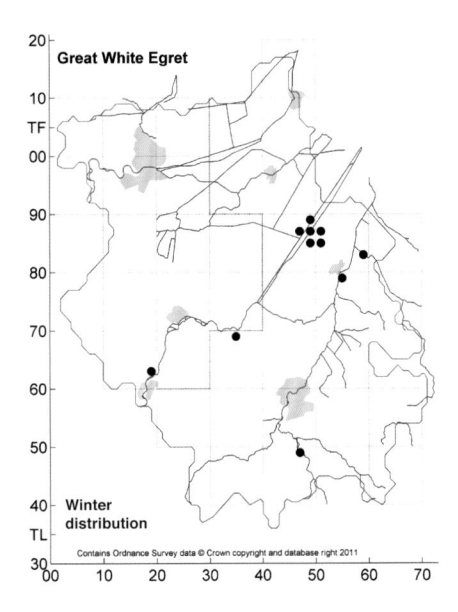

LITTLE EGRET *Egretta garzetta*
Amber List. Fairly common, and increasing, resident

Breeding population estimate: 5-10 pairs
Wintering population estimate: 100-300 individuals

Nationally and locally Little Egret has colonised since the last atlas period. It has gone from being an official rarity to a widespread resident and localised breeder. Breeding in the county was first confirmed in 2004 and now occurs on both the Nene and Ouse Washes, with birds showing signs of breeding in other locations. It is also a widespread non-breeding species present throughout the year around well-vegetated lakes, along rivers and washland and in fenland drains, birds sometimes being flushed from quite minor ditches.

Breeding requirements are similar to those of Grey Heron and is often in heronies, but the breeding period is later so it is possible that breeding is missed even in well-studied heronies. Breeders are likely to use existing heronries – in other parts of the UK mixed-species heronries are becoming a familiar sight. The population is likely to continue to increase and there are plenty of heronries and other areas suitable for colonisation.

Most breeding-season TTVs only recorded small numbers of birds, up to four individuals in summer, but the two main washes recorded higher counts than this on TTVs; the peak TTV count of 27 birds was in the Ouse valley.

In winter, birds are found on both well-watched WeBS sites and also in the wider countryside such as rivers, streams and drainage ditches and even in arable fields, especially those close to waterways. This, combined with the rapid recent changes, makes their population hard to estimate. The National Atlas will provide a clearer picture. WeBS data alone give a national total of 4,500 for 2010 but the real total is likely to be higher than this. Winter TTVs recorded a maximum of only four in any TTV timed count.

A record count of 233 Little Egrets for the county was made in the summer of 2012, after the atlas period, by concerted counting across the whole Ouse Washes. A winter count in late 2012 of 45 birds at Grafham Water continues to reflect the good fortunes of this species. The peak count during the atlas period was 96 birds in March 2011, again at the Ouse Washes.

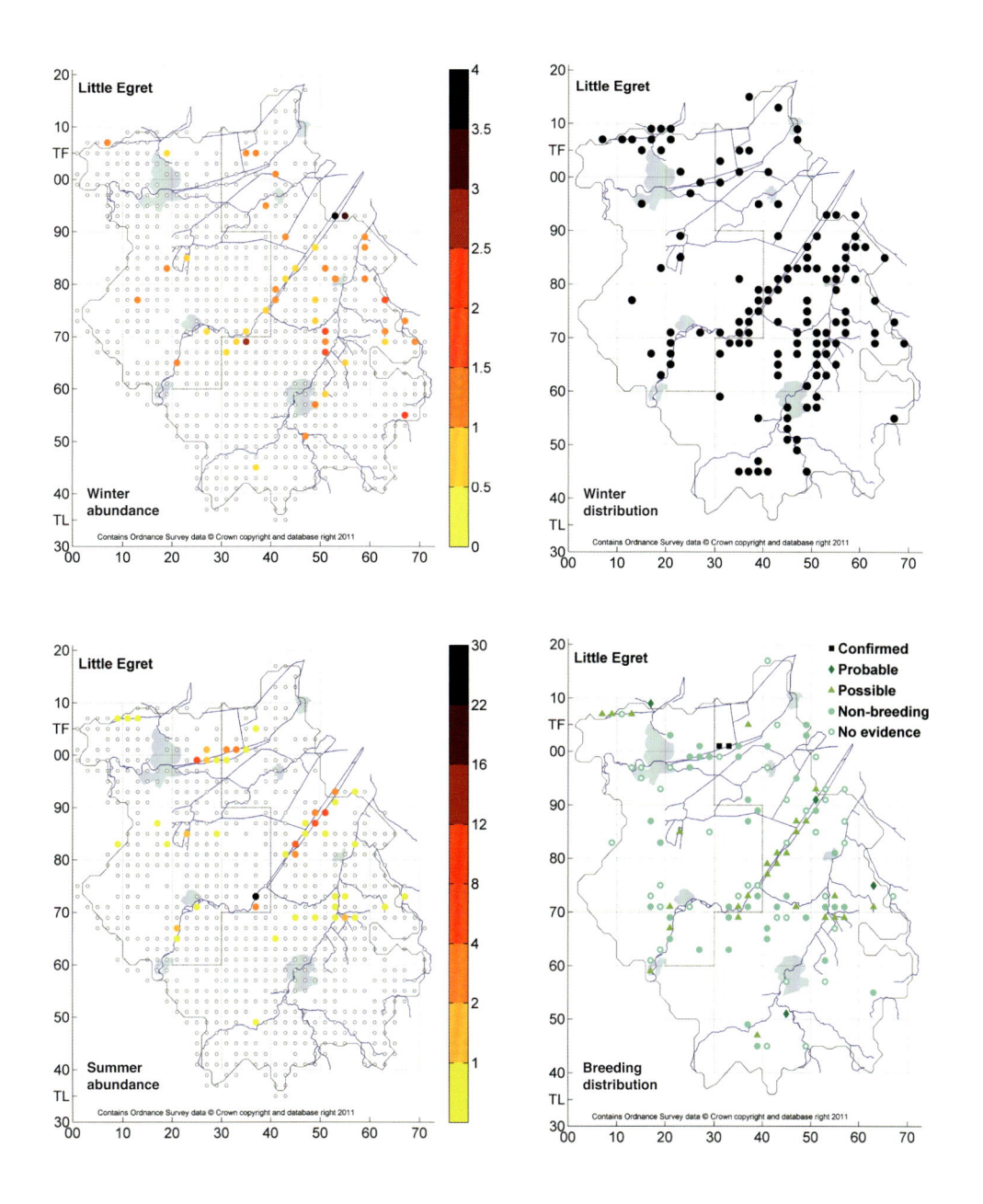

	Confirmed	Probable	Possible	Non-breeding	No evidence	Total summer (% county)	Total winter (% county)
Total tetrads	2	4	27	40	40	113 (12%)	128 (13%)

GREY HERON *Ardea cinerea*
Green List. Fairly common resident and passage migrant, mainly in the autumn

Breeding population estimate: 150-250 pairs
Wintering population estimate: 300-600 individuals

This is a widespread and well-studied species, with most heronies monitored for the BTO Heronries Census, which recorded excellent counts within Cambridgeshire up to 2007, but rather patchily since then (CBR 85). The possible breeding records most likely refer to dispersing breeding birds or non-breeding birds present in suitable habitat. Birds first breed at two years old, hence there is a significant non-breeding population of second-calendar-year birds, supplemented by foraging birds, failed breeders and post-breeding dispersal within the atlas breeding period. Birds can be found in any habitat with open water, from the shores of large lakes to small farm ponds and from large rivers to minor streams and drainage ditches. Presence on the Washes in both seasons is largely dependent on water levels.

Grey Heron is likely to be under-represented as a confirmed breeding species in the atlas records as it breeds early, with active colonies in late February–March. Most confirmed breeding records thus come from roving records and those submitted to the BTO via Bird Club records and nest recording.

The distribution of records is consistent along river valleys and patchy in-between, reflecting the distribution of suitable ponds and ditches. The open-water habitats are well watched but birds could remain undetected in ditches without access and on farm reservoirs. During TTV visits the species was seen in just over a third of all tetrads across the county in winter, with the greatest numbers present along the Ouse Washes.

Nationally the species is increasing gradually due to a range of factors, including milder winters, improved water quality, reduced persecution, and habitat creation schemes.

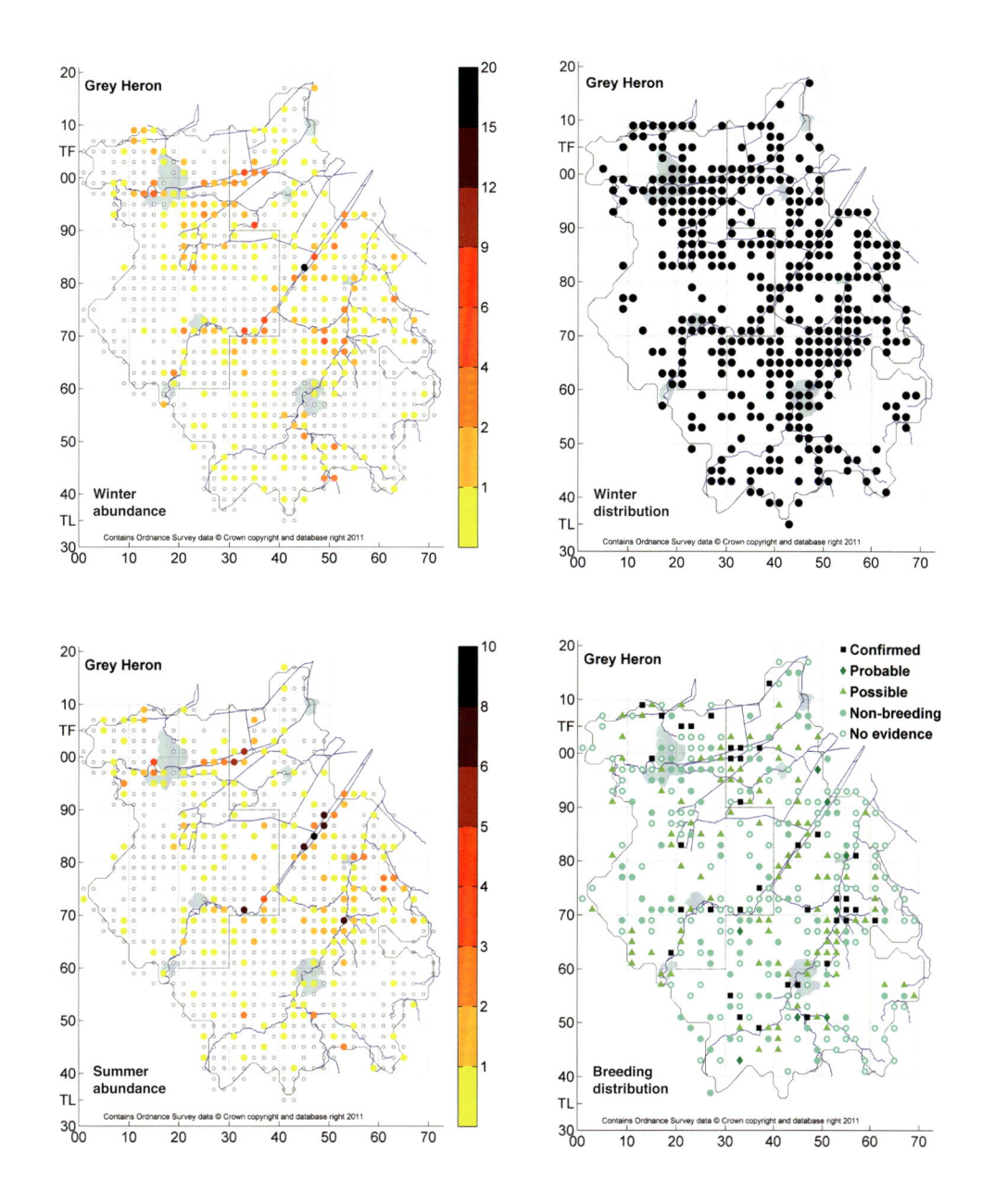

	Confirmed	Probable	Possible	Non-breeding	No evidence	Total summer (% county)	Total winter (% county)
Total tetrads	37	8	105	86	153	389 (40%)	396 (41%)

LITTLE GREBE *Tachybaptus ruficollis*
Amber List. Fairly common resident, breeding mainly on lakes

Breeding population estimate: 150-250 pairs
Wintering population estimate: 300-750 individuals

The Little Grebe is a bird of marshes, lakes, ponds and slow-flowing rivers. It feeds mainly on insects, molluscs, tadpoles and small fish, diving up to a metre to reach them. It can be found on relatively small and shallow water bodies. It prefers areas with muddy bottoms and submerged vegetation. On larger lakes it tends to favour the shallow sheltered margins. It nests on an anchored platform of floating vegetation, but is more secretive during the breeding season than its larger cousin the Great Crested Grebe, resulting in a lower proportion of confirmed breeding records.

The habitat requirements of Little Grebe lead to a widespread but patchy distribution. The maps show concentrations around wetland areas but also outlying breeding records on small farm ponds and reservoirs. The winter distribution, swelled by immigrants, is more widespread and follows the river valleys more strongly. Little Grebe is a familiar, if unobtrusive, sight along the slow-flowing rivers of Cambridgeshire in winter. Their trilling calls will also give away their presence on an unseen pool or drain in larger wetland areas. In cold spells they may congregate on areas of open water, especially along ice-free sections of rivers with well-vegetated banks, or move to the coast.

The county distribution is similar to the previous atlases. There are some gains in breeding-season distribution, especially in the south-east of the county, due to birds colonising new farm ponds. Nationally the species is amber-listed due to a long-term population decline, with BBS population trends showing a 4% increase since 1995 (Risely *et al.*, 2012). The 30-year trend (Eaton *et al.*, 2012) also shows a 45% increase in numbers during summer. The UK non-breeding population is estimated at 17,000 individuals, again with an increase during the last 10 years (Eaton *et al.*, 2012), although the wide distribution of Little Grebe, often away from WeBS sites, makes the accuracy of this estimate uncertain.

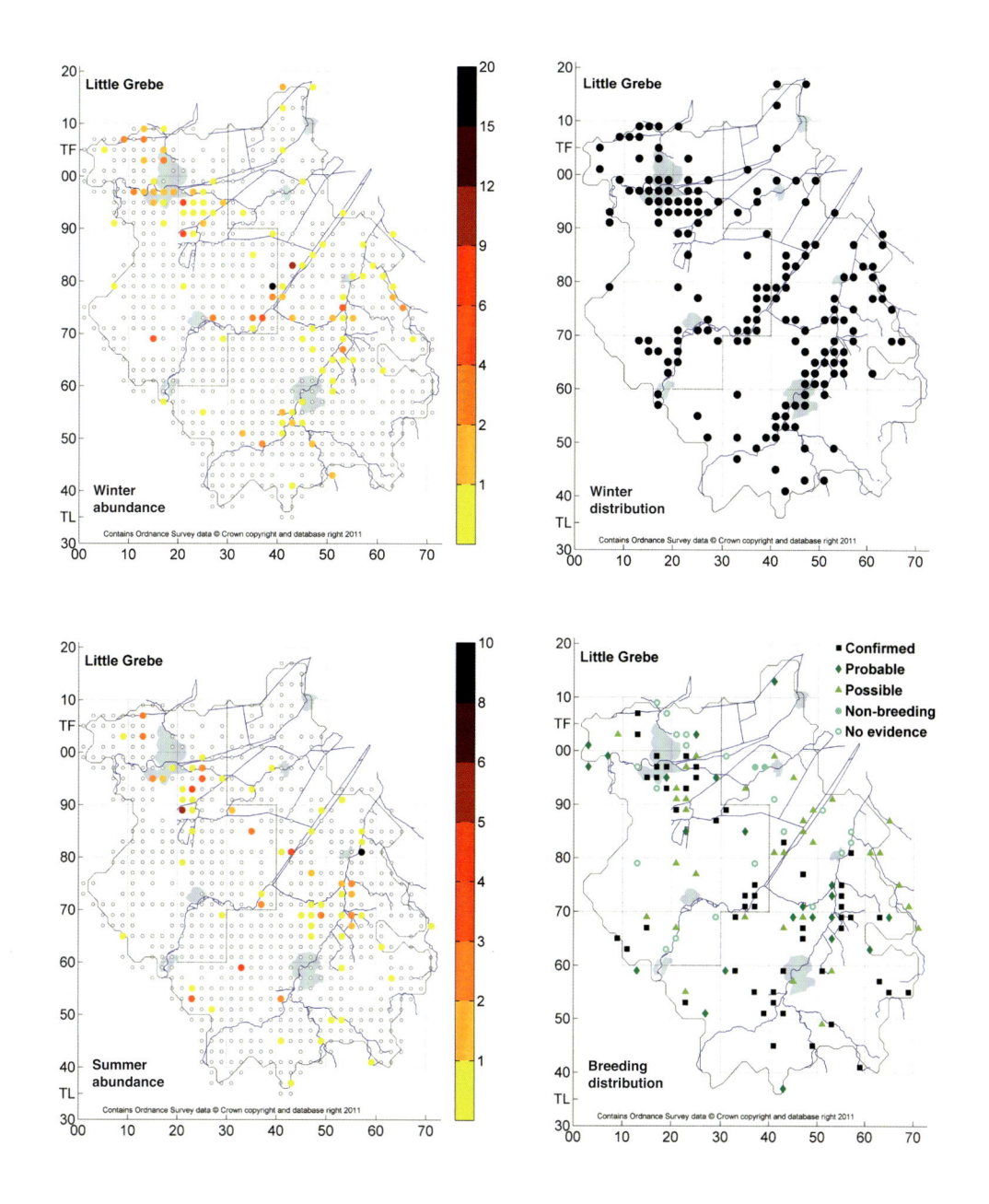

	Confirmed	Probable	Possible	Non-breeding	No evidence	Total summer (% county)	Total winter (% county)
Total tetrads	52	22	34	2	20	130 (13%)	169 (17%)

GREAT CRESTED GREBE *Podiceps cristatus*
Green List. Fairly common resident; some immigration in cold winters

Breeding population estimate: 150-300 pairs
Wintering population estimate: 500-1,000 individuals

Great Crested Grebes are clearly limited to areas with sufficient water for diving and catching fish. These habitats range from large lakes and reservoirs to deep farm reservoirs and ponds, rivers, washland when flooded, and large fenland drains.

The species requires vegetated lakes, rivers and drains for constructing its floating nest. The maps show distribution tied to water courses or other wetland areas. The young, and sometimes the nest, are easily visible, leading to a high number of confirmed breeding records; approximately 50% of the tetrads in which Great Crested Grebe was recorded had confirmed breeding status. In winter birds are more widely dispersed, to areas of deeper open water (particularly Grafham Water and Fen Drayton Lakes), along fenland drains and on the Ouse Washes (depending on flood conditions). Winter numbers are swelled by immigrants as the species is partially migratory (Wernham *et al.*, 2002). In cold spells Great Crested Grebes congregate on open waterbodies or move to the coast. In warmer conditions the maps suggest that birds can be more dispersed.

There is no significant difference in the distribution of Great Crested Grebes compared to previous atlases. Wetland creation, through gravel extraction or direct habitat creation, has led to some additional tetrads being occupied. This patchy distribution, varying little between summer and winter, reflects relatively specific habitat requirements but the bird is a common sight in suitable areas, even where rivers pass through sizeable human settlements. Similar densities were recorded on summer TTVs to winter ones, with very few counts above three individuals.

Nationally the species is stable, being found wherever suitable habitat exists. BBS data show a 9% increase in the UK from 1995 to 2010; no Eastern England trend was available (Risely *et al.*, 2012). This is in contrast to the situation just over 100 years ago when the species was close to being exterminated from the UK due to hunting for its feathers. Protests against this led to the founding of the RSPB. The national wintering trend of Great Crested Grebe shows a slight decline (5%) over 10 years, with a longer-term trend not available (Eaton *et al.*, 2012).

Great Crested Grebe

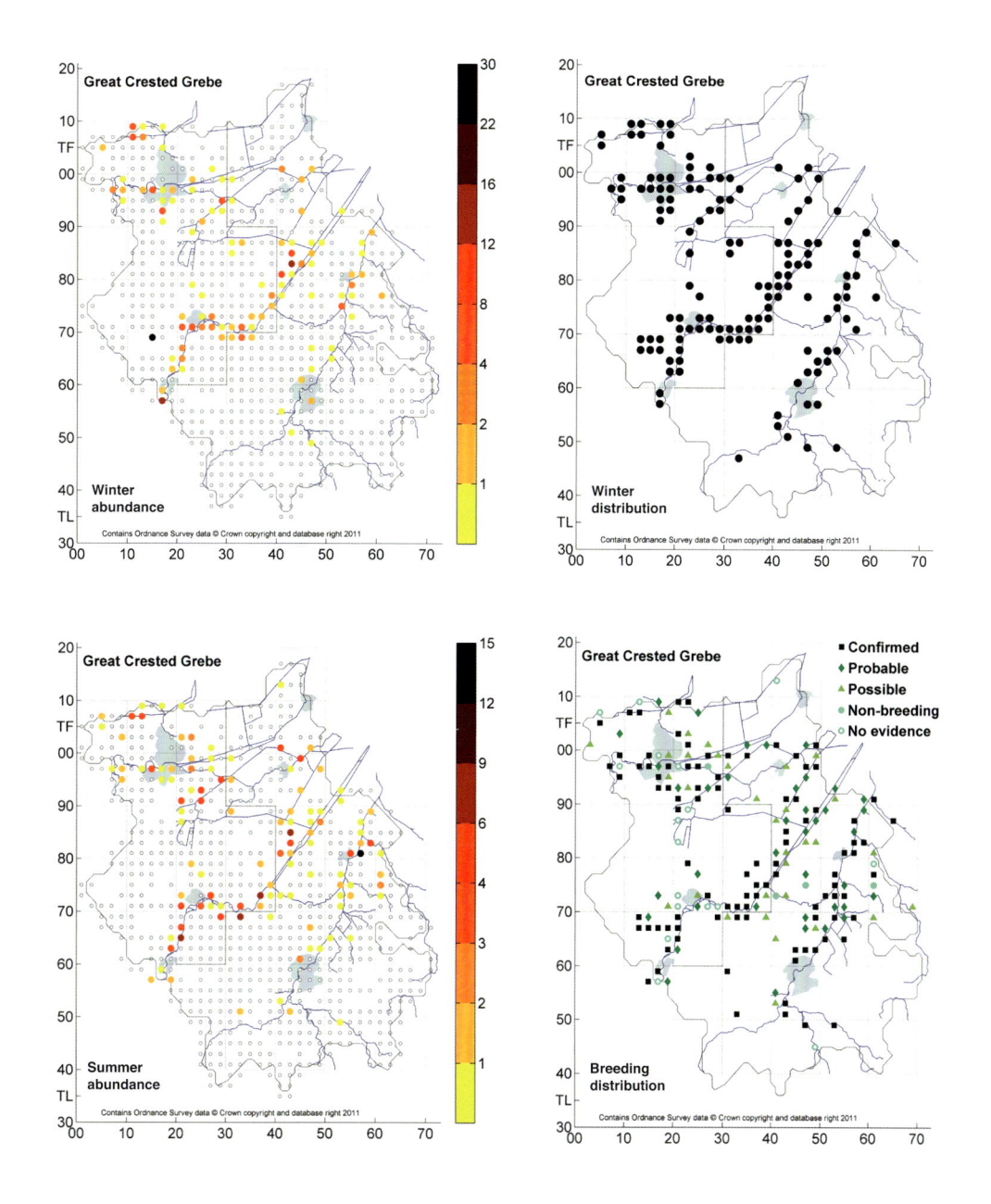

Winter abundance

Winter distribution

Summer abundance

Breeding distribution

	Confirmed	Probable	Possible	Non-breeding	No evidence	Total summer (% county)	Total winter (% county)
Total tetrads	96	39	32	4	17	188 (19%)	139 (14%)

BLACK-NECKED GREBE *Podiceps nigricollis*
Amber List. Scarce annual visitor, mainly passage/summer

Breeding population estimate: 0-3 pairs
Wintering population estimate: 5-20 records annually

Black-necked Grebe is a sporadic breeder in the county that nested successfully during the atlas period. Due to its tenuous foothold as a breeding species, maps are not included. There were also occasional records of non-breeding birds in summer, in total from 13 tetrads. A secretive breeding species, it is unclear how well recorded it was during the breeding season. In the previous Cambs Atlas it was confirmed as a breeder from one site and noted as present at a second, in different 10 km squares. It was noted as present in the previous Hunts Atlas.

Winter records are not unusual but there is no established regular wintering population. Black-necked Grebe was recorded from six winter tetrads. All records come from waterbodies in our major river valleys where gravel and brick pits provide suitable habitat.

	Confirmed	Probable	Possible	Non-breeding	No evidence	Total summer (% county)	Total winter (% county)
Total tetrads	3	2	0	7	1	13 (1%)	6 (1%)

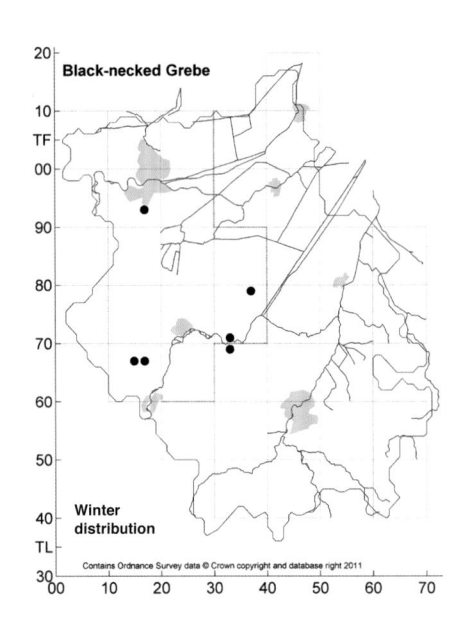

Black-necked Grebe
Winter distribution

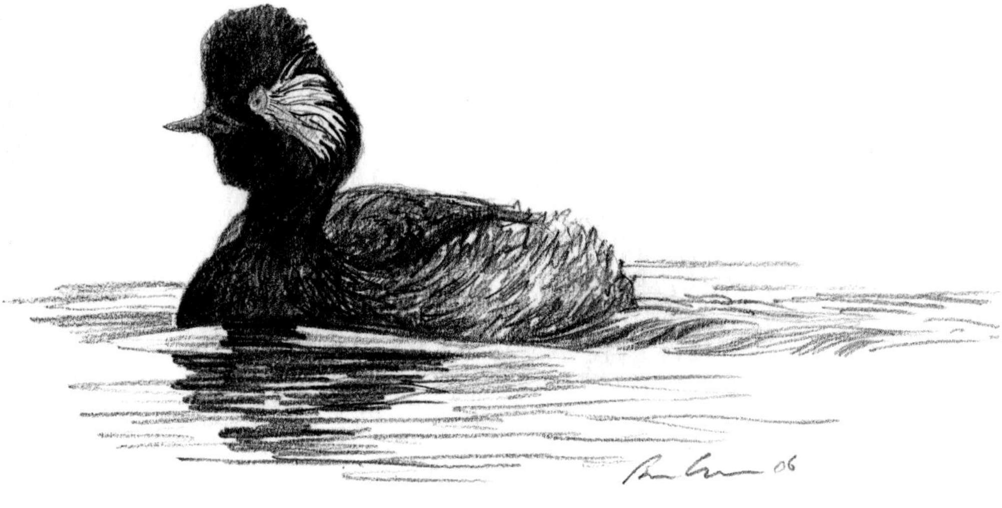

RED KITE *Milvus milvus*
Amber List. Increasing, but local, resident; has bred regularly since 2004

Breeding population estimate: 25-50 pairs
Wintering population estimate: 100-200 individuals

The Red Kite was said to breed in Cambridgeshire in previous centuries but by the 1850s it had declined and ceased nesting; thereafter it was recorded very rarely until the 1970s when a series of records began, possibly related to the increasing Welsh population and the resulting dispersal of young birds. The re-introductions in the Chilterns in 1989 and the East Midlands in 1995 saw the number of records in Cambridgeshire increase dramatically; breeding was confirmed by 2002 and has been regular since 2004 with 2–11 pairs present (CBR 85).

The breeding distribution map shows the population largely centred on the north-western rim of the county, closest to the East Midlands release site; one confirmed pair close to Cambridge appears to be out on a limb. With breeding confirmed in 23 tetrads and probable in another 20 the potential population may be more than three times that reported previously. There are also a number of outliers in the far south and south-east of the county which may be the beginning of new breeding populations. Unsurprisingly, given such a clear western geographic distribution of breeding birds in Cambridgeshire, the densities shown on the map are highest in that area.

Given that established breeding pairs tend to remain close to their breeding site throughout the year (Brown & Grice, 2005), the wintering distribution maps display the same pattern as those for summer with records mainly in the north-west of the county and numbers exceeding single individuals recorded in that area. Elsewhere the occasional bird was seen in winter.

The largest numbers were recorded in winter: 8 on a single occasion, 7 twice, 6 four times, 5 once and the remaining records were of 1–3. It is reasonable to suggest that the population in Cambridgeshire in general is still small, excluding the higher numbers recorded in gatherings at the core release areas around the north-west county boundary. In summer the largest count was four.

The atlas project will almost certainly provide a marker from which future population growth may be measured; if the current trend continues this species ought to become a more widespread breeding bird in the next 10–20 years.

Red Kite

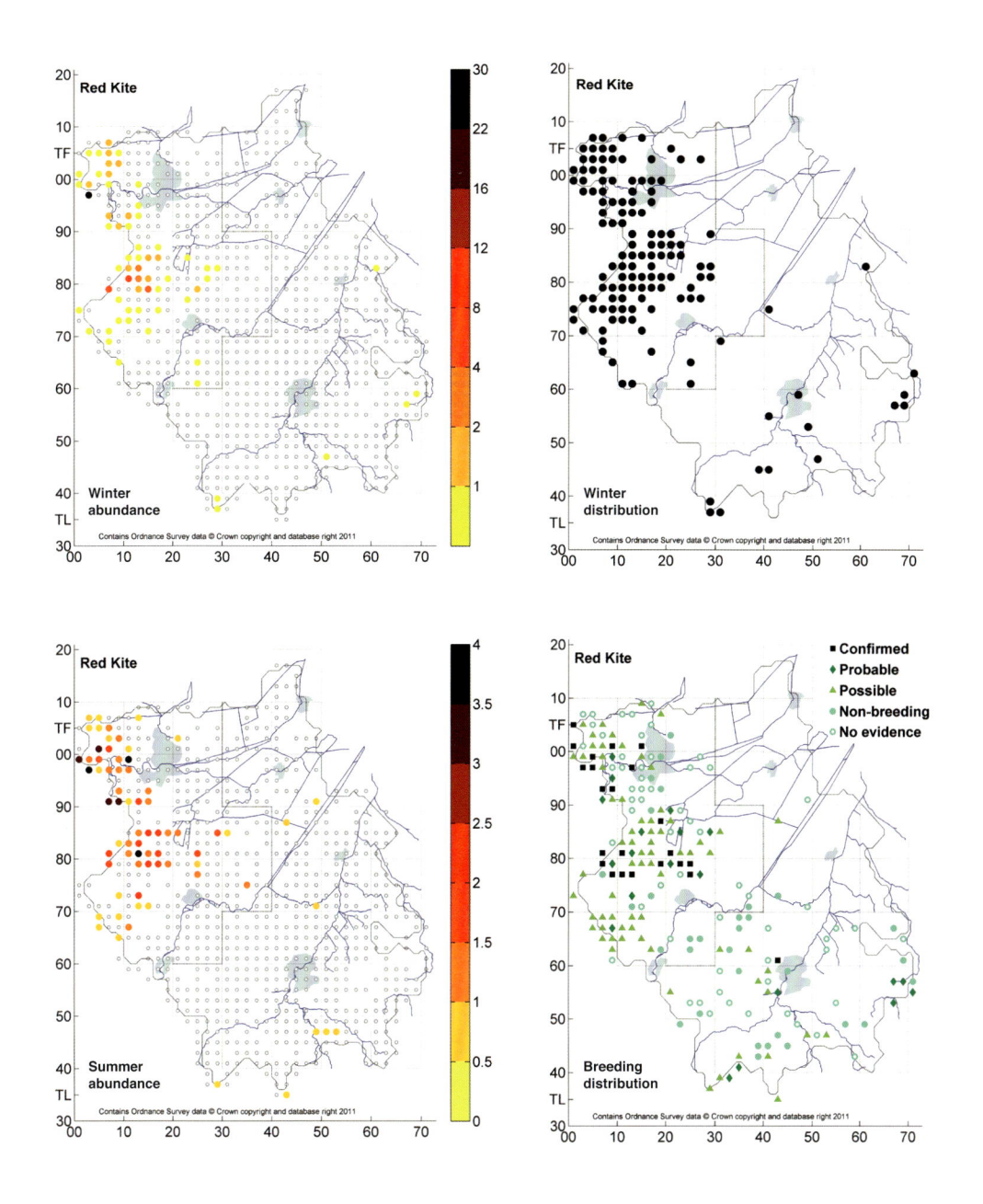

	Confirmed	Probable	Possible	Non-breeding	No evidence	Total summer (% county)	Total winter (% county)
Total tetrads	23	20	70	32	60	205 (21%)	132 (14%)

MARSH HARRIER (Western Marsh Harrier) *Circus aeruginosus*
Amber List. Uncommon passage migrant and migrant breeder; scarce in winter

Breeding population estimate: 40-80 breeding females
Wintering population estimate: 10-50 individuals

Formerly a rare visitor after numbers declined in the 19th century; Marsh Harriers bred in the county up to about 1850. After a low point of a single breeding pair in Suffolk in 1971, the population increased steadily and spread. The number of records in Cambridgeshire consequently increased until breeding was recorded in 1981. Since then Marsh Harrier numbers have improved gradually. From being solely a summer visitor, this species has become resident and this may be significant in their population increase.

The breeding-season map (not shown) indicates that Marsh Harriers are distributed largely along the river systems and adjacent wetlands. Confirmed breeding was recorded in 36 tetrads, a remarkable number that shows the scale of the increase in the 30-year period since the first recent record; probable breeding was recorded in a further 25 tetrads. This represents a healthy population which could comprise as many as 50 females. Marsh Harriers, which can be polygynous where conditions allow, breed almost exclusively in reedbeds; some recent nesting in arable crops – oilseed rape for example – has been reported but this latter habitat may be sub-optimal and adopted by birds unable to find reedbed sites. There is some suggestion that reedbed conservation action directed at Bitterns has had a positive effect on Marsh Harriers. Most of the atlas breeding records were from the fenland basin and the area north of Cambridge but confirmed breeding was reported in three tetrads south of Cambridge and probable breeding was recorded there in a further two tetrads, a situation unthinkable 30 years ago. Records are generally for 1–2 birds, but up to four in summer, presumably adults and juveniles; the density was greatest in the core breeding areas.

The winter distribution shows a similar pattern with birds using mainly the larger wetlands and land adjacent to the main river systems north of Cambridge. Numbers per tetrad remain low, as might be expected; there are fewer birds in the winter as part of the population still presumably migrates to warmer climes. Underhill-Day (in Wernham *et al.*, 2002) suggests that females are more likely to overwinter and males more likely to migrate.

Ringing results include a juvenile ringed at Wicken Fen that was found dead in Mauritania; the national figures show migration along the north-west coast of Africa and that some continental birds may pass through the UK or even overwinter here.

Marsh Harrier

Winter abundance

Winter distribution

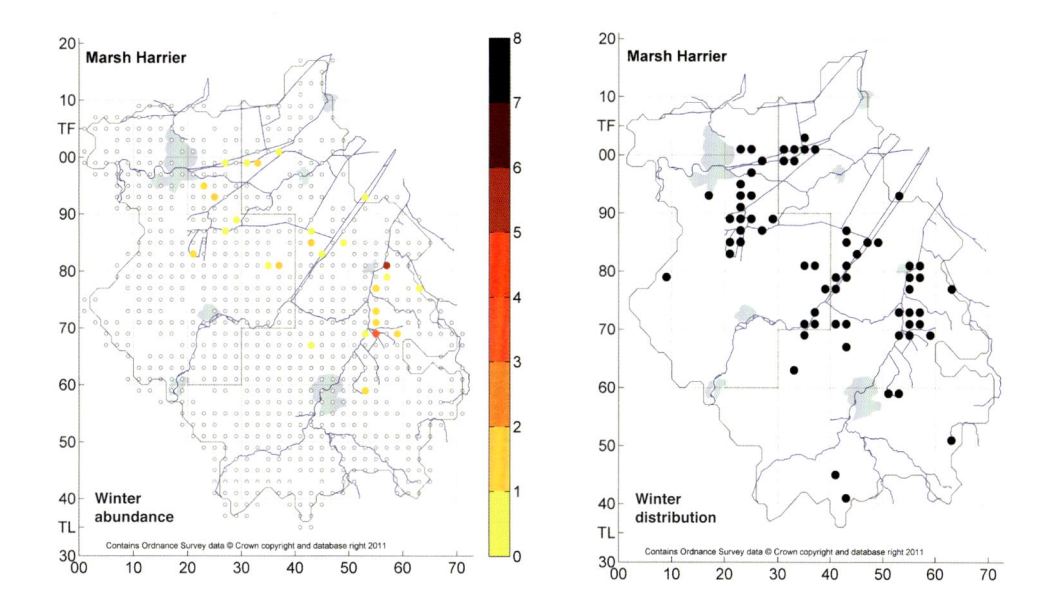

	Confirmed	Probable	Possible	Non-breeding	No evidence	Total summer (% county)	Total winter (% county)
Total tetrads	36	25	55	43	44	203 (21%)	66 (7%)

HEN HARRIER (Northern Harrier) *Circus cyaneus*
Red List. Uncommon winter visitor and passage migrant; has summered

Not a breeding species
Wintering population estimate: 10-20 individuals

Historically this species may have bred in the county but the evidence is unconvincing; even if accepted there have been no such records since the early 19th century. The population of English Hen Harriers is under serious threat, only the Welsh and Scottish populations remain viable in the UK (Holling *et al.*, 2012). The Hen Harrier is a much-persecuted bird as a result of conflict with the grouse-shooting fraternity and, despite legal protection, it is still illegally killed on its breeding sites. Up to the mid-1970s Hen Harriers were something of a rarity in Cambridgeshire but over the following decade a number of now-traditional roost sites in reedbeds such as at Wicken and Woodwalton Fens and on the Ouse and Nene Washes became established and as a consequence birds were seen wandering quite widely.

The winter distribution map shows a similar pattern to that of Marsh Harrier with most records along the main river systems north of Cambridge, mainly within the fenland basin; a few records in tetrads south of Cambridge indicate a presence there. Roosting at traditional sites continues but possibly in slightly reduced numbers from a peak of 25–30 birds in the mid-1980s; it seems likely that Cambridgeshire still holds up to 20 birds. Highest counts during the atlas period were in the region of 6–8 birds (at roost sites).

There are few national ringing results but those that do exist suggest that most birds wintering in lowland England, and by implication those in Cambridgeshire, are from northern regions of the UK. Limited evidence indicates the presence of some Continental birds from France and two long-distance recoveries were for Scandinavian birds.

Hen Harriers were recorded in 90 tetrads during the winter period.

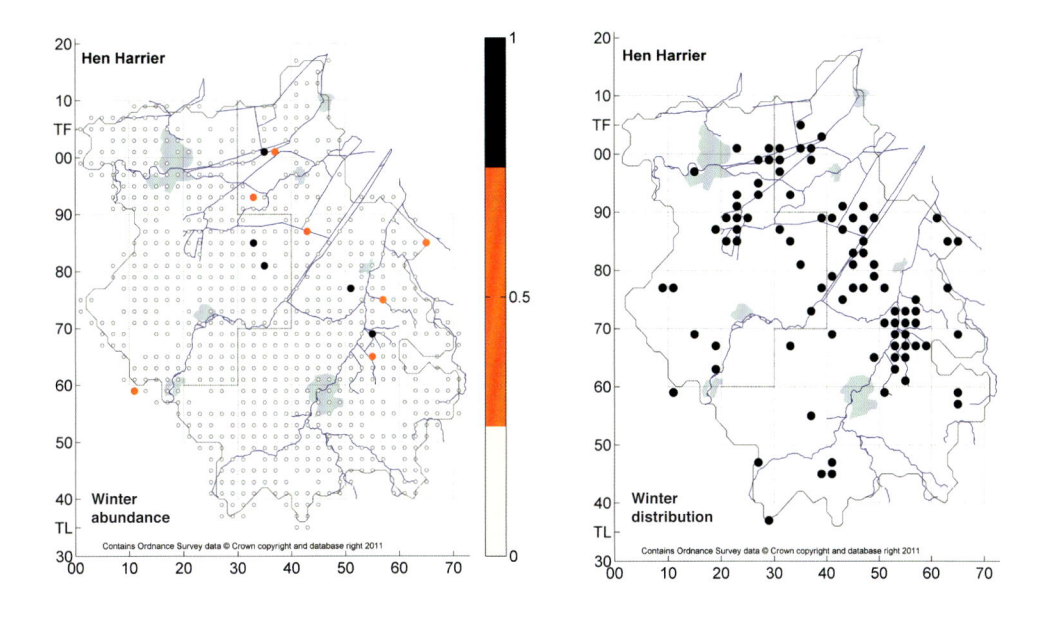

MONTAGU'S HARRIER *Circus pygargus*
Amber List. Scarce, almost annual, passage migrant and former migratory breeder

Breeding population estimate: occasional breeder, last confirmed 1995
Not a wintering species

This species has a record of sporadic breeding in Cambridgeshire including records at the fen sites of Wicken and Woodwalton in the immediate post-war period. More recently a number of reports have been received of birds in possible breeding sites. As well as reedbeds, recent putative breeding records relate to cereal crops. Nationally Montagu's Harrier is a rare breeding species with fewer than 20 pairs in the UK. Despite a stronghold in neighbouring Norfolk there seems to be no sign of regular breeding in Cambridgeshire where the last confirmed record was in 1995.

The summer distribution map (maps not shown) indicated a handful of widespread records all of which related to passage birds (non-breeding). Often such limited records are a reflection of the distribution of well-watched sites and migrants almost certainly pass through the entire county.

SPARROWHAWK (Eurasian Sparrowhawk) *Accipiter nisus*
Green List. Fairly common resident; some passage migrants and winter visitors

Breeding population estimate: 150-500 pairs
Wintering population estimate: 300-1,200 individuals

The Sparrowhawk is traditionally a bird that nests in woodland and hunts both there and in open country. It has been persecuted since the rise of gamekeeping in the early 19th century and this has, to some extent, dictated its abundance and distribution. Most analysts were able to show an increase during the war years, when gamekeepers were otherwise occupied, but numbers fell on the resumption of persecution and were then drastically affected by organochlorine poisoning in the late 1950s. By 1961 the Sparrowhawk had ceased to breed in Cambridgeshire: indeed there was not a single record. The situation was so dire that it took 20 years for breeding birds to return but their recovery, when it came, was rapid, probably due to immigration from counties to the west where the effects had been less dramatic and the recovery faster. Eastern England was most affected by the decline in numbers due to the preponderance of cereal crops on which the toxic chemicals were used. Population trends show that Sparrowhawks probably reached their optimal breeding numbers by the early 1990s since when the population has been stable (Brown & Grice, 2005).

The summer breeding map shows confirmed breeding in 73 tetrads and probable breeding in a further 59. Sparrowhawks are highly secretive during the breeding season leading to potential under-recording of breeding activity; while early-season displays can indicate a potential territory, the most likely method of confirming breeding is to see adults carrying prey items. Unsurprisingly the main population centres are in areas of woodland, parkland and suburbia; there are also records across the fens, where the generally open landscape also includes trees in villages and around isolated houses. Numbers recorded were between one and four – higher numbers presumably representing an adult pair and fledglings.

The winter distribution is similar to the summer distribution, although perhaps slightly more extensive. This is most likely due to post-natal dispersal which takes place in autumn, most birds remaining within a 20 km radius of their natal site. A further possibility is the arrival of overwintering birds from Scandinavia (Newton in Wernham *et al.*, 2002). Winter numbers were almost always singles or twos; very occasionally up to four were noted.

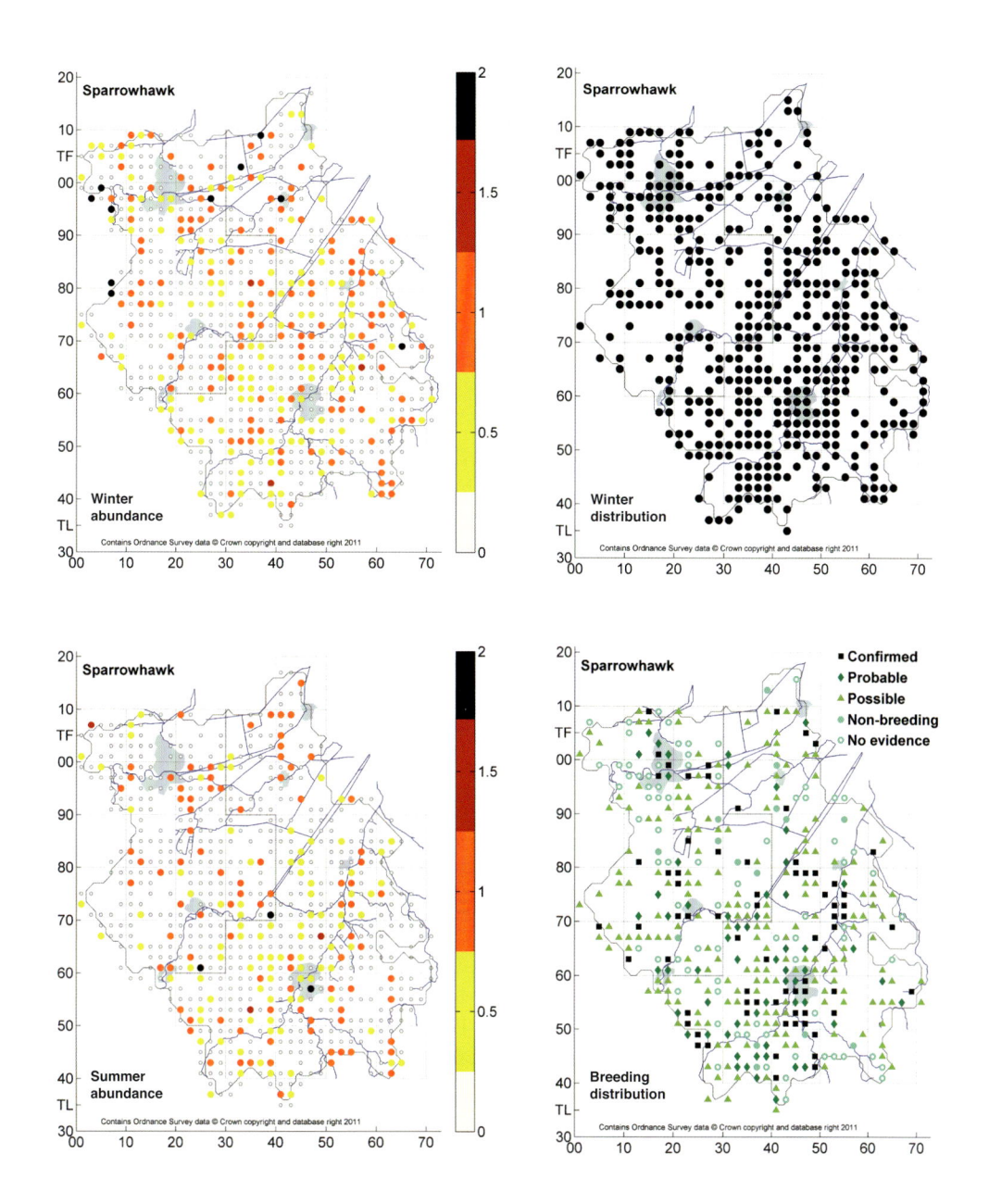

	Confirmed	Probable	Possible	Non-breeding	No evidence	Total summer (% county)	Total winter (% county)
Total tetrads	73	59	196	15	78	421 (43%)	464 (48%)

BUZZARD (Common Buzzard) *Buteo buteo*
Green List. Fairly common resident, passage migrant in variable numbers

Breeding population estimate: 200-400 pairs
Wintering population estimate: 400-1,000 individuals

The spread of the Buzzard into eastern England in recent decades has been spectacular. Buzzards were common and widespread throughout the UK 200 years ago, yet by 1860 had been eliminated by persecution from all but the most western areas. Two world wars resulted in a decrease in keepering activities and Buzzards began to spread, although this was limited in the 1950s and 1960s by the effects of myxomatosis on the rabbit population and organochlorines affecting reproductive success (Brown & Grice, 2005; Parkin & Knox, 2010). There was a major range expansion in eastern England in the 1990s, with breeding in Essex in 1994, Bedfordshire in 1995 and Hertfordshire in 1996 (Clements, 2000).

Isolated instances of breeding in Cambridgeshire occurred in 1959–60 and 1976 (Clark, 2000). A pair was seen carrying sticks at a site in the north of the county in 1992 but did not stay to breed (CBR 66). Records started to increase significantly in the mid-1990s, possibly as a consequence of releases of captive birds in Norfolk as well as natural colonisation from neighbouring counties (CBR 71; Clements, 2000), and breeding was confirmed in the south-east of the county in 1999 (CBR 73). The numbers of confirmed and suspected breeding pairs in the annual CBRs suggest a gradual increase to about 40 pairs over the following decade, but suspicions that the real extent of the increase was being significantly under-recorded (CBR 82,83) are confirmed by the results of the atlas fieldwork.

Breeding was confirmed in 68 tetrads and probable/possible breeding noted in a further 402 tetrads, which together make up almost half of the 969 tetrads in the county. Buzzards display relatively early in the spring and can be very secretive at the nest, so firm evidence of breeding can be difficult to obtain. A survey of displaying Buzzards in an area around Melbourn, South Cambs, covering approximately 70 tetrads in ideal weather conditions on 25th March 2012 revealed 31 pairs (S.L. Cooper, pers. comm.).

The maps for both summer and winter show that Buzzards were recorded much less frequently in the fens, where suitable nest sites and food are probably lacking. Despite Cambridgeshire being the least wooded county in England, there are clearly sufficient copses and small woods in the arable farmland in the south and west of the county to provide suitable nest sites, and nests have been found in isolated trees. The Buzzard's ability to take a wide range of mammalian and avian prey, carrion and invertebrates has enabled it to thrive here.

The extent to which the resident population is supplemented outside of the breeding season by individuals from elsewhere is uncertain. Despite regular winter influxes of Buzzards on the east coast, there has been only one record of a bird that was ringed outside the UK being recovered in this country (Wernham *et al.*, 2002; BTO, 2013). The general view of several authors is that many young Buzzards disperse eastwards from their natal areas in Wales and western England; this is supported by one found dead in Cambridgeshire in March 1994 that had been ringed as a nestling in Gwent, Wales (CBR 68).

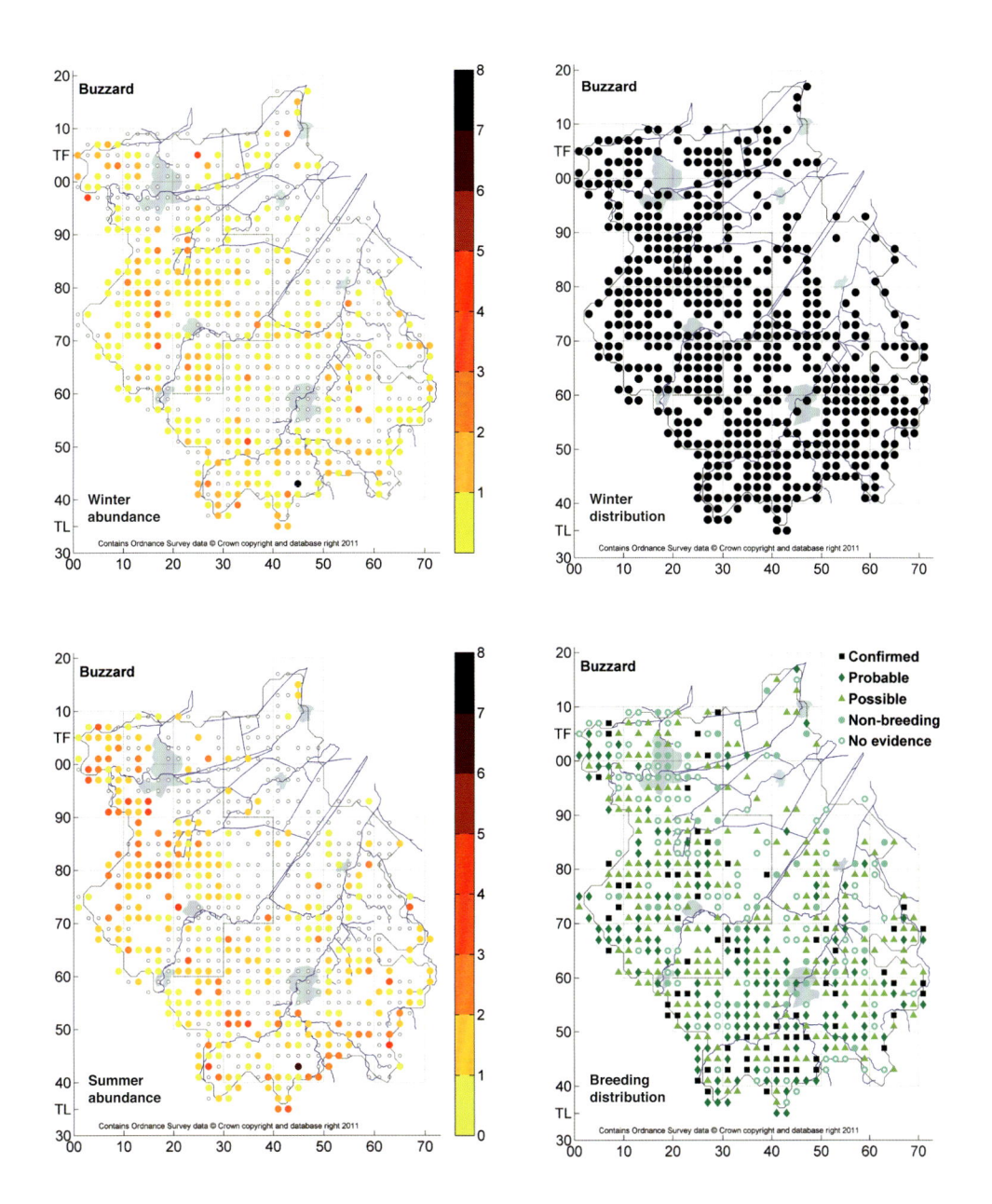

	Confirmed	Probable	Possible	Non-breeding	No evidence	Total summer (% county)	Total winter (% county)
Total tetrads	68	152	250	43	103	616 (64%)	565 (58%)

KESTREL (Common Kestrel) *Falco tinnunculus*
Amber List. Fairly common resident; winter visitor and autumn passage migrant

Breeding population estimate: 300-500 pairs
Wintering population estimate: 600-1,200 individuals

Until the return of the Sparrowhawk, the Kestrel was undoubtedly the most common and most widespread raptor in Cambridgeshire. This was not always the case; numbers fell in the immediate post-war period due to persecution exacerbated by poisoning with organochlorine chemicals in the late 1950 and 1960s. Clark (1996) reported that the Kestrel was virtually extinct in Huntingdonshire with no breeding birds recorded at all in 1960 and Bircham (1989) suggested that the population in old Cambridgeshire fell to as few as 11 pairs. The recovery in the 1970s was slow but by 1983 the population was estimated to be 100 pairs in old Cambridgeshire (still well below the 300 pairs estimated in the 1930s). CBC records suggest a recent decline in breeding birds but it is likely that they fail to reflect the true situation. Putative restrictions on breeding success include a reduction in nest sites and the cyclical nature of vole populations. BBS data for the UK show a 32% decline since 1995, with a slightly lower decline of 17% in Eastern England (Risely et al., 2012).

The breeding-distribution map shows confirmed breeding records in 167 tetrads which together with the 126 tetrads in which probable breeding was reported suggests a minimum breeding population of nearly 300 pairs; with more than one pair in a tetrad the breeding population could be larger. Counts of more than two birds were only recorded during the four months of winter.

Supplementation of the resident population by overwintering birds is implied in both the distribution and density maps for winter. While Kestrels breeding in lowland England are known to be sedentary, upland birds usually winter at lower altitudes and birds from northern Europe are known to move south, sometimes as far as north Africa, often passing through the UK on passage. Some of these birds overwinter in Eastern England (Brown & Grice, 2005). According to the winter distribution map Kestrels appear to be both slightly more widespread and slightly more numerous in this season. Certainly any car journey in winter of more than a few miles will reveal a Kestrel perched on overhead wires surveying the ground: a method preferred at that time of the year as being more energy efficient than flight-hunting (Pettifor, 1984).

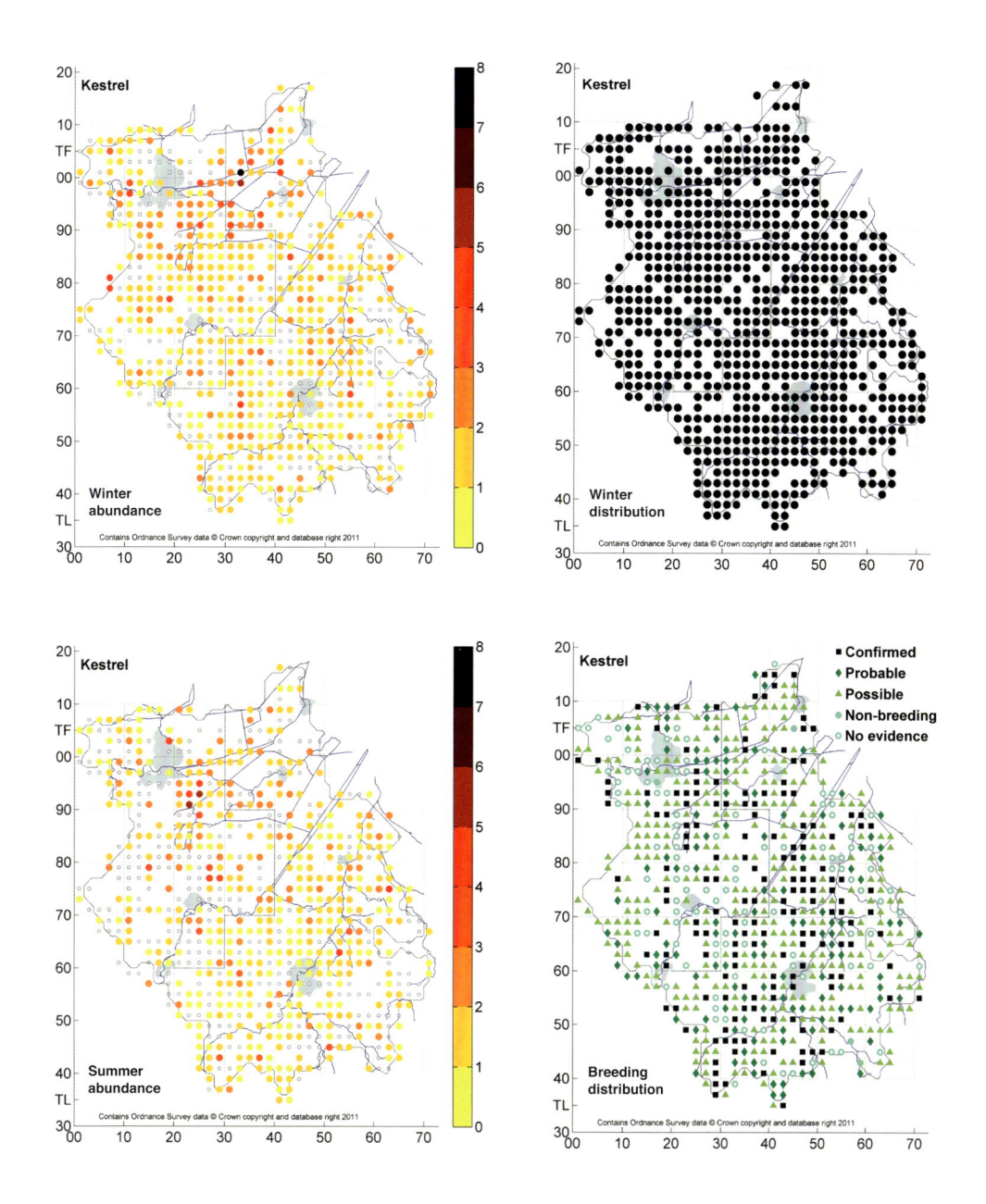

	Confirmed	Probable	Possible	Non-breeding	No evidence	Total summer (% county)	Total winter (% county)
Total tetrads	167	126	333	4	105	735 (76%)	765 (79%)

MERLIN *Falco columbarius*
Amber List. **Uncommon winter visitor and passage migrant**

Not a breeding species
Wintering population estimate: 5-20 individuals

Merlins in Cambridgeshire are winter visitors seen mainly in the fens but also occasionally over arable land in the southern half of the county, typically preying on small passerines such as Skylarks and Meadow Pipits. Nationally, numbers appear to be relatively stable, not least due to a change in habits. Many pairs have moved from open moorland to post-thicket conifer plantations in which they utilise old crows nests (Rebecca, 2011).

The distribution map shows two main areas where Merlins are recorded, along the river systems in the fens and on the arable land along the southern chalk ridge. Both these areas are notable for predominantly open habitats with large fields and some fallow stubble land where small passerines might be expected to feed. The density map shows the very small numbers of Merlins involved: most reports are of single birds. Merlins are by no means common.

Ringing recoveries suggest that the birds wintering in the county are of UK origin. Birds from Iceland have been reported but not in eastern England; the number of Icelandic birds is thought to be small (Wernham *et al.*, 2002).

Merlins were recorded from 83 tetrads during the atlas (9%).

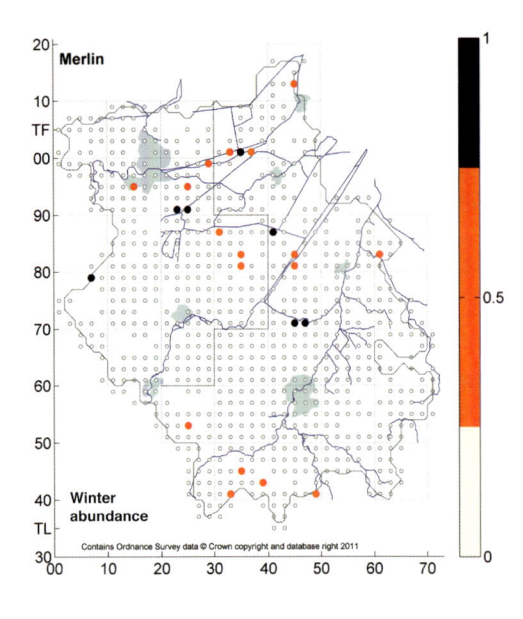

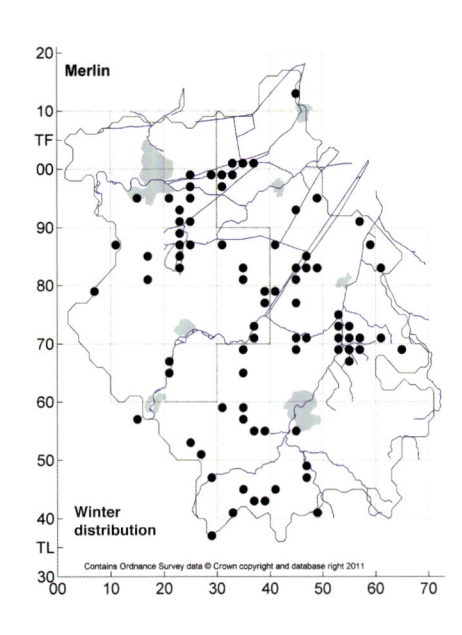

HOBBY (Eurasian Hobby) *Falco subbuteo*
Green List. Uncommon migratory breeder

Breeding population estimate: 60-100 pairs
Not a wintering species

The Hobby is a summer migrant that winters in Africa. Hobbies were traditionally birds of heathland in England which might explain their historical scarcity in Cambridgeshire: breeding was recorded sporadically in both old Cambridgeshire and Huntingdonshire. A dramatic change began in the late 1970s and early 1980s when breeding not only became regular but numbers increased almost annually such that between the two previous National Atlas projects of 1968–72 and 1988–92 an increase in occupied 10 km squares of 136% was noted. The exact reason is not entirely clear beyond a supposed increase in dragonfly abundance due to an increase in the number of gravel pits, and even garden ponds, and a change in breeding sites to woodland abutting arable farmland. The increase in populations of late-summer dragonflies was considered by Prince & Clarke (1993) to be a driver behind this increase as the provision of a good food source increased post-fledging survival.

The breeding-distribution map shows 30 tetrads in which there was confirmed breeding and a further 37 in which probable breeding was reported. This would suggest a minimum of over 60 pairs which compares favourably with the estimate of 40–50 pairs by Prince & Clarke (1993) and suggests that the Hobby population is relatively stable in the county. Hobbies are notoriously secretive during much of the breeding process; the best way to obtain evidence of successful breeding is when the young birds leave the nest in late summer. This late fledging could mean that confirmed breeding was not recorded during TTVs, although roving records may have supplied these data. Surprisingly the density map shows no great aggregations despite frequent reports of 10–20 birds at wetland sites usually, but not always, in spring. Some of these birds may be on passage; national ringing returns provide no information on where these birds settle although breeding now extends to the north of England as far as Northumberland (Holling *et al.*, 2012).

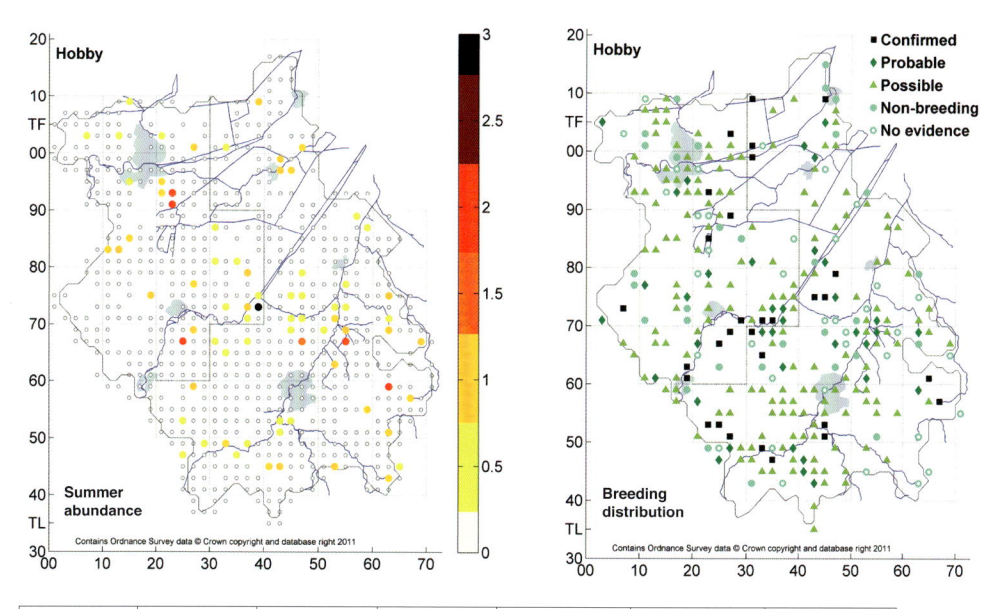

	Confirmed	Probable	Possible	Non-breeding	No evidence	Total summer (% county)
Total tetrads	30	37	163	31	37	298 (31%)

PEREGRINE (Peregrine Falcon) *Falco peregrinus*
Green List. Uncommon winter visitor and passage migrant; now scarce breeder

Breeding population estimate: 4-6 pairs
Wintering population estimate: 5-20 individuals

The status of the Peregrine in Cambridgeshire is a reflection of the national situation. In the immediate post-war period it was heavily persecuted and then a victim of organochlorine pesticide poisoning; the national breeding population had all but collapsed by the 1960s with around 400 pairs remaining, mostly in upland areas. Following conservation measures the population recovered and expanded to give a breeding estimate of approximately 1,500 pairs in 2002 (Holling *et al.*, 2012); this led to increased sightings in Cambridgeshire of wintering and passage birds. From being a rare bird sighted only in some winters, it became a scarce bird, seen regularly, almost always in the fens. As the number of wintering birds increased it became possible that breeding might occur and in 2007 a pair bred successfully at Peterborough Power Station.

The summer distribution data (breeding-season maps not shown) indicate confirmed breeding in four tetrads scattered across the county, with a single record of probable breeding. This suggests a county population of 4–6 pairs as reported in CBR 85. Other summer records will relate to hunting breeding birds from known sites, or to non-breeders. It is likely that the county population will continue to increase.

In winter the distribution is related to the river systems, mainly in the fens where birds hunt over the pits and washlands preying on wildfowl and waders. Numbers remain low, usually single birds but occasionally two are seen. Interestingly a group of records came from south Cambridgeshire, where traditionally the Peregrine was an extremely rare bird; this may reflect increased numbers in the county as a result of the increase in the national population.

Ringing recoveries show a few records of wintering birds from Scandinavia, but the likelihood is that the birds wintering in Cambridgeshire are dispersing young birds from within the UK (Brown & Grice, 2005).

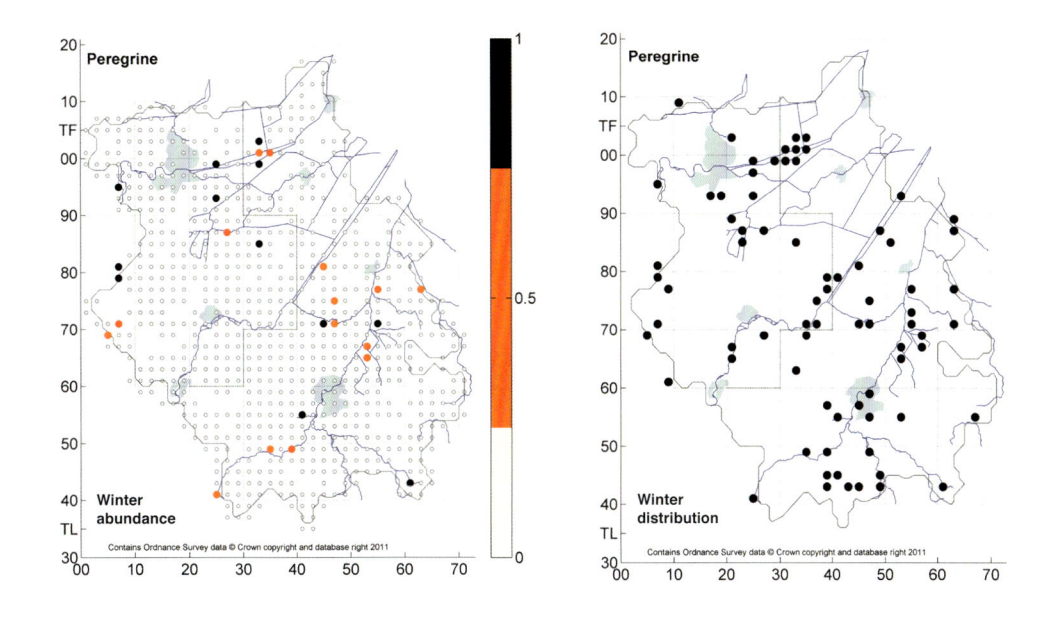

	Confirmed	Probable	Possible	Non-breeding	No evidence	Total summer (% county)	Total winter (% county)
Total tetrads	4	1	1	5	11	22 (2%)	75 (8%)

WATER RAIL *Rallus aquaticus*
Green List. Uncommon, much declined, resident, winter visitor and passage migrant

Breeding population estimate: 20-50 pairs
Wintering population estimate: 50-150 individuals

The winter maps show a wider distribution of Water Rails compared with the breeding season, probably as a result of an influx of birds from frozen parts of the continent. This is illustrated by one bird ringed at the Falsterbo Observatory in Sweden that was recovered at Sawston in the last winter of the atlas period (this individual is not mapped; no ringing data for the last season were added to the atlas data due to the delay in processing this information). During the breeding season, Water Rails were recorded at a smaller number of sites, most of which remained occupied in the winter period. The key areas are around Wicken Fen and Kingfishers Bridge, Ely Beet Factory pools and Chippenham Fen in the east, Fowlmere in the south, Grafham Water in the west, the pits around Peterborough in the north, and the wetlands in the Ouse valley and the upper stretch of the Ouse Washes. Rather surprisingly, they were recorded infrequently in the summer in the main areas of the Ouse and Nene Washes, and at Woodwalton Fen; these sites were more likely to be occupied in the winter.

The winter distribution includes major wetland reserves but also general countryside wherever wet vegetation can be found. This includes many of the river valleys including those in the major conurbations.

The dense wetland habitats occupied by Water Rails – fens, reedbed and similar – make seeing this species very difficult but fortunately they regularly give distinctive loud calls, making detection relatively straightforward. The habitat density means that proof of breeding was rather difficult to achieve, although their distinctive black chicks are somewhat easier to see than the more camouflaged adults. Due to the general under-recording of what is essentially an uncommon species, records of breeding are considered by the RBBP (Holling *et al.*, 2012). Water Rails show a widespread distribution across the whole of the UK, but accurate information on trends is difficult to establish. It is thought that major losses occurred before the modern era of bird monitoring, resulting from increased efficiency of land drainage.

Compared with the old atlases there has been relatively little change. The main losses seem to be from the Ouse Washes, where they were present during the 1988–92 survey. It is possible that more frequent summer flooding at the Washes has caused them to abandon this site in the breeding season. On the positive side, new habitats such as Kingfishers Bridge and the wetlands by the River Cam at Hinxton have contributed to an increased breeding distribution.

The highest counts of the atlas period came from Fowlmere RSPB reserve, TL44C, with a summer peak of 10 and a winter peak of 16. This probably reflects the fact that well-placed hides allow observation of Water Rails at this site, as well as there being a high density of this species there. Other good habitats, such as Chippenham Fen, are much less readily studied. In the winter period, Water Rails were recorded in 84 tetrads (9%), and 29 10 km squares (57%).

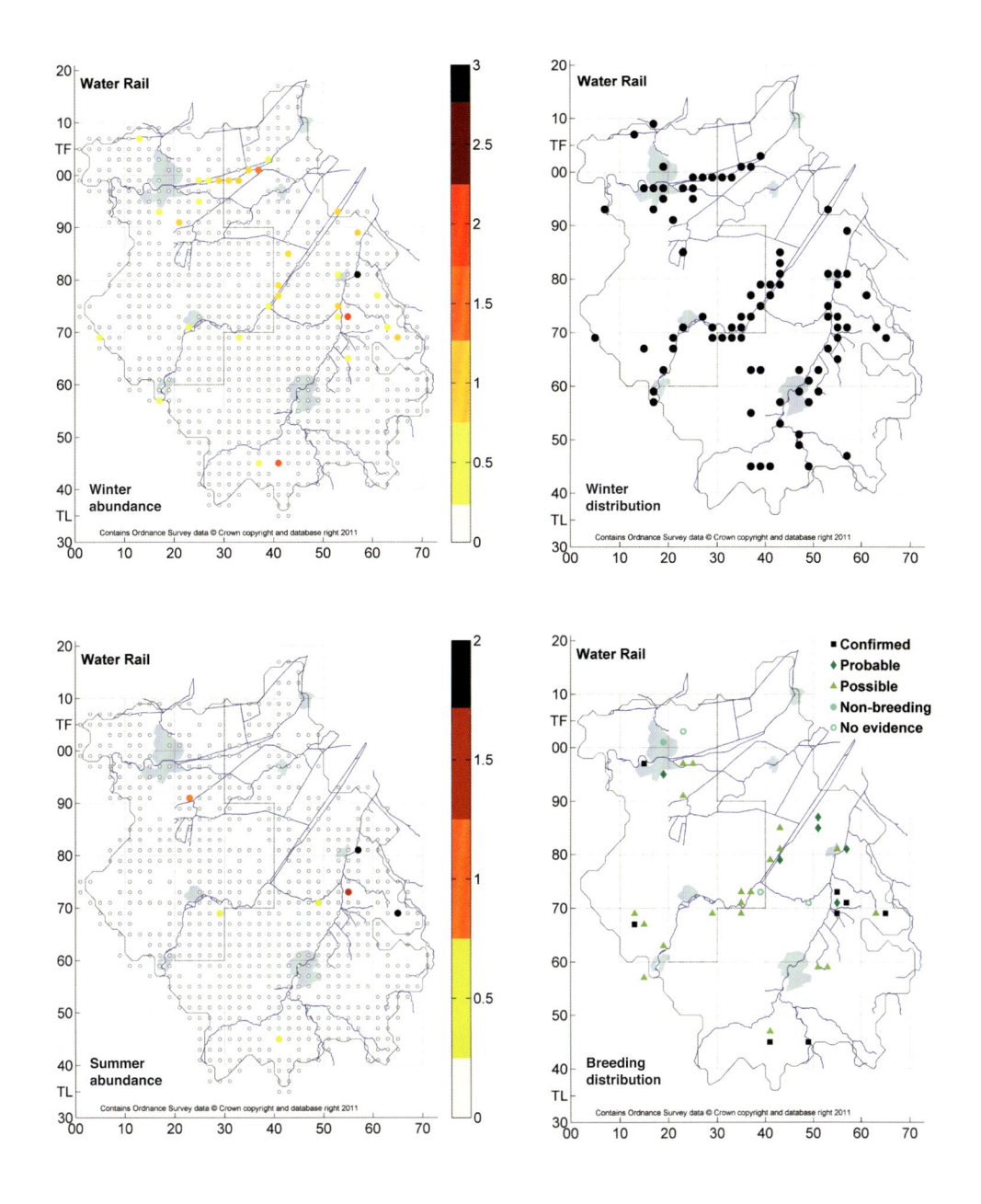

	Confirmed	Probable	Possible	Non-breeding	No evidence	Total summer (% county)	Total winter (% county)
Total tetrads	8	6	20	1	3	38 (4%)	84 (9%)

SPOTTED CRAKE *Porzana porzana*
Amber List. Scarce annual summer visitor/passage migrant; breeding has been confirmed in past years

Breeding population estimate: 0-3 pairs
Not a wintering species

This is a rare breeding bird, both locally and nationally, requiring extensive areas of wetland habitat. It is a summer visitor, and was not detected on any of the TTVs, but was regularly recorded at the Ouse and Nene Washes, so there are a few dots on the summer distribution map. They are difficult to see in their breeding habitats, most of which are inaccessible; the best chance of observing one is if they drop in at a smaller wetland site on migration. The main means of detection is by hearing their far-carrying distinctive calls. Even this, however, requires a fairly determined effort, as they are primarily nocturnal callers, which during the summer means really late at night! Whether they occur at any of our other large wetlands is perhaps, therefore, a debatable issue. Certainly the expansion of fenland reserves has the potential to produce more suitable habitat for this species in the future, and the next atlas may show an increase in distribution.

Although males singing against each other or in one spot for an extended period make classification of probable breeding relatively straightforward, observations of nesting behaviour for confirmation of breeding are more or less out of the question, and proof of breeding was not achieved during the atlas period. Young were seen during the previous Cambs Atlas, at the Ouse Washes, along with records from the Nene Washes, Wicken Fen and the Cam Washes, but there were no records in the Hunts Atlas.

This species occurs at a handful of sites across the UK, in variable numbers from year to year, and is sporadically recorded anywhere from south-west England to Shetland. Cambridgeshire is one of the few counties in the UK with a consistent presence. A special survey in 2012 will shed further light on the national picture but came too late for this atlas.

The highest count during the atlas period was of four on the Ouse Washes, in June 2008. The three tetrads (0.3%) with species records were assigned probable or possible breeding, and they occured in three different 10 km squares (6%).

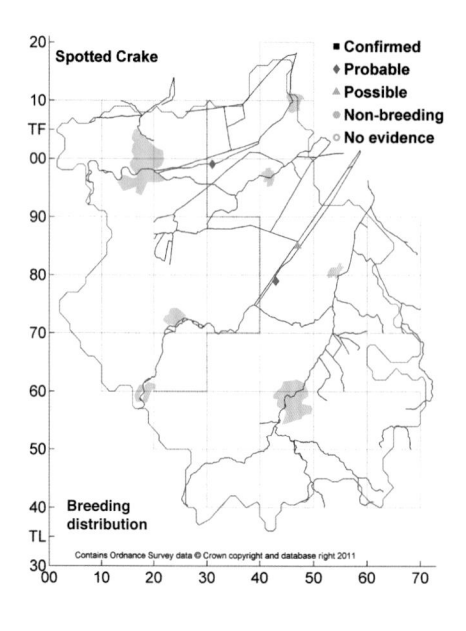

CORNCRAKE (Corn Crake) *Crex crex*
Red List. Rare re-introduced breeding species and rare passage migrant

Breeding population estimate: 21 singing males
Not a wintering species

All records received for this species came from the area around the Nene Washes, where an attempted re-introduction programme is underway. While it is too early to declare this project a success, there are encouraging signs, with released individuals returning from their winter migration and breeding successfully. However, return rates are only 50% of that required for a short-lived species with high mortality. The biggest threat seems to be the risk of summer floods destroying nests. In total, 45 records were submitted during the atlas period, but 17 of these were not assigned to a specific tetrad. Of the three tetrads specifically cited for this species, TL29Z had confirmed breeding status and the highest count of individuals with 10 on the 12th May 2011 (young were netted for ringing in counts during the breeding season). To the west, TL29U had a maximum count of four individuals, and territorial males raised the breeding status to probable. To the east, TL39E had a record of three individuals, and singing males gave this square possible breeding status.

There were also records not ascribed to specific tetrads. The most impressive count in this category was of 16 individuals on the 30th June 2009. Unfortunately these were logged as 'Nene Washes'. CBC placed these records in TF30, in the absence of any other clues, because TF30 contains the largest portion of the Nene Washes. They may actually have been in the core squares of TL29. One record was ascribed to TF20, which has about one tenth of a 1 km grid square in the Nene Washes with the other 99.9% of the 10 km square being agricultural fenland; if this bird was in the area away from the Nene Washes it would be particularly interesting.

There were no records in the previous two county atlases, and indeed this is a unique experiment in England, as the main Corncrake remnant populations are in north and west Scotland. Nationally, it is rare but the population is slowly increasing.

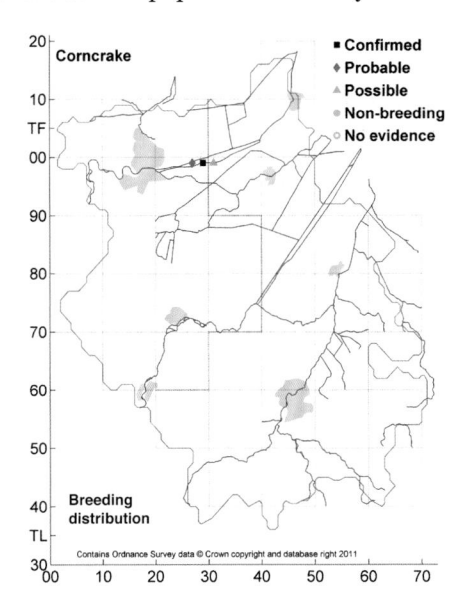

	Confirmed	Probable	Possible	Non-breeding	No evidence	Total summer (% county)
Total tetrads	1	1	1	0	0	3 (0.3%)

MOORHEN (Common Moorhen) *Gallinula chloropus*
Green List. Fairly common resident and probable autumn immigrant

Breeding population estimate: 2,000-4,000 pairs
Wintering population estimate: 4,000-10,000 individuals

This is a widespread and adaptable waterbird, equally likely to be seen in cities as it is out on the expanses of the major washlands, and it may be found on village ponds or farmland with permanent water in the form of ditches, streams or ponds. The maps reflect its ubiquity, with the only unpopulated areas being the higher ground of the western regions and, more noticeably, the chalk areas of the south-east. For much of the county, however, the density of Moorhens is rather low, with single-figure counts per hour on TTVs. Particularly important areas have much higher densities especially in the winter months when, according to ringing data, there is some local movement and immigration from abroad; favoured locations attract large numbers of birds. The main centres of importance are the Cam valley, between Cambridge and Ely, the Ouse valley and Washes below St. Ives, and the fens south and east of Peterborough around the old course of the Nene.

The breeding-season map shows that at the majority of sites where Moorhens were seen, they were likely to be breeding. There were just a few outlying 10 km squares where breeding was not confirmed. At the tetrad level, lower levels of breeding status tend to be associated with less-visited areas of the county. This illustrates the relative ease of detection of this species and its young, making confidence in the maps very high. The fact that the percentage of TTV and of roving-record tetrads was similar for winter and summer adds weight to this conclusion.

A greater number of occupied tetrads was recorded in the previous Hunts Atlas, but the Cambs Atlas shows a similar distribution to the current maps. This may reflect the trends detected nationally – a long-term decline of 17% since 1970 has stabilised, with no change detected since 1995.

The highest summer count was in TL58D, at Littleport, where 80 were recorded during a late-May visit. In the winter, 200 were counted between Earith and Bluntisham in TL37; TL37X held 120 and also had nearly the highest single TTV count, narrowly beaten by TL48S a little further down the Ouse Washes, which recorded 72 in one hour. In the winter period, Moorhens were recorded in 571 tetrads (59%), and 47 10 km squares (92%).

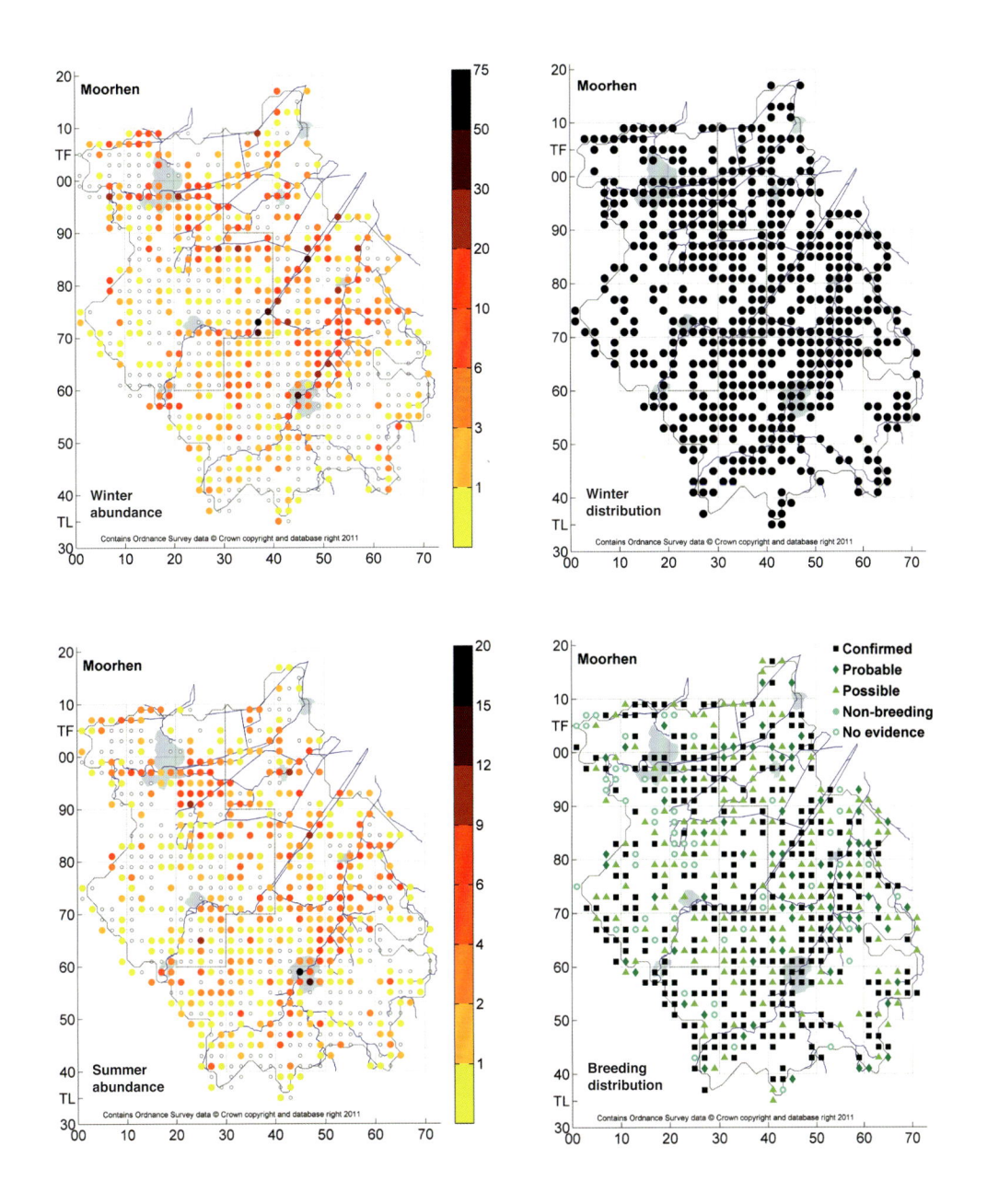

	Confirmed	Probable	Possible	Non-breeding	No evidence	Total summer (% county)	Total winter (% county)
Total tetrads	320	75	180	0	56	631 (65%)	571 (59%)

COOT (Common Coot) *Fulica atra*
Green List. Common resident and winter visitor on open water

Breeding population estimate: 1,000-2,000 pairs
Wintering population estimate: 7,500-15,000 individuals

The distribution and density maps for Coot reflect the availability of suitable habitat; they occur on almost any waterbody with a reasonable quantity of aquatic vegetation. The winter and summer TTV maps appear rather similar; Coots are found on slightly fewer sites in the winter but in higher numbers, reflecting that they form large congregations on favoured waterbodies and that local birds are joined by reinforcements from the continent. While they are found in many locations, the density maps show a strong concentration in the Ouse Washes and nearby Ouse valley pits. In the breeding season they are highly aggressive towards each other, in contrast to their gregarious winter behaviour, and disperse to breed on any suitable waterbody, sometimes as isolated pairs. They require larger and deeper waterbodies than Moorhens, so the the main drains and rivers in the fens are ideal breeding habitat; in the higher and drier rest of the county they are largely confined to the Ouse, Nene and any lakes or gravel pits.

There is little trouble in spotting Coots on their open-water habitats as they are conspicuous and noisy; their nests can sometimes be quite exposed and the young leave the nest early making them obvious. As the major wetlands are also well frequented by birdwatchers, there is a high degree of confidence in the maps produced.

There has been a slight increase in the distributional range of Coots in the summer compared with the previous atlases. This is particularly noticeable in the south-east of the county, presumably as a consequence of the small agricultural reservoirs that have been constructed in this drier corner of the county. National monitoring programmes also suggest that Coots are increasing in number, by 32% over the past 15 years.

The peak summer (July) count over the four years of the atlas was 827 at Fen Drayton Lakes. Average peak winter counts at key sites were: Ouse Washes (Cambs only) 3,821, Grafham Water 1,170, and Fen Drayton Lakes 1,556. In the winter period, Coots were recorded in 266 tetrads (27%) and 41 10 km squares (80%).

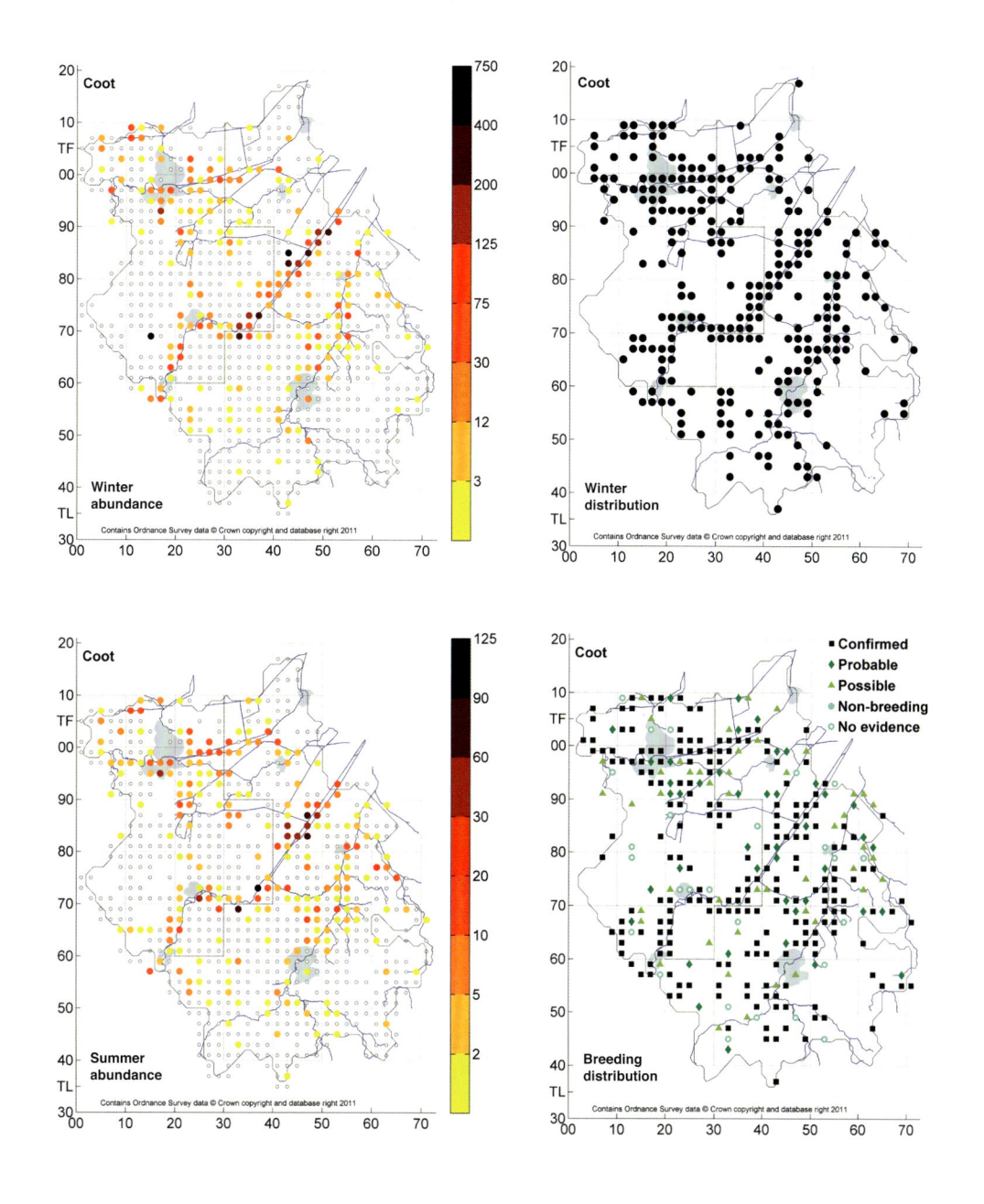

	Confirmed	Probable	Possible	Non-breeding	No evidence	Total summer (% county)	Total winter (% county)
Total tetrads	215	43	47	0	26	331 (34%)	266 (27%)

CRANE (Common Crane) *Grus grus*
Amber List. Scarce, but annual passage visitor, rare breeder (may have bred up to the 17th century, and again in 2010-2011)

Breeding population estimate: 1-2 pairs plus non-breeding birds
Wintering population estimate: 5-10 individuals

The summer distribution map shows that if you stand in one of our major river valleys for long enough, you have a chance of encountering a Crane in flight. Most of the non-breeding records that make up the majority of occupied tetrads were of flying birds. Even more exciting is the prospect of seeing them on their breeding grounds and watching their courtship display; this is now a distinct possibility in our large wetlands. They have particularly taken to the extensive wet grassland habitat and network of ditches and pools of the RSPB's Nene Washes, with Woodwalton Fen – and the extension being created by the Wildlife Trust – their second site of choice. One pair raised a chick in 2010 – the first recorded breeding in the county in over 300 years coinciding with the fieldwork for this atlas.

There were about half the number of records of Cranes during the winter atlas period compared to summer, with the vast majority coming from the same locations favoured during the summer. There were no flight records during this period.

Studying the 162 Crane records from the atlas illustrates the colonisation of the county during this period. In the first winter, there were just three records, all from the Norfolk border. The first summer had 70 records, which were widely scattered about the county, ending up in the Nene Washes. These two periods had the lowest and highest number of Crane records of the entire eight recording periods. In the second winter Cranes were recorded regularly at the Nene Washes for the first three months, then moved to Woodwalton Fen. In the second summer they started at Woodwalton Fen then moved to the Nene Washes where they spent the third winter. In the third summer, records came from five locations, and breeding was confirmed on the Nene Washes. It is likely that records were suppressed at this time due to the sensitivity of this species to disturbance, and further atlas records were not necessary from their regular haunts. In the fourth winter, Cranes were recorded at Woodwalton Fen in November, then returned to the Nene Washes. In the fourth summer the majority of records came from the Ouse Washes but with no indication of breeding.

It is possible that, when not at the well-watched reserves, our Cranes spend time on remote areas of open farmland in the fens, where they may remain undetected. Despite their large size and distinctive appearance they can be very unobtrusive; with slow steady movements and wary habits they can blend into the background, especially as the more expansive farmed fenland areas are relatively underwatched and thus undisturbed.

Cranes were recorded during the period of the previous Cambs Atlas, but only as vagrant status. The UK native population is centred around the Norfolk Broads, but has been growing and expanding slowly into other parts of eastern England, while a re-introduction programme in western England also supplements our records as occasional captive-bred individuals join the local population. Increasingly, passage migrants en route to Scandinavia may also feature as summer flight records.

The highest count in the atlas period was of five birds, recorded during the winter period in the Nene Washes at TF30F; the summer peak count was of four, seen in flight over St. Neots and Little Paxton heading north-east (logged as TL16V). In the winter period, Cranes were recorded in nine tetrads (1%), and five 10 km squares (10%) but one of these records was from Welney in the Ouse Washes, where the tetrad is predominantly in Norfolk, and another came from Brandon Creek, of which half is also in Norfolk.

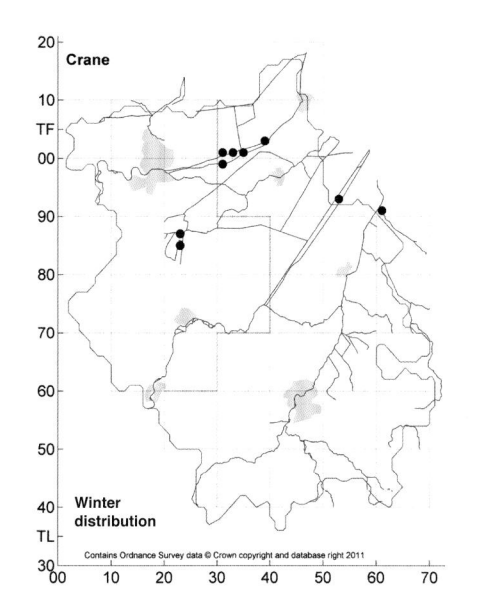

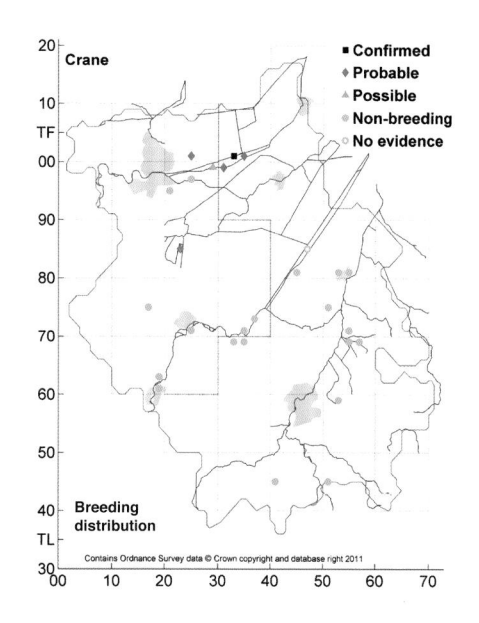

	Confirmed	Probable	Possible	Non-breeding	No evidence	Total summer (% county)	Total winter (% county)
Total tetrads	1	4	1	20	1	27 (3%)	9 (1%)

OYSTERCATCHER (Eurasian Oystercatcher)
Haematopus ostralegus
Amber List. Uncommon passage migrant, scarce winter visitor and local breeder

Breeding population estimate: 50-100 pairs
Wintering population estimate: 25-75 individuals

The previous Cambs Atlas noted a shift in behaviour in the Oystercatcher, which had started breeding inland along major river valleys. This spread has continued, and Oystercatchers are more common now than in the previous atlas period; they now also breed in arable fields, especially in the stonier, open vistas of the Breckland and similar parts of Cambridgeshire.

Breeding-season records were largely limited to areas along major rivers, particularly along the Ouse Washes, Nene Washes, River Great Ouse and the River Cam. The availability of wet grassland for feeding is probably important in this distribution. The scattering of records along the Cambridgeshire-Suffolk (or Norfolk) border possibly represent arable-breeding birds, although some records are from the Isleham Washes and one nesting attempt took place on a roof in Wisbech. A distinctive and noisy bird, it is not likely that many went unrecorded at breeding sites in well-watched river valleys, although further breeding birds in arable sites may not have been noticed as these districts often had poorer coverage.

Oystercatchers are rare in Cambridgeshire during the winter, reflected by their occurrence on only 1.6% of TTVs. There were only 67 winter records during atlas work, spread across 36 tetrads. Counts were typically of one or two birds, the highest count being 11. The record count in Cambridgeshire up to 2011 is 55 birds (CBR 85). Reinforcing the rarity of Oystercatchers in Cambridgeshire during the winter, most atlas records (60 out of 67, 90%) were from February, especially the second half of the month when birds disperse inland to breed. The UK wintering population of Oystercatcher is estimated to be 320,000 (Musgrove *et al.*, 2011). Compatible with the low numbers seen in winter in Cambridgeshire, only around 2% of these are found inland during early winter (Musgrove *et al.*, 2011).

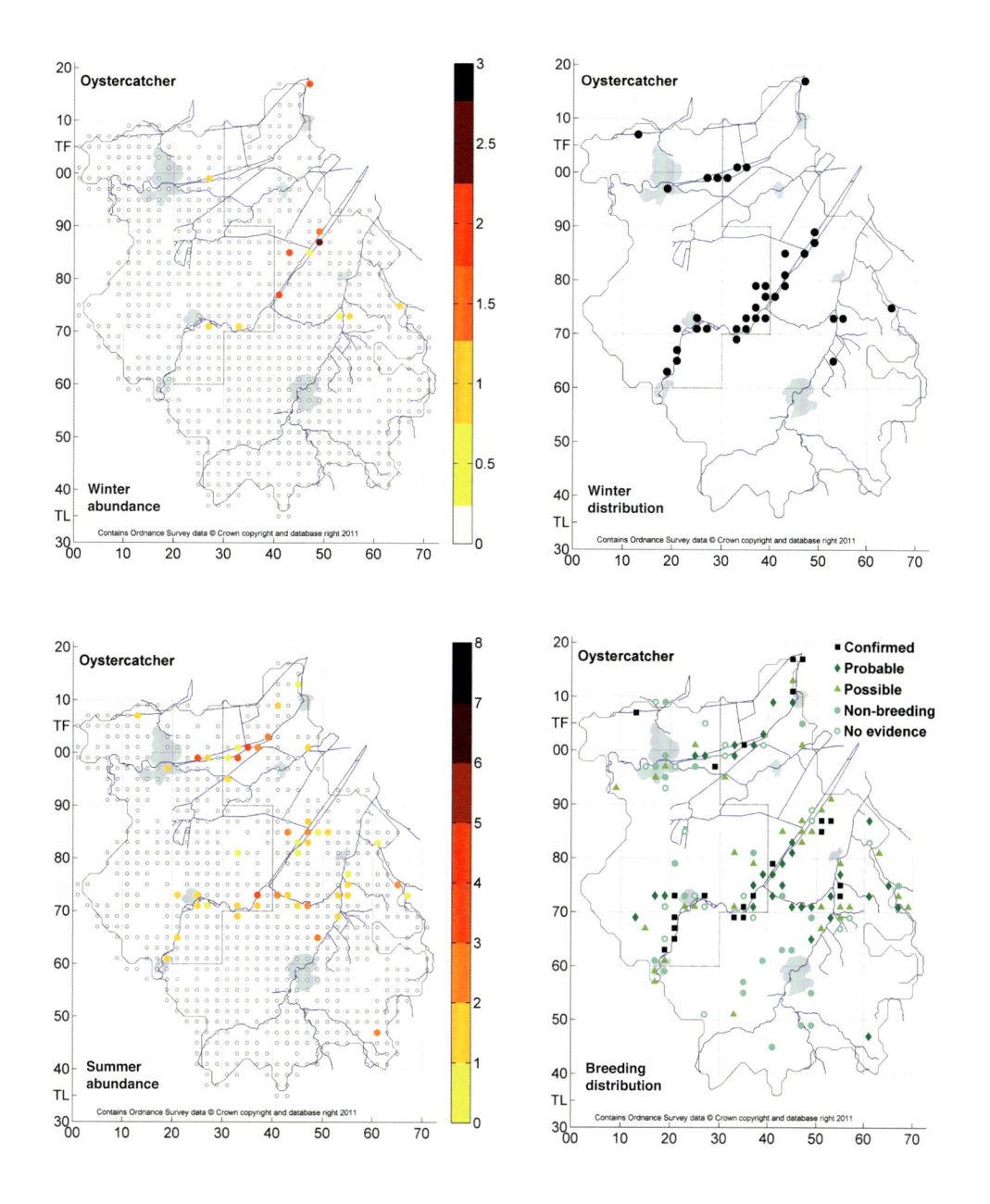

	Confirmed	Probable	Possible	Non-breeding	No evidence	Total summer (% county)	Total winter (% county)
Total tetrads	22	32	33	23	21	131 (14%)	36 (4%)

AVOCET (Pied Avocet) *Recurvirostra avosetta*
Amber List. Uncommon passage migrant and migratory breeder

Breeding population estimate: 30-60 pairs
Not a wintering species

Avocet is one of the more unexpected additions to the breeding avifauna of Cambridgeshire; at the time of the previous atlases it was a rare breeding bird on the East Anglian coast. It only became a regular breeding species in 2001 and remains very scarce and localised. Where it occurs it seems to be relatively successful and there is potential for it to spread to other sites in the county. It is also a regular passage migrant in both spring and autumn, mostly at sites where breeding now occurs.

During the atlas, it was confirmed breeding in 15 tetrads, probable in eight, possible in a further four and recorded as a non-breeder in one additional tetrad. The highest density of breeding was achieved at a private wetland creation project in the centre of the county, where 15–20 pairs breed and many chicks are colour-ringed. This has in part enabled some of the post-breeding movements of our birds to be monitored; they seem to congregate on river washlands in late summer and in the spring and autumn. Virtually none remain during winter, however, with only one recorded in a tetrad at Fen Drayton.

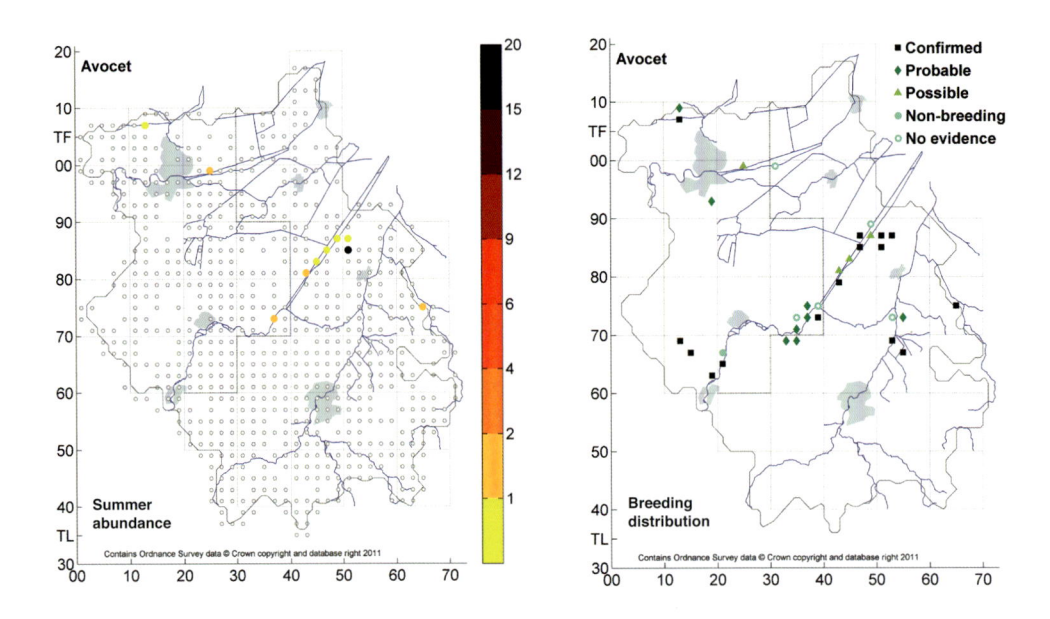

	Confirmed	Probable	Possible	Non-breeding	No evidence	Total summer (% county)
Total tetrads	15	8	4	1	5	33 (3%)

LITTLE RINGED PLOVER *Charadrius dubius*
Green List. Uncommon migratory breeder and passage migrant

Breeding population estimate: 30-50 pairs
Not a wintering species

A strictly summer visitor, the Little Ringed Plover is far less site-faithful than the Ringed Plover; although it is a regular breeder on our gravel pits, it is also to be found near small waterbodies such as farm pools, roadside balancing ponds and similar suitably bare transient habitats. These will be used for a year or two, but as soon as they become too vegetated the Little Ringed Plovers will move on. They seem tolerant of human settlements, if the habitat suits them, with several of the atlas records coming from pools on large city-edge development areas or road-scheme pools. Birds will also occasionally breed in arable areas – this is more common in the Brecks but was also noted on spring-sown, stony fields in the county on occasions. This transitory nature may mean that the number of tetrads in which breeding was recorded is an exaggeration of the true population, but close examination of the records shows that many of the sites used were large gravel-pit complexes, where it is likely that breeding would occur regularly; relatively few were from more-transient habitats.

Little Ringed Plover is probably a slightly more abundant breeder now than it was during the previous atlas period (Cambs Atlas 1994: 16 confirmed plus eight tetrads possible/probable; Hunts Atlas 1988: 23 confirmed, seven probable and seven possible tetrads). Numbers in the county have been increasing since they first colonised in the 1950s.

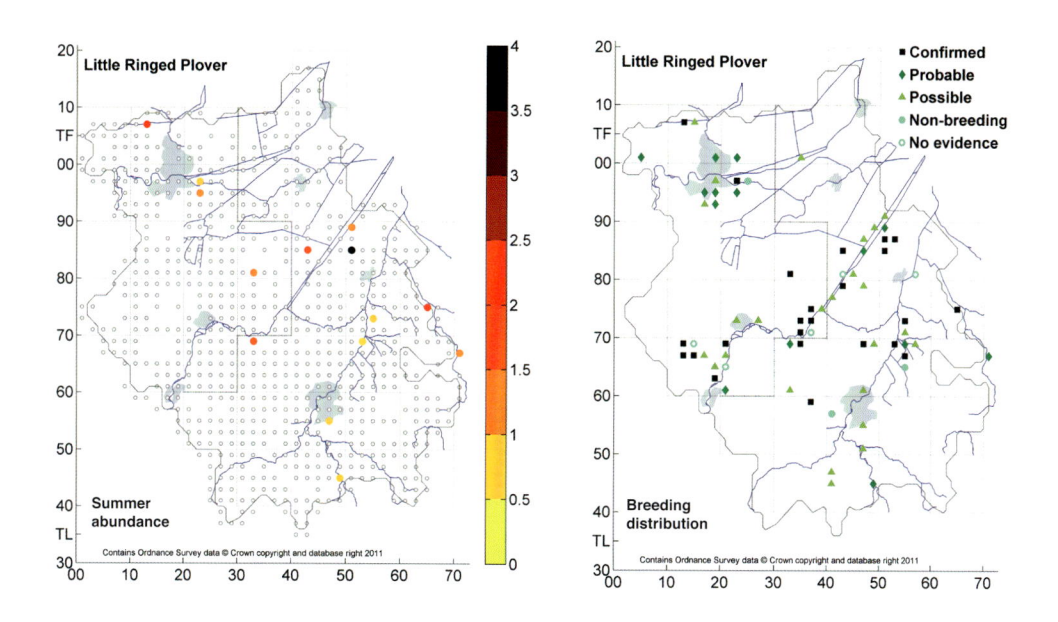

	Confirmed	Probable	Possible	Non-breeding	No evidence	Total summer (% county)
Total tetrads	24	14	25	3	5	71 (7%)

RINGED PLOVER (Common Ringed Plover) *Charadrius hiaticula*
Amber List. Scarce migratory breeder (recent sharp decline) and fairly common passage migrant; very occasional in winter

Breeding population estimate: 10-20 pairs
Wintering population estimate: 5-15 records annually

Ringed Plover has always been a comparatively scarce breeding bird: the previous Cambs Atlas implied that it had been a very sporadic breeder but had become more regular. Across the UK, Ringed Plover has been declining in recent years, and it would seem from the distribution maps that we have fewer breeding sites in Cambridgeshire than 20 years ago.

It is a species mostly confined to the major gravel-pit complexes or wetlands with a network of pools and islands. The newer wetland-creation projects such as Kingfishers Bridge are typical localities away from core sites in the gravel pits of the Ouse valley, Maxey Pits, Kings Dyke, etc. It appears to have been lost as a breeder from the Nene Washes, where several tetrads contained possible breeders and one with confirmed breeding in the previous atlas; only one tetrad here logged summer birds in the present fieldwork. Of 14 winter records (maps not shown) in eight tetrads, all bar one were in the last week of February – these are likely to be the first passage migrants of the season. Two of these winter records also logged displaying behaviour, which would be expected of passage birds heading for their breeding grounds. The other winter record was logged in November on an airfield on a TTV in the south of the county away from significant waterbodies; it is likely to have been a late migrant.

Most Ringed Plovers are recorded on passage, so do not appear as atlas records, but the county retains a small breeding population. The previous Hunts Atlas noted 18 confirmed, 12 probable and seven possible breeding tetrads, focussed on the Nene Washes, the pits south of Peterborough and a scattering throughout the Ouse valley; the Cambs Atlas showed eight confirmed and a further six present in summer tetrads, centred on the Nene Washes with smaller clusters elsewhere.

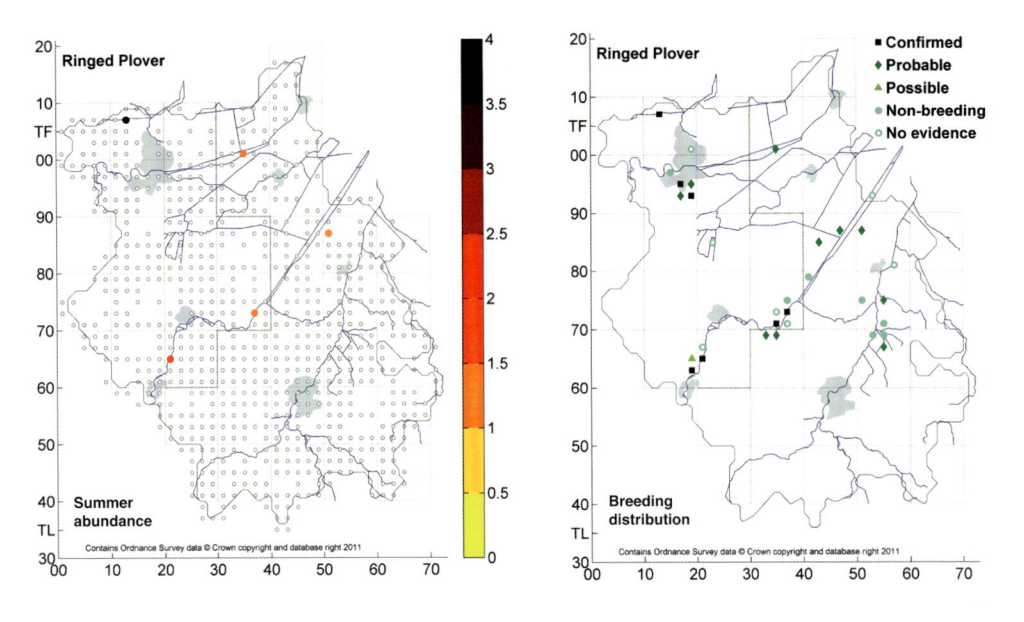

	Confirmed	Probable	Possible	Non-breeding	No evidence	Total summer (% county)	Total winter (% county)
Total tetrads	7	10	1	7	7	32 (3%)	8 (1%)

GOLDEN PLOVER (European Golden Plover) *Pluvialis apricaria*
Amber list. Very common winter visitor and passage migrant

Not a breeding species
Wintering population estimate: 10,000-30,000 individuals

The Golden Plover is a familiar winter bird across Cambridgeshire, utilising both arable and wetland habitats. Often to be found on arable fields in mixed flocks with Lapwing, the fields of southern Cambridgeshire and fenland areas are a valuable feeding resource. The drier areas of western Huntingdonshire and the south-eastern chalklands hold far fewer records of this species. Large flocks can also be found at our major wetland sites, the Ouse and Nene Washes and the Cam and Ouse valleys.

Golden Plover are relatively widespread in Cambridgeshire during the winter, being found in 249 (26%) tetrads. Of these, 23 (9%) had counts of 1,000 or more birds, with the highest count during the atlas fieldwork being 2,850. The highest count reported in Cambridgeshire during 2007–11 was 8,000 at the Nene Washes in December 2008 (CBR 82); the highest recorded count ever in Cambridgeshire is 13,000 at the Nene Washes in February 2005 (CBR 85). Indeed, the Nene Washes holds nationally important numbers of wintering Golden Plover (regularly 1% or more of the estimated national population, a threshold currently set at 4,000 birds; Holt *et al.*, 2012).

The UK wintering population was estimated by Baker *et al.* (2006) to be 310,000 birds while Gillings & Fuller (2009), in a large-scale survey, estimated a peak of 400,000 birds in the UK during the winter 2006/07. The 30-year trend shows a significant increase of 321%, but with a decline in recent years of 12% across the UK as a whole (Eaton *et al.*, 2012).

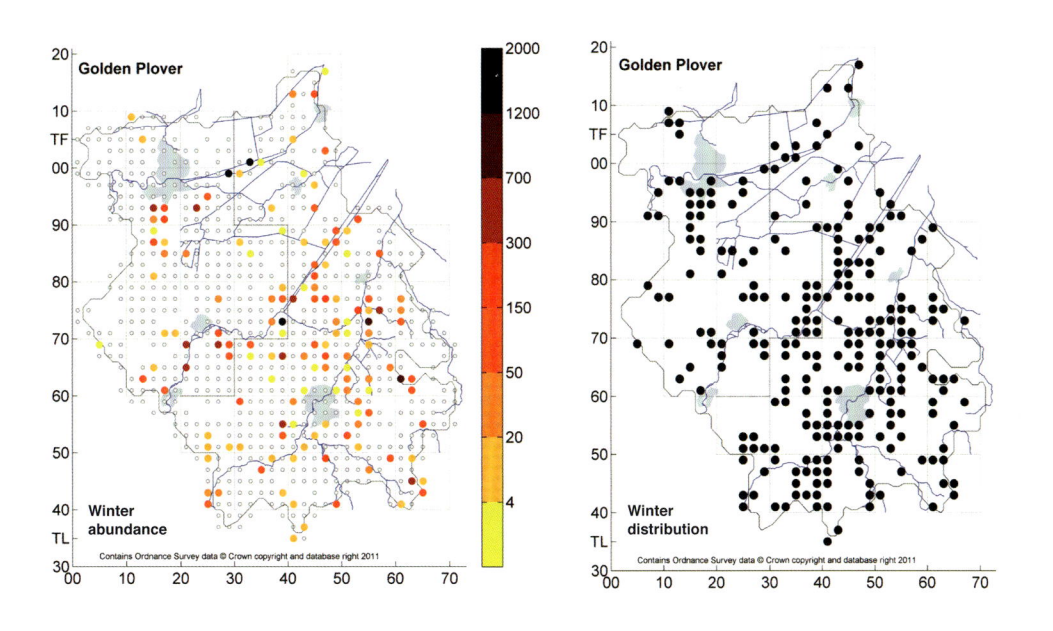

LAPWING (Northern Lapwing) *Vanellus vanellus*
Red list. Fairly common but decreased resident; abundant winter visitor/passage migrant

Breeding population estimate: 500-2,000 pairs
Wintering population estimate: 10,000-50,000 individuals

Now red-listed in the UK, the Lapwing is one of the most strongly declining bird species in Europe; national Common Birds Census/BBS surveys have estimated a 49% decline in England and Wales over the decade 1987–98. These declines continue in Eastern England, with BBS returns recording a further 45% regional losses in 2010–11. Lapwings nevertheless remain familiar and widespread breeding birds in Cambridgeshire. Wherever present, they are unlikely to be overlooked due to the open habitats they frequent, their tumbling display flights, persistent calling and their vigilant mobbing of marauding corvids.

Recorded during the breeding season in 422 (14%) tetrads, breeding was confirmed in 103 and probable in 159. This compares with scores combined from the previous atlases of 471 tetrads with birds present, 284 with confirmed breeding and 121 with probable breeding. These continuing losses are concentrated in Huntingdonshire, fenland away from the river washland reserves, and both to the east and west of Cambridge. Confirmed breeding densities were highest around the Ouse and Nene Washes; over 100 pairs of Lapwing were recorded breeding at both locations during each year of the atlas, accounting for some 77% of breeding pairs or territorial individuals in 2011. However, both Washes are susceptible to spring and summer flooding which can result in high failure rates of all nesting waders. Other areas of good density lie along the River Cam and its tributaries, and along the River Great Ouse – in particular at reserves such as Fen Drayton Lakes, Wicken Fen and Kingfishers Bridge.

Away from these fragile strongholds, mostly sustained by intensive wetland and farmland conservation management, it can sadly no longer be said (Cambs Atlas 1994) that 'Lapwings seem to breed successfully on even the smallest suitable field'. There is good evidence that, nationally, these declines have resulted from habitat loss and degradation due to changes in agricultural practices, in particular change from spring to autumn sowing, drainage of grasslands and loss of mixed farmland, which have led to breeding productivity dropping below a sustainable level. Cambridgeshire has been no exception. Chick mortality and predation is thought to be the main determinant of their population decline. Long-term nest record card analysis has shown that nest predation rates, possibly also resulting from habitat changes due to agricultural intensification, were substantially higher in the 1990s than in previous decades. Recent empirical evidence also suggests that levels of predation on wader nests may now be unsustainably high in many cases, even in some situations where breeding habitat, for example on managed reserves, is otherwise favourable.

In winter, Lapwings were also widespread in Cambridgeshire, being recorded in 436 (45%) tetrads. Large flocks are not uncommon and counts of 1,000 or more were recorded in 19 tetrads during atlas surveying, the largest being 6,600 in TF30F in February 2008. As with breeding, high densities in Cambridgeshire were again seen around the Ouse and Nene Washes; both sites are deemed to hold nationally important numbers of Lapwings during winter (Holt *et al.*, 2012). This threshold is defined as regularly holding 1% or more of the national population, currently 6,200 birds for Lapwing (Holt *et al.*, 2012). The highest ever count in the county is 35,520 at the Ouse Washes in December 2007.

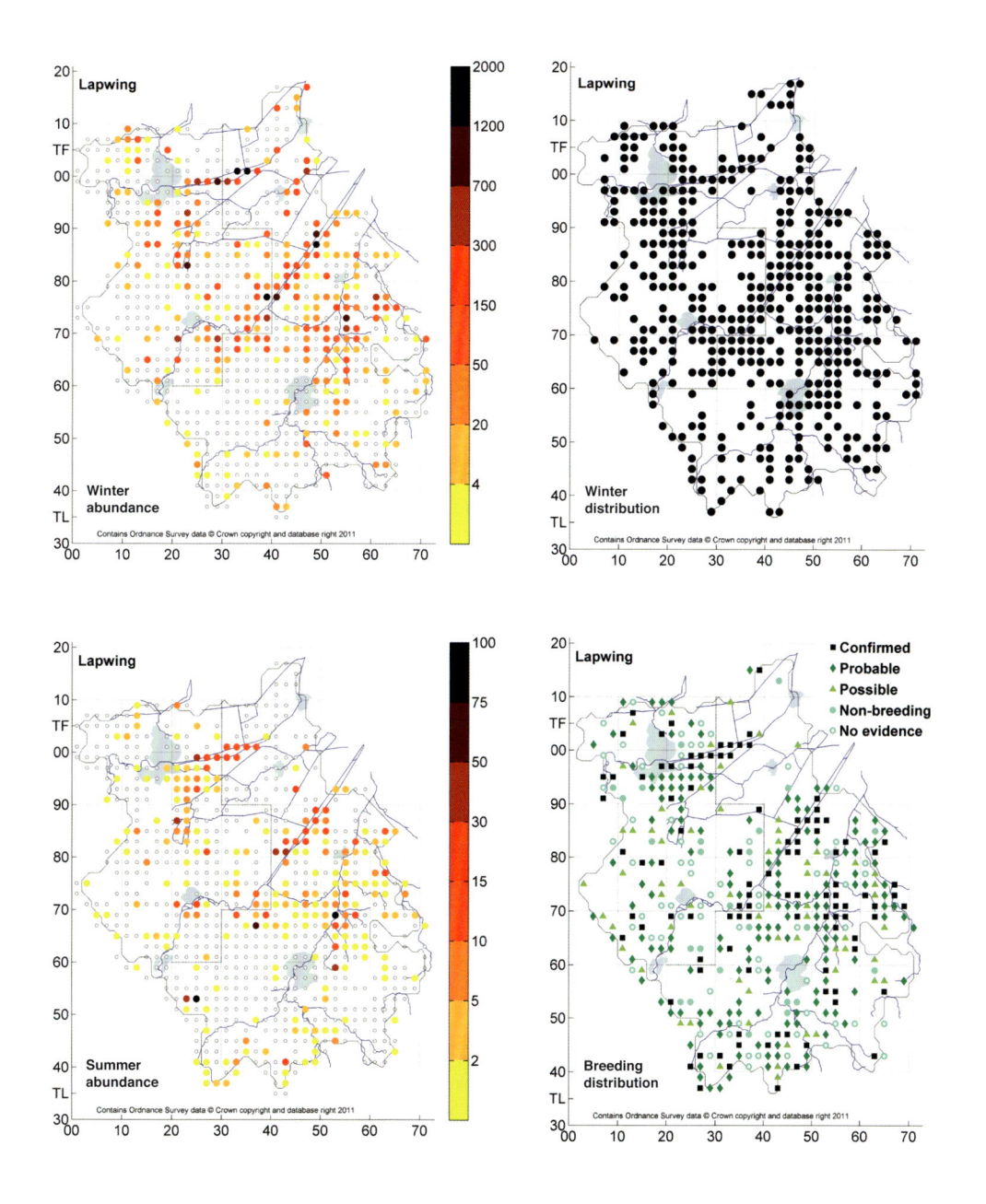

	Confirmed	Probable	Possible	Non-breeding	No evidence	Total summer (% county)	Total winter (% county)
Total tetrads	103	159	65	25	70	422 (44%)	436 (45%)

DUNLIN *Calidris alpina*
Red List. Uncommon passage migrant and winter visitor

Not a breeding species
Wintering population estimate: 50 individuals

Dunlin breed in a wide range of habitats, from coastal grasslands and saltmarsh to upland moorland and tundra wetlands. The UK breeding population is relatively small at 8,600–10,600 pairs (Musgrove, 2013) but the number of wintering birds, the majority of them on estuaries, is vast at around 350,000 individuals (Musgrove *et al.*, 2011). Thousands more pass through on spring and autumn migration: their precise numbers are unknown.

Fewer than 1% of wintering Dunlin use inland sites and in Cambridgeshire, while they may vary, numbers are generally very small. The atlas maps reflect this, and also show how records were largely concentrated in the Ouse valley and, to a lesser extent, on the Nene Washes. Shallow wetland edges with exposed mud are normally the favoured habitat, but wet fields or pools on flooded arable land are often attractive too, and it is then that Dunlin sometimes surprise observers by appearing with Lapwing and Golden Plover flocks.

The nature of atlas recording may give a somewhat misleading impression of winter numbers of Dunlin; it will not capture maximum flock sizes where they are short-lived or occur in March. Reference to recent CBRs reveals that at times there can be several hundred birds in the county. The CBRs also provide a good indication of passage numbers, which do not show up in atlas returns. These can vary enormously and can occasionally be surprisingly large even at individual sites – e.g. 200 at Little Paxton in May 2007.

It is generally thought that most of our wintering birds are of the nominate race *alpina*, breeding in northern Scandinavia and north-western Russia, probably including some of the race *schinzii*, which breed in the UK, south-east Greenland, Iceland and the Baltic area. The latter are better represented on passage when birds showing their characteristics occur in Cambridgeshire, as, much more rarely, do *arctica* birds from north-east Greenland.

Winter records came from 29 tetrads.

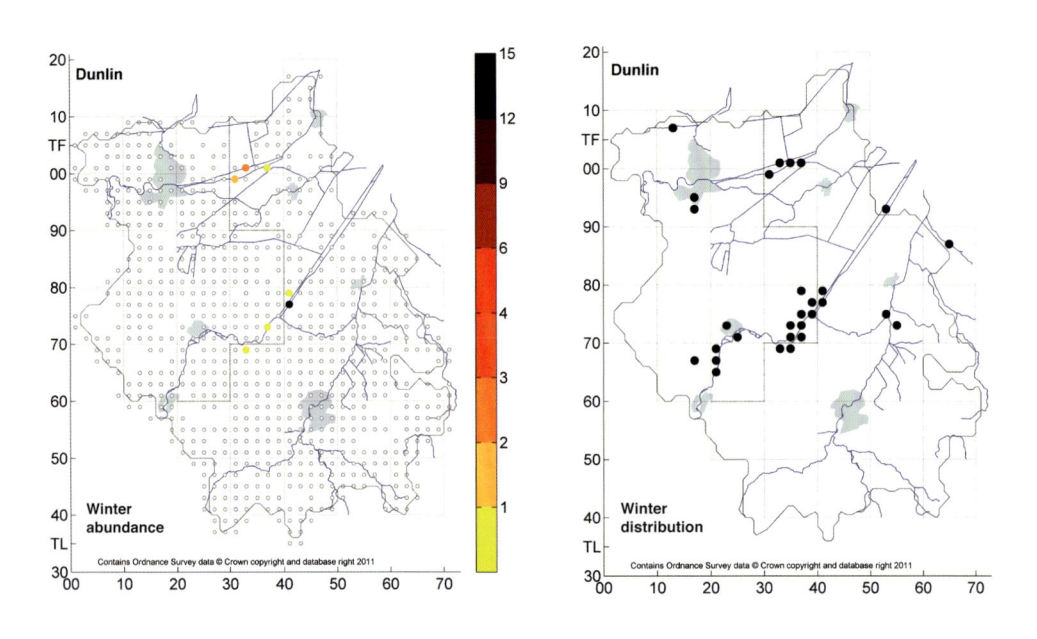

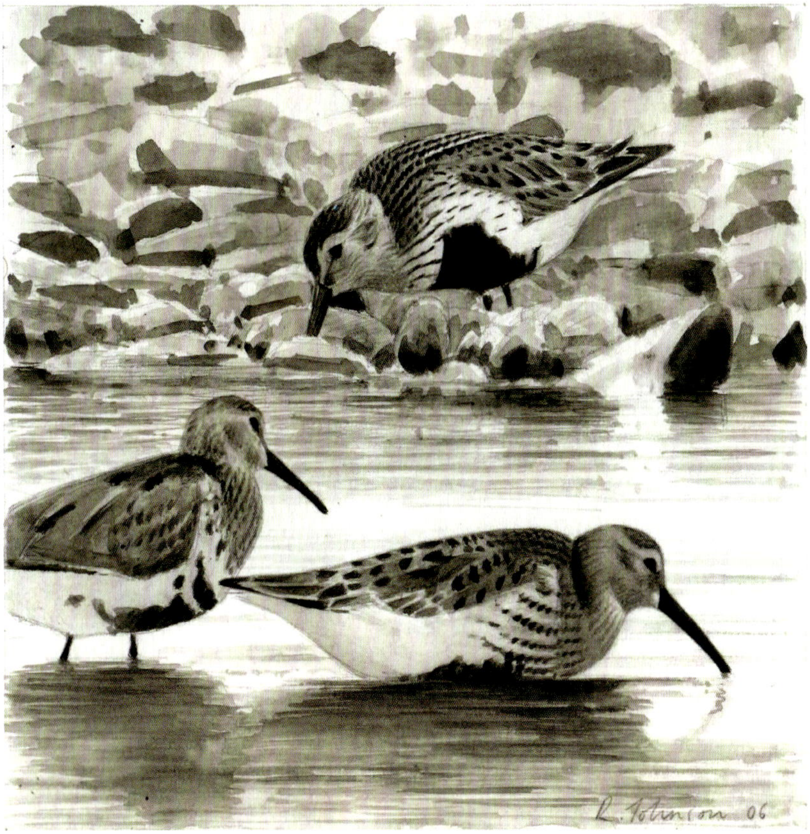
R. Johnson 06

RUFF *Philomachus pugnax*
Red List. Fairly common passage migrant/local winter visitor

Not a breeding species, last confirmed 1991
Wintering population estimate: 10-100 individuals

Fifty years ago, the finding of a nest proved that Ruffs were breeding on the Ouse Washes. This was the first authenticated record for 40 years: Ruffs were once fairly common but, owing to drainage and widespread killing for food, numbers declined until, by the middle of the 19th century, they had become virtually extinct as a nesting species, with just a few isolated breeding records thereafter (Parslow, 1973).

For a time, the Ouse Washes were the Ruff's UK stronghold: it became one of Cambridgeshire's most iconic breeding species. The Washes provided classic nesting habitat, with their low-lying meadows, often flooded in winter and used for grazing in summer. Proving breeding was never easy, but it was known or strongly suspected to have occurred in most years up to the mid-1980s. During the 1970s, the number of reeves was at least five, often more, and reached an exceptional 21 in 1971. In the 1980s, however, it became clear that a decline had taken place, to just 1–6 birds (Bircham, 1989; Gibbons et al., 1993). Reserve status and habitat management on the Washes improved the available habitat, but spring flooding remained a problem. The present situation is that breeding has not been proved in Cambridgeshire since 1991.

There has also been a marked reduction in the number of reports of lekking birds in spring. There was a lek of over 50 birds at the Ouse Washes in April 2007, but the birds were gone by May. Since then, there were no further records until a dozen displaying birds were seen there in April 2011. The reasons for this changed situation are unclear, but may be connected to the spring floods which are still a huge problem on the Washes. The national picture is no more rosy: there are still widely scattered records of breeding away from the old Cambridgeshire stronghold, but the 2010 report of the RBBP (Holling et al., 2012) noted that there had been no confirmed breeding in the UK for four years.

The breeding-season map shows a typical spread of records, with perhaps an encouraging single record of probable breeding. Atlas methods, unfortunately, do not lend themselves to a detailed description of spring passage, which in the not-too-distant past would be when there was a chance of encountering spectacular bouts of lekking behaviour. Numbers of spring migrants through the county vary greatly and sometimes reach well into three figures. The same can be said of autumn passage, which can be most impressive. The birds are often widespread, but the highest numbers are usually found on the Ouse Washes.

The winter maps show the county situation well in terms of distribution. The Ouse and Nene Washes usually hold the largest numbers, but much depends on winter flooding. Numbers can vary enormously; a recent noteworthy maximum was 183 on the Ouse Washes in March 2011, but it is likely that some early spring movement was involved. To put winter numbers in Cambridgeshire in context – the UK overwintering population estimate is only around 800 birds (Musgrove et al., 2011). Wintering Ruffs were recorded in 29 tetrads.

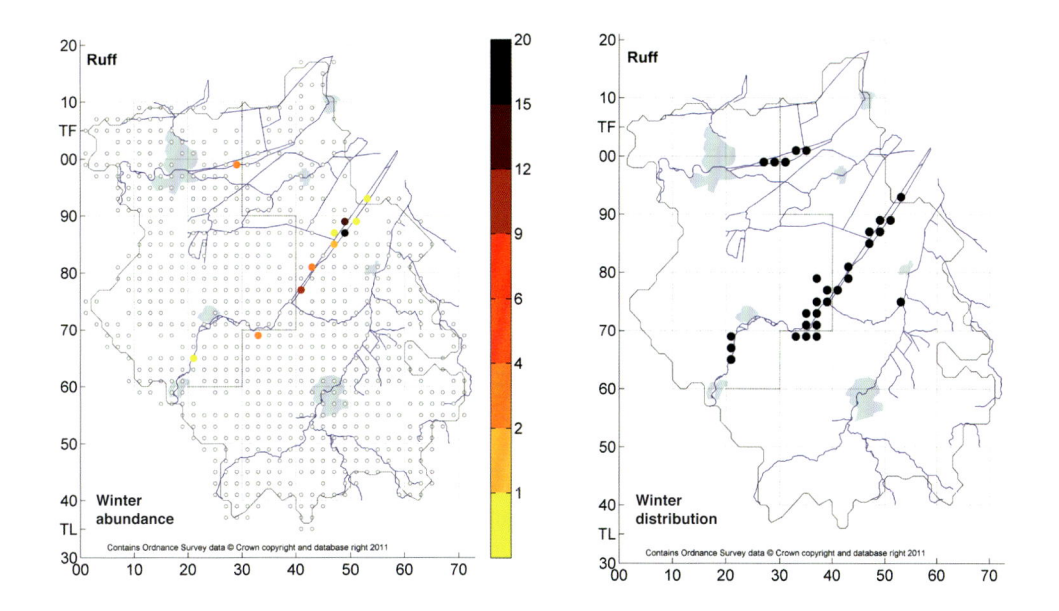

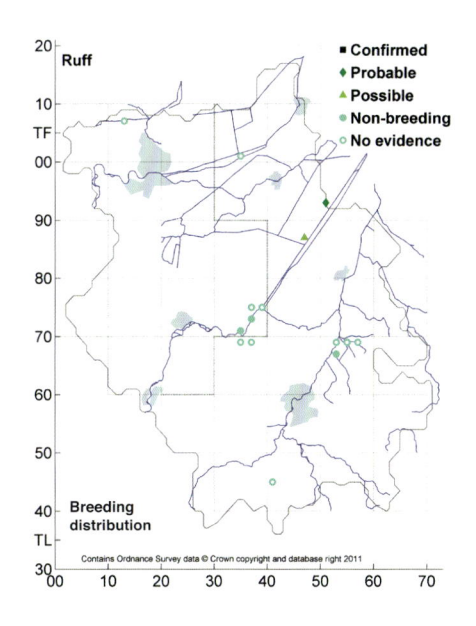

	Confirmed	Probable	Possible	Non-breeding	No evidence	Total summer (% county)	Total winter (% county)
Total tetrads	0	1	1	3	10	15 (2%)	29 (3%)

JACK SNIPE *Lymnocryptes minimus*
Amber List. **Uncommon winter visitor and passage migrant**

Not a breeding species
Wintering population estimate: 10-50 individuals

Jack Snipe are one of those winter treats, a species which birdwatchers can usually manage to see, but that often require a special effort to visit known sites. Nonetheless, they can be encountered by chance in wetland habitats, including wet grassland away from nature reserves. The main concentrations of records are the Nene and Ouse valleys, in the gravel-pit zones upstream of the main washlands, where marsh, reed fringe and wet grass habitats are to be found. There is a very small number of TTV records, which come from more varied locations, showing that this species is thinly distributed in fen ditches, flooded meadows and similar locations.

Jack Snipe is very likely to be under-recorded due to its small size, cryptic plumage and reliance on cover. It spends much of its time in thick vegetation away from regular human activity, and there are really only two ways they can be seen. One is by scrutinising suitable marshy habitats very carefully from a vantage point – this is where nature reserves with well-placed hides are invaluable – and the second is by walking through such habitat hoping to flush the birds out. Jack Snipe are extremely hard to flush, however, and may be almost trodden on before they will fly, so thorough searching of suitable habitat is required to find them. On the other hand, suitable habitat is dwindling in extent, and much of what remains is likely to be designated as reserves where birdwatchers may well ensure reasonable coverage.

In the winter period, Jack Snipe were recorded in 34 tetrads (4%), and 23 10 km squares (45%). Note that two of the 10 km squares (TL16 and TL44) had no tetrad data supplied so these records do not appear on the distribution map.

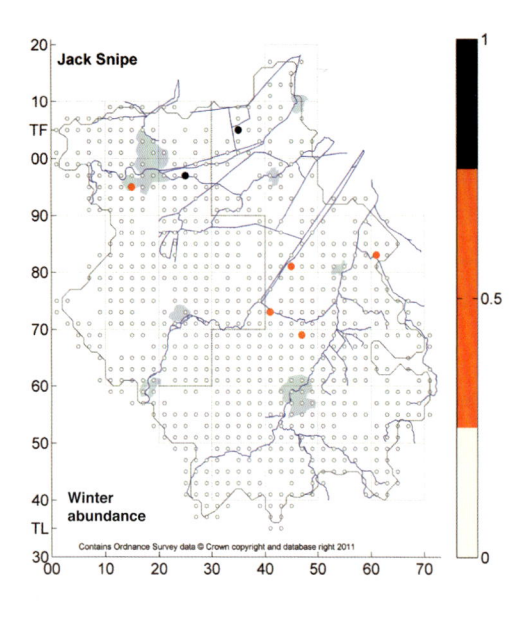

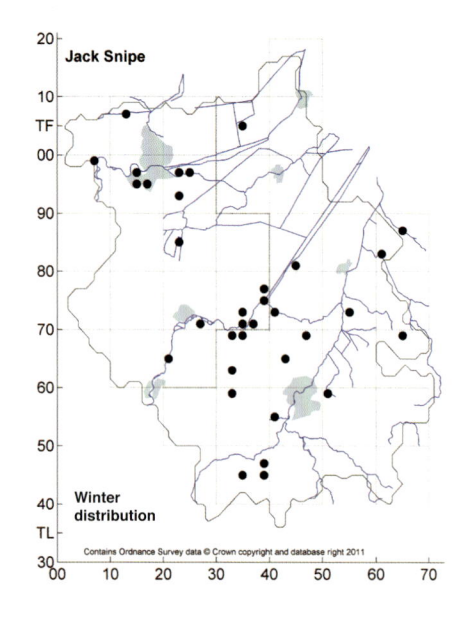

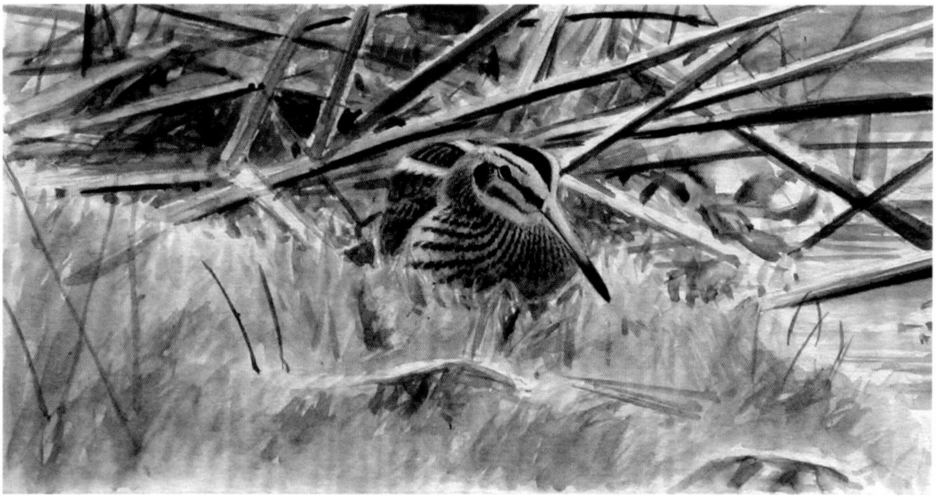

SNIPE (Common Snipe) *Gallinago gallinago*
Amber List. Local breeder; common winter visitor and passage migrant

Breeding population estimate: 100-500 pairs
Wintering population estimate: 200-1,500 individuals

Snipe is a specialised wader, dependent on damp soft ground where it can probe for earthworms. They rely on their cryptic plumage and ability to hide in light cover to avoid predation. In the breeding season, Snipe are largely found in the main washlands, with TTV maps showing that the chance of coming across this species on a visit anywhere else in the county is pretty low. A few are found in some of the other major wetlands, particularly Wicken Fen and surrounding areas. Many of the other summer distribution map entries represent birds which were probably not breeding, such as late migrants. In the Ouse and Nene Washes strongholds, Snipe densities are quite high, with several double-figure counts coming from tetrads in these areas.

In the winter months, Snipe are far more likely to be found in the general countryside, with a much wider distribution and relatively small patches of habitat proving suitable – a damp meadow, muddy river bank or even a tiny ditch can hold one or two birds. Hard weather, such as that encountered during the atlas period, often causes movement and additional influxes of birds, bringing records to new areas where they may only find temporary refuge for a few days before moving on. In the winter, the main Washes are often completely underwater, making them unsuitable for Snipe, so densities are rather more evenly spread around the county, although higher in the river valleys with washlands or flood meadows than on drier ground.

The difficulty of observing Snipe at any distance – due to their ability to remain motionless and camouflaged among the vegetation – means that this species is probably under-recorded. During the breeding season, display flights and other activity make them more easily observed, while in the winter they can occur in places where we are more likely to walk close enough to flush them. Overall the maps are probably a good estimation of the distribution and density of this species, but confirmation of breeding is so difficult that this is certainly under-estimated; there were no confirmed breeding records for the Ouse Washes area, which seems unlikely to be correct.

The summer distribution has not changed greatly since the previous county atlases, although there has been some loss of occupied and confirmed breeding sites. In the previous Cambs Atlas, the Cam Washes were the third most important site, with around 30 pairs; this site is now largely deserted. Previous county atlas estimates of breeding populations from the three main sites suggested the presence of over 500 pairs of Snipe, so as well as loss of some breeding sites, there may also be a decline in density at the strongholds. The current CBR data suggest a total population fluctuating between under 200 pairs in 2011 and over 300 pairs in both 2008 and 2009 (CBR 85).

The highest summer count was of 120 from TL29U in the Nene Washes in May 2008, but this was way ahead of the next highest count (30, on a TTV also in the Nene Washes). In the winter, 98 was the peak count, from Holywell in the Ouse valley (TL37K), while 45 from the Cam meadows, between Milton and Waterbeach (TL46W), was the highest TTV count.

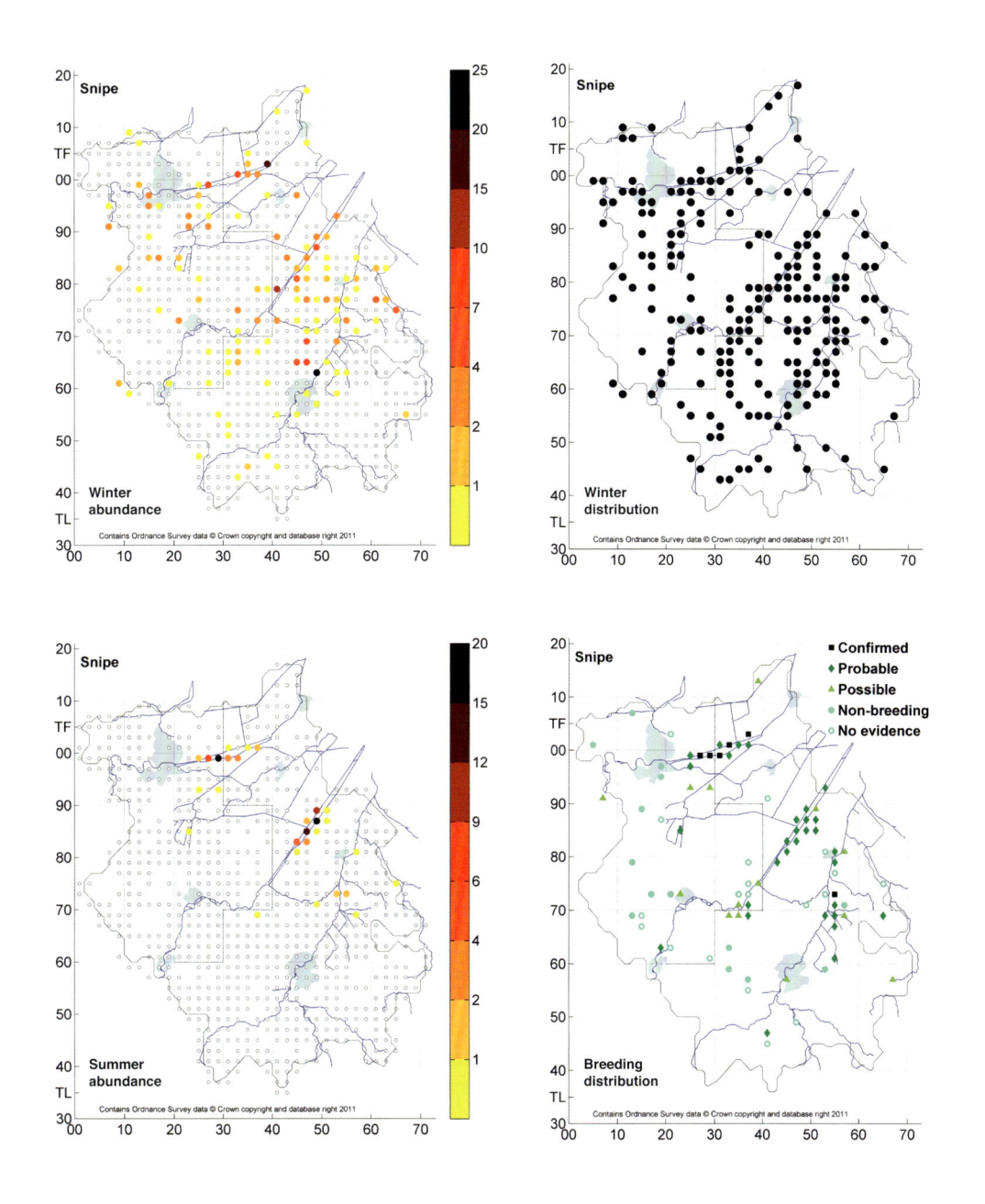

	Confirmed	Probable	Possible	Non-breeding	No evidence	Total summer (% county)	Total winter (% county)
Total tetrads	6	31	14	14	19	84 (9%)	213 (22%)

WOODCOCK (Eurasian Woodcock) *Scolopax rusticola*
Amber List. Uncommon resident, winter visitor and passage migrant

Breeding population estimate: 10-50 pairs
Wintering population estimate: 100-500 individuals

Confirmed or probable breeding of Woodcock was only recorded from four of our larger nature reserves: Monks Wood, our largest tract of woodland, and the fen reserves of Wicken, Woodwalton and Chippenham, all of which have considerable areas of woodland or scrub as well as fen habitats hence providing a combination of breeding cover and soft, wet peaty ground for feeding. There was a small number of other locations recording Woodcock during the summer period; no TTVs recorded Woodcock during the summer. They were found during the winter period mostly in small numbers at random, widely distributed locations; this is reflected in the maps. The main gaps in distribution are in the farmed fenland and the south-east corner of the county, both regions that are relatively underwatched but also less wooded, so it is hard to be certain if these are genuine absences.

This species occurs widely but thinly distributed across the countryside in winter, inhabiting small patches of habitat on farmland and rough vegetation almost anywhere, feeding at night and remaining camouflaged under cover by day. Unless one is flushed, Woodcocks are likely to remain undetected. In the breeding season, they are equally inconspicuous for most of the time, except for the distinctive roding flights of the males at dusk. A visit to a breeding site at dusk is almost certain to reveal their presence, but for any sites that did not receive this level of observation they may have been overlooked. Some of the present/possible records in the south of the county may represent late-staying wintering birds, for example a couple of displaying birds in March at Fowlmere in 2009 given as a possible breeding record for TL44C. Two other possible breeding records away from the core regions of the larger fen and woodland reserves, at TL66J and TL25Q, were roding birds in May which may well represent territorial birds and such sites may have held an undiscovered successful pair.

This species is clearly declining as a breeding bird in the county. The previous Hunts Atlas showed ten confirmed breeding tetrads, and 39 with probable breeding, while the previous Cambs Atlas had 23 probable/confirmed breeding tetrads. They were found in the major woodland areas that are still present in the south-eastern, south-western and north-western parts of the modern county, so perhaps some change has occurred which reduces these woods' suitability for breeding. Such factors are likely to be a combination of drying of soils in summer, deer browsing removing the understorey, reduced woodland management leading to a less-varied structure, a lack of open areas for flight displays, and perhaps increased disturbance from dog walkers as nature reserves drift towards becoming public amenity sites.

The highest summer count was of eight in May 2008 at Chippenham Fen, while in winter, there were 35 at Kingfishers Bridge on one count, and a TTV maximum of six in TL37Z. In the winter, Woodcocks were recorded from 150 tetrads which were distributed across 41 10 km squares. Note that one summer record (Bradley Fen) was provided at a 10-km square resolution only; this was probably for TL29I and inclusion of this record would boost the 'No evidence' column in the table to two records.

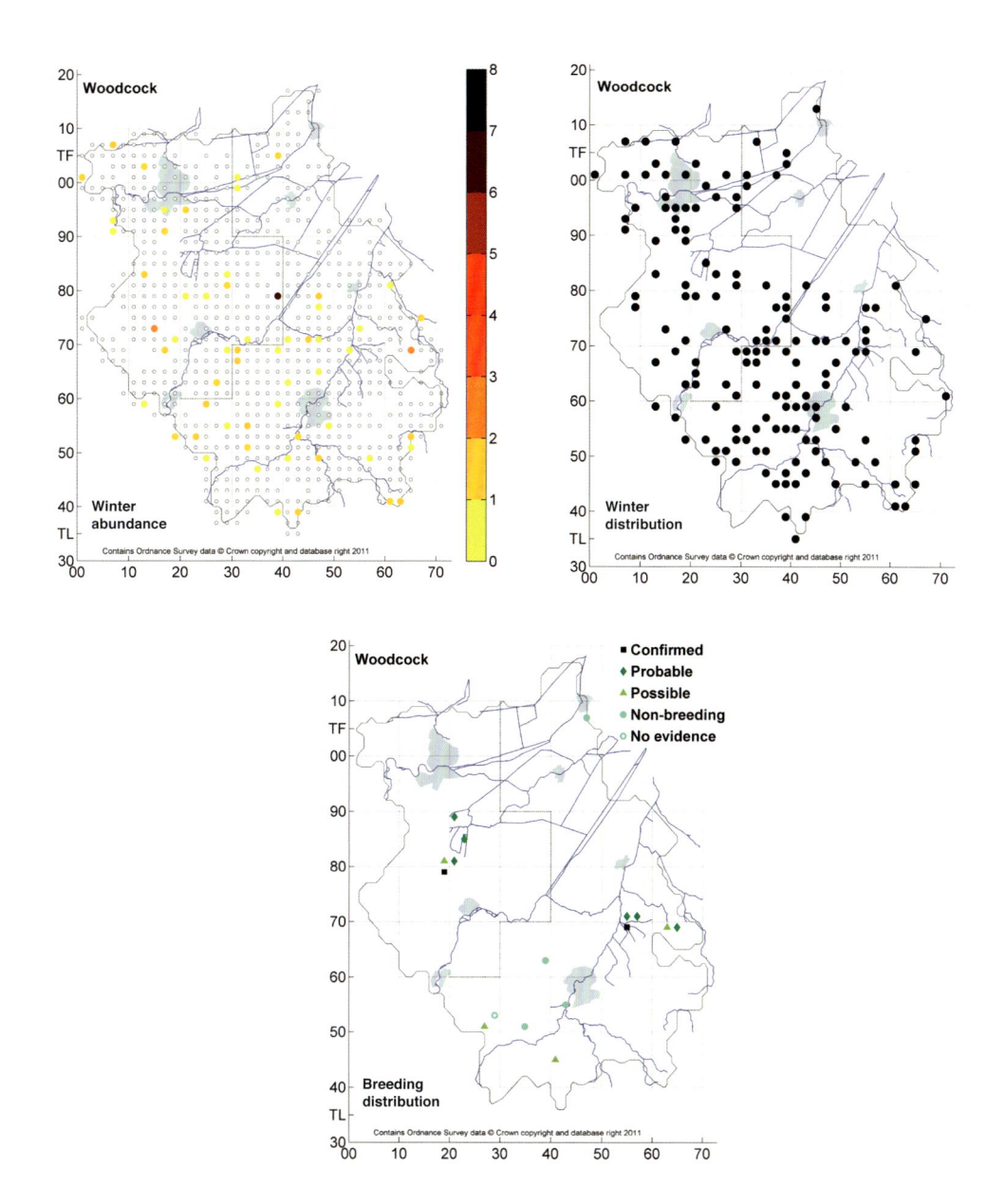

	Confirmed	Probable	Possible	Non-breeding	No evidence	Total summer (% county)	Total winter (% county)
Total tetrads	2	6	4	4	1	17 (2%)	150 (15%)

BLACK-TAILED GODWIT *Limosa limosa*
Red List. Very local, uncommon breeder; fairly common passage migrant and winter visitor

Breeding population estimate: 20-40 pairs
Wintering population estimate: 100-4,000 individuals

The Black-tailed Godwit remains something of a 'flagship' bird for Cambridgeshire. It was first discovered breeding on the Ouse Washes in 1952 – returning to a county where it had bred historically up until the early 19th century. Hopes were high for a sustained increase in both numbers and distribution when, by the mid 1970s, up to 65 pairs nested (Bircham, 1989); breeding was also recorded on the Nene Washes around this time. However, as the CBRs show, that proved to be the peak; the total number of pairs has since remained at around 20–40, with most recently all of these birds on the Nene Washes. Since 1998 there has been no confirmed breeding on the Ouse Washes where seasonal flooding has undoubtedly increased breeding failure. Recent assessment from the RBBP suggests that the Nene Washes area holds 84% of the total UK breeding population (Holling *et al.*, 2012). The RSPB has purchased agricultural land adjacent to the Ouse Washes and is currently creating suitable breeding habitat away from the washlands and the risk of summer flooding.

The breeding distribution map shows clearly the two tetrads where breeding currently takes place with three tetrads in which breeding probably took place – one on the Nene and two on the Ouse Washes. Elsewhere a few possible breeding tetrads are scattered along the path of the Ouse. Most other records are likely to relate to non-breeding birds, foraging individuals, and passage migrants.

While the breeding birds are of the race *limosa*, most passage birds are of the race *islandica* and, as their name suggests, originate from Iceland. These passage flocks often arrive in Cambridgeshire in mid-winter and thus counts in the December–March period can be high – thousands – on the Ouse and Nene Washes and occasionally at other sites. The winter distribution is mainly along the Ouse valley and Nene Washes with one or two records on the Cam washlands and at Wicken Fen. Black-tailed Godwits were recorded from a total of 33 winter tetrads.

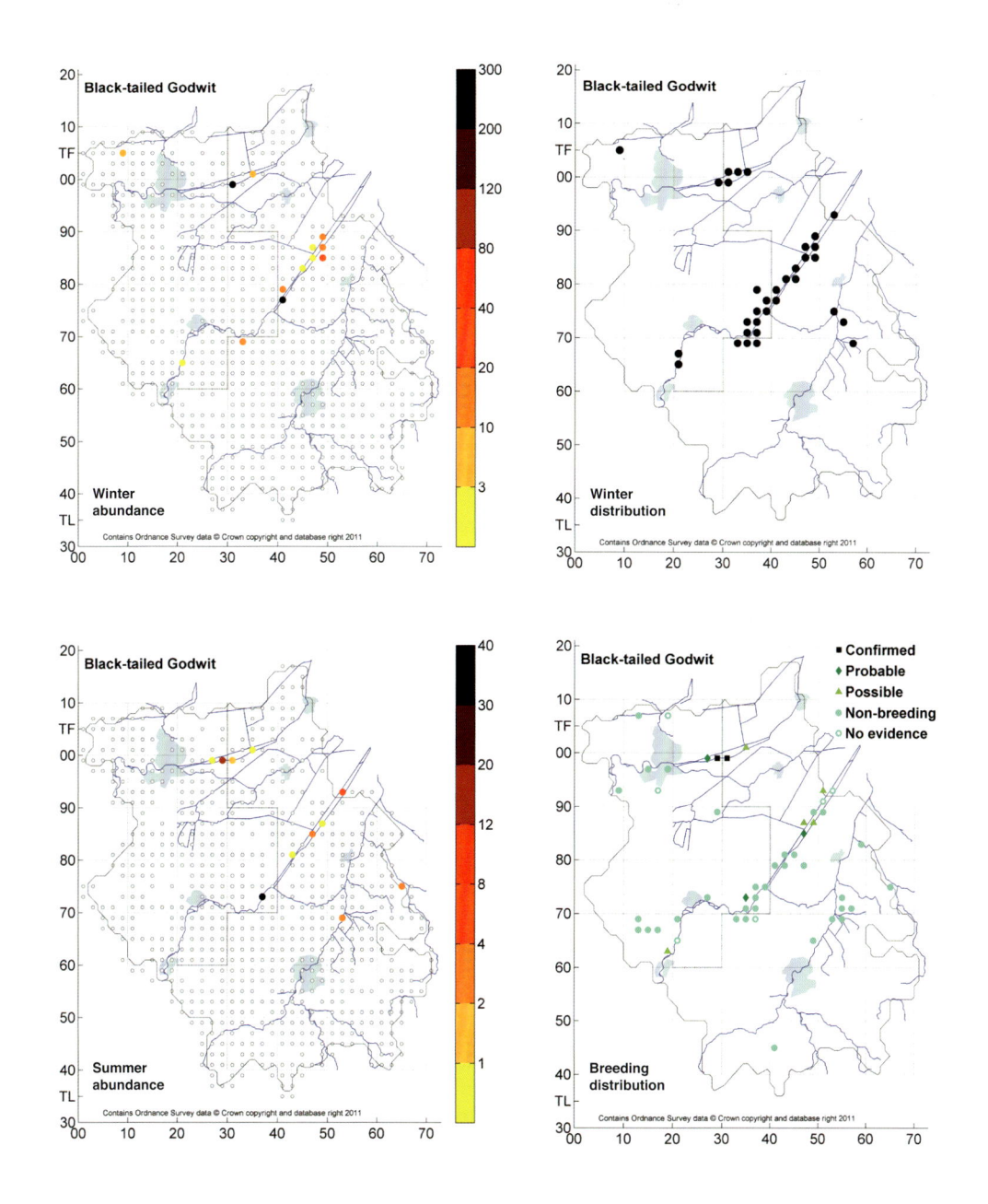

	Confirmed	Probable	Possible	Non-breeding	No evidence	Total summer (% county)	Total winter (% county)
Total tetrads	2	3	5	34	6	50 (5%)	33 (3%)

CURLEW (Eurasian Curlew) *Numenius arquata*
Amber List. Uncommon passage migrant and winter visitor

Not a breeding species
Wintering population estimate: 10-50 individuals

Curlews are associated with wetland areas such as the main washlands of the Ouse, Nene and Cam, but they are also recorded at the larger gravel-pit complexes and at Grafham Water. The winter distribution map shows that apart from one or two isolated records in the west of the county and a single record in the south, all the remaining sightings were on, or very close to, rivers and waterways. Wet fenland sites such as Wicken Fen or the Great Fen also attract individuals. Curlews breed mainly on upland pasture, often a significant distance from the coast, so it is not surprising that some passage birds occur on farmland away from water.

Single birds are most common. The density map shows a maximum of two, although county records reached a maximum of seven during December 2010 when bad weather may have forced birds inland. Most birds do not stay for long periods either on passage or in winter.

As a very prominent bird it is likely that most individuals are recorded; even when they venture into arable land or away from well-watched areas of wetland they draw attention to their presence by calling or by their size. A number of records refer to birds flying over.

Although birds pass through on passage until May and return in July there were no summering records. There are reports that breeding took place on the Nene Washes in the period 1940–50 with a maximum of 20 pairs (Bircham, 1989), but otherwise there are no known breeding records. Gibbons *et al.* (1993) shows a paucity of breeding records south of a line from the Wash to the Severn and almost none in inland East Anglia except on the Breckland of Norfolk/Suffolk. Breeding was confirmed in 2010 less than 1 km over the border in Northamptonshire, on an active MOD site. BBS data show this species to be in decline, by 44% since 1995 (Risely *et al.*, 2012) and a wintering population decline over 10 years of 20%.

Wintering Curlews were recorded from 45 tetrads (5%).

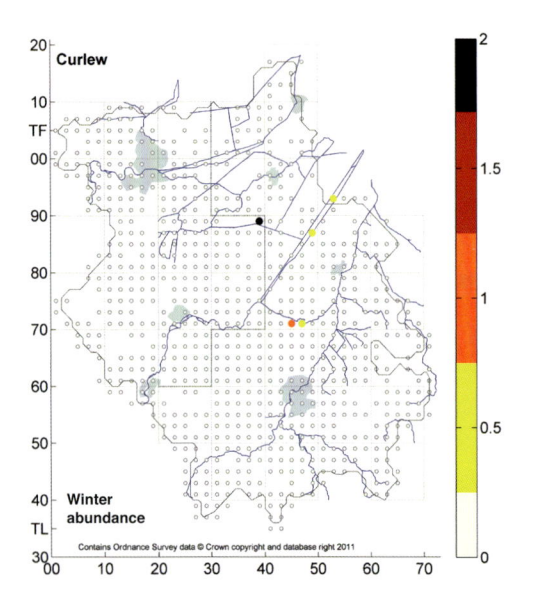

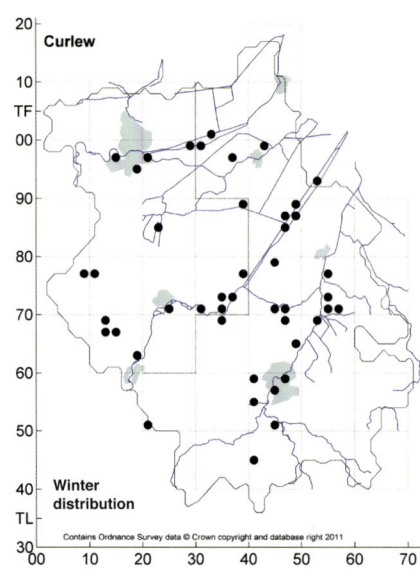

COMMON SANDPIPER *Actitis hypoleucos*
Green List. **Fairly common passage migrant, occasionally overwinters**

Not a breeding species
Wintering population estimate: 1-5 individuals

Common Sandpipers are frequent passage migrants in both spring and autumn, recorded mostly on gravel-pit complexes and at Grafham Water. Some individuals are also found on the washlands but this is probably a less-desirable habitat except when flood provides a shallow edge. Common Sandpipers may be present but unrecorded on the river systems in the south when water levels are low.

In winter there are no atlas records south of the Ouse valley and the very small number of records overall shows how unusual it is to find this species – a sub-Saharan migrant – anywhere in Cambridgeshire in the winter months. This is somewhat surprising given that its congener the Green Sandpiper is regularly found in winter, albeit in small numbers. Those Common Sandpipers that are recorded in winter are often single instances of birds or occasionally late-staying birds recorded until December. True overwintering is rarely, if ever, recorded.

There are no breeding records of Common Sandpiper in Cambridgeshire, which is not surprising when the waterways – mostly broad and slow-moving with steep-sided banks – contrast so obviously with those in this species' breeding strongholds – narrower, shallower and fast-moving. Gibbons *et al.* (1993) records their distribution as restricted almost entirely to the uplands of the UK and Ireland. Individuals are recorded in summer on passage, some as late as May, and returning birds in the first week of July. National BBS data show this species to be in sharp decline for reasons that are not entirely clear (a 7% decline since 1995; Risely *et al.*, 2012).

Ringing results from Ely Beet Factory in the 1980s showed that some individuals use the same site on passage in successive years.

Wintering records were noted from five tetrads (0.5%).

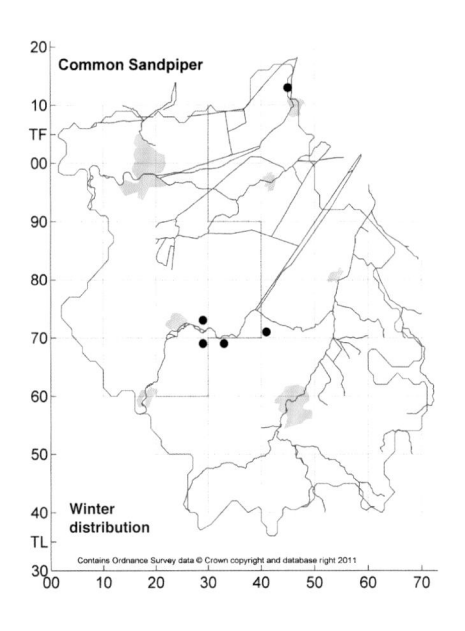

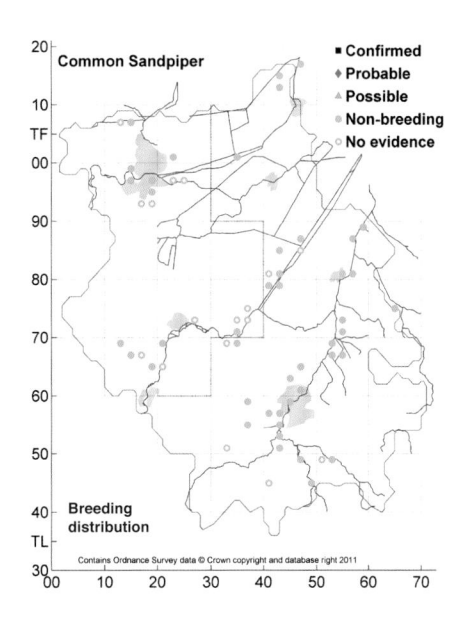

GREEN SANDPIPER *Tringa ochropus*
Amber List. Fairly common passage migrant, mainly autumn; regularly winters

Not a breeding species
Wintering population estimate: 20-60 individuals

Many a winter day's birding is enlivened by the sudden flushing of this northern wader from a pool or a fen ditch, flashing black and white as it climbs away, calling excitedly. There will be days too when a 'Green Sand' is found pottering about at the water's edge at some lake or gravel pit. However, this is a difficult bird to count with much accuracy, not least because it so often uses the sort of wet spots birders seldom get to. The atlas gives us a picture of a wide winter distribution and small total numbers – although the latter should be treated with some caution. Reference to WeBS reports shows that here too the methodology does not lend itself to accurate Green Sandpiper counts. The latest estimate for the national wintering population is a conservative 910 birds (Musgrove *et al.*, 2011).

In Cambridgeshire, most of our Green Sandpipers appear as passage migrants, probably moving to and from the nearer parts of their breeding range in Scandinavia and north-east Europe. Numbers vary, but are highest from fairly late in July to the end of August. CBRs for recent years suggest that in either month totals may reach or even exceed 100 birds. Smallish, loose groups of birds are not unusual, but the word 'flock' can scarcely be applied to this species. A good total for one of the larger wetlands in the county would be 20–30 birds.

As in winter, passage migrants are essentially birds of freshwater pools, marshes and watercourses. Although they do turn up in saltmarsh gutters, they are generally very rare in any intertidal habitat. Wet woodland is their typical northern breeding habitat; most Green Sandpipers nest in trees, using the old nests of thrushes or Woodpigeons, or small natural platforms – a curious habit, but not unique among waders. It is shared by their New World counterpart the Solitary Sandpiper *T. solitarius*, and occasionally also by Wood Sandpipers *T. glareola*. In recent years a few pairs have nested in the Scottish Highlands.

Recorded from 70 winter tetrads (7%).

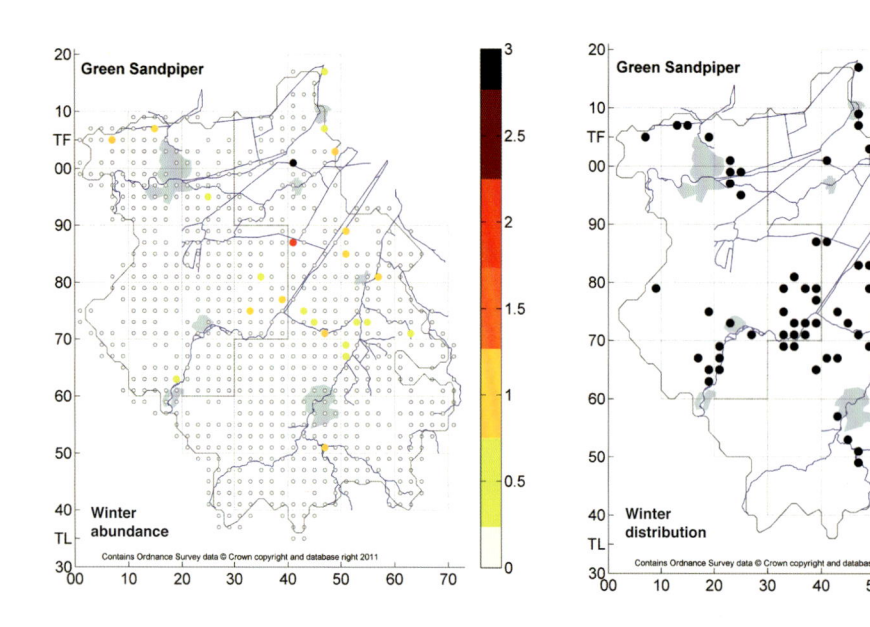

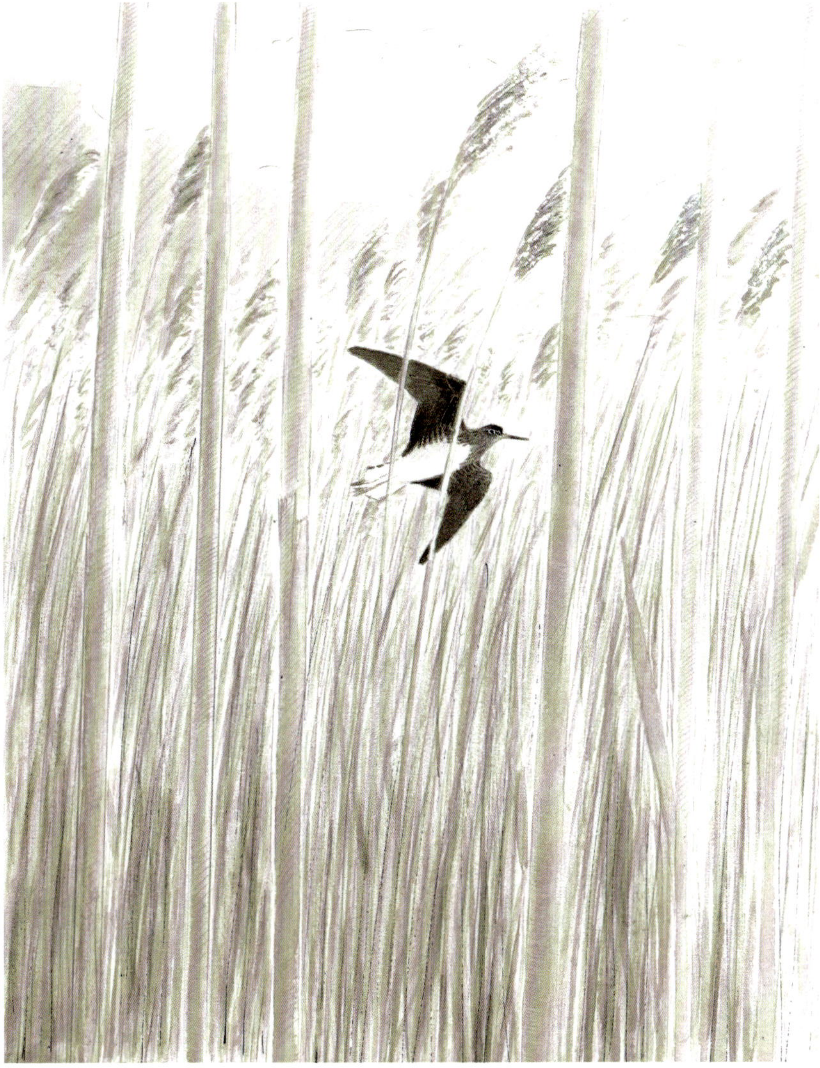

REDSHANK (Common Redshank) *Tringa totanus*
Amber List. Fairly common, but local and declined breeder; passage migrant/winter visitor

Breeding population estimate: 300-400 pairs
Wintering population estimate: 50-250 individuals

Redshanks are quite conspicuous waders, generally working the water's edge; they are also quite vocal and thus relatively easily recorded. In Cambridgeshire they occur across the full range of wetland sites: washlands, fen, gravel pits and reservoirs. Redshanks tend to defend their feeding space and where they occur in large numbers these are aggregations rather than flocks; high counts are recorded almost exclusively at the larger wetland sites such as the Ouse and Nene Washes.

Data from CBRs show breeding at around 6–12 sites centred on the Nene (c. 180 pairs) and Ouse Washes (c. 150 pairs) with 1–10 pairs at other sites. The atlas breeding map shows that taking the confirmed and probable breeding records together (it is never easy to obtain confirmation of breeding for waders) there is little decline in distribution since the previous Cambs Atlas. The tetrads in which Redshanks occur in the breeding season all lie along the river systems apart from an outlier in the Chippenham area. All the tetrads in which possible breeding was recorded lie close to known breeding sites. This may reflect feeding grounds of birds breeding close by; alternatively it may indicate a potential expansion of the current breeding sites. On the Ouse Washes a project to create suitable breeding habitat away from the risk of summer flooding is underway. Cadbury & Rooney (1982) estimated that Cambridgeshire supports around 10% of the breeding population in lowland England and Wales. Brown & Grice (2005) report that a survey in 2002 showed that numbers had increased on both large washlands (Ouse by 22.5%, Nene 16.7%).

The maps show that the winter distribution is almost identical to that of summer; however, at some sites there is a noticeable absence of this species once the breeding season is complete with birds returning in late autumn and winter. There are only a handful of records away from river systems.

Ringing results yield very little information specific to Cambridgeshire. Movements to and from the Wash suggest that birds breeding in Cambridgeshire move to the coast. A bird ringed in May 1976 at Wicken Fen was found in the Gironde district of France the following March. Wernham *et al.* (2002) shows movement between East Anglia and Iceland, the near Continent or Scandinavia but these appear to be birds wintering along the coast.

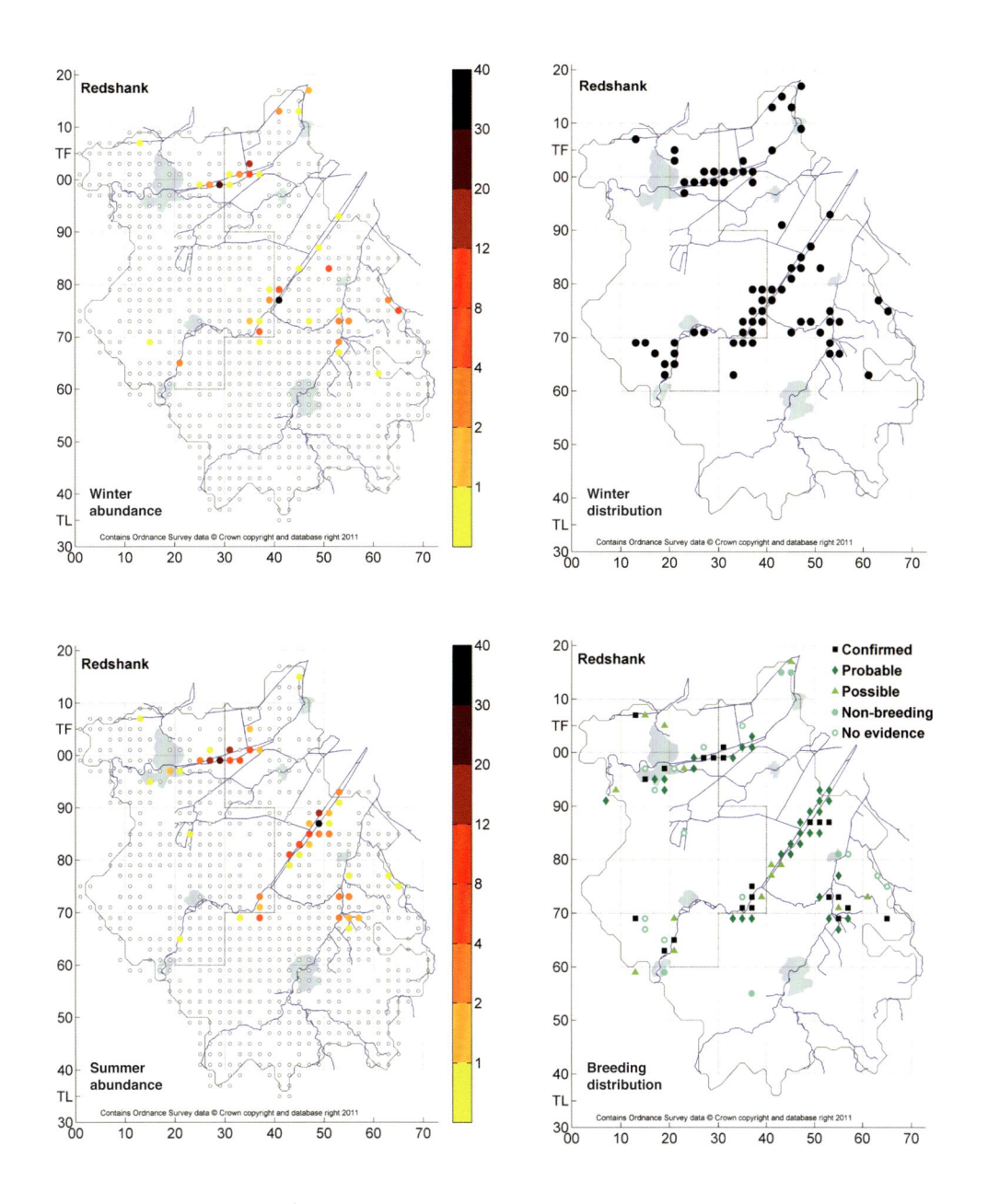

	Confirmed	Probable	Possible	Non-breeding	No evidence	Total summer (% county)	Total winter (% county)
Total tetrads	22	32	14	5	13	86 (9%)	71 (7%)

BLACK-HEADED GULL *Chroicocephalus ridibundus*
Amber List. Fairly common but very local breeder; abundant passage migrant/winter visitor

Breeding population estimate: 300-600 pairs
Wintering population estimate: 10,000-40,000 individuals

This is the most widespread gull in Cambridgeshire and the most numerous. They are found predominantly, but by no means exclusively, at wetland sites such as the washlands, larger gravel pits and river systems. Away from the breeding period individuals can be seen almost anywhere with parties of 20–30 often observed flying to and from feeding grounds and roost sites. They are often found as gatherings of over 100 birds following a tractor or feeding on newly ploughed farmland.

There is an estimated breeding population of around 500 pairs restricted to a handful of sites close to the river systems: the map shows confirmed breeding in 12 tetrads along the Ouse, five on or near the Nene and the Peterborough brickpits, four along the lower reaches of the Cam and three on the Welland river basin. A couple of probable sites close to the Ouse and a few other sites at which possible breeding was recorded are in the same main areas with the exception of a tetrad in south Cambridgeshire, an area where breeding has not yet been confirmed. The density map shows that records in summer are almost entirely close to river systems and breeding sites and generally of small numbers (1–30), although there are some large counts (100+). These are almost certainly foraging birds and/or non-breeding individuals, or even birds on passage. Non-breeders were scattered across the county.

Nationally numbers rose in the second half of the 20th century, partly due to cessation of persecution; they probably peaked in the early 1980s since when they have fallen slightly and are now around 80,000 breeding pairs (Brown & Grice 2005). The previous Cambs Atlas shows confirmed breeding in only three tetrads with birds recorded in another 41. Clark (1996) reports that in old Huntingdonshire a strong breeding population was established by the 1970s which peaked at around 900 pairs in 1988.

In winter Black-headed Gulls are widespread across the county. A significant proportion of these birds are immigrants from Continental Europe. Gull ringing at Cambridgeshire landfill sites between 1984 and 1991 revealed that over half the birds for which information of origin was obtained came from Denmark, the Netherlands and Finland; other birds were traced to Belgium, Germany, the Baltic States, Scandinavia, Czechoslovakia (as it was then), Russia and Poland. Recaptures over a series of winters showed that Cambridgeshire represents a regular wintering area. Some individuals moved further south in England, as far as Devon, and some remained within East Anglia but seemed quite mobile, turning up in Essex, Norfolk and Suffolk. Numbers up to 500 were recorded during the present atlas period, but roost counts on the Ouse Washes are usually in the region of 10,000–20,000, exceptionally 100,000 in 1975 (Clark, 2000). The Cambridgeshire Gull Ringing Group handled just over 19,000 birds during the eight years of their existence.

Some passage occurs in both spring and autumn but this is quite difficult to measure due to the background of both breeding and wintering birds in spring and autumn.

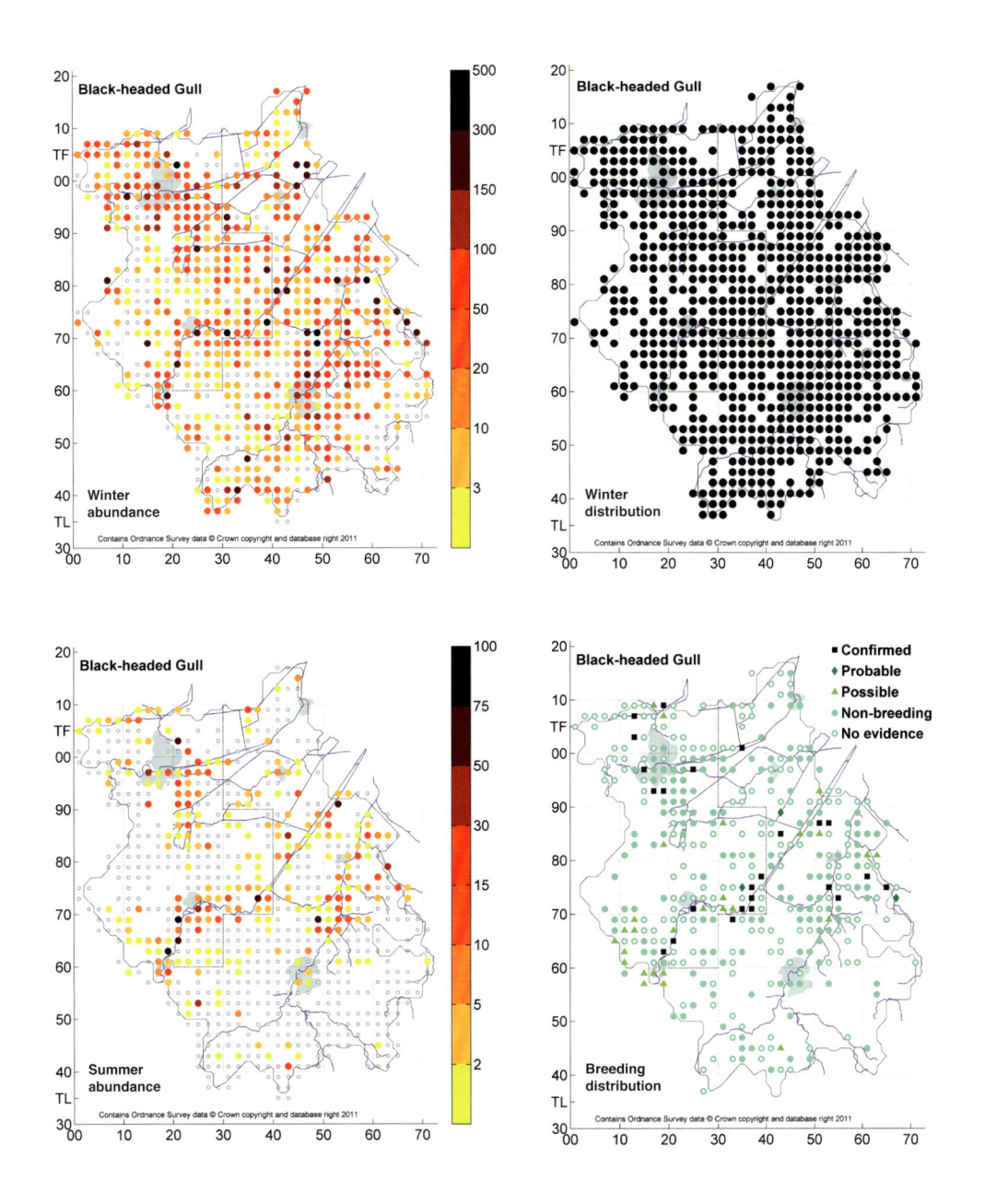

	Confirmed	Probable	Possible	Non-breeding	No evidence	Total summer (% county)	Total winter (% county)
Total tetrads	24	3	27	146	190	390 (40%)	742 (77%)

MEDITERRANEAN GULL *Larus melanocephalus*
Amber List. Uncommon, annual passage migrant and winter visitor; has bred

Breeding population estimate: 0-2 pairs, last confirmed 2007
Wintering population estimate: occasional visitor only

First seen in 1974, then increasingly in the 1980s, Mediterranean Gull is still not a commonly recorded bird. It is usually noted in small numbers (1–5) at the larger wetland sites, mainly on passage and in winter. Away from the larger washlands, gravel pits and reservoirs this species may occur within gull flocks and for that reason may escape scrutiny. Following an increase in records and national establishment as a breeding species, Mediterranean Gull was considered to be a likely colonist to Cambridgeshire with breeding expected to take place leading to increasing numbers. However, this does not seem to have happened.

Mediterranean Gull first bred (unsuccessfully) in Cambridgeshire in 1998, but subsequent records have been erratic with 1–2 pairs recorded, although not annually; recent CBRs suggest that no breeding has taken place since 2007. Nationally the original breeding colonisation was exclusively at coastal sites (Gibbons *et al.*, 1993), following the first record in 1968 which was thought to be the result of expanding breeding colonies on the Black Sea. For unknown reasons this species has failed to establish a breeding population in the county and is now an uncommon visitor in almost any month.

The winter distribution map shows presence in only five tetrads (1%), three close to Peterborough and two in the south close to Cambridge, doubtless at gravel-pit sites or refuse tips. There were records from 18 tetrads (2%) during the summer, none with evidence of breeding; these are likely to be passage birds.

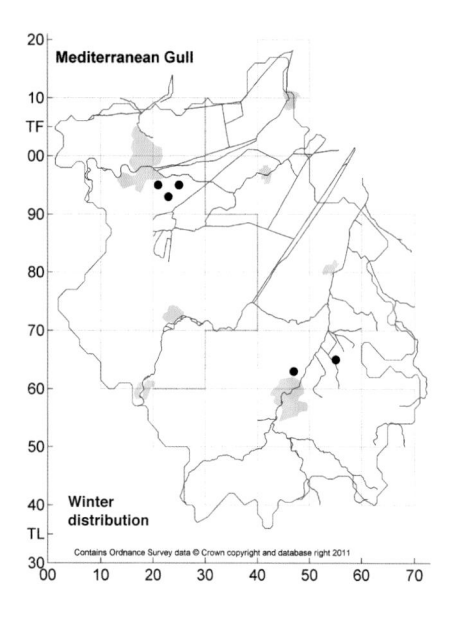

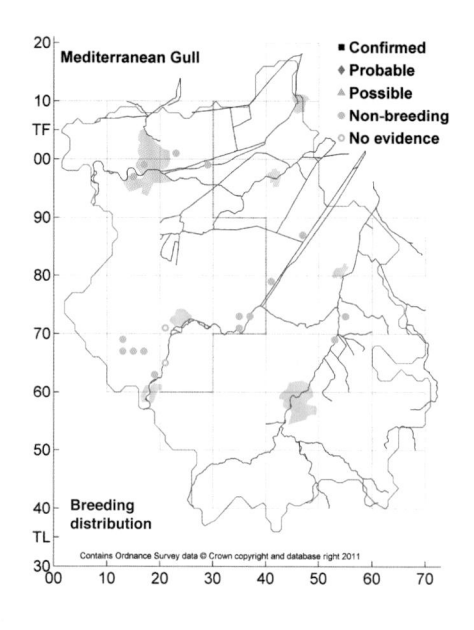

COMMON GULL *Larus canus*
Amber List. Common winter visitor and passage migrant

Not a breeding species
Wintering population estimate: 3,000-10,000 individuals

Nowhere near as common (despite the name) as the Black-headed Gull in winter, this species is also slightly more restricted in its distribution. It may be overlooked as small numbers can occur among larger flocks of Black-headed Gulls and it is a rather less conspicuous bird than its congener. Numbers wintering inland in the UK have increased during the 20th century but Brown & Grice (2005) stated that there were, surprisingly, comparatively few in East Anglia. Ringing by the Cambridgeshire Gull Group revealed the source of these Cambridgeshire birds to be Denmark, Germany, Norway, Sweden, the Netherlands, Finland, the Baltic States and Poland.

In Cambridgeshire winter peak counts are mostly at roosts on the Washes. CBRs give counts of flocks numbering between 50 and 200 in winter on arable sites or gravel pits such as Paxton Pits and at Grafham Water. The distribution map shows a broad spread of tetrads in which this species is recorded, but the density map shows counts below 50 in most tetrads away from water, presumably on arable land. Mixed flocks can be seen on recreational areas in towns and villages with Black-headed Gulls representing the greater part but Common Gulls present in tens and twenties. In this context they may be under-recorded since observers assume that only Black-headed Gulls are present. The largest winter count in the atlas, of 400, was on the Ouse Washes, as might be expected.

Common Gull was recorded in 514 winter tetrads (53%). Additionally, there were records of non-breeding birds from 80 summer tetrads (8%).

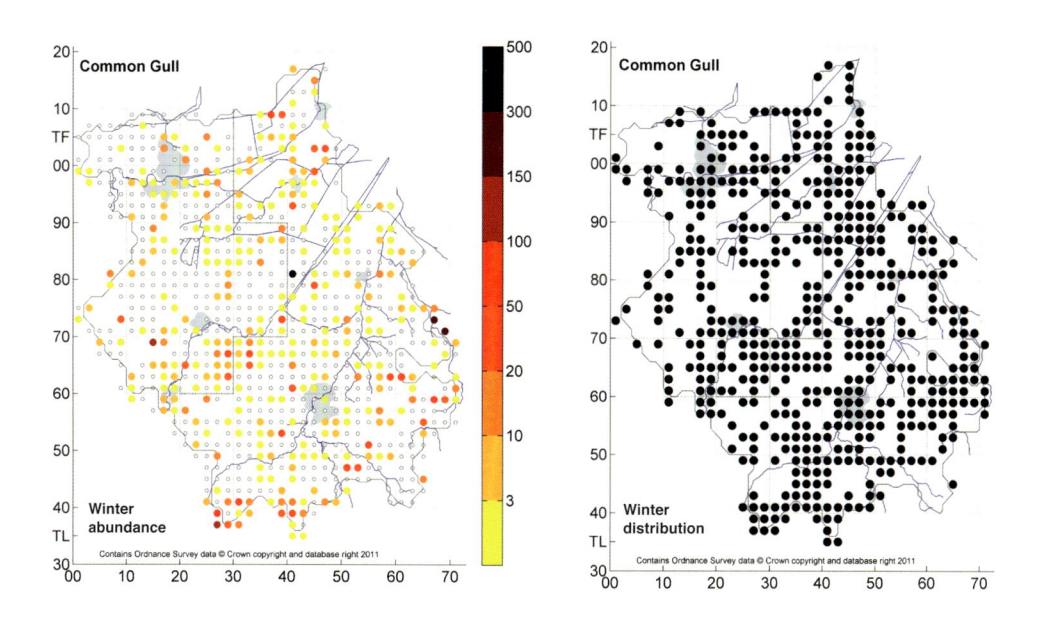

LESSER BLACK-BACKED GULL *Larus fuscus*
Amber List. Very common passage migrant; increased summer/winter visitor. Small breeding population

Breeding population estimate: 10-50 pairs
Wintering population estimate: 2,000-5,000 individuals

For most observers Lesser Black-backed Gulls are seen on passage or for periods in the autumn when more significant numbers gather on recently harvested or ploughed land where their superior size makes them stand out from Black-headed Gulls. Many of these birds are of the race *intermedius* from Scandinavia and appear darker on the back than the British race *graellsii*, some almost as dark as Great Black-backed Gulls. Throughout the winter individuals and small groups can be seen flying to and from feeding grounds – mostly on farmland or refuse tips – and roosting sites; in much of the county there is a daily passage of this kind.

Ringing results show that Cambridgeshire birds come from the Netherlands, Norway and the Faeroe Islands, and also move to France and Morocco. Two individuals identified in Cambridgeshire by their colour rings had been ringed at Orfordness. One had previously been sighted in Gloucestershire and Portugal, the other in Germany and then back in Suffolk.

Roosting occurs at sites such as the Ouse Washes and Grafham Water; at the latter, the largest roost count of 5,200 was recorded in 1991 (Clark, 2000).

The winter distribution map shows widespread records, although not quite as broadly distributed as the Black-headed Gull, and the density map indicates that the largest numbers (>20) are found almost always on or close to the river systems. Elsewhere numbers are at or below 20.

After some speculation breeding was first confirmed in 1996 and has continued since, now at four or five wetland sites and on one industrial roof-top site in Wisbech (CBR 85), with a total of around 10–50 pairs of the race *graellsii*. Brown & Grice (2005) reported a significant increase in numbers at the Orfordness colony from 150 pairs in 1969–70 to 7,000 pairs by 1998–2002; this may have been partly responsible for the arrival of breeding birds in Cambridgeshire. This increase is part of a wider expansion in western Europe with numbers in the UK now causing such concern that some colonies have been subjected to culls for a variety of reasons, including predation of nests and eggs of species of higher conservation priority.

The breeding-distribution map reveals confirmed breeding in 12 tetrads, all close to river systems, at gravel pits and at Kingfishers Bridge, probable breeding at four further tetrads and possible at another nine, almost all of these close to existing sites and restricted to the northern half of the county. Perhaps of significance is the recording of non-breeding birds across the county as a whole, although some of these may refer to passage birds. It is difficult to see potential expansion to the southern half of the county due to the lack of suitable breeding sites.

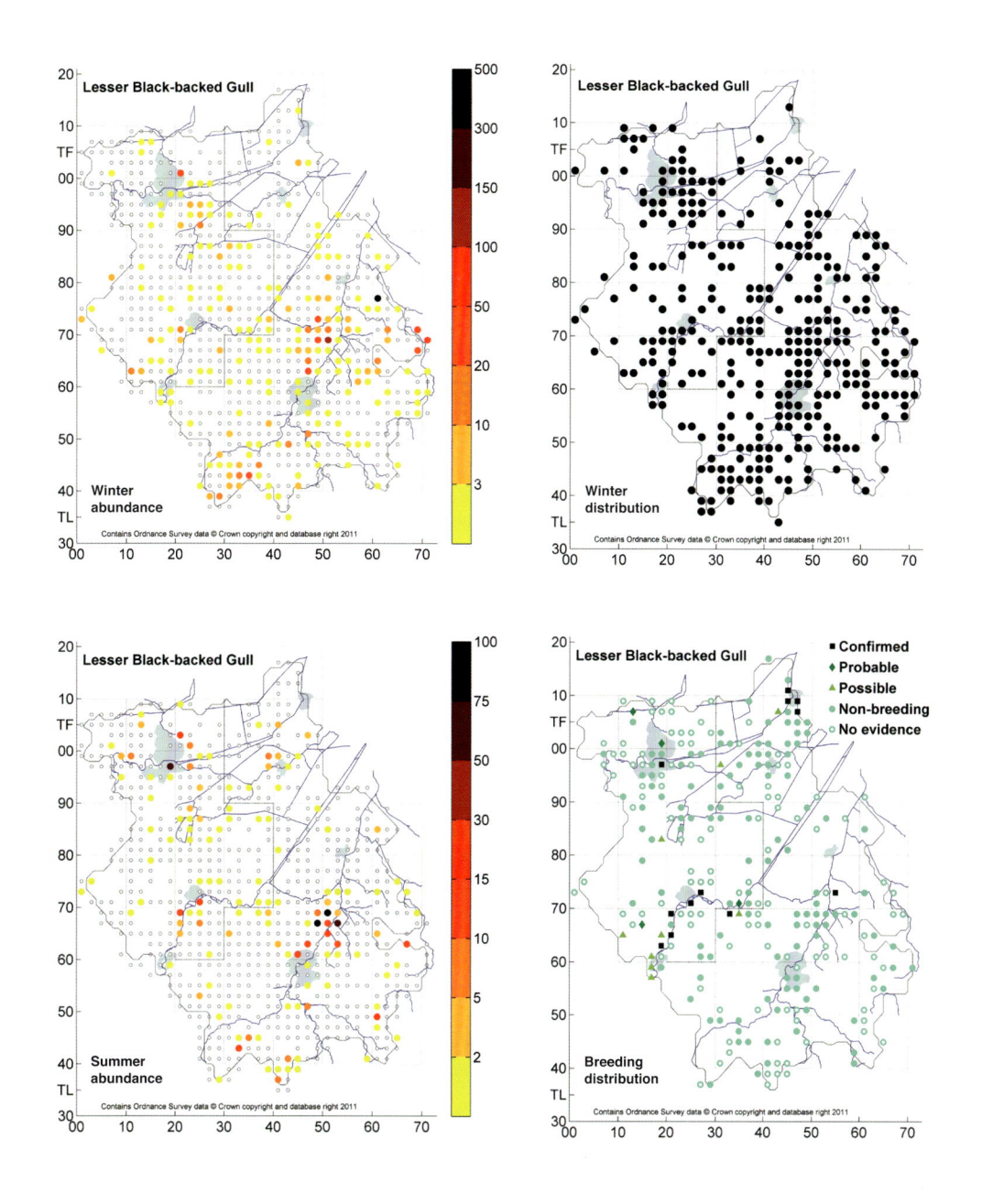

	Confirmed	Probable	Possible	Non-breeding	No evidence	Total summer (% county)	Total winter (% county)
Total tetrads	12	4	9	121	116	262 (27%)	331 (34%)

HERRING GULL (European Herring Gull) *Larus argentatus*
Red List. Very common winter visitor and passage migrant; small breeding population

Breeding population estimate: 1-20 pairs
Wintering population estimate: 2,000-5,000 individuals

Historically the most coastal of all gulls, Herring Gull numbers began to increase in numbers nationally in the post-war period, enhanced by the availability of food on refuse tips.

The winter distribution map shows birds on or close to the main river systems, but, as with other gulls, wintering birds frequently make use of agricultural land, especially where it has been recently ploughed, and thus can be seen in any part of the county, albeit in small numbers and associating with other gull species. The CBRs show some aggregations in the hundreds at a few sites, mainly refuse tips and gravel pits, and at Grafham Water.

Ringing results specific to Cambridgeshire show birds coming from the Netherlands, Germany and Denmark. However, there is also some evidence that UK-bred, or breeding, Herring Gulls move inland to Cambridgeshire. One bird colour-ringed at Orfordness in July 1999 was subsequently recorded at Milton tip, then in France in March and August 2000 before being seen at Milton in December 2000 and January 2001, back at Orfordness in April 2001 and Milton again in December 2001. This may be a typical pattern.

Breeding in the county began in 2005 and has continued at Godmanchester and Wisbech with a county maximum to date of 11 pairs in 2007. Nationally the breeding population increased up to the 1970s, but by the late 1980s there had been a significant decline of over 50%. More recently there has been a recovery but not to the earlier numbers. Conversely, and significantly for Cambridgeshire, the Orfordness colony has shown a rapid increase (Brown & Grice, 2005).

The breeding map shows confirmed breeding in five tetrads, probable in one and possible in one; all other records refer to non-breeding birds or birds for which there was no evidence of breeding. A significant proportion of entries on the density map are likely to refer to non-breeding or passage birds. In general, these birds are seen on or near the main watercourses with a few exceptions. The main breeding colony is on industrial buildings in Wisbech.

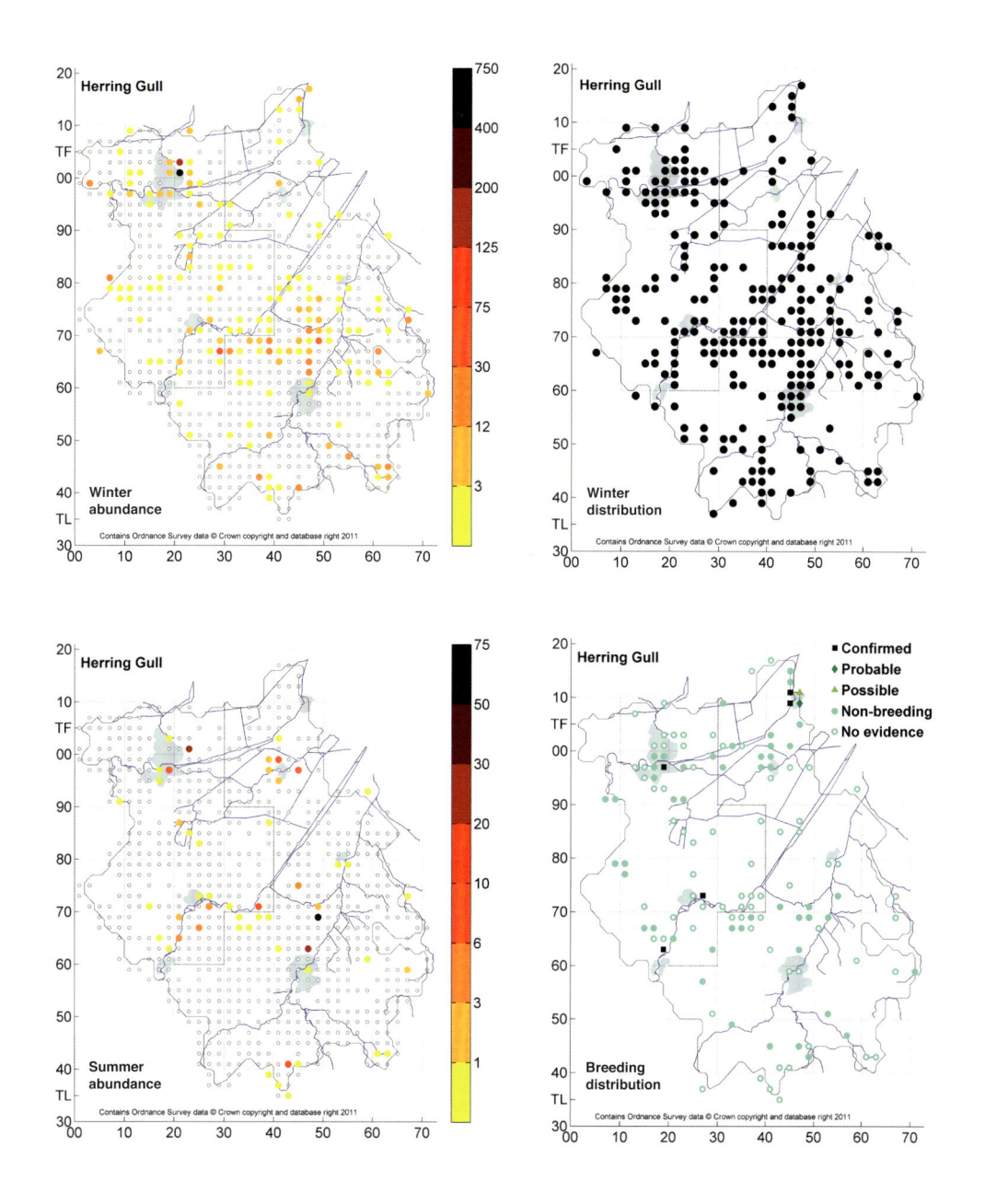

	Confirmed	Probable	Possible	Non-breeding	No evidence	Total summer (% county)	Total winter (% county)
Total tetrads	5	1	1	48	71	126 (13%)	249 (26%)

YELLOW-LEGGED GULL *Larus michahellis*
Amber List. Fairly common visitor, mainly summer and autumn

Not a breeding species
Wintering population estimate: 10-50 individuals

This distinctive and elegant Mediterranean/Atlantic large gull is regularly reported in Cambridgeshire, particularly as birds disperse north post-breeding, although it is increasingly encountered at various times of the year.

From the 1970s onwards, adult-type birds approximating to what was at the time regarded as one of the southern races of Herring Gull were recorded in English gull roosts on an infrequent basis; this race was not formally recorded in Cambridgeshire until 1987. It was not until the wholesale revision of large white-headed gull systematics in the 1990s that this taxon was elevated to species status.

During the atlas period, a total of 136 Yellow-legged Gulls were recorded in Cambridgeshire, from 27 tetrads (3%). The most important site for this species was easily Grafham Water (76 records). Other notable sites included Milton tip (21), Swavesey (16) and Colne Fen (10). More Yellow-legged Gulls occur in the county in autumn, so the atlas maps do not represent the peak season for this species, although increasing numbers are to be found in November, December and January.

Yellow-legged Gulls were recorded during the atlas period displaying and pairing with Lesser Black-backed and Herring Gulls, although there was no evidence of successful or attempted breeding beyond pairing in the county.

Yellow-legged Gull has been increasing in western Europe since at least 1980 and in 2006 this species' status in Cambridgeshire was upgraded from 'uncommon' to 'fairly common'. This increase, combined with observer awareness and interest, is likely to see a continued rise in the numbers of this species recorded in Cambridgeshire.

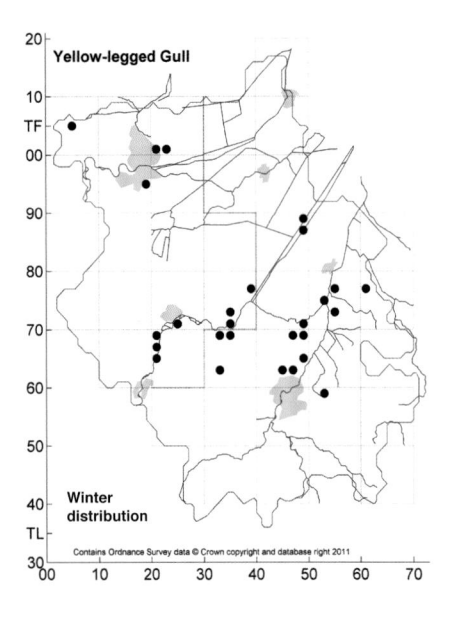

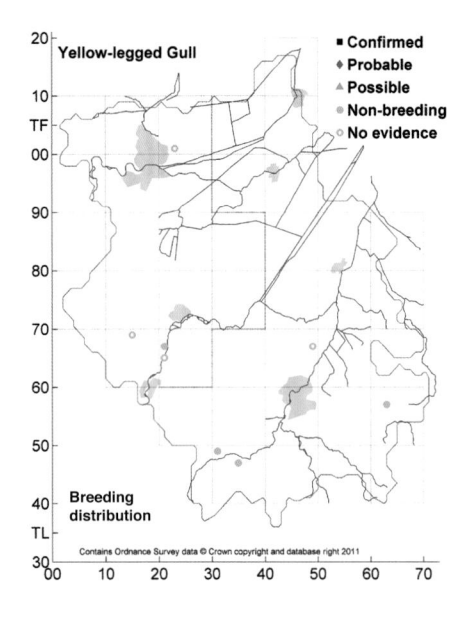

CASPIAN GULL *Larus cachinnans*
Uncommon visitor, mainly winter

Not a breeding species
Wintering population estimate: 5-20 individuals

Cambridgeshire has gained a reputation in recent years as one of the best counties in the UK to find and study this enigmatic species, which, as recently as the early 1990s, was considered nothing more than an exotic, poorly known south-eastern race of Herring Gull. Caspian Gull is moving westwards, with increasingly significant populations in several eastern European countries, in particular Poland, where hybridisation with both nominate *argentatus* Herring Gull and Yellow-legged Gull continues to produce identification headaches for gull fans. There has been a remarkable rise in the numbers of this species being reported in the south and east of the UK since ground-breaking identification work was undertaken in the mid-1990s. Following additional evidence from the burgeoning discipline of DNA analysis, an increasing number of birdwatchers have taken a keen interest in big gulls.

During the atlas period, a total of 66 Caspian Gulls were reported in Cambridgeshire, from 13 tetrads; the majority of birds being logged between November and February, and most at established rubbish-tip/wetland-roost locations staked out by dedicated gull-watchers. Milton tip, Dogsthorpe tip and the Grafham Water gull roost boast the majority of the records over the atlas period, although other sites, including Cottenham Long Drove and Tanholt gravel pits are also important sites for this species, which could now conceivably turn up anywhere in the county.

Given the westward expansion of this species, coupled with increased observer awareness, interest and knowledge, the number of Caspian Gull records in Cambridgeshire is expected to continue rising. Despite the winter bias of records over the atlas period, this species is increasingly being recorded at all times of the year.

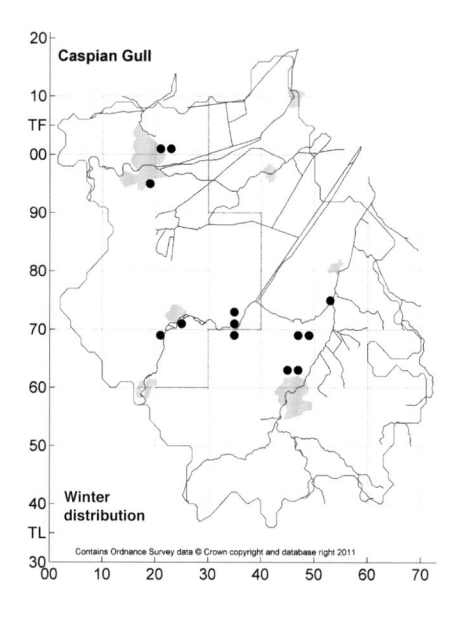

ICELAND GULL *Larus glaucoides*
Amber List. Scarce, annual winter visitor and passage migrant

Not a breeding species
Winter population estimate: 1-10 records annually

This species has been recorded in England increasingly since the 1970s (Brown & Grice, 2005), perhaps due to greater observer awareness of identification features. Bircham (1989) listed only five records for old Cambridgeshire but there were more records in Huntingdonshire, a situation that continues to reflect the favoured sites for this species. CBRs show that numbers recorded during the last 15 years vary between two and 12 (in 2009, an exceptional year).

Some individuals of the race *kumlieni*, also known as Kumlien's Gull, have been recorded. These birds originate from North America, whereas the origin of the nominate birds is southern Greenland. Toms (in Wernham *et al.*, 2002) estimates the total number of Iceland Gulls in the UK to be between 100 and 200.

The winter distribution map shows presence in six tetrads at three main points, close to the Old West River (Cottenham Long Drove/Smithey Fen), close to the Ouse, and near Peterborough.

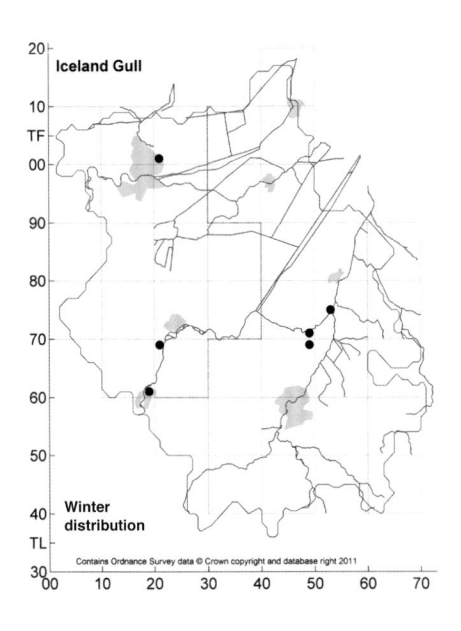

GLAUCOUS GULL *Larus hyperboreus*
Amber List. Scarce, almost annual winter visitor and passage migrant

Not a breeding species
Wintering population estimate: 1-10 records annually

Glaucous Gulls are found in small numbers in the UK; Brown & Grice (2005) report them as four times as common as Iceland Gulls, a statistic that is not reflected by the Cambridgeshire records where numbers of both species are similar: there are between two and eight Glaucous Gull records per annum. As with Iceland Gull the main locations where this species is recorded are Grafham Water (although no reports were submitted to the atlas for this site), gravel pits and refuse tips; they usually occur as singles, often first year or sub-adult in age. Brown & Grice (2005) report site fidelity of a number of individuals over a period of years at coastal sites.

Ringing results yield only a little information. Toms (in Wernham *et al.*, 2002) states that birds reported in the UK originated from Iccland (three), Bear Island, Svalbard (one), and Norway (one).

The winter distribution map shows records in nine tetrads at much the same sites as the Iceland Gull records (Cottenham Long Drove and around Peterborough).

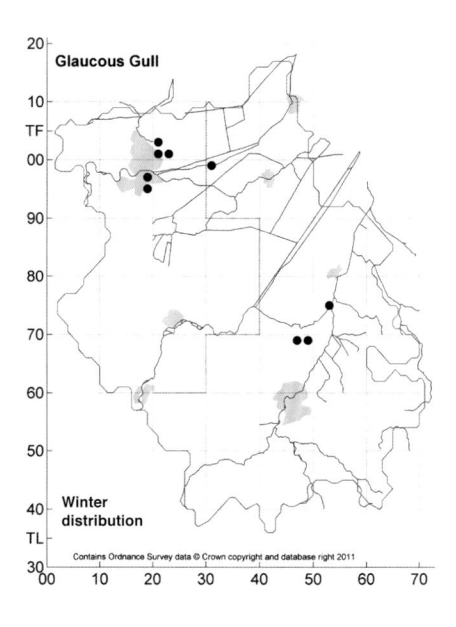

GREAT BLACK-BACKED GULL *Larus marinus*
Amber List. **Fairly common winter visitor and passage migrant**

Not a breeding species
Wintering population estimate: 500-1,000 individuals

Great Black-backed Gulls are less widespread in Cambridgeshire than most of the other large gulls. Historically this was a rare visitor to the county and, as with its congeners, Great Black-backed Gull numbers began to increase in the middle of the 20th century with the adoption of feeding at refuse tips. Up to 20 birds were recorded at several sites, and reports of roost numbers in excess of 100 on the Ouse and Nene Washes and some gravel pits (Bircham, 1989).

Brown & Grice (2005) show numbers at inland roosts in East Anglia rising from c. 1,700 in 1983 to over 10,000 ten years later, while over the same period coastal roost numbers fell dramatically from 8,600 to just under 1,000; this suggests a change in strategy for birds wintering in our area. CBRs show that recently the highest numbers have been at Kingfishers Bridge, including up to 500 in 2009 and 2010. A count of 500 was recorded at Fletton BP in both 1977 and 1981 (Clark, 1996) and 600 at Grafham Water in January 1999.

The distribution map shows birds along the main river systems, less widely distributed than the other regular wintering gulls, numbering generally 1–10 birds with one high count in Peterborough. However, as with the other gulls there are records in tetrads some distance from the rivers, presumably on agricultural land and a reflection of the fact that ploughing can take place in almost any month from September to April when soil conditions allow.

Ringing results show the origins of some Cambridgeshire birds to be Norway and the Netherlands. Reid (in Wernham *et al.*, 2002) states that UK breeding birds are mainly sedentary and that many birds that winter in the UK originate from Fennoscandia and the Baltic States. There is also evidence of wintering-site fidelity.

Great Black-backed Gulls were reported from 121 winter tetrads (12%).

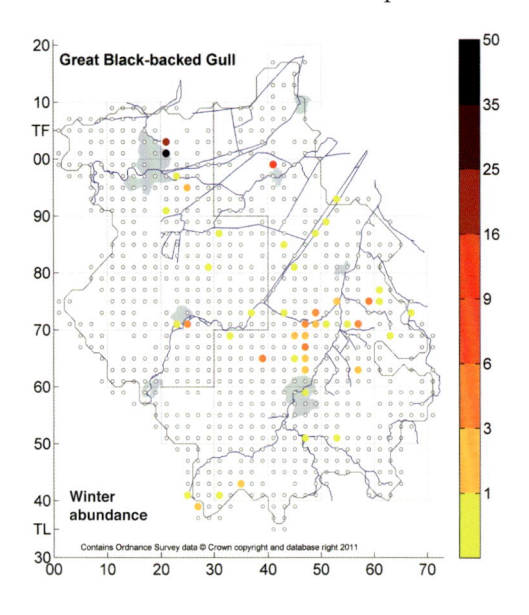

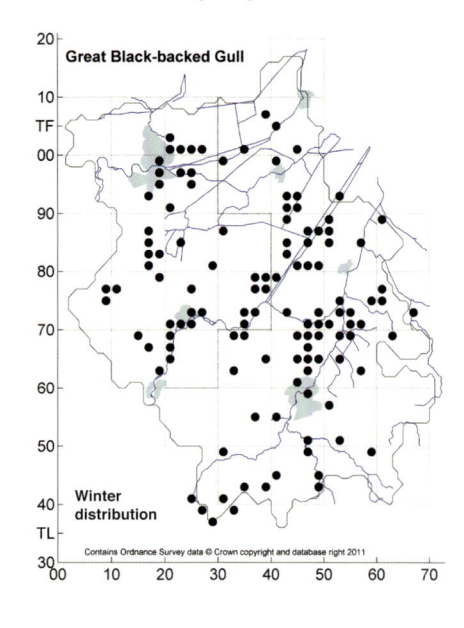

COMMON TERN *Sterna hirundo*
Amber List. Fairly common migratory breeder and passage migrant

Breeding population estimate: 50-150 pairs
Not a wintering species

This species is associated with our main river systems and areas of open water such as gravel pits, Grafham Water and fenland meres. Both noisy and obvious, Common Tern is easily recorded wherever it is present. Generally birds arrive in April and the latest depart in September.

Breeding was first confirmed in 1954 at Orton Pit; subsequently there was such a slow expansion that even by 1969 there were only eight pairs at three sites. The first breeding record in old Cambridgeshire was in 1971 at Chatteris gravel pits. The following years saw the population rise with most breeding sites in the pits along the Ouse valley so that by 1987 there were 94 pairs at seven sites; recently the total number of pairs has probably been around 70–100.

The expansion of inland breeding has been due to the increasing number of gravel pits with islands and also to the provision of artificial nesting rafts. Brown & Grice (2005) report a decline in coastal breeding populations and an element of variability in numbers at traditional coastal sites; they suggest that the decline in coastal colonies has been offset by the increasing inland population.

The maps show breeding confirmed in 25 tetrads, probable breeding in a further nine and possible breeding in 24 amounting to 58 tetrads, rather greater than numbers given in recent CBRs. Records of non-breeding birds are in tetrads that lie mainly along the Rivers Ouse, Nene, Welland and Cam. The density map shows that counts greater than 1–3 birds are exclusively along the rivers and close to breeding sites. Comparison with the previous Cambs Atlas shows an increase from around five tetrads with positive evidence of breeding in old Cambs to 10–11 in the same area for this atlas. There may be potential for further increase given the addition of artificial nest sites to existing gravel pits.

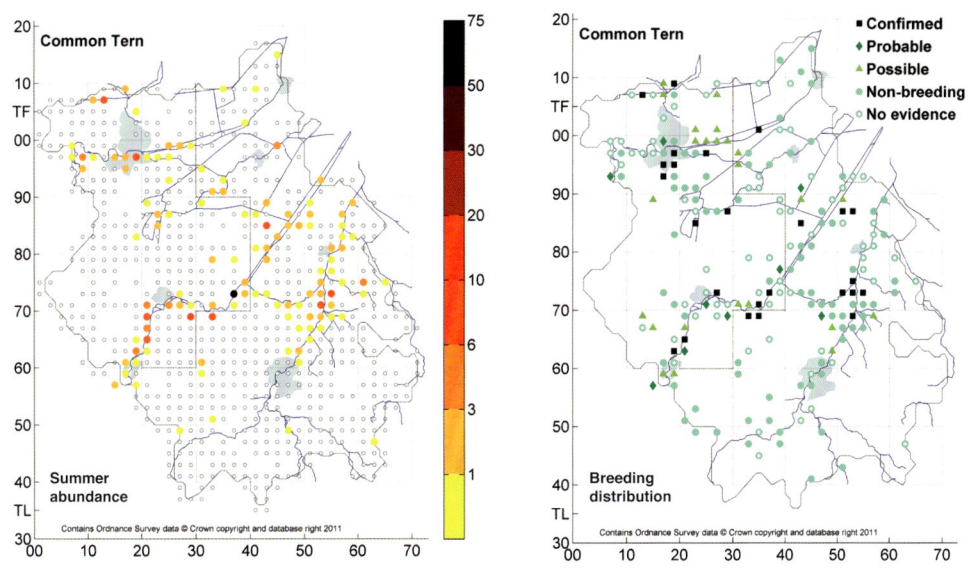

	Confirmed	Probable	Possible	Non-breeding	No evidence	Total summer (% county)
Total tetrads	25	9	24	81	70	209 (22%)

ROCK DOVE/FERAL PIGEON *Columba livia (forma domestica)*
Green List. Common feral resident, increased in rural but not urban areas (where control measures are often used)

Breeding population estimate: 2,000-4,000 pairs, many non-breeding birds
Wintering population estimate: 5,000-10,000 individuals

The Feral Pigeon, the feral form of the domesticated form of the Rock Dove, is widely distributed in the UK, with strongholds in cities and towns. On the Scottish and Irish coasts, away from urban areas, the majority of birds still resemble the original Rock Doves in terms of plumage and probably also genetically. In Cambridgeshire, the Feral Pigeon may be one of the least-understood bird species regarding its breeding distribution, population trends and breeding ecology. Birdwatchers and ornithologists tend to ignore it. Only a small proportion of the birds in urban populations nest regularly; the Feral Pigeon flocks in our towns and cities are likely to consist of many non-breeders (Cramp, 1985). The flocks are also likely to contain a small number of 'escaped' racing pigeons. Away from urban centres it is even more difficult to distinguish between truly feral and free-flying captive birds.

Despite these caveats, the atlas fieldwork reveals some clear patterns. The breeding and winter distribution in Cambridgeshire is rather patchy. TTVs recorded the species in both seasons in only 26% of tetrads, with low average densities of 1.1 birds per hour in the breeding season and 1.8 birds per hour in winter. There is no clear picture of population strongholds in the county but remarkably the cities of Cambridge and Peterborough do not stand out as such, except on the map of roving records in winter. Expansion into rural areas in Huntingdonshire was noted by the mid-1990s (Clark, 1996).

Probable and confirmed breeding was recorded only in 84 tetrads (9%), compared to 17% in the previous Hunts Atlas. The BBS 15-year trends show significant declines for the UK (1%), for England (20%) and Eastern England (10%) (Risely *et al.*, 2012).

According to the TTV maps, some fen areas in the north and east of the county show higher densities in both seasons, in addition to the urban centres of Cambridge and Peterborough. These are likely to be birds from villages and towns that feed regularly in the open agricultural areas. Unlike the fens, the western clay plateau and the southern chalk escarpment of the county show lower densities (with few exceptions) and large gaps, in particular on the TTV maps. Confirmed breeding is rather restricted to the cities and towns although nesting also takes place at more isolated farm buildings. It is, however, likely that many breeding attempts went unnoticed during atlas fieldwork.

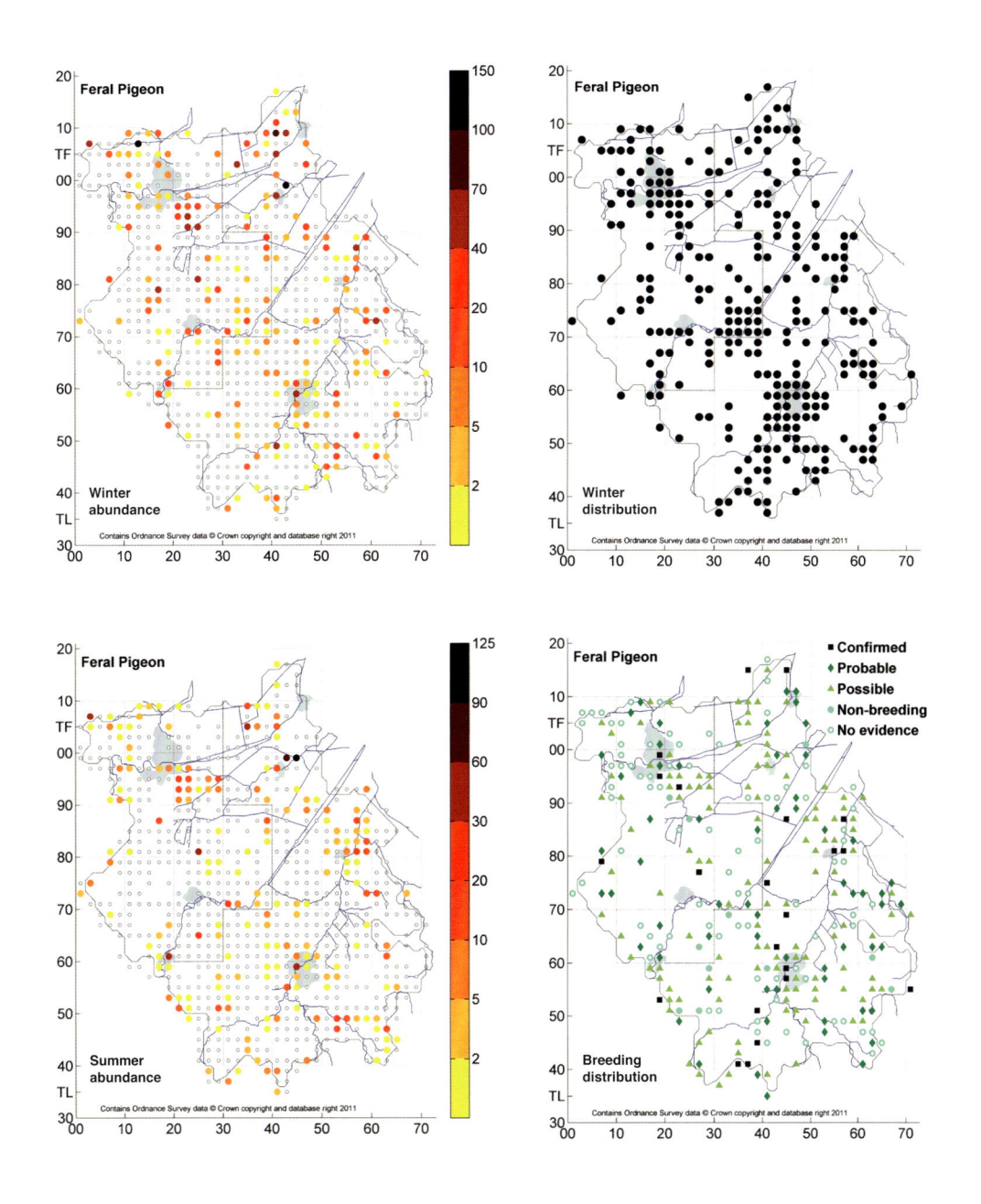

	Confirmed	Probable	Possible	Non-breeding	No evidence	Total summer (% county)	Total winter (% county)
Total tetrads	22	62	126	11	85	306 (32%)	272 (28%)

STOCK DOVE *Columba oenas*
Amber List. Common resident and winter visitor

Breeding population estimate: 2,000-4,000 pairs
Wintering population estimate: 4,000-10,000 individuals

The UK is, in a European context, the stronghold of the Stock Dove's breeding population (Hagemeijer & Blair, 1997). While the species is widely distributed, the breeding-season distribution in the county is somewhat patchy. Stock Dove was recorded in 71% of TTVs, with gaps evident particularly in the more hilly western and southern areas; the fens seem to be a stronghold for this species.

Breeding was confirmed or found probable in 482 tetrads (50%), compared with only 27% in the old Cambs Atlas and 56% in the old Hunts Atlas.

Nationally, the Stock Dove has increased by an estimated 92% between 1970 and 2010 (Eaton *et al.*, 2012), with a rather stable population between 1995 and 2010. It is, nevertheless, amber-listed on the basis of the importance of the UK populations in a European context. Over the past decades, the Stock Dove population has clearly expanded. For old Cambridgeshire, Bircham (1989) found the species 'thinly distributed ... across the county' and in the previous Cambs Atlas the species was 'absent from some large open fenland areas' due to the lack of suitable nesting sites. This is clearly no longer the case, perhaps due to an increased use of nestboxes provided for Barn Owls and Kestrels and of buildings for nesting.

In winter, Stock Doves were recorded in 57% of TTVs, fewer than in the breeding season. The average density, however, was higher in winter (2.3 birds per hour) than in the breeding season (1.4 birds per hour), reflecting the tendency of this species to form flocks outside of the breeding season. These flocks are likely to contain resident birds and those from other parts of the country; there is little evidence for a substantial influx into the UK from the continent (Wernham *et al.*, 2002). The distribution throughout the county is markedly different in winter: the species is clearly concentrated in the fens, with fewer birds and even larger gaps than in the breeding season in the western and southern parts of the county. Cambridgeshire holds a substantial proportion (5.5%) of the national wintering population of Stock Doves, again reflecting the attractiveness of the agricultural areas in the fens for this species.

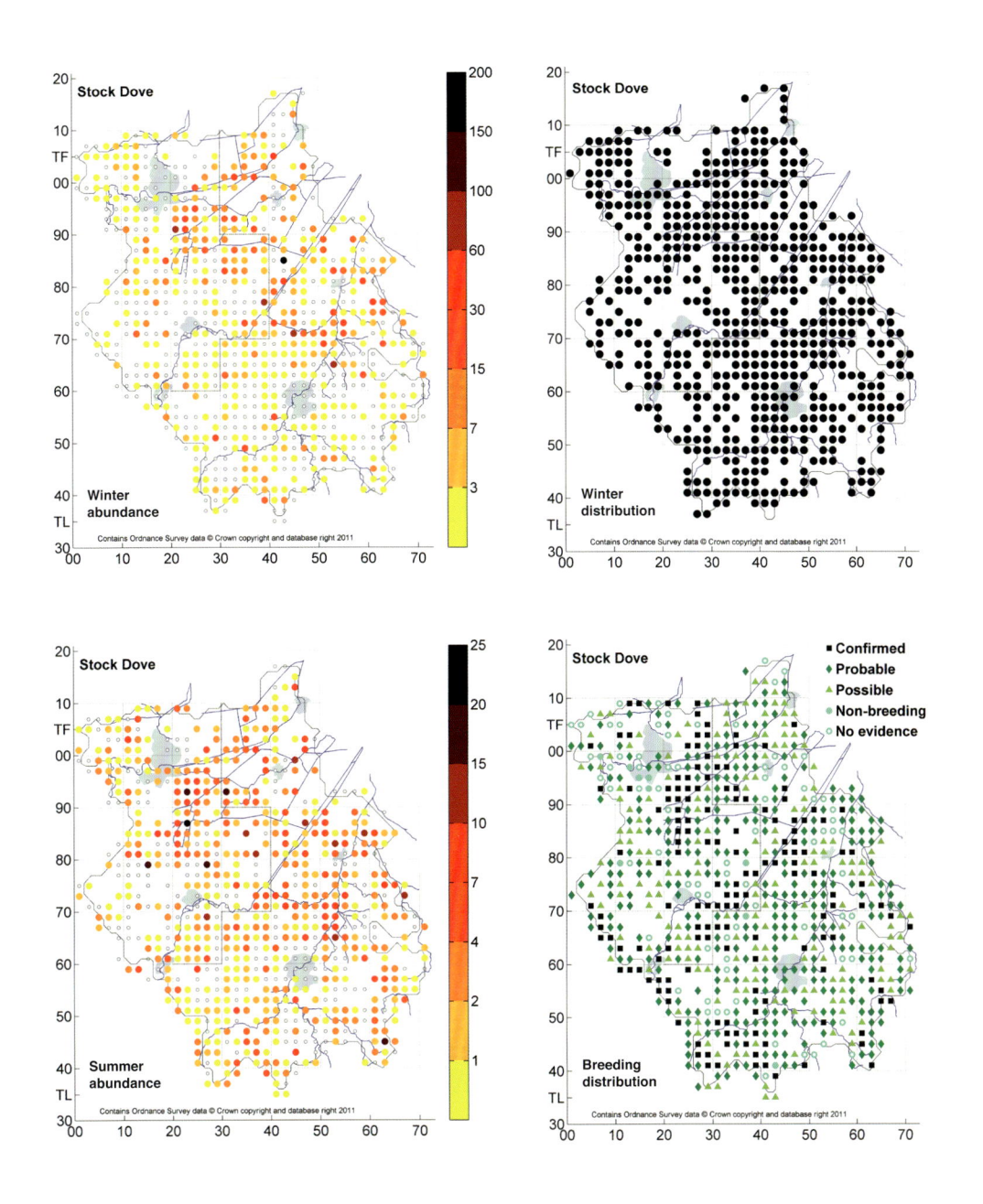

	Confirmed	Probable	Possible	Non-breeding	No evidence	Total summer (% county)	Total winter (% county)
Total tetrads	157	325	183	9	79	753 (78%)	607 (63%)

WOODPIGEON (Common Wood Pigeon) *Columba palumbus*
Green List. Abundant resident and winter visitor

Breeding population estimate: 100,000-200,000 pairs
Wintering population estimate: 200,000-500,000 individuals

The Woodpigeon is one of the most abundant birds in the UK; this is mirrored in our county, where it was the most abundant species found in both seasons during the atlas fieldwork. TTVs both in the breeding season and in winter recorded the species in all tetrads. It is difficult to make out any differences in density between the fens and the more hilly areas. Clearly our landscape, dominated by agriculture, provides optimal conditions for this adaptable species. The Cambridgeshire population is estimated to represent 3.6% of the national population, more than three times the expected figure if Woodpigeons were distributed evenly across the UK.

Whilst Woodpigeons are able to nest all year round, the peak of the breeding season falls between July and September, when in arable landscapes grain provides a high-quality food source for raising their young. This period is only partly covered by the timing of the atlas TTVs, although roving records recording breeding evidence could be submitted during this time. The density maps reflect the fact that Woodpigeons can be found in flocks well into summer. Nevertheless, with such a common species it was possible to state confirmed or probable breeding in 678 tetrads (70%); this figure was 81% in the previous Cambs Atlas and 95% in the Hunts Atlas.

Nationally, the Woodpigeon population is estimated to have increased by 130% between 1970 and 2010 (Risely *et al.*, 2012); the BBS shows a 44% increase between 1995 and 2010. Cambridgeshire BBS data also exhibit a strong increase over the same period and previous atlases also showed the bird to be very widely distributed. By the 19th century, agricultural changes resulted in the Woodpigeon being very common throughout the country, in particular in low-lying regions (Holloway, 1996).

The winter population is likely to be made up of residents and wintering birds from other areas in the UK. There is little evidence of large-scale wintering of continental birds in the UK (Wernham *et al.*, 2002). The maps demonstrate that the winter population in Cambridgeshire is substantially higher than that in the breeding season (TTV counts in summer average 30 birds per hour, compared to 120 birds per hour in winter); this is not surprising for a county offering a large-scale winter food supply in the agricultural landscape. The atlas data show that with 5.3%, the county holds a substantial proportion of the national wintering population of this species.

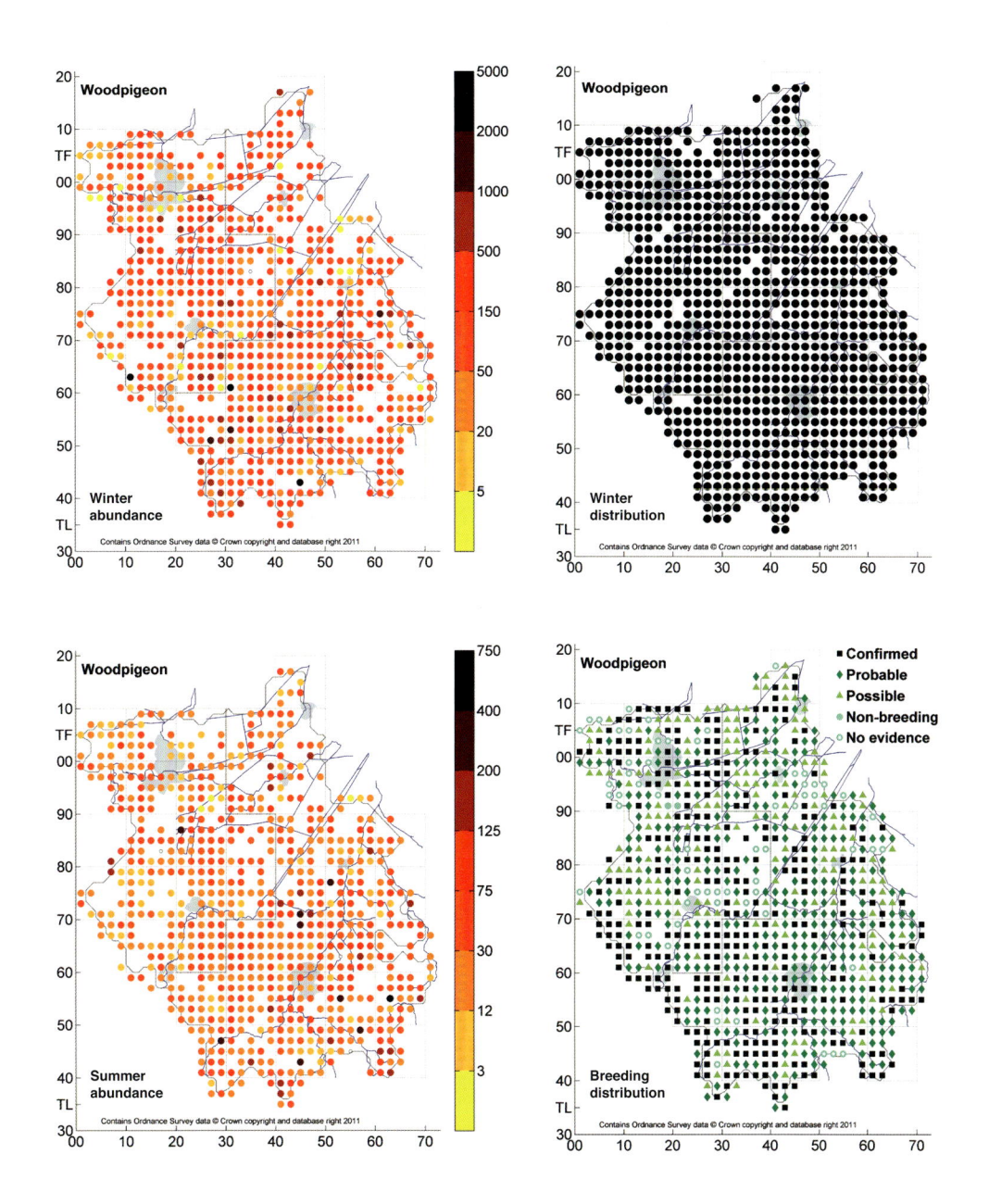

	Confirmed	Probable	Possible	Non-breeding	No evidence	Total summer (% county)	Total winter (% county)
Total tetrads	332	346	190	2	63	933 (96%)	925 (95%)

COLLARED DOVE (Eurasian Collared Dove) *Streptopelia decaocto*
Green List. Very common resident

Breeding population estimate: 10,000-30,000 pairs
Wintering population estimate: 20,000-75,000 individuals

The Collared Dove is a familiar bird in towns and villages but also at farm buildings in the open countryside. Colonising Europe originally from India via Turkey, it was first recorded in the UK in 1952 and began breeding in 1955. The first record for Cambridgeshire dates from 1960 in Cambridge, and the first breeding was noticed in 1961 in Littleport. During the previous atlas period, Collared Doves were already widespread but gaps in the fens were still apparent. TTVs during the current atlas work recorded Collared Doves in 82% of tetrads surveyed during the breeding season and in 76% of TTVs in winter. Some small gaps are still apparent, in particular in the western clay plateau and the south-eastern chalk escarpment.

Cambridgeshire holds a substantial proportion of the UK population, with a higher than average proportion in both the breeding season and winter. As with Woodpigeon, this reflects that our county, dominated by agricultural (in particular arable) land use, is very attractive for this predominantly seed-feeding species. Compared with Woodpigeon, Collared Dove densities are generally low, with four birds per hour counted during TTVs in summer and 5.1 birds per hour in winter. Higher counts seem to dominate in winter and in the fens, where flocks can be found foraging near villages and farm buildings. The distribution in the breeding season is not very different from that in winter; not surprising for a sedentary species.

Probable or confirmed breeding was recorded in 531 tetrads (55% of the county's tetrads), compared to 47% in the previous Cambs Atlas and 72% in the Hunts Atlas (when different definitions were used for probable and confirmed breeding). Confirmed breeding records have been made predominantly in cities and towns, reflecting the species' tendency to nest in gardens, parks and generally close to human settlements. The breeding season of Collared Dove lasts from late winter to autumn and most pairs undertake several breeding attempts per season.

Collared Doves have shown one of the most dramatic increases in the UK over the past decades, estimated at 333% between 1970 and 2010 and 23% between 1995 and 2010. The population was estimated at 990,000 breeding pairs in 2009 (Eaton *et al.*, 2012). This is in contrast to Central Europe, where after decades of dramatic increases the species has more recently undergone a severe reduction, e.g. in Germany by 40% between 1990 and 2007 (ADEBAR, in preparation). It remains to be seen whether the next atlas will continue to show Collared Dove as a very common resident.

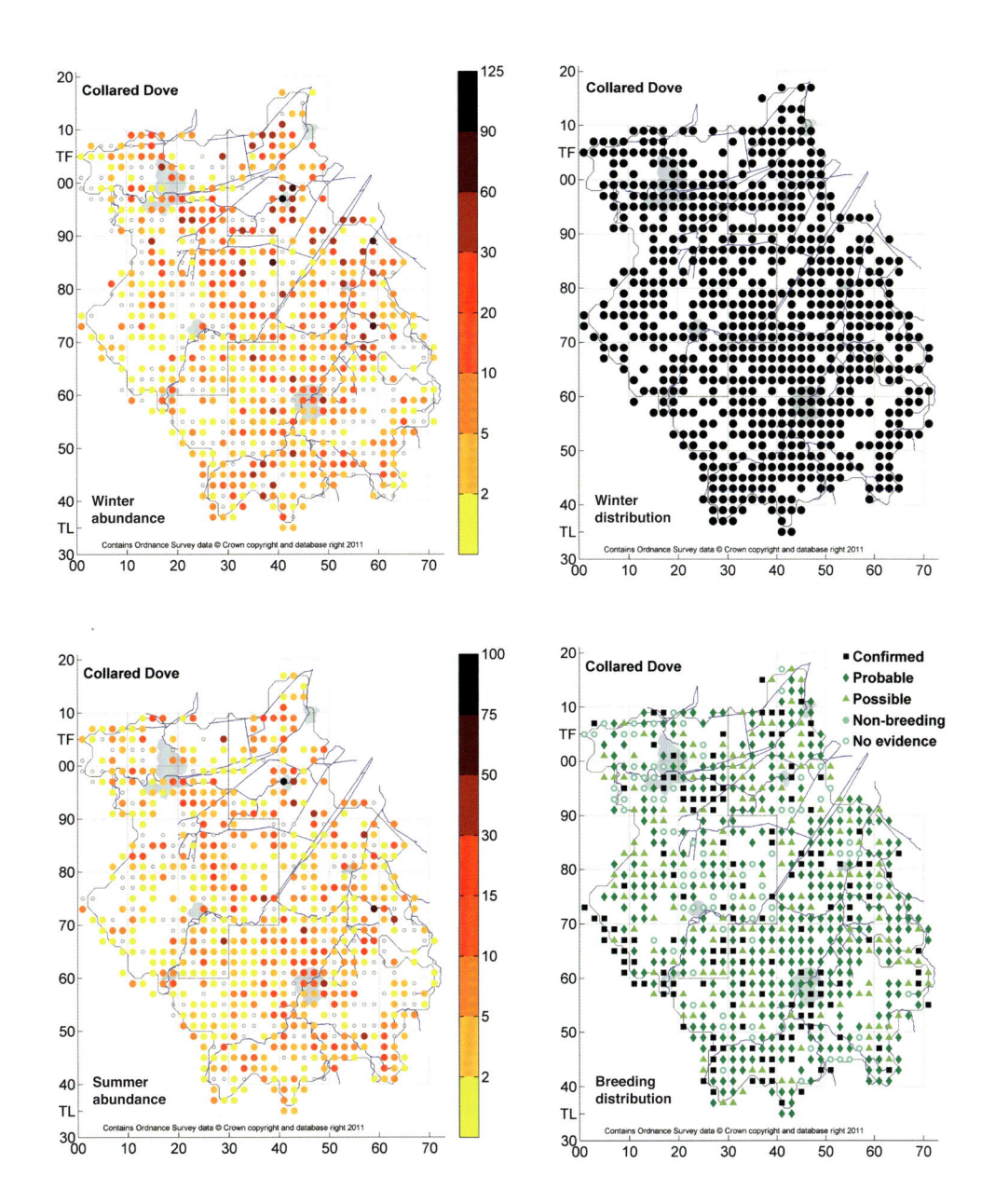

	Confirmed	Probable	Possible	Non-breeding	No evidence	Total summer (% county)	Total winter (% county)
Total tetrads	144	387	170	0	82	783 (81%)	719 (74%)

TURTLE DOVE (European Turtle Dove) *Streptopelia turtur*
Red List. Fairly common passage migrant and recently much declined migratory breeder

Breeding population estimate: 150-300 pairs
Not a wintering species

The Turtle Dove used to be a common feature of our countryside in spring and summer, attracting attention with its purring song, but has recently shown significant declines. It was recorded in just 21% of TTVs in the breeding season, with a patchy distribution throughout the county. The majority of these records come from the fens but the species clearly occurs in all landscapes, although with large gaps, as the distribution map demonstrates. Probable or confirmed breeding in the atlas period was recorded only in 112 tetrads (12%). Cambridgeshire holds a higher than average proportion of the UK population. This is no surprise for a species with a southern and south-eastern bias in national distribution. It is the rarest of the five species of pigeons and doves, with a mere 0.14 birds per hour recorded during breeding-season TTVs.

During the previous atlas periods, the Turtle Dove was much more widespread across the county, recorded in the previous Cambs Atlas in 48% of tetrads with probable or confirmed breeding and in the Hunts Atlas with an impressive 88%. During the 1980s and 1990s, the species underwent a severe decline. This decline has continued, with the national population trend from the Common Bird Census/BBS being -80% between 1995 and 2010 and -93% between 1970 and 2010. The UK population was estimated in 2009 to comprise just 14,000 pairs (Eaton *et al.*, 2012). The main reason for the decline seems to be reduced food availability due to herbicide use in agriculture, resulting in a shorter breeding period with fewer nesting attempts. Severe hunting pressure and habitat loss along the migration route and in the African wintering areas are also likely to play a role. The decline is also evident in the decreasing number of records during autumn migration, with a concurrent decrease in flock size. In 2011, for the first time in recent years, no flock of more than six birds was recorded in the county (CBR 85). It is hoped that recent conservation measures targeted at the Turtle Dove will stem this decline so that this species will not be lost from our countryside by the next atlas.

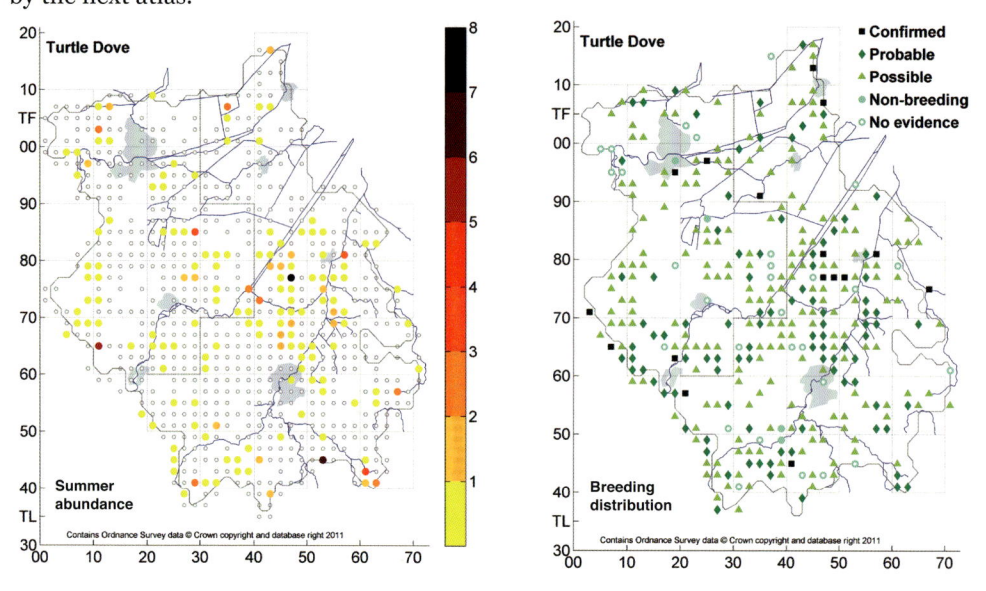

	Confirmed	Probable	Possible	Non-breeding	No evidence	Total summer (% county)
Total tetrads	16	96	200	4	29	345 (36%)

CUCKOO (Common Cuckoo) *Cuculus canorus*
Red List. Fairly common but declined migratory breeder and passage migrant

Breeding population estimate: 50-100 calling males
Not a wintering species

The Cuckoo's well-known song is still widely regarded as a sign of spring despite it being heard less and less frequently. It is nowadays absent from large parts of our countryside, having been recorded in just 21% of TTVs. The atlas records show a concentration in the fens and the north-west limestone area west of Peterborough. The distribution in the fens, however, shows large gaps, and the atlas maps indicate that most of our Cuckoos occur in the Nene and Ouse valleys and at and around key fen sites such as Wicken and Woodwalton Fen. This distribution may reflect the higher densities of its host species, particularly Reed Warbler and Meadow Pipit, at these fen sites; another possibility is that the large, hairy caterpillars which form a substantial part of the adult Cuckoo's diet are of several moth species which themselves are undergoing very significant declines away from wetland sites.

Not surprisingly for a brood parasite, there are probable or confirmed breeding records only for 73 tetrads (8%). With 0.13 birds per hour recorded during breeding-season TTVs, density is generally very low, with exceptions again from the above-mentioned key fen sites. The species has clearly declined in the county; in particular its recent scarcity in the south-west is striking when compared to the distribution demonstrated by previous atlases. The previous Cambs Atlas found probable or confirmed breeding in 38% of tetrads, with Cuckoos present in a further 5%. For the previous Hunts Atlas, breeding was confirmed or found probable in 61% of tetrads and found possible in a further 20%.

The Cuckoo is still widely distributed throughout the UK and therefore Cambridgeshire only holds approximately 1.5% of the national population, according to atlas data. BBS data suggest a national decline of 62% between 1970 and 2010, and 49% between 1995 and 2010 (Risely *et al.*, 2012). The reasons for the decline are not clear and research increasingly focuses on their African staging and wintering grounds. The BTO has recently satellite-tagged several Cuckoos to investigate their migration routes and durations and identify their wintering areas.

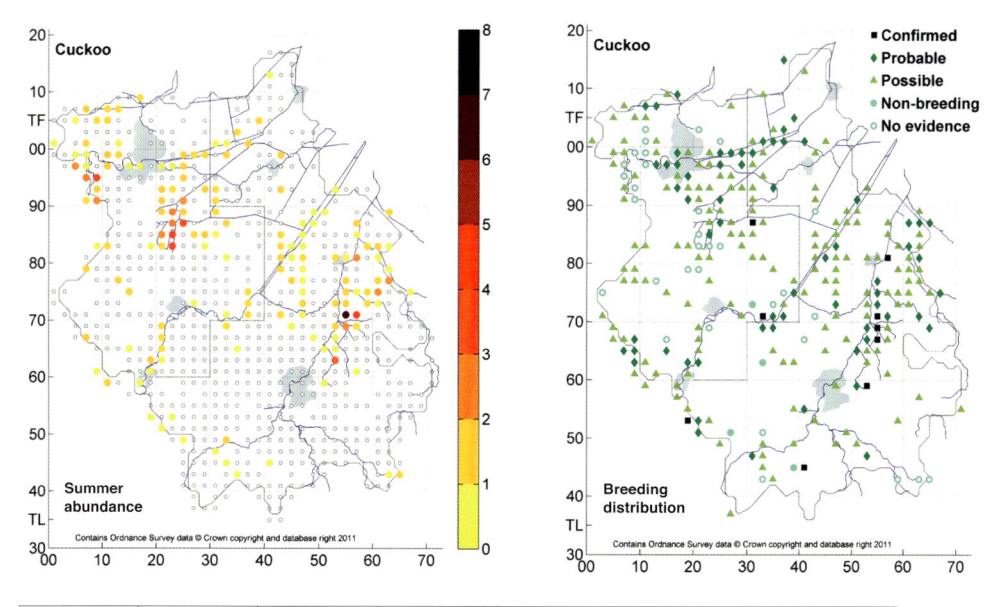

	Confirmed	Probable	Possible	Non-breeding	No evidence	Total summer (% county)
Total tetrads	9	64	161	4	32	270 (28%)

BARN OWL *Tyto alba*
Amber List. Fairly common widespread resident with highest concentrations in fenland

Breeding population estimate: 200-400 pairs
Wintering population estimate: 500-1,000 individuals

The Barn Owl, charismatic, ghostly hunter over grassland and arable-edge landscapes at dusk, is possibly the most expanded in range of the owls since the previous atlas periods. It has undergone a significant expansion in rural parts of the county, and is found in a large proportion of fenland tetrads. It has a scattered distribution in the rest of the county, away from significant population centres. This expansion is due to several factors – the provision of nest boxes across the agricultural landscape, which are well monitored with many chicks ringed, and the increase in rough-grass farm-field headlands and farm plantations surrounded by long grass. These features provide ideal habitat for field voles, the main prey of the Barn Owl. This provision of nest boxes means that a good network of nest sites is available, and the reasonably high reproduction rate of breeding pairs means that there is a reasonable recruitment of young birds into the population.

Largely sedentary, its summer and winter distributions are similar; the slight differences between the maps probably reflect observer differences and chance rather than any true seasonal change in distribution.

Most of the summer tetrads had confirmed breeding rather than lower categories – a pale bird visiting a box at dusk or seen carrying prey is relatively easy to identify, so the high proportion of confirmed breeding is not surprising. Only a handful of pairs were breeding in the county in the 1970s; by the time of the previous Cambs Atlas this had increased to around 40–50 pairs. The population was estimated at around 300 pairs in the early years of the 21st century (Bacon *et al.*, 2007) when the CBC carried out a comprehensive survey of breeding owls. Of our four breeding owls, the Barn Owl is probably the most easy to find – a pale bird, often hunting over open ground at dusk or earlier if feeding has been sparse, is far more noticeable than a brown owl hunting in woodland after dark.

The figures from the previous atlases showed 17 (Hunts Atlas) and 49 (Cambs Atlas) confirmed tetrads, with a further 17 probable and 47 possible for Huntingdonshire and a further 18 (possible/probable, reflecting the different definitions used) for old Cambridgeshire. This amounted to only 15% of the county. The increases in distribution have been in the south of the county; there has been an increase in abundance throughout their range.

The BBS data (Risely *et al.*, 2012) show a 15-year (1995–2010) increase for the UK of 390% and for England 369%.

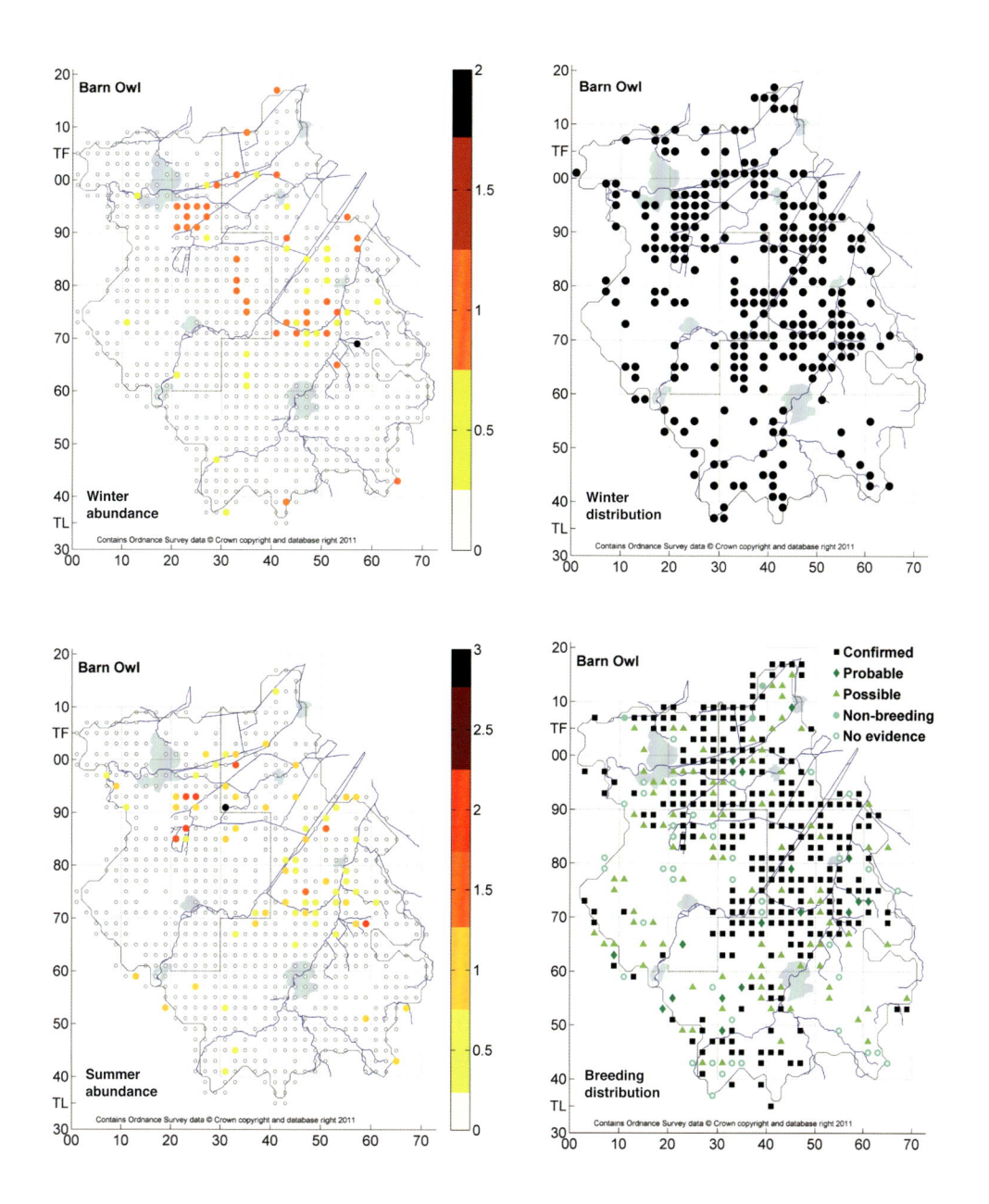

	Confirmed	Probable	Possible	Non-breeding	No evidence	Total summer (% county)	Total winter (% county)
Total tetrads	270	17	96	3	41	427 (44%)	262 (27%)

LITTLE OWL *Athene noctua*
Fairly common, introduced, naturalised resident

Breeding population estimate: 200-400 pairs
Wintering population estimate: 400-800 individuals

A fairly widespread owl species, the Little Owl is likely to be out in daylight or early dusk/dawn, making recording easier. Typically an owl of parkland, orchards and other lightly wooded areas such as pasture with hedges containing large old trees, the Little Owl uses natural holes. It has not taken to box-nesting, unlike the Barn Owl, and despite being nearly diurnal is not the most obvious of hunters. It is often overlooked although it has a noisy phase during the late summer when the young are dispersing, and this can be a good season to collect records.

It appears to have decreased, or at least altered its range from the last two atlases. However, how much this can be attributed to recorder effort is uncertain; the present dataset is very dependent on roving records and ad hoc observations, although in a few parts of the county hours of field time were devoted to connecting with this species.

It would appear to be recorded far less often in winter than in summer, based on our distribution maps; as it is a sedentary species, the summer and winter distributions combined may reflect better their true distribution. The distribution does not noticeably coincide with any habitat or landscape types. There seem to be striking gaps; for instance to the west of Peterborough. This is a landscape of well-connected woods and parkland where we would expect this species to occur, but it was only recorded on a single winter tetrad. The highest density seems to be on the southern edge of Peterborough out into the fens – a group of TTVs here all recorded at least two birds. The other cluster in an otherwise widely scattered distribution is to the south-west of Cambridge – an area of villages with pasture, connected woodlands, and some parkland areas. This shows up most clearly on the summer distribution map. There is also a good swathe of records from the orchard belt, through the southern edge of the fens, in villages such as Bluntisham, Earith, etc. This distribution must be due in part to chance – Little Owl was not often encountered on TTVs and some observers were presumably more crepuscular than others. The previous Hunts Atlas showed an extremely wide distribution across west and central Hunts, which seems to have nearly entirely disappeared; this must reflect a true change in distribution rather than observer effects.

Little Owls have a strong affinity with grassland, but also need nest holes: the correct combination of grassland, for hunting invertebrates and small mammals, and tree-holes is not of high abundance in the county.

The BBS data (Risely et al., 2012) show a 15-year (1995–2010) decrease of 40% for the UK and a similar reduction of 38% for England.

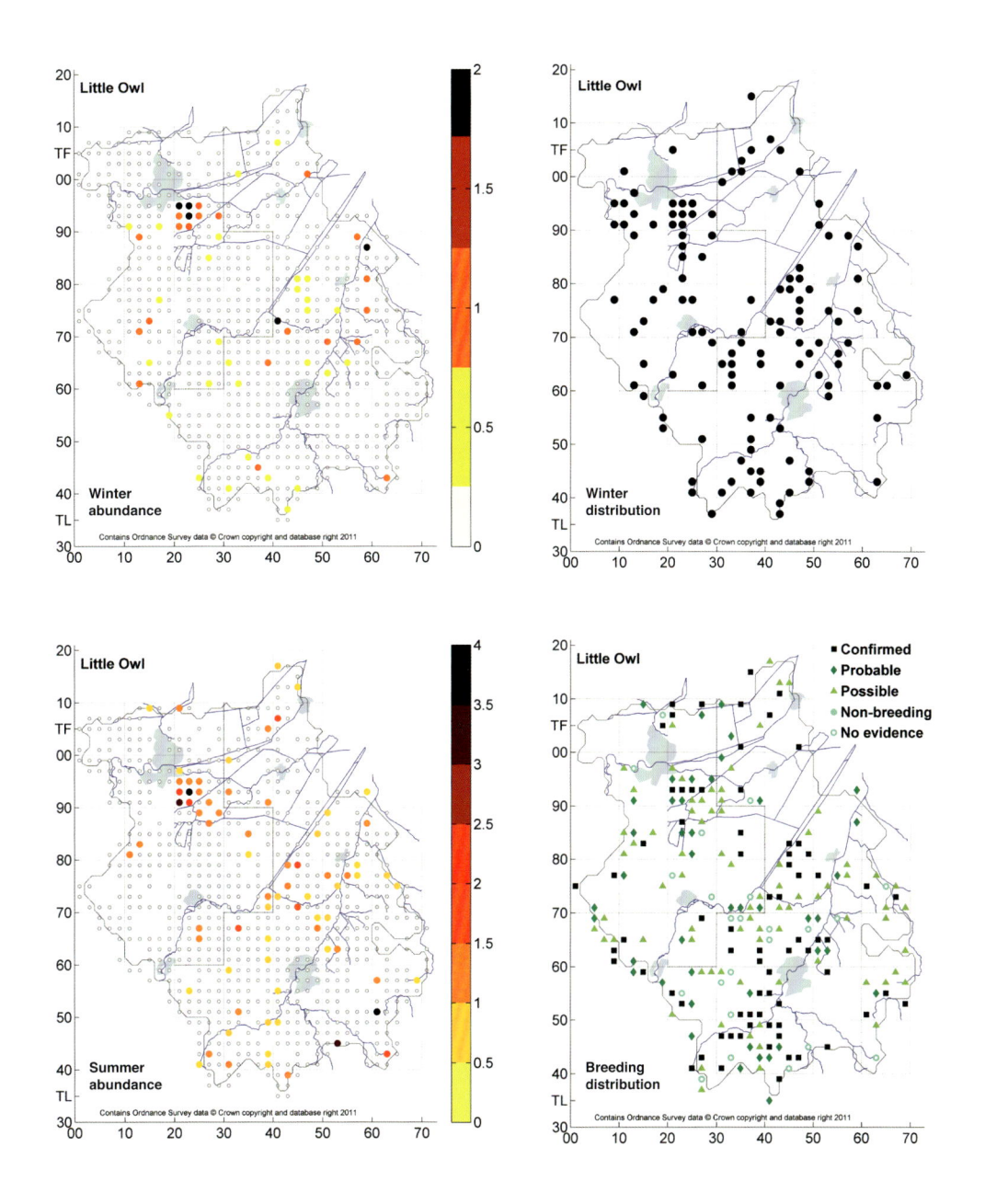

	Confirmed	Probable	Possible	Non-breeding	No evidence	Total summer (% county)	Total winter (% county)
Total tetrads	74	44	79	0	23	220 (23%)	120 (12%)

TAWNY OWL *Strix aluco*
Green List. Fairly common widespread resident

Breeding population estimate: 200-300 pairs
Wintering population estimate: 400-800 individuals

Tawny Owls prefer mature woodland and the distribution maps reflect this to some extent. The maps indicate this species' near-absence from the treeless fens, with strong centres of distribution in the wooded south-west of the county and to the west of Peterborough. Tawny Owls tend to breed in woodland, but also in wooded parts of towns. Their nocturnal habits no doubt lead to under-representation other than in roving records; the very sparse TTV maps reflect this.

As hole nesters, Tawny Owls readily take to nestboxes; most nests are in woodland or in a landscape which includes plenty of trees and suitable hunting grounds. They breed early in the year, often starting in February, with a season somewhat skewed from the core atlas periods. Young owls can be quite noticeable when they fledge in mid-summer; birds are vocal in late summer when dispersing into new territories and when pairs hoot to each other. Little has changed since the previous atlas in a broad sense: Tawny Owls are mostly found in the south and west, with far fewer in fenland areas. The number of occupied tetrads in Huntingdonshire has decreased since the previous Hunts Atlas.

It is the most urban of the owls, being found through Cambridge and parts of Peterborough, where there are suitable trees/boxes and food resources.

The BBS data (Risely *et al.*, 2012) show a 15-year (1995–2010) decrease for the UK of 23% and a similar reduction for England of 14%.

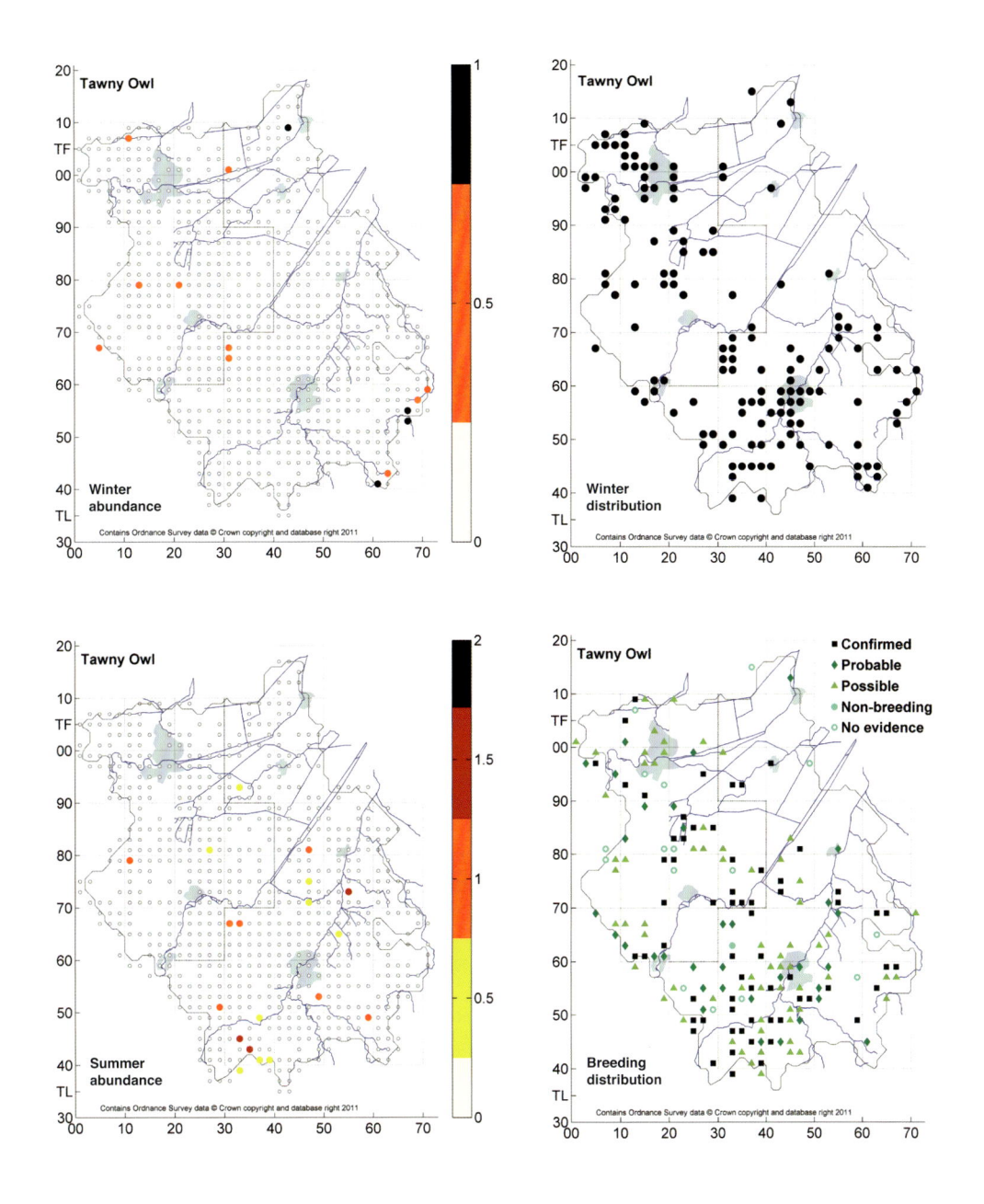

	Confirmed	Probable	Possible	Non-breeding	No evidence	Total summer (% county)	Total winter (% county)
Total tetrads	65	34	66	1	16	182 (19%)	140 (14%)

LONG-EARED OWL *Asio otus*
Green List. Scarce and very local resident; uncommon winter visitor/passage migrant (occasional influxes)

Breeding population estimate: 5-20 pairs
Wintering population estimate: 10-50 individuals

The Long-eared Owl is our most elusive owl, and is a scarce county species in both winter and summer. In the last atlas period it was a scarce breeding species, with records from only 14 (Hunts Atlas) and 19 tetrads (Cambs Atlas). This atlas provides records from 32 tetrads which is very similar. The secretive nature of the Long-eared Owl means that it was unlikely to be encountered on TTVs – there were only three TTV encounters in summer and two in winter, hence these records have not been mapped. The total number of winter tetrads was 10, compared to 32 for summer. This is somewhat surprising for a resident species often augmented in winter by immigrant birds from further north.

The Long-eared Owl is a breeding bird of wet woodlands in the county; many of its long-standing breeding sites are in reserves such as Woodwalton Fen. This habitat is not typical of all Long-eared Owls in the UK; it can be a species of heathlands and coniferous woods. Interestingly, research has shown that it tends to be found in sites with no Tawny Owls.

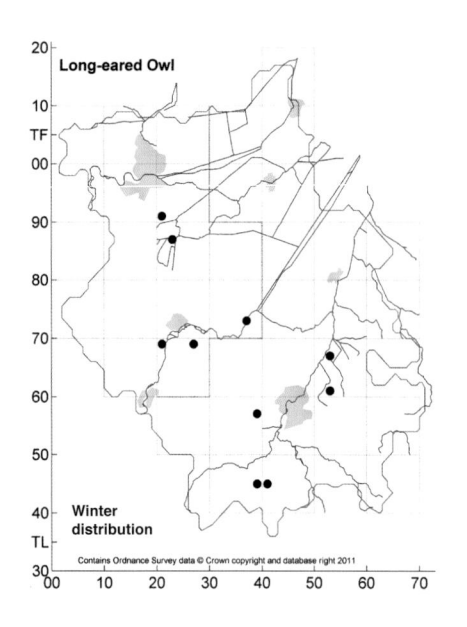

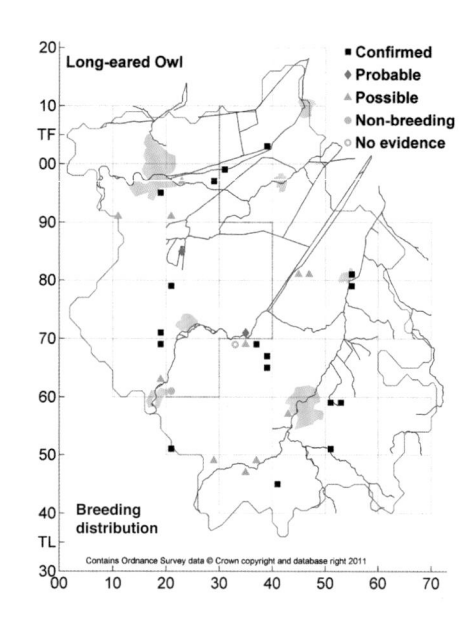

	Confirmed	Probable	Possible	Non-breeding	No evidence	Total summer (% county)	Total winter (% county)
Total tetrads	17	2	11	1	1	32 (3%)	10 (1%)

Cambridgeshire Bird Club Breeding Owl Survey 2004-2006
(Bacon *et al.*, 2007)

In 2004–06 the Cambridgeshire Bird Club carried out an Owl survey, in anticipation of the National Atlas and the likelihood that the standard atlas survey methods would not provide comprehensive coverage of the owl species. The Club designed the survey to focus on Barn Owl and Long-eared Owl, surveying farmland and other habitats as comprehensively as possible across the county. Volunteers surveyed at dusk at times of their own choosing between March and July, covering any likely habitat in their selected area. There is also an extensive nest-box ringing and monitoring project in the county, especially in fenland areas, and the Club had access to their data. Records submitted to the Bird Club's annual dataset were also incorporated. Whilst not focusing on Little or Tawny Owl, records of these species were also collected, but coverage was not likely to have been as comprehensive. There was a general paucity of records from Huntingdonshire which may affect species maps.

Tawny Owls form their territories and breeding partnerships in the winter and breed very early. This species appears to be widespread outside the fens, and its population is similar or has possibly decreased slightly since the previous atlases. A full population survey would require specifically targeted methods, probably involving surveying for calling birds in late winter and for birds after they have left the nest in early summer, when they can be very vocal.

The Barn Owl had good years and bad years, linked to population cycles of its primary food, voles. 2004 was an excellent year, with pairs having two or three broods, and five or six young being reared from a number of nests. By contrast 2006 was a poor year over much of the county except the far south, with few voles; most birds concentrated on feeding themselves rather than breeding. The birds are sufficiently long-lived for this to be a reasonable strategy in a poor year. In suitable habitat birds can reach quite high densities; occupation of nest boxes only 100 yards apart has been recorded. Most Barn Owls are in the fens, although the populations in south Cambridgeshire, new since the previous atlases, appear to be doing well.

Little Owl distribution appeared from this survey to be unchanged since the previous Cambs and Hunts atlases; few were present in the east of the county but it is widespread in the western half.

Long-eared Owls were very restricted in range as in previous atlases.

The maps below show the breeding season records mapped using three dot sizes for confirmed (largest), probable breeding or present.

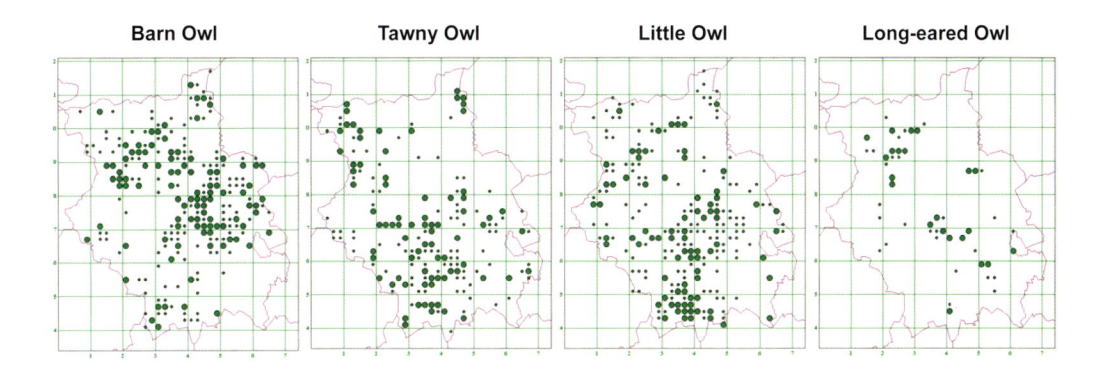

| Barn Owl | Tawny Owl | Little Owl | Long-eared Owl |

SHORT-EARED OWL *Asio flammeus*
Amber List. Uncommon winter visitor, passage migrant and occasional breeder

Not a breeding species
Wintering population estimate: 10-50 individuals

Short-eared Owls are most familiar to us as winter visitors – in Cambridgeshire we play host to birds from the north of the UK and northern Europe each winter, but in very variable numbers. The number depends on breeding success (based on small rodent availability), and on weather and food availability at migration time. The atlas years were average for numbers of this species but the following winter (2011/12) saw near-record numbers arrive in the county; some mid-winter counts at single sites reached well into double figures. The numbers during the atlas period were much more modest. Peak counts were nine during a two-hour TTV on the Nene Washes – this site regularly provides good winter numbers; other sites are far less reliable. The best way to enjoy the spectacle of this erratic visitor is to watch for it hunting over rough, often damp, grassland in mid- to late afternoon in mid-winter. This precluded large roost counts from TTVs, as they are usually finished by then; roving records, however, may have included evening visits to key sites.

Short-eared Owls occasionally breed in the county, usually as opportunistic breeders after a large-influx winter; none was thought to be have bred during the atlas period. There were 29 summer records of non-breeding birds.

In the previous Hunts Atlas, there were 10 tetrads with summer birds, five probable breeders and five possible breeders. Short-eared Owl was not mapped in the previous Cambs Atlas, but was recorded as a late-staying winterer. It bred in 1985 (in the Hunts Atlas period); presumably following a vole-year influx the preceding winter.

There were 45 tetrads (5%) with winter Short-eared Owl records through the atlas period.

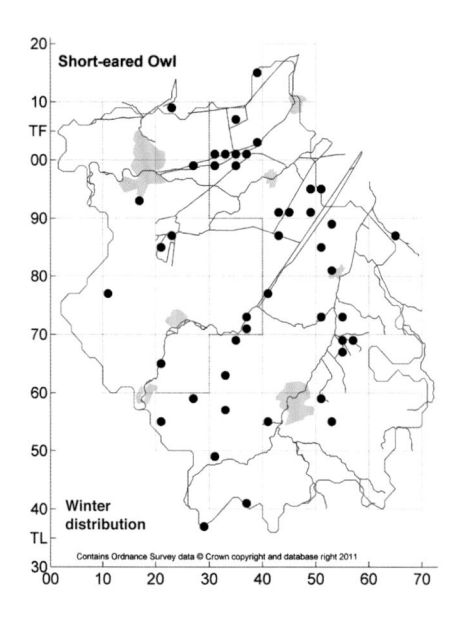

SWIFT (Common Swift) *Apus apus*
Amber list. Common but declining migratory breeder and passage migrant

Breeding population estimate: 2,000-5,000 pairs
Not a wintering species

During the breeding season, Swifts were reported from 608 (63%) tetrads, spread throughout the county, but seemingly more densely distributed in and around Cambridge, and more sparsely in the north-western half of the county. Breeding was confirmed in fewer than 10% of tetrads in which the species was recorded – probably reflecting the limited number of suitable breeding sites and the difficulty in confirming the presence of occupied nests (particularly during TTVs). Overall, some evidence of potential breeding was provided for 369 tetrads. The relatively high proportion of tetrads without any breeding evidence (39% of those tetrads with Swift records) presumably reflects the long distances that breeding adults can travel from their nests to forage, and the large numbers of non-breeding individuals that are present in the population (Baillie *et al.*, 2012). Although numbers of breeding birds are difficult to estimate from the atlas data, counts of c. 300–1,000 individuals were reported on several occasions from three tetrads encompassing parts of Grafham Water.

Comparison of the current breeding distribution with the previous Hunts Atlas (records from 241 tetrads) and Cambs Atlas (281 tetrads) shows a slight increase in the number of occupied tetrads but a reduction of more than half in the number where breeding was confirmed or probable (156 and 164 tetrads, respectively, in the previous atlases).

Nationally, the most up-to-date estimate of the population of Swifts in the UK is 87,000 (64,000–111,000) pairs, although this figure probably underestimates breeding numbers (Musgrove *et al.*, 2013). The 15-year (1995–2010) BBS trend for the UK is a decrease of 38%, although regional data suggest it may be faring slightly better in Eastern England (a 10% decline) than in other regions (Risely *et al.*, 2012).

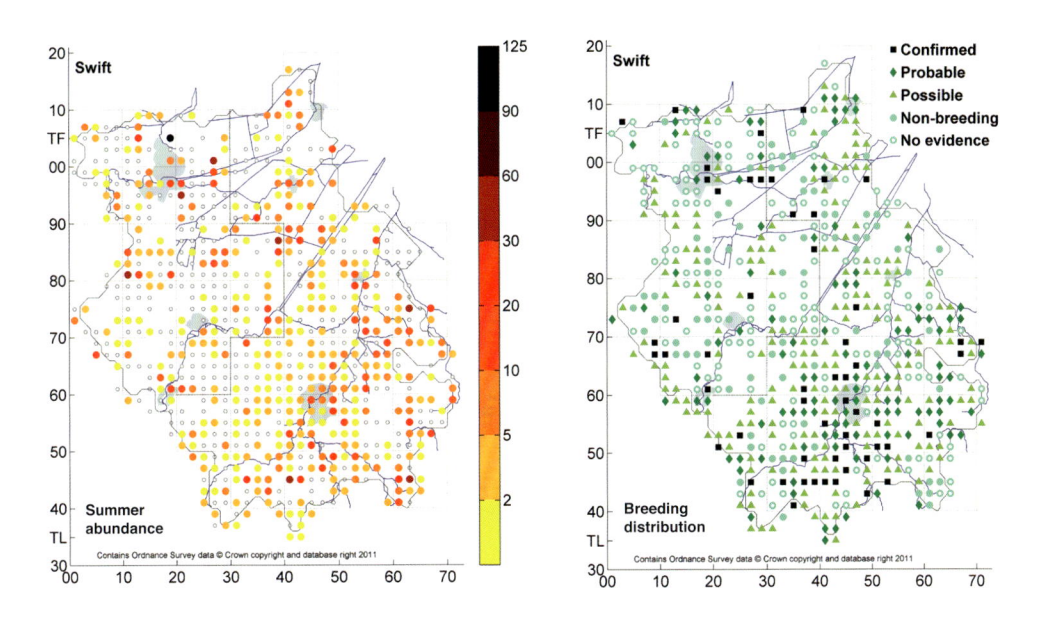

	Confirmed	Probable	Possible	Non-breeding	No evidence	Total summer (% county)
Total tetrads	56	112	201	81	158	608 (63%)

KINGFISHER (Common Kingfisher) *Alcedo atthis*
Amber List. Fairly common, but local resident; numbers affected by severity of winters

Breeding population estimate: 50-200 pairs
Wintering population estimate: 100-500 individuals

During the breeding season, Kingfishers were reported from 183 (19%) tetrads, clustered – as one might expect for a characteristic species of riparian habitats – mainly along the Rivers Nene, Great Ouse and Cam and their tributaries, and the artificial waterways of the Nene and Ouse Washes. The paucity of records from the chalk escarpment in the south-east and the western clay plateau reflects the general absence of streams and rivers in these areas; the cluster of records to the south-west of Huntingdon are from Grafham Water. Breeding was confirmed in 23% of tetrads in which the species was recorded, with some evidence of potential breeding provided for 163 tetrads overall. The majority of breeding-season records related to one or two individuals, but two or three pairs were reported from a small number of tetrads, including those encompassing parts of Fen Drayton Lakes, Roswell Pits and Wicken Fen.

Based on an average of one pair per occupied tetrad and the overall number of tetrads where breeding was confirmed, probable or possible, the breeding population of Kingfishers in the county may number in the region of 50–200 pairs. This broadly coincides with the figure of *c.* 190–210 pairs derived using a recent BTO estimate of the proportion of the national population (Musgrove *et al.*, 2013) occurring within Cambridgeshire.

During the winter, the species was reported from 168 (17%) tetrads, with the overall pattern of records showing considerable similarity with the breeding-season distribution, as might be expected for a relatively sedentary species. The most notable differences were the apparent abandonment of Grafham Water and a potential expansion or redistribution in northern fenland. As in the breeding season, the vast majority of winter records related to just one or two birds, although three individuals were recorded in a handful of tetrads.

Comparison of the current breeding distribution with the previous Hunts Atlas (records from 62 tetrads) and Cambs Atlas (99 tetrads) shows a slight increase in the number of occupied tetrads. Compared with the Wintering Atlas 1981–84 (Lack, 1986), the current winter distribution also appears to be more extensive, with a net gain of six 10-km squares, particularly in northern fenland.

Nationally, the most recent estimate of the breeding population of Kingfishers in the UK is 3,800–6,400 pairs, which was derived from an initial estimate in the Breeding Atlas 1988–91 (Gibbons *et al.*, 1993) based on an approximate figure of 3–5 pairs per 10-km square, extrapolated forward (to 2009) using the WeBS/WBBS trend (Musgrove *et al.*, 2013). Officially, the long-term UK trend is described as 'fluctuating', with the species suffering severe mortality during harsh winters, but the WeBS/WBBS data show a general increase since the 1980s, when the population was at its most recent low (Baillie *et al.*, 2012).

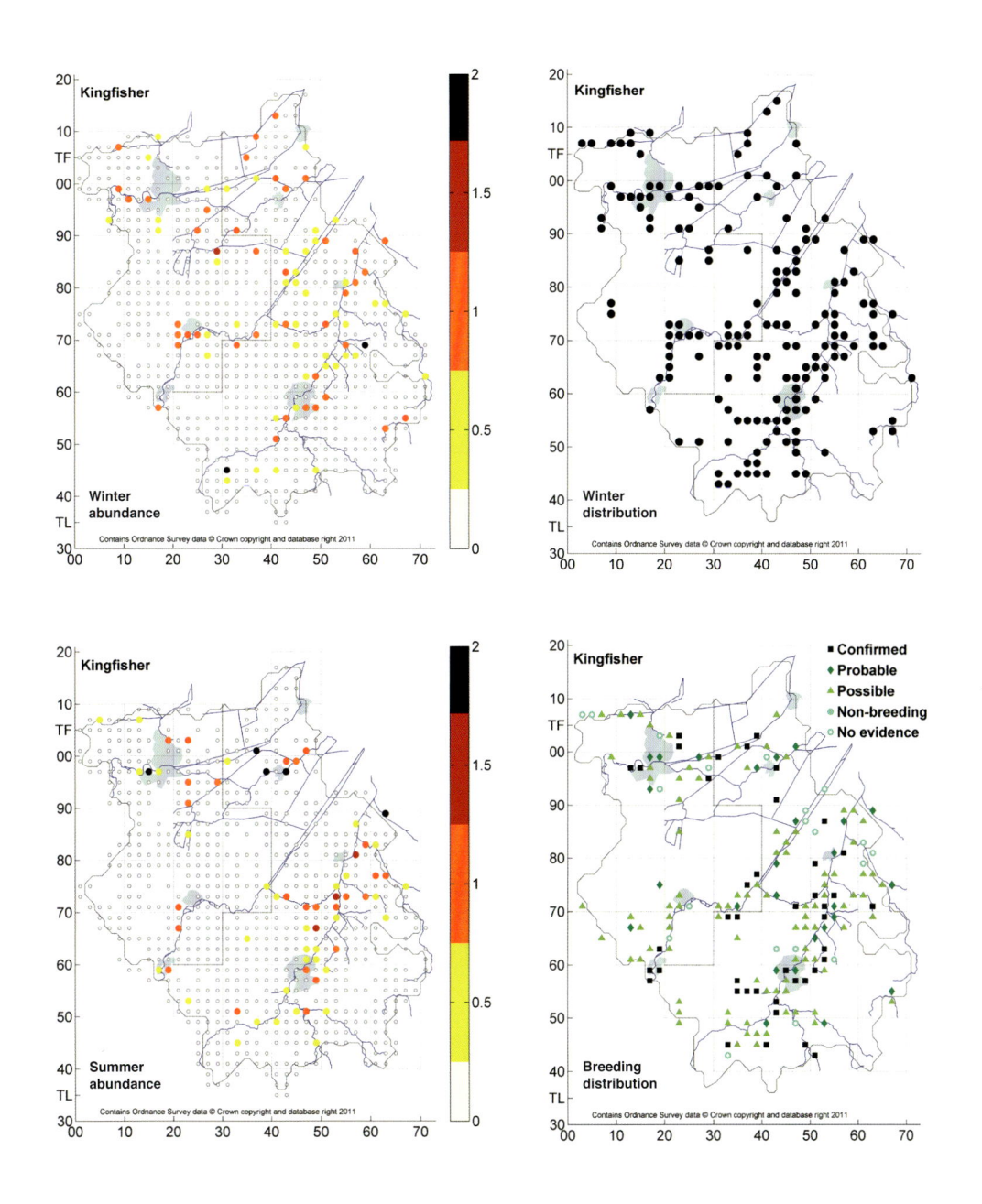

	Confirmed	Probable	Possible	Non-breeding	No evidence	Total summer (% county)	Total winter (% county)
Total tetrads	43	27	93	0	20	183 (19%)	168 (17%)

GREEN WOODPECKER (European Green Woodpecker)
Picus viridis
Amber List. Fairly common resident, widespread except in fenland

Breeding population estimate: 500-1,500 pairs
Wintering population estimate: 1,000-4,000 individuals

During the breeding season, Green Woodpeckers were reported from 670 (69%) tetrads, spread throughout the county but distributed more densely in the south and seemingly more sparsely in parts of the northern fens and less-wooded parts of the western clay plateau (e.g. to the north-west of Huntingdon). Breeding was confirmed in 24% of tetrads in which the species was recorded, with some evidence of potential breeding provided for 598 tetrads overall. The vast majority of breeding-season records related to between one and four individuals, but as many as 12–13 were reported from certain sites, including Hinchingbrooke Country Park and a tetrad (on the border with Bedfordshire) to the south-west of Gamlingay.

Based on an estimate of 1.5 pairs per occupied tetrad (Cambs Atlas), and the overall number of tetrads where breeding was confirmed, probable or possible, the breeding population of Green Woodpecker in the county now falls within the range 500–1,500 pairs; the density estimate used above may now be somewhat of an underestimate, due to this species' recent population expansion.

During the winter, Green Woodpeckers were reported from 591 (61%) tetrads, with the overall pattern of records broadly similar to the breeding-season distribution, the strip of fenland between Ramsey and Chatteris remaining a notable gap. Although the far-carrying 'yaffling' call is given by both sexes throughout much of the year, vocal activity is higher during the spring which probably partly explains the seemingly reduced distribution of this largely sedentary species during the winter. As in the breeding season, the vast majority of winter records related to one to four individuals, although up to 12 individuals were reported from a few sites.

Comparison of the current breeding distribution with the results from the previous Hunts Atlas (records from 153 tetrads) and Cambs Atlas (68 tetrads) shows an approximate tripling in the number of occupied tetrads. Compared with the Wintering Atlas in 1981–84 (Lack, 1986), the current winter distribution is also far more extensive, with a gain of 21 10-km squares, particularly in the fens.

Nationally, the most up-to-date estimate of the breeding population of Green Woodpecker in the UK is 52,000 (47,000–58,000) pairs, which was derived from an initial estimate by Newson *et al.* (2008), extrapolated forward (to 2009) using the BBS trend (Musgrove *et al.*, 2013). The long-term trend for the UK is a 115% increase during 1970–2010 (Eaton *et al.*, 2012), with the BBS trend for Eastern England an increase of 151% between 1995 and 2010 (Risely *et al.*, 2012).

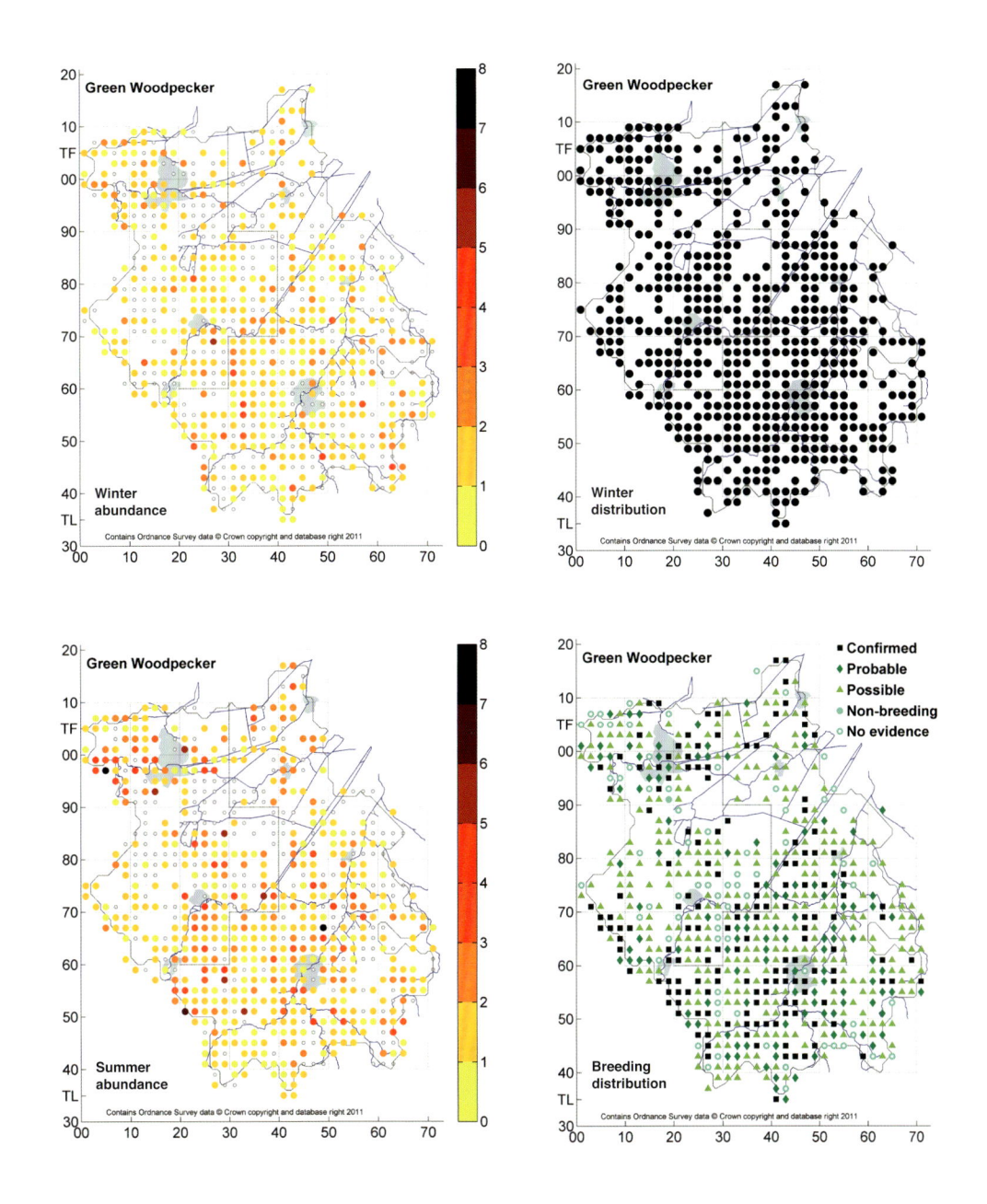

	Confirmed	Probable	Possible	Non-breeding	No evidence	Total summer (% county)	Total winter (% county)
Total tetrads	159	119	320	1	71	670 (69%)	591 (61%)

GREAT SPOTTED WOODPECKER *Dendrocopos major*
Green List. Fairly common, increased, resident, except in central fenland

Breeding population estimate: 250-1,000 pairs
Wintering population estimate: 500-3,000 individuals

During the breeding season, Great Spotted Woodpeckers were reported from 538 (56%) tetrads, spread throughout the county, but seemingly more sparsely distributed in the northern fens and in less-wooded parts of the western clay plateau (e.g. between Huntingdon and Peterborough). Breeding was confirmed in 28% of tetrads in which the species was recorded, with some evidence of potential breeding provided for 472 tetrads overall. The vast majority of breeding-season records related to between one and four individuals, although nine individuals were recorded during one hour in a tetrad near East Hatley, and five to eight birds were reported from a few other tetrads (including two tetrads within Monks Wood).

Based on an estimate of 1.5 pairs per occupied tetrad (Cambs Atlas), and the overall number of tetrads where breeding was confirmed, probable or possible, the breeding population of Great Spotted Woodpeckers in the county is probably now in the range 250–1,000 pairs.

During the winter, the species was reported from 584 (60%) tetrads, with the overall pattern of records broadly similar to the breeding-season distribution, albeit with an apparent expansion in parts of the northern fens (with the exception of the area between Ramsey and Chatteris, which remains a notable gap). As in the breeding season, the vast majority of winter records related to 1–4 individuals, although 8–10 individuals were reported from a few sites (e.g. Hinchingbrooke Country Park and Hatley Park).

Comparison of the current breeding distribution with the results from the previous Hunts Atlas (records from 140 tetrads) and Cambs Atlas (128 tetrads) shows an approximate doubling in the number of occupied tetrads. Compared with the Wintering Atlas in 1981–84 (Lack, 1986), the current winter distribution appears slightly more extensive, with a gain of five 10-km squares in the northern fens.

Nationally, the most up-to-date estimate of the breeding population of Great Spotted Woodpecker in the UK is 140,000 (130,000–150,000) pairs, which was derived from an initial estimate by Newson *et al.* (2008), extrapolated forward (to 2009) using the BBS trend (Musgrove *et al.*, 2013). The long-term trend for the UK is a 368% increase during 1970–2010 (Eaton *et al.*, 2012), with the BBS trend for Eastern England being an increase of 80% between 1995 and 2010 (Risely *et al.*, 2012).

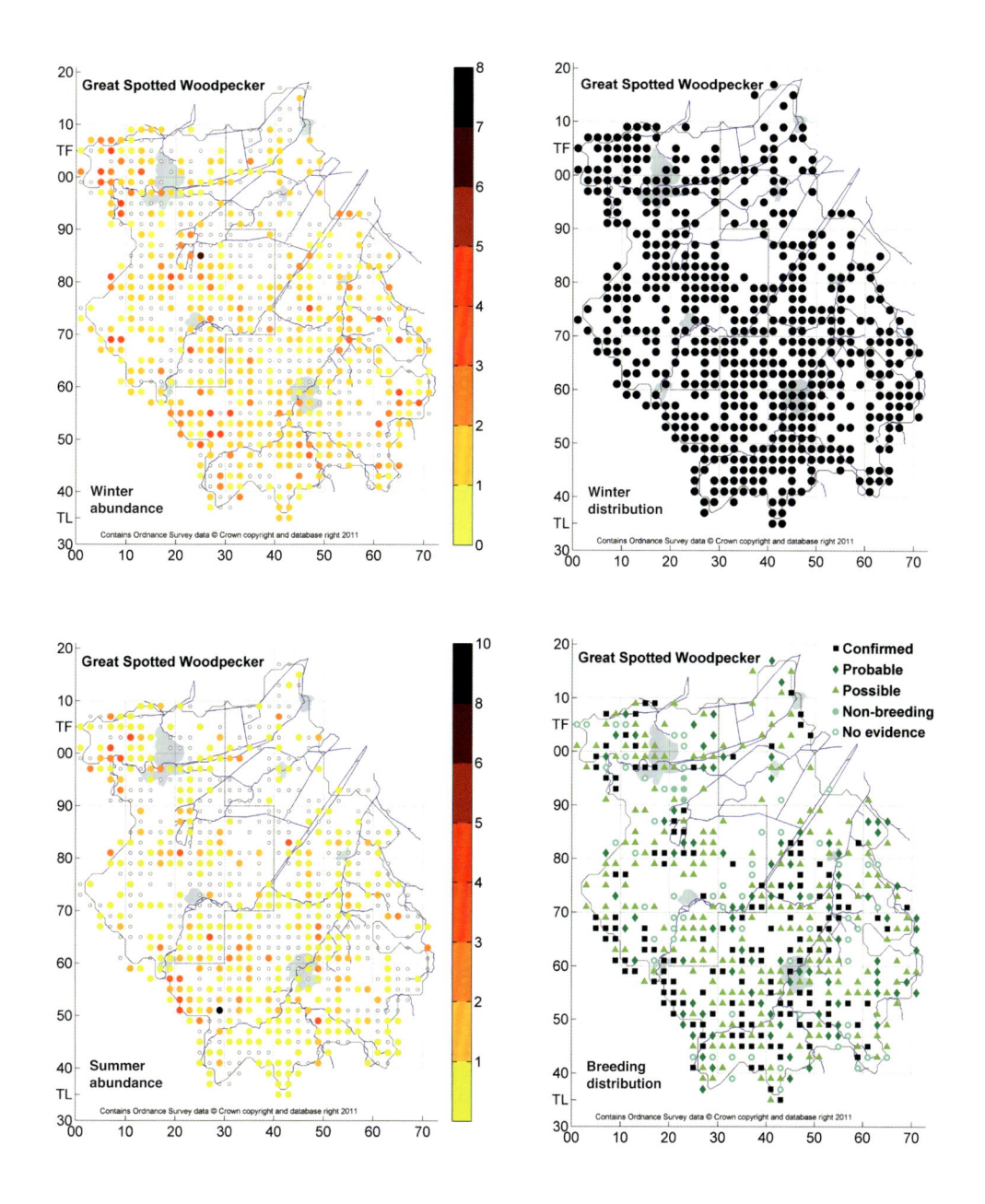

	Confirmed	Probable	Possible	Non-breeding	No evidence	Total summer (% county)	Total winter (% county)
Total tetrads	150	94	228	5	61	538 (56%)	584 (60%)

LESSER SPOTTED WOODPECKER *Dendrocopos minor*
Red List. Scarce resident, now very local after marked recent decline

Breeding population estimate: 5-15 pairs
Wintering population estimate: 10-35 individuals

During the breeding season, Lesser Spotted Woodpeckers were reported from 22 (2%) tetrads, confined to the west and south of the county, with a complete absence of records from the fens. Confirmation of breeding was provided for just two tetrads (in the Wimpole area and near Great Chishill), which probably reflects the secretive nature of this species, and the difficulty involved in detecting individuals following the typical burst of territorial activity during March and April (Charman et al., 2010). Although the records are not mapped here, breeding was also confirmed at Milton Park (Peterborough) during the atlas period (in 2008 and 2010, but not included in the table as a tetrad was not defined for this breeding record). In addition, probable breeding was reported for four tetrads (near Bedford Purlieus, Sawston Hall and two tetrads encompassing parts of Hinchingbrooke Country Park), with possible breeding reported for a further 11 tetrads (including three near Grafham Water, Monks Wood, St. Neots, Brampton and Waresley Wood). No breeding evidence was provided for the remaining five tetrads in which this species was present (e.g. Croxton Park). The majority of breeding-season records related to just one individual, although two to four individuals (the latter probably including fledged young) were reported from a small number of tetrads.

Based on an average of one pair per occupied tetrad, and the overall number of tetrads where breeding was confirmed, probable or possible, the breeding population of Lesser Spotted Woodpeckers in the county may now number as few as 5–15 pairs. This coincides fairly closely with the figure of c. 7–13 pairs derived using a recent BTO estimate of the proportion of the national population occurring within Cambridgeshire. A total of nine pairs was given for the county by the RBBP in their 2010 report (Holling et al., 2012).

During the winter, the species was reported from just 14 (1%) tetrads, with the overall distribution of records broadly similar to that during the breeding season, with apparent clusters to the west of Peterborough (e.g. Bedford Purlieus), near Monks Wood, in and around St. Neots (including Priory Park), and a few scattered records to the south of Cambridge (e.g. near Balsham). Although not attributable to a single tetrad (and hence not mapped here), there were also a number of winter records from Hinchingbrooke Country Park. As in the breeding season, the vast majority of winter records related to just one or two individuals.

Comparison of the current breeding distribution with the results from the previous Hunts Atlas (records from 117 tetrads) and Cambs Atlas (64 tetrads) reveals a severe (>80%) decline in the number of occupied tetrads. Compared with the Wintering Atlas in 1981–84 (Lack, 1986), the current winter distribution is also significantly reduced, with a net loss of 27 10-km squares (throughout the county, but particularly in the southern half). Nationally, the most recent estimate of the breeding population of Lesser Spotted Woodpeckers in the UK is 1,000–2,000 pairs, which was derived from an initial estimate in the 1988–91 Breeding Atlas (Gibbons et al., 1993), extrapolated forward (to 2009) using the long-term trend (Musgrove et al., 2013). In 2010 (the first year that they covered the species), records of 446 pairs were received by the RBBP (Holling et al., 2012).

The long-term trend for the UK is a 71% decline during 1970–2010 (Eaton et al., 2012), with the increasing scarcity of this species meaning that it is no longer monitored effectively by the BBS (Holling et al., 2012). Although the reasons for the decline remain unclear, a number of factors have been suggested, including the general loss of mature, open woodland and traditional orchards, potential changes in phenology – and hence breeding-season food availability – owing to climatic changes, and competition with the increasing population of Great Spotted Woodpeckers (Baillie et al., 2012; Charman et al., 2010; Jarman, 2012; Smith & Charman, 2012).

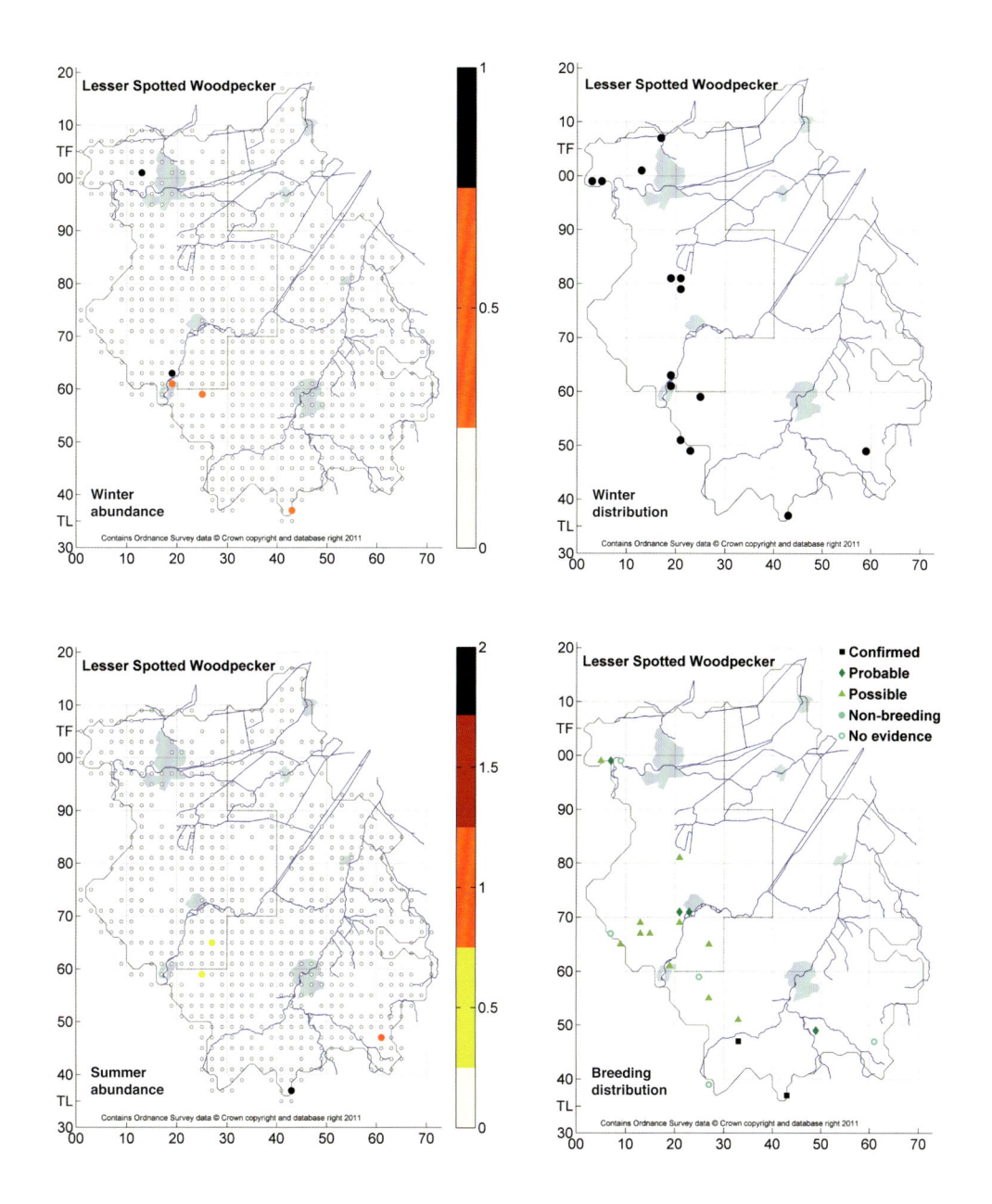

	Confirmed	Probable	Possible	Non-breeding	No evidence	Total summer (% county)	Total winter (% county)
Total tetrads	2	4	11	0	5	22 (2%)	14 (1%)

MAGPIE (Eurasian Magpie) *Pica pica*
Green List. **Common and widespread resident**

Breeding population estimate: 2,000-4,000 pairs
Wintering population estimate: 4,000-10,000 individuals

The Magpie is a common and widespread resident, well known in our cities and towns as well as in the countryside. The atlas fieldwork confirmed its presence throughout the county; it was recorded in 85% of TTVs in the breeding season and 91% in winter. Particularly high densities were recorded in the breeding season in Cambridge and some fen areas, such as south-east of Peterborough. The preference for urban areas is even more clear in winter, when Cambridge and Peterborough recorded the highest densities. Urban sites provide Magpies with protection from pest-control activity, a good range of nesting sites in tall trees, and plenty of food in gardens and streets. There are few gaps in their distribution but an area in central Huntingdonshire lacks Magpies in both the breeding season and winter, possibly as a consequence of land-management approaches. Clark (1996) reported that Magpies were remarkably scarce in the old county of Huntingdonshire in the 1970s. That population recovered during the 1980s and 1990s. The previous Cambs Atlas showed large gaps in the fens. However, already at that time the species had increased substantially over the previous decades.

Magpie nests are relatively obvious and observers will often notice nest-building behaviour. Nevertheless, breeding was confirmed or found probable only in 354, or 37% of all tetrads throughout the county, a figure similar to the previous Cambs Atlas (38%) but double that of the Hunts Atlas (18%). In winter, Magpies may form small flocks and roam more widely, as reflected by the high number of birds recorded during TTVs, an average of 2.3 birds per hour, compared with 1.6 birds per hour during the breeding season.

Magpies are widely distributed over England, Wales and southern Scotland, with the highest densities found in the southern parts of the country. According to atlas data, Cambridgeshire has 1.4% of the national population in the breeding season and 1.6% during winter. The long-term national trend is highly positive, with an estimated 97% increase from 1970 to 2010 (Risely *et al.*, 2012), while the population seems stable in the shorter term (1995–2010).

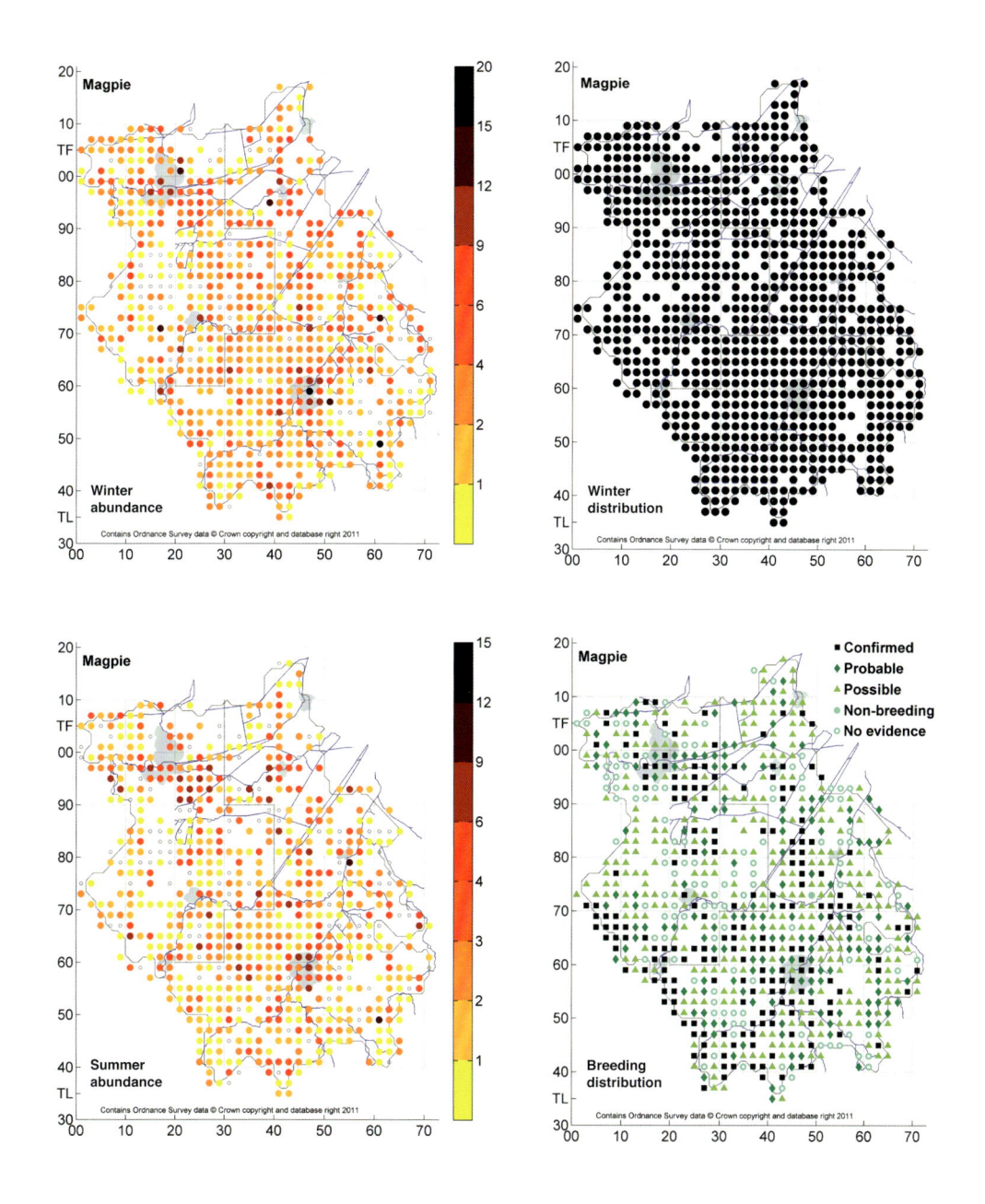

	Confirmed	Probable	Possible	Non-breeding	No evidence	Total summer (% county)	Total winter (% county)
Total tetrads	196	158	311	1	117	783 (81%)	828 (85%)

JAY (Eurasian Jay) *Garrulus glandarius*
Green List. Fairly common resident; some autumn influxes

Breeding population estimate: 500-1,000 pairs
Wintering population estimate: 1,000-2,500 individuals

The Jay is predominantly a woodland species, widely distributed throughout the UK, in particular in England and Wales but less common in Scotland. Atlas data suggest that Cambridgeshire holds 1.1% of the breeding population and 1.2% of the wintering population in the UK, perhaps more than expected for a county with very little tree cover. In the breeding season, Jays were found in 30% of TTVs, with gaps in particular in the fens and also the western clay plateau. Higher densities were recorded in and around Cambridge, to the west of Peterborough, Ely, along the river Cam, and at and around Wicken Fen and Woodwalton Fen. All those areas provide small woodlands or large gardens where Jays can breed. Confirmed breeding records come also, as expected, from the more wooded areas in the west of the county. Confirmation of breeding is not easy, as birds roam widely in search of food; many breeding-season records refer to possible breeding only. In total, breeding was found probable or confirmed in only 95 (10%) tetrads, a similar figure to that of the previous Cambs Atlas (11%), but much lower than in the Hunts Atlas (27%). Absence from most of the fens was also recorded by the previous county atlases, with Wicken Fen noted as an exception. It seems that this species is slightly more widespread now than in the 1970s and 1980s.

In winter, Jays are more widespread than in the breeding season, with records during TTVs in 40% of surveyed tetrads. The areas of higher densities are similar to those in the breeding season, again with large gaps in the fens and in the west and south of the county. The number of birds recorded per hour during TTVs was twice as high in winter (0.36) than in the breeding season (0.19) but is overall rather low, as expected for a species that rarely occurs in flocks.

The national population has shown a slight increase both in the long term (1970–2010) and during the last 15 years (1995–2010). This seems to align well with the situation in our county (Risely *et al.*, 2012).

British Jays are sedentary so we can expect that the winter population in Cambridgeshire is made up mainly of local birds. The extent to which foreign Jays form part of the winter population is not known. In some years there are apparent influxes of northern European Jays into the UK (Brown & Grice, 2005; Wernham *et al.*, 2002) (as seemed to be the case most recently in the autumn of 2012), but in most years it is unlikely that more than a tiny proportion of our wintering Jays originates from the Continent. The Migration Atlas (Wernham *et al.*, 2002) noted the complete lack of recovery of foreign-ringed Jays in the UK and Ireland.

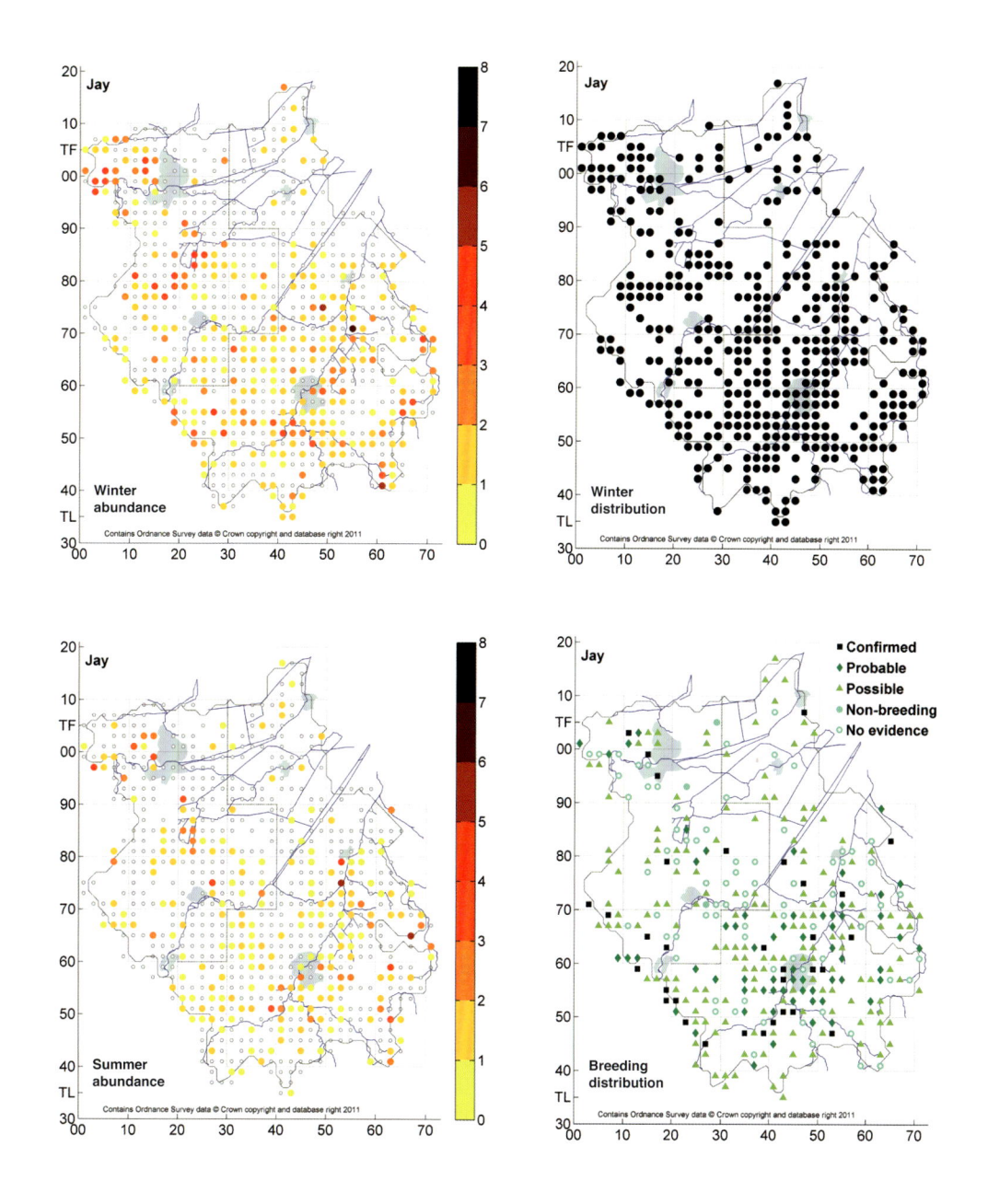

	Confirmed	Probable	Possible	Non-breeding	No evidence	Total summer (% county)	Total winter (% county)
Total tetrads	33	62	166	3	76	340 (35%)	416 (43%)

JACKDAW (Western Jackdaw) *Corvus monedula*
Green List. Very common and widespread resident, winter visitor and passage migrant

Breeding population estimate: 10,000-20,000 pairs
Wintering population estimate: 25,000-50,000 individuals

The Jackdaw is a familiar bird of our towns and villages, often nesting in chimneys and visiting bird tables in gardens. It is widely distributed in the county in both the breeding season and in winter. The atlas maps show some gaps, in particular in the breeding season in the open fens, where buildings or trees providing nest sites might be missing. The maps for the breeding season and winter are rather similar, with the species recorded on 84% of TTVs in the breeding season and 83% in winter. 52% of atlas records refer to probable or confirmed breeding; nesting evidence is relatively easy to obtain by watching birds entering nesting sites. With different definitions of probable and confirmed breeding, the previous Cambs Atlas found breeding evidence in 33% of tetrads and the Hunts Atlas in 49%.

The gregarious nature of Jackdaws outside the breeding season is reflected in the much higher average encounter rate during TTVs in winter (13 birds per hour) as opposed to during the breeding season, although with 5.6 birds per hour it is still a common bird. Jackdaws tend to forage in flocks outside the breeding season, often with Rooks, and form huge roosts. Even casual observers will have noticed the stream of birds over our towns and villages and in the open countryside before or at dusk, flying to pre-roost gathering sites and to woodland roosts.

The previous county atlases show much larger gaps in Jackdaw distribution in the breeding season, in particular in the fens; it seems that this species has increased in abundance and extended its range in the county. Jackdaws are common throughout England, Wales and southern and eastern Scotland and atlas data suggest that Cambridgeshire holds 1.4% of the national breeding population and 1.8% of the winter population.

Nationally, Jackdaw numbers have increased between 1970 and 2010, by an estimated 131%, and in the shorter term (1995–2010) this trend has continued with a 44% increase (Risely *et al.*, 2012). This is not surprising given that Jackdaws are highly adaptable to changes in urban and rural landscapes.

The higher wintering than breeding population in the county indicates an influx of birds from elsewhere, presumably including birds from the Continent. It is well known that continental birds form part of the national winter population of Jackdaws and ringing recoveries show these birds to originate from Scandinavia and the Netherlands. Occasionally, birds showing characteristics of the eastern or northern European subspecies (*soemmerringii* and *monedula*, respectively; our birds belong to the subspecies *spermologus*) are recognised in the county but an exact allocation to subspecies is difficult.

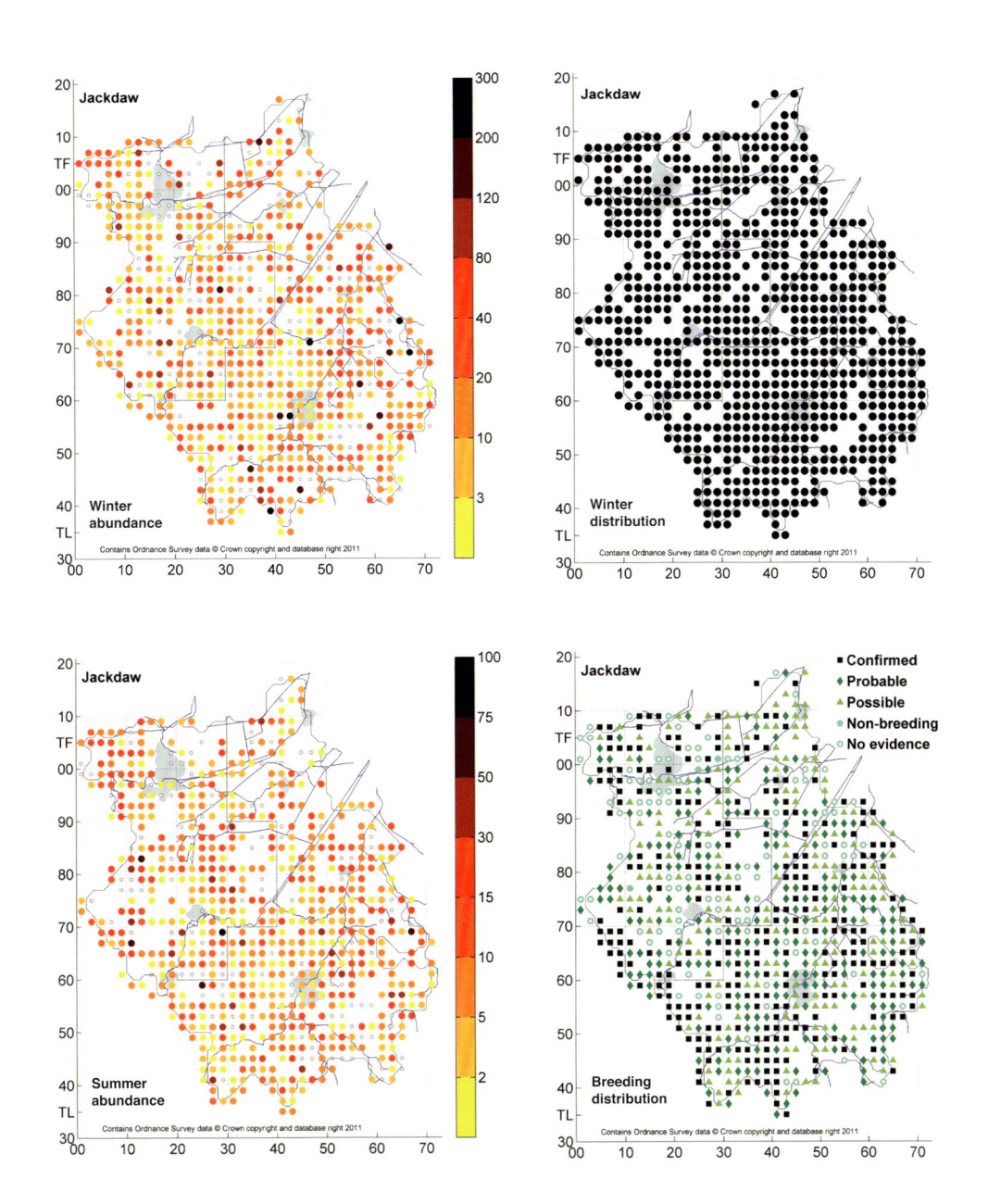

	Confirmed	Probable	Possible	Non-breeding	No evidence	Total summer (% county)	Total winter (% county)
Total tetrads	281	227	191	3	98	800 (83%)	782 (81%)

ROOK *Corvus frugilegus*
Green List. Very common and widespread resident

Breeding population estimate: 20,000-30,000 pairs
Wintering population estimate: 40,000-60,000 individuals

The Rook is a common and widespread resident bird of our villages and the open countryside, often forming large and conspicuous flocks that include many Jackdaws. It was recorded in 71% of breeding-season TTVs, with some gaps in the northern half of the county, in the fens and the western clay plateau. These gaps presumably mirror the lack of suitable stands of trees for nesting. With rookeries an obvious feature of our countryside, the number of tetrads with probable and confirmed breeding records is 377, or 39% of all tetrads. With a different definition of probable or confirmed breeding, the corresponding figure from the previous Hunts Atlas was similar (42%) but was much lower in the Cambs Atlas at 27%.

The gaps in distribution are still obvious, but to a smaller extent, in winter, when the encounter rate during TTVs increased to 80%. Atlas data suggest that Cambridgeshire holds 1.7% of the national population during the breeding season. The species is widely distributed throughout England, Wales, and southern and eastern Scotland, concentrated in agricultural areas where birds have easy access to food.

With an average of 26 birds per hour, the encounter rate during TTVs was much higher in winter than in the breeding season (9.7 birds per hour), reflecting their more pronounced gregarious behaviour outside the breeding season. At 2.7% the proportion of the national population to be found in winter in the county is quite high.

During the previous atlases, Rooks were largely absent from the fens and some areas in central Huntingdonshire and south-east Cambridgeshire. It was found that the species had undergone a strong decline due to the loss of nesting sites in elms to Dutch Elm disease, the loss of grassland to cultivation and the large-scale use of pesticides in the post-World War II decades (Clark, 1996). Easy (1996) documented the decline of this species in old Cambridgeshire. Counts of Rook nests in the fens and south Cambridgeshire plummeted from 11,000 in 1944/45 to just 4,200 in 1989 but recovered to 6,600 in 1995. Obviously, the gaps found by the previous atlases have now been filled to a good extent and the species is much more common than 20 or 30 years ago.

It is worrying, though, that BBS data show a national decline of 16% from 1995 to 2010 (Risely et al., 2012) (no long-term trend data are available). It is not clear whether this is reflected in the county. The CBC undertook a census of rookeries in 2010 but this remained incomplete so no full comparison with Easy's (1996) data is possible; these data are incorporated into the present atlas. It is hoped that more complete rookery surveys can be undertaken in the future in order to detect any problems that the species might encounter.

The winter flocks of Rooks in the county consist mainly of local resident birds, likely to be enriched by birds from other regions in the UK and abroad. Ringing recoveries show a winter influx of birds into the UK from western and eastern Europe but this seems to have become less regular with more continental birds wintering nearer to their breeding areas recently due to milder winters.

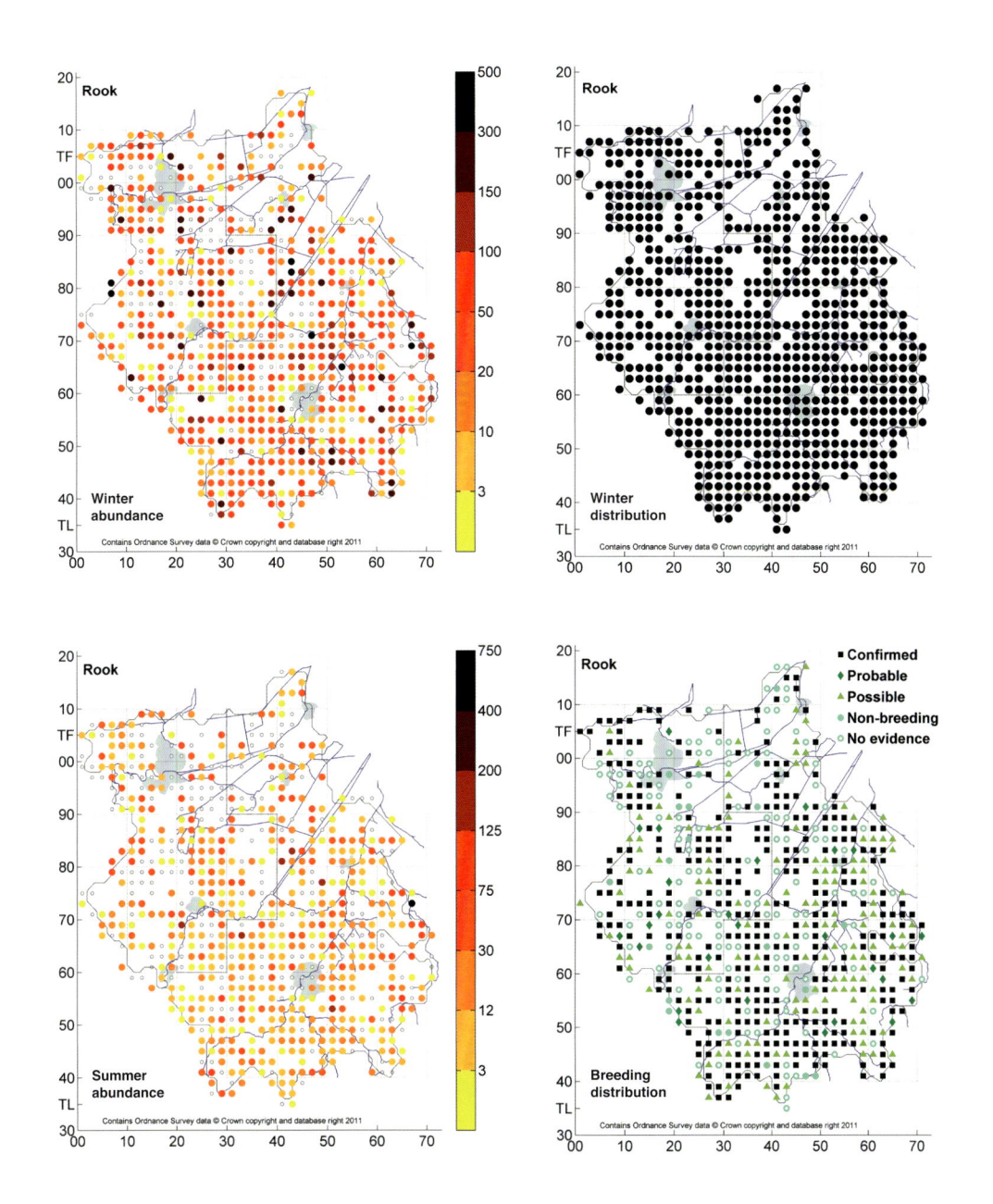

	Confirmed	Probable	Possible	Non-breeding	No evidence	Total summer (% county)	Total winter (% county)
Total tetrads	350	27	153	21	141	692 (71%)	749 (77%)

CARRION CROW *Corvus corone*
Green List. Common, increased resident and winter visitor

Breeding population estimate: 5,000-10,000 pairs
Wintering population estimate: 10,000-30,000 individuals

The Carrion Crow is a very common and widespread resident species, inhabiting both urban and open countryside habitats. Carrion Crows were recorded during TTVs in 95% and 98% of the surveyed tetrads in the breeding season and winter, respectively. The species occurs throughout the county, in all landscapes, with no apparent differences between the breeding season and winter. It is difficult to make out areas with lower densities but this may be the case for the fens, perhaps due to a lack of trees as nesting sites. Throughout the county, probable or confirmed breeding was found in 57% of all tetrads, the corresponding figures being 43% and 63%, respectively, for the previous Cambs Atlas and Hunts Atlas.

With 4.3 birds per hour, the average encounter rate during TTVs was lower in the breeding season than in winter (6.4 birds per hour), when Carrion Crows can form small flocks. Being an extremely sedentary species, it is unlikely that the winter population in the county includes a significant number of birds originating from further afield.

The previous atlases recorded the Carrion Crow much less regularly, with gaps in the breeding season apparent in the south-east of old Cambridgeshire, in the fens and in the Peterborough area. The Cambs Atlas noted a decrease compared to the 1968–72 National Atlas, which clearly has been reversed. The birds' ability to settle in all kinds of habitat as long as there are trees for nesting together with a possible decrease in control measures seem to be the most likely reasons for their range expansion and increase in numbers. This is in line with the national picture: the long-term trend shows an 89% increase from 1970 to 2010 (Eaton *et al.*, 2012) and a 10% increase from 1995 to 2010 (Risely *et al.*, 2012).

Nationally, densities are highest in England and Wales, with slightly higher figures in the low-lying more pastoral western English and Welsh landscapes.

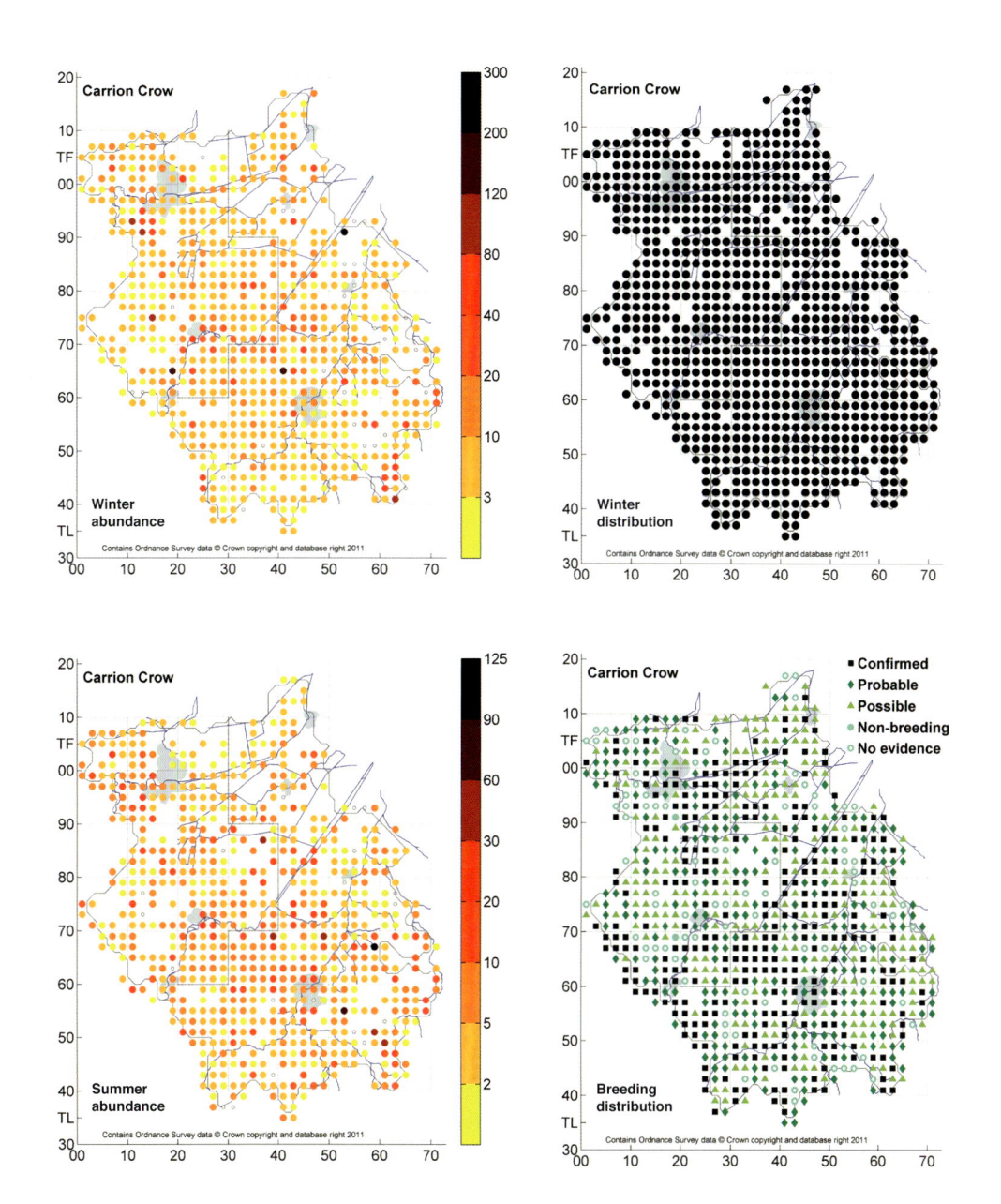

	Confirmed	Probable	Possible	Non-breeding	No evidence	Total summer (% county)	Total winter (% county)
Total tetrads	304	247	262	2	89	904 (93%)	890 (92%)

RAVEN (Northern Raven) *Corvus corax*
Green List. Scarce visitor of British or continental origin

Not a breeding species
Wintering population estimate: 1-5 records annually

The Raven was once a widespread species in the UK, breeding in the early 19th century in most counties but subsequently suffering local extinction in many southern areas due to persecution. There is limited evidence for historic breeding in Cambridgeshire and Peterborough from the first half of the 19th century. The UK stronghold by the mid-20th century was Wales but parts of England and most of Scotland were also inhabited. A slow recovery occurred throughout the 20th century and this has reached Cambridgeshire, with an increasing number of sightings over the past decade and breeding occurring in some of our neighbouring counties.

During the atlas fieldwork, ten records were submitted in the breeding season and five in winter, all from the western parts of the county or just into the fens. While these birds are presumed to be non-breeding visitors originating from neighbouring breeding populations, breeding in the area west of Peterborough or close to the Bedfordshire border cannot be ruled out as Ravens breed early and these areas have several inaccessible, private woodlands. However, the increase in records suggests that we can expect the Raven to nest once again in the county in the near future, with the woodlands in the western parts of Cambridgeshire providing potentially suitable nesting habitat.

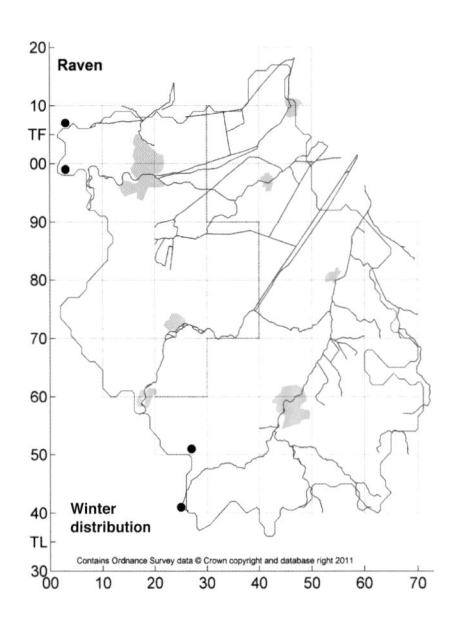

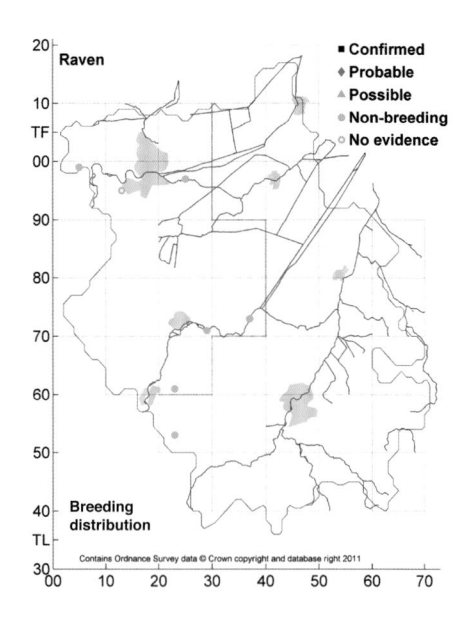

	Confirmed	Probable	Possible	Non-breeding	No evidence	Total summer (% county)	Total winter (% county)
Total tetrads	0	0	0	6	1	7 (1%)	4 (0.4%)

FIRECREST (Common Firecrest) *Regulus ignicapilla*
Amber List. Scarce annual passage migrant, and rare breeder

Breeding population estimate: 1-10 territorial males
Wintering population estimate: 1-10 individuals

Firecrests are scarce birds in Cambridgeshire, records comprise a very restricted mix of winter visitors, passage migrants and summer visitors. Breeding is very occasionally confirmed or suspected; Firecrest bred in the southern part of the county during the atlas period, this location was withheld and is not mapped. Brown & Grice (2005) show a continuing rise in the breeding population in England and the population in Norfolk and Suffolk is increasing, so it is likely that occurrences of this species will become more frequent. For records of breeding activity, males singing on migration are difficult to tell apart from males taking up territory, but repeated singing at the same location would provide stronger evidence (many of the possible/probable breeders in the table could be lone singing males). Firecrest is likely to be very elusive as a breeding species, so any activity beyond singing would require luck or many hours in the field.

Wintering birds seemed, as for Goldcrest, much scarcer in the second half of the atlas period when the winters were harsher; most Firecrest records were from the second winter and none from the final winter. Records were received from six tetrads in winter.

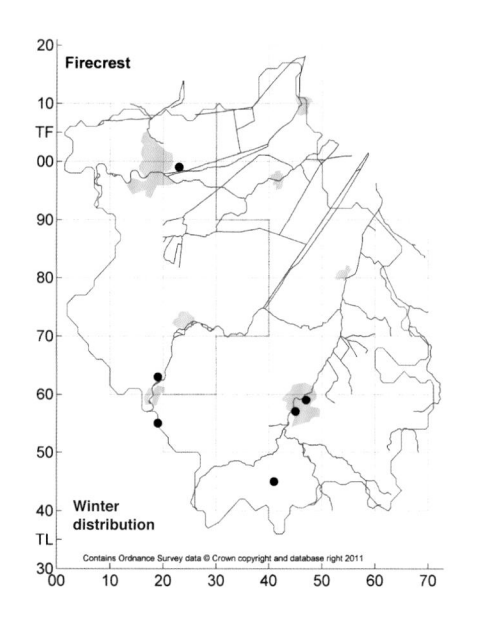

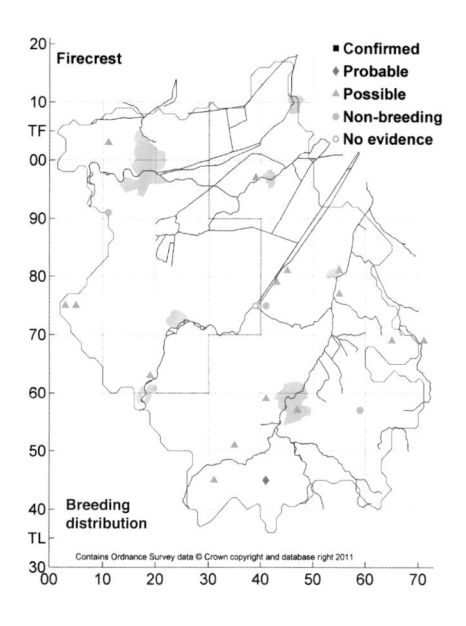

	Confirmed	Probable	Possible	Non-breeding	No evidence	Total summer (% county)	Total winter (% county)
Total tetrads	0	1	15	3	1	20 (2%)	6 (1%)

GOLDCREST *Regulus regulus*
Green List. Common, but local, resident; widespread autumn passage migrant and winter visitor

Breeding population estimate: 500-1,000 pairs
Wintering population estimate: 1,000-2,500 individuals

The Goldcrest has a breeding distribution strongly biased towards the villages and woods to the west and south of Cambridge, in wooded or breck-like areas on the south-eastern edge of the county, and in wooded and parkland zones to the west of Peterborough. It is not absent from the fens, but is encountered far less frequently, and is probably tied to towns or villages with suitable (usually coniferous) woodland or parkland habitat. In winter, Goldcrest distribution is wider: woodland birds tend to be more noticeable in winter when the trees are bare, and in most winters the resident population is supplemented by birds from further north in the UK and from the continent.

Recording Goldcrests is laden with pitfalls – their high-pitched call and song is difficult or impossible for a significant proportion of birdwatchers to hear and relying on visual clues to their presence makes recording and particularly providing breeding evidence difficult. This may have led to an element of under-recording, although the roving distributions in winter and summer probably fairly represent the species in the county. Hard winters always impact small birds, and Goldcrests are likely to suffer in prolonged cold weather. It is possible that the total number of records per winter provide evidence of this with 236, 282, 77 and 124 records of Goldcrest in the four winters of the atlas period; the third winter was the hardest, and the first two were notably mild.

BTO national population trends suggest a slight decline over the last five years but in the medium term the population seems to be stable. BBS data show a 15-year trend (1995–2010) of -15% for the UK, 5% for England and 23% for Eastern England (Risely *et al.*, 2012).

In the previous atlases there were breeding season records in 100 tetrads (Cambs Atlas) and 96 (Hunts Atlas), making a total of approximately 21% of the modern county; this is only slightly lower than the current 25% of tetrads in the breeding season.

National ringing results show that many of our wintering Goldcrests come from the near Continent but some travel from as far as Eastern Europe. There is also evidence of birds moving further south to France and Iberia.

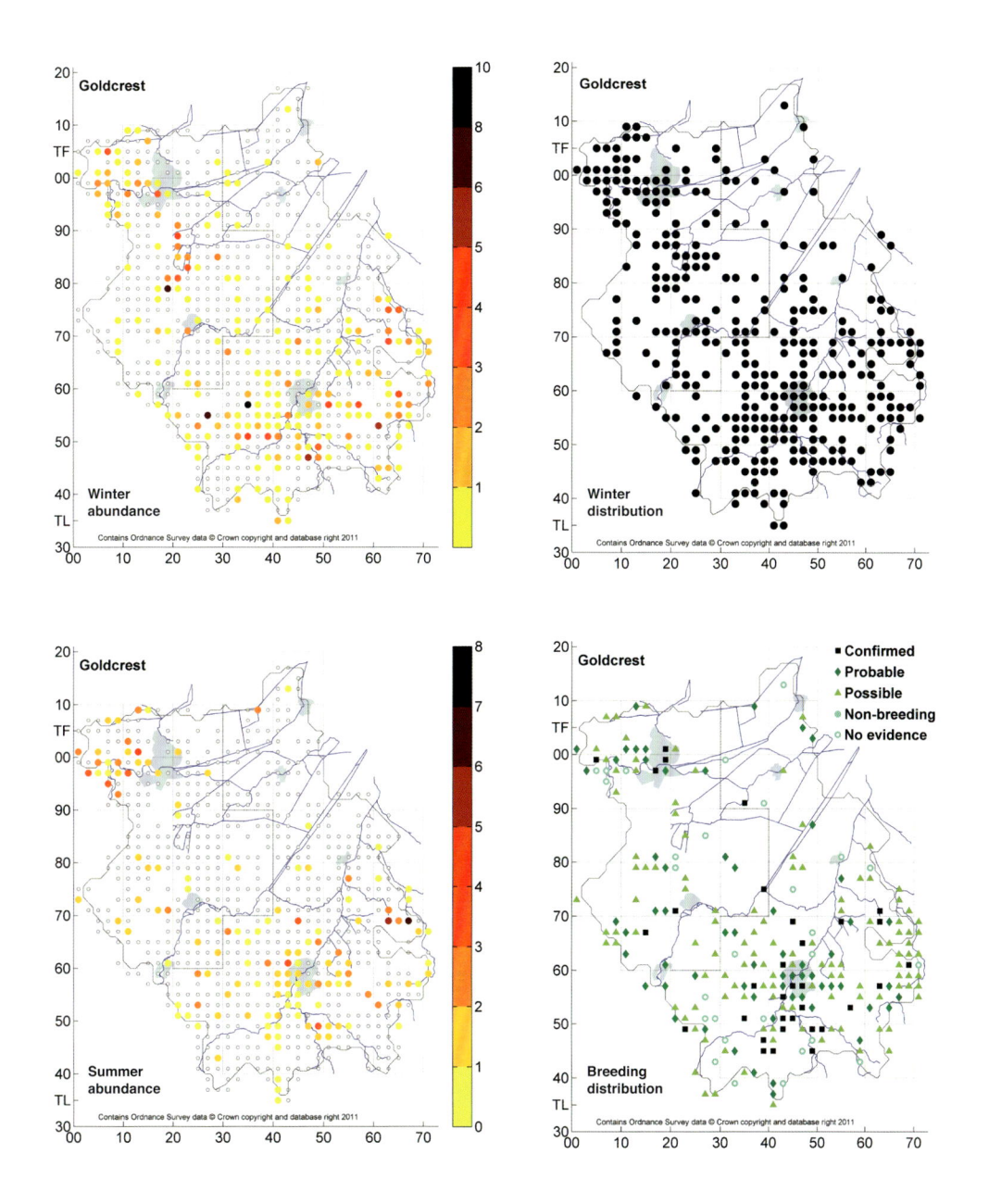

	Confirmed	Probable	Possible	Non-breeding	No evidence	Total summer (% county)	Total winter (% county)
Total tetrads	33	62	120	0	28	243 (25%)	337 (35%)

BLUE TIT *Cyanistes caeruleus*
Green List. Abundant and widespread resident

Breeding population estimate: 30,000-60,000 pairs
Wintering population estimate: 50,000-150,000 individuals

The Blue Tit is the most common member of the tit family, and has the least demanding requirements – a small patch of trees, scrub, gardens or a thick hedgerow with a few taller trees will suffice. The few gaps on the maps reflect either totally treeless tracts of the fens, or areas with no coverage. For example, the lack of records from the western part of Peterborough in both seasons coincides with an absence of records for other species that are probably present. Parts of remote farmed fenland are likely genuinely to lack Blue Tits in both winter and summer. A small number of nil returns came from TTVs in the south-eastern corner of the county, where some large estates are managed as studs or prairie-style agriculture and the woods are privately owned and inaccessible.

The density of Blue Tits is highest in the north-west of the county, between Peterborough and the Northamptonshire boundary, but the western and southern part of the county in general has a high population density, including urban areas. Blue Tits probably breed almost everywhere they occur in summer, but confirmed breeding was recorded from just over half of occupied tetrads. With 959 confirmed breeding records (some tetrads had multiple records of confirmed breeding), it is possible to see which behaviours are used most commonly by observers. All of the possible confirmed breeding categories were used except 'distraction display' (not Blue Tit behaviour); 'used nest' was recorded on just three occasions, whereas 606 records related to 'fledged young'. Despite their readiness to use nest boxes, and the widespread availability of such, records relating to nests represented only 28% of confirmed breeding records. 'Adult carrying faecal sac or food' was recorded 86 times.

Blue Tit distribution has not changed since the previous two atlases; the fens have always been a poor area for this species. Interestingly, the area of Peterborough with no records in this work also lacked records in the Hunts Atlas. Nationally, Blue Tits are increasing, and this rate of increase is highest in the eastern region; in Cambridgeshire, BBS squares show an increase in both occupancy and density.

The highest counts during the breeding season came from two tetrads in Monks Wood: TL18V had 58 and TL28A had 50; both counts came from TTVs on 13th June 2008, when there would have been many fledged young present. Aversley Wood, which straddles four tetrads in TL18 had a winter roving record of 90 Blue Tits.

In the winter period, Blue Tits were recorded in 869 tetrads (90%), and 50 10-km squares (98%), with no records from the Cambridgeshire part of peripheral square TF31.

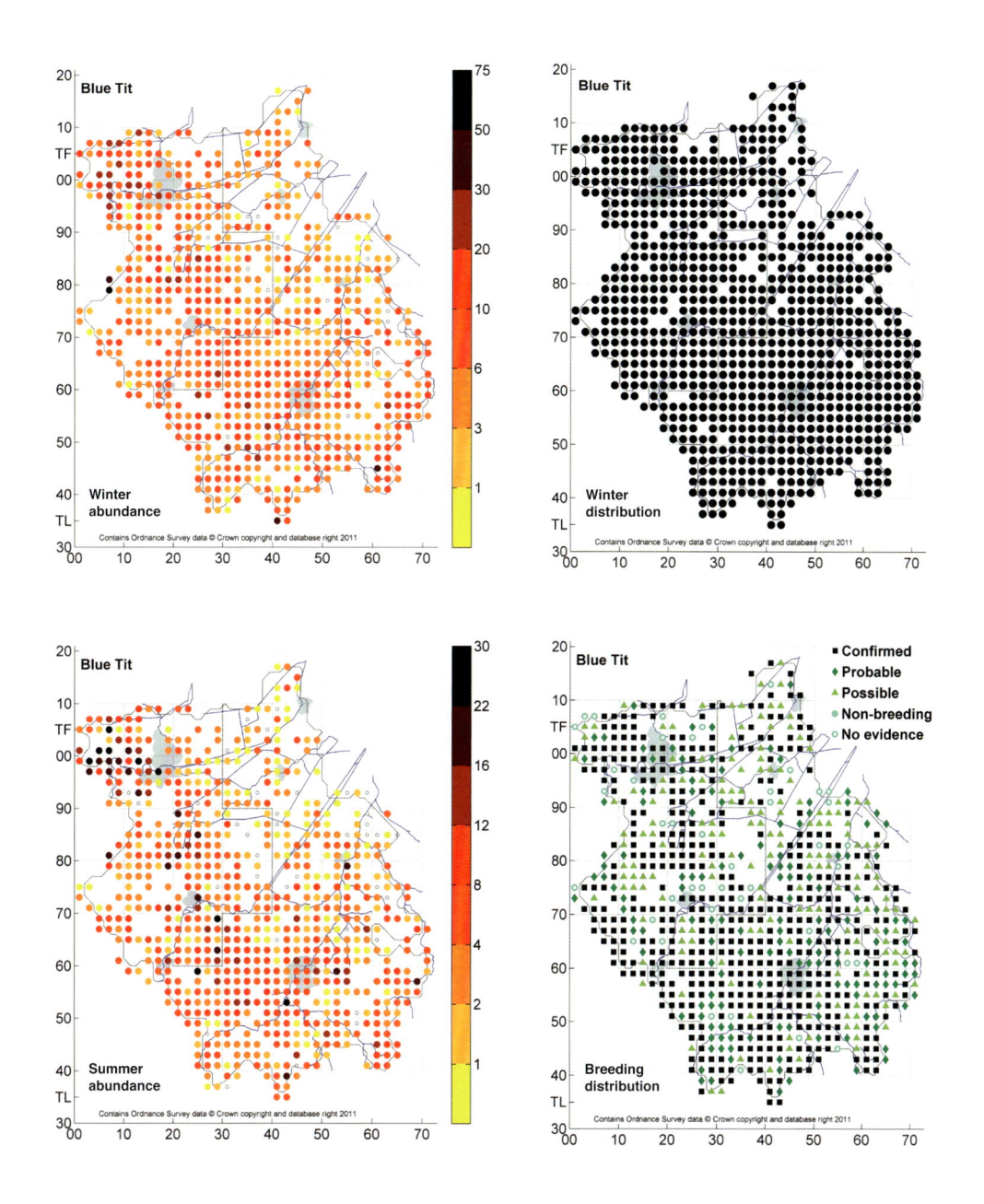

	Confirmed	Probable	Possible	Non-breeding	No evidence	Total summer (% county)	Total winter (% county)
Total tetrads	479	148	175	0	43	845 (87%)	869 (90%)

GREAT TIT *Parus major*
Green List. Abundant and widespread resident

Breeding population estimate: 25,000-50,000 pairs
Wintering population estimate: 50,000-150,000 individuals

The distribution of the Great Tit is very similar to that of the Blue Tit; the two species occupy the same broad mix of habitats with an element of tree cover. Great Tits are fractionally less abundant and widespread, with 2–3% fewer TTV visits recording this species.

This species is very easy to observe in all seasons and breeding activity is also conspicuous, particularly the presence of noisy fledged broods in the early summer. Hence, the maps are likely to be a good reflection of the distribution of this species. A total of 3,747 summer records of Great Tit were received (slightly more than the winter period) but effort was not uniformly distributed. There are some conspicuous gaps: the west-Huntingdon tetrad TL27G was not visited for a TTV; roving records were submitted but with no confirmed breeding. In fact, it appears that no Great Tits bred anywhere in the town. This illustrates the effects of local variations in recording effort during the atlas.

There has been a detectable increase in occupancy of old Cambridgeshire since the Cambs Atlas, but little change since the earlier Hunts Atlas. The main factor leading to the increase in old Cambridgeshire is a consolidation of the previous distribution.

BBS data show this species to be increasing both nationally (46% increase for 1995–2010) and regionally (30% in Eastern England over the same time period) while locally it has increased from 55% to 80% of Cambridgeshire BBS squares, and more than doubled in density of birds per square during this time (Risely *et al.*, 2012).

In the summer period, the highest counts were of 40 birds – a count achieved on three separate visits to Hinchingbrooke CP in TL27, and on one TTV visit to TL36G (Overhall Grove & Knapwell). Aversley Wood, in TL18, spans four tetrads, but one winter visit there recorded 60 Great Tits, while the highest tetrad count was of 47 from TL34E. Winter TTV counts of 37 were recorded from TL25S and TL34E.

In the winter period, Great Tits were recorded in 841 tetrads (87%), and 50 10-km squares (no county records from the peripheral TF31).

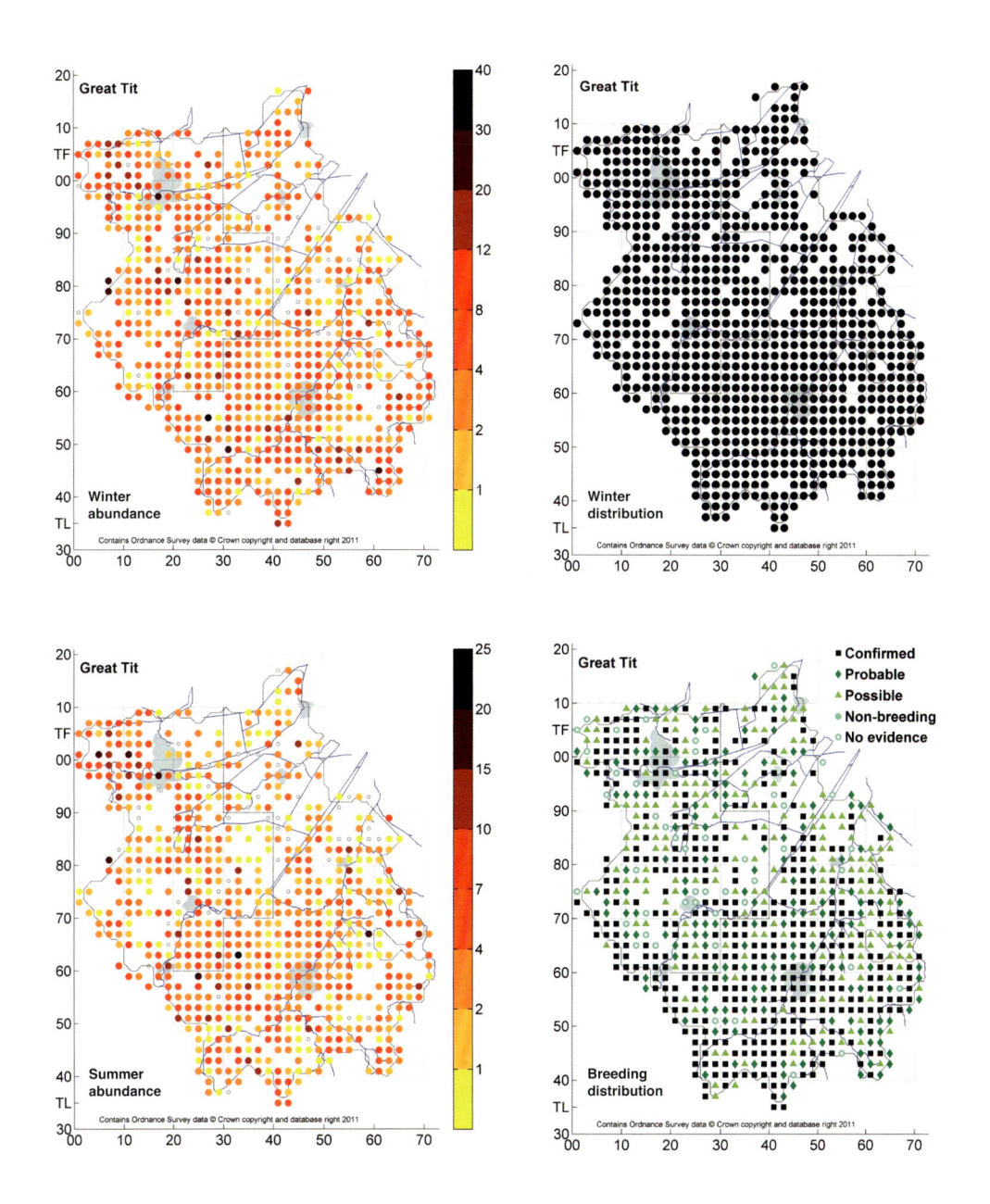

	Confirmed	Probable	Possible	Non-breeding	No evidence	Total summer (% county)	Total winter (% county)
Total tetrads	421	163	207	0	48	839 (87%)	841 (87%)

COAL TIT *Periparus ater*
Green List. Fairly common, but local, resident; occasional influxes

Breeding population estimate: 1,000-2,000 pairs
Wintering population estimate: 2,000-5,000 individuals

Coal Tits are strongly associated with coniferous woodland. They also breed in mixed woodland, well-wooded gardens and broadleaved woodland, but at a much lower density due to the dominance of Blue Tits and Great Tits which are stronger competitors for food and nest sites in those habitats. In the winter months, they are more mobile than the other tits, probably a behavioural adaptation to the unpredictable winter food supplies of their ancestral coniferous woodland habitat. In Cambridgeshire they are most abundant in the south-eastern woods, many of which have undergone a certain amount of coniferisation, but they occur throughout the wooded areas of the county. The fens are largely lacking in Coal Tits although there are a few scattered records, particularly from the edge of towns such as March and Wisbech. Even in their strongholds, Coal Tits were not found in every tetrad; their distribution is quite patchy, reflecting large areas without suitable woodland.

Coal Tits can be quiet and unobtrusive, with the birds spending much of their time in the tree canopy. It is possible that this species was overlooked on some site visits, but there are no identification difficulties and breeding behaviour, particularly family parties and adults carrying food, is fairly easy to observe, so the maps are considered to be an accurate reflection of the current distribution. Their distribution is relatively unchanged since the previous two county atlases.

Coal Tits have been increasing steadily in the UK; BBS data suggest a 17% increase since 1995 (Risely *et al.*, 2012). Although they only occur on a few Cambridgeshire BBS squares, both the proportion occupied and the density per square in our county show increasing trends. This may result from a combination of factors, such as food provision in gardens, milder winters, and increasing woodland cover, but as a species of no conservation concern there is little research to explain these trends.

The highest summer count was of 20 birds in TL28A (Monks Wood); this was at the end of May and could have included fledged young. Three winter visits also had counts of 20, one of which was from Monks Wood (TL18V) and the other two from separate visits to Hinchingbrooke Country Park (TL27). As this species can have fledged young during May, only timed counts made in April will truly reflect the number of pairs present. The highest April TTV count was of eight in TL25A, in the Gamlingay area.

In the winter period, Coal Tits were recorded in 227 tetrads (23%), and 41 10-km squares (80%).

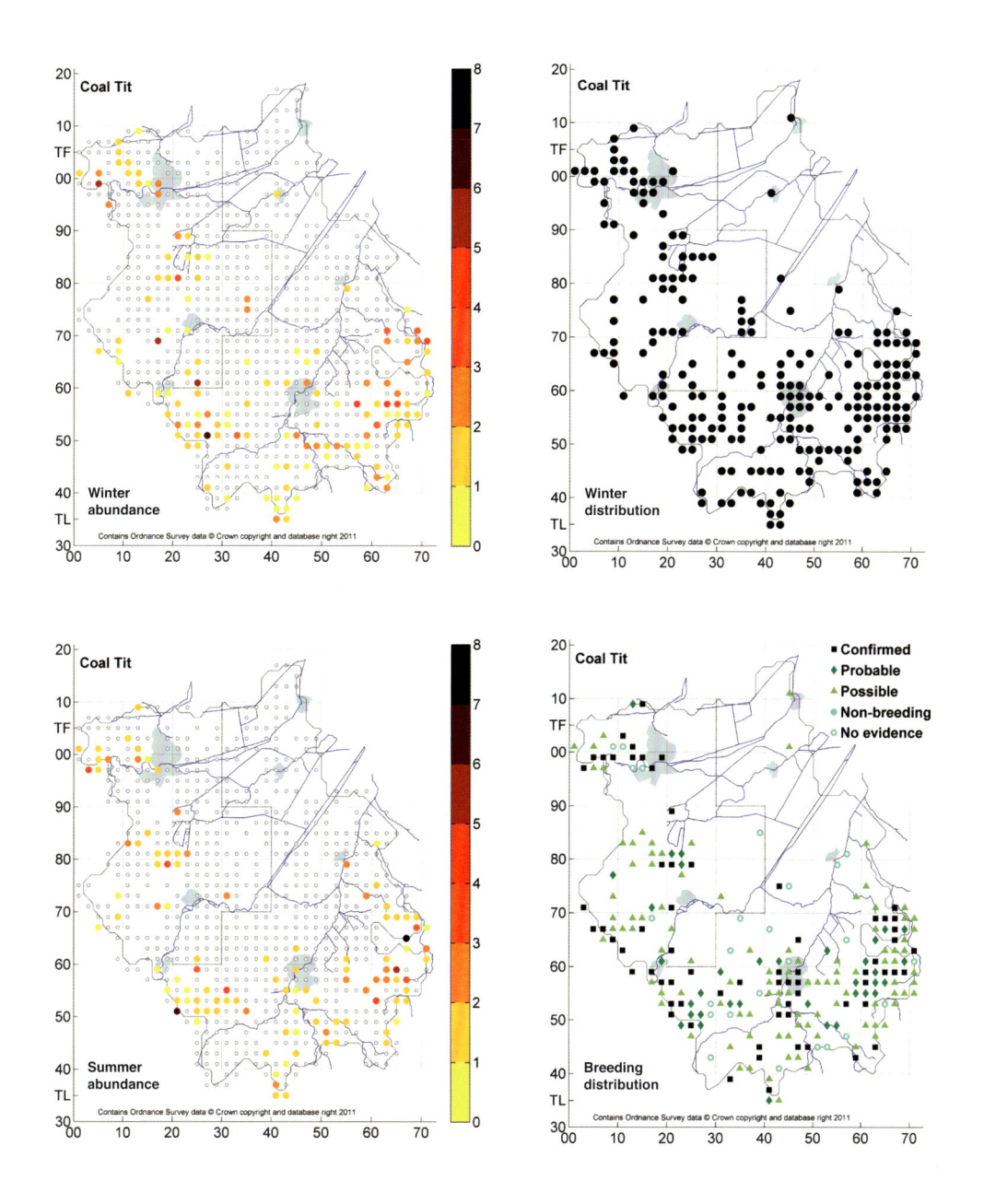

	Confirmed	Probable	Possible	Non-breeding	No evidence	Total summer (% county)	Total winter (% county)
Total tetrads	68	35	102	0	25	230 (24%)	227 (23%)

MARSH TIT *Poecile palustris*
Red List. Fairly common, but declined, local resident

Breeding population estimate: 250-500 pairs
Wintering population estimate: 500-1,500 individuals

Marsh Tit is a woodland species, requiring larger areas of natural broadleaved woodland than the other tits, hence its distribution reflects the main woodland areas in the county. It is absent from agricultural fenland, but occurs in some nature reserves in the fens, such as Woodwalton and Chippenham Fens, where there is substantial tree cover. The main concentrations are west of Peterborough, with sites such as Castor Hanglands and Bedford Purlieus; north of Huntingdon, including Monks Wood and Woodwalton Fen; around Grafham Water in sites such as Brampton Wood; the south-west boulder clay area from Gamlingay to Hardwick Wood and the Wimpole Estate; the small woods and old orchards of the extreme south of the county around Chishill; and the boulder clay woods of south-east Cambridgeshire including Balsham, Borley and Ditton Park woods north to Chippenham Fen. Larger woods are probably essential for maintaining a handful of pairs each, acting as genetic mixing bowls, where young from the smaller surrounding woods can pair up; many smaller woods can only support a single pair in good years and may lose the species in poor years, with large woods nearby allowing recolonisation.

The winter and summer maps are very similar, with a hint of a slightly larger range in winter when some birds may roam in search of new sites. The density maps show that those areas consisting of blocks of large woodlands are the most important for Marsh Tit, although the summer TTVs showed lower densities to the west of Peterborough than in the winter visits. Intensive fieldwork around Monks Wood led to high levels of confirmed breeding there. Generally, however, breeding evidence was relatively easy to gather: over a third of tetrads with summer records had confirmed breeding.

The species is fairly unobtrusive and lives at low densities, so it may be missed by observers not familiar with its distinctive call. Occasionally Great Tits impersonate Marsh Tit calls, which may lead to false entries on the map, although this tends to occur when they have learned the call from nearby Marsh Tits. The risk of misidentification of Willow Tits has practically disappeared with that species' dramatic decline. In some parts of the county, woods are largely in private ownership with difficult access, so some almost certainly went undetected.

Compared with the previous Cambs Atlas, the distribution has changed very little. Comparison with the Hunts Atlas, however, indicates a marked loss of occupied area. In that earlier work, 130 occupied breeding-season tetrads were recorded, compared with 105 in the larger modern county of Cambridgeshire. TL07, 08, 17 and 18 were particularly well occupied by Marsh Tits in the past compared to now. This loss of range probably occurred at the time of the steepest decline in this species shown by the Common Bird Census in the 1970s, but on-going BBS monitoring has shown that Marsh Tit has continued to decline at a steady rate: 22% since 1995. Locally, it does not occur on enough Cambridgeshire or Eastern England BBS squares to reveal a trend (Risely *et al.*, 2012).

The highest counts were recorded during the early summer months, when family parties appear post-fledging. The most impressive counts were made on 19th June 2009, when the four quarters of Monks Wood (which spans four tetrads, each in a different 10-km square) held 30, 25, 20, and 20. Monks Wood also had the highest winter count, with 25 in TL18V.

Several records are in the database at 10-km resolution but with no tetrad assigned, which means that for TL44, 19 and 26 it was not possible to produce mappable tetrad records, one of which was for confirmed breeding (TL26, Offord). In the winter period, Marsh Tits were recorded in 106 tetrads (11%), and 31 10-km squares (61%).

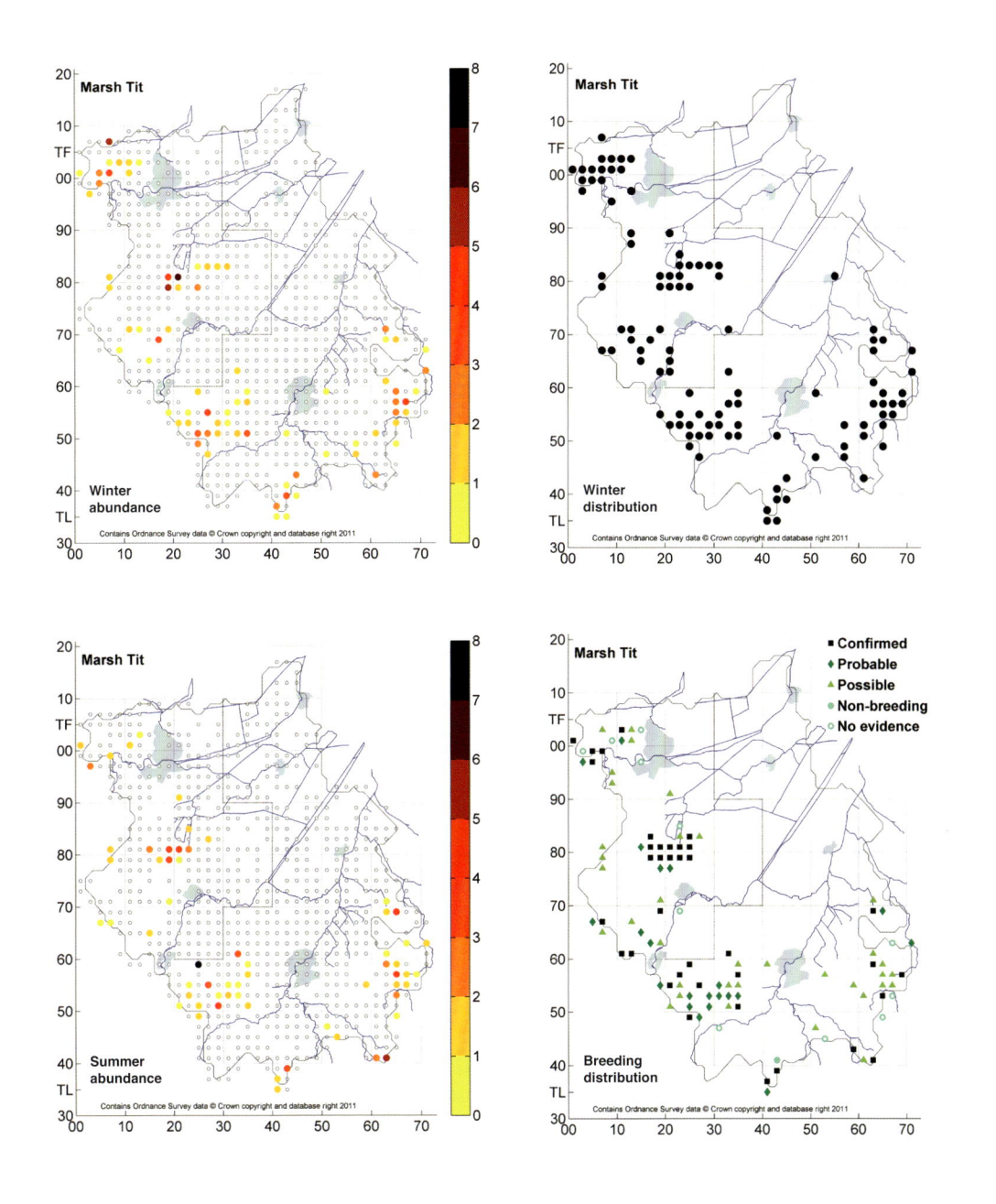

	Confirmed	Probable	Possible	Non-breeding	No evidence	Total summer (% county)	Total winter (% county)
Total tetrads	37	21	35	1	11	105 (11%)	106 (11%)

BEARDED TIT (Bearded Reedling) *Panurus biarmicus*
Amber List. Scarce, very local resident; passage migrant and winter visitor

Breeding population estimate: 5-15 pairs
Wintering population estimate: 10-30 individuals

This species occurs in extensive *Phragmites* reedbeds, which provide a rich food supply of invertebrates and suitable nesting sites in summer and essential winter food of reed seeds. The distribution of Bearded Tit is limited climatically, with cold winters setting the population back significantly. These factors combine to make it a rare bird in the UK (the RBBP estimate 718 breeding pairs; Holling *et al.*, 2012). Cambridgeshire probably benefits from being close to the largest concentrations of this species, which are in Norfolk and Suffolk.

In Cambridgeshire, the core breeding area is around Wicken Fen, with two tetrads on the National Trust reserve having confirmed breeding activity, and two with possible/probable breeding; the nearby Kingfishers Bridge also recorded confirmed breeding activity. Confirmed breeding was also noted at the Ely Beet Factory and at Ouse Fen (CBR 85). Away from this core area, the species was recorded at three other localities during the breeding period: a pair at Teversham Fen, birds in two different years around Fen Drayton Lakes, and an observation from the Ouse Washes area (note that this latter observation was supplied at 10 km resolution and therefore is not mapped).

There appears to be a large amount of potential habitat in the county currently unoccupied by breeding Bearded Tits, for example at Woodwalton Fen, Fowlmere RSPB reserve and the many reedbeds around gravel pits, washes and dykes. If climate favours this species, its future should be secure, as reedbed-creation projects continue. Many such potential breeding sites were visited by Bearded Tits during the atlas winter period. They can be extremely productive in good breeding seasons, with fledglings dispersing throughout the summer and roving widely in search of suitable sites. The majority of such sightings were from just a few occasions. Only three locations managed to log the species on TTVs in the winter, most abundantly at the two sites where it was also present on summer TTVs; the core area between Wicken and Ely remains the most important area for the species throughout the year.

Most Bearded Tits observed during the atlas period probably made it into the database as a consequence of their 'birder appeal'. The species could, however, be under-represented on the maps on account of its unobtrusiveness during windy and wet conditions. They can hide deep within reedbeds, and if they remain silent will not be noted. The large extent of some of our reedbeds means that birds could pass unnoticed, particularly for less-visited sites such as Chippenham Fen (no atlas records). Young from early broods may move away from their breeding sites, so it is possible that some confirmed breeding records were generated for birds from a different tetrad, but this is unlikely to be a major cause of error in the maps. It is difficult to count this species accurately in large reedbed areas, due to the sporadic nature of sightings and uncertainty in how they move around a site.

Bearded Tit has increased from a low point since the previous atlases: it was only recorded in the previous Cambs Atlas (it remains absent from Huntingdonshire in the summer), and only a single tetrad (Wicken Fen) had possible/probable breeding. The maximum population in the previous period was five pairs. Nationally, monitoring for this species is via the RBBP, who consider coverage to be moderate and report a slowly increasing trend.

Peak counts for both seasons were in TL58Q, part of the Wicken complex, with 20 in summer and 10 in winter.

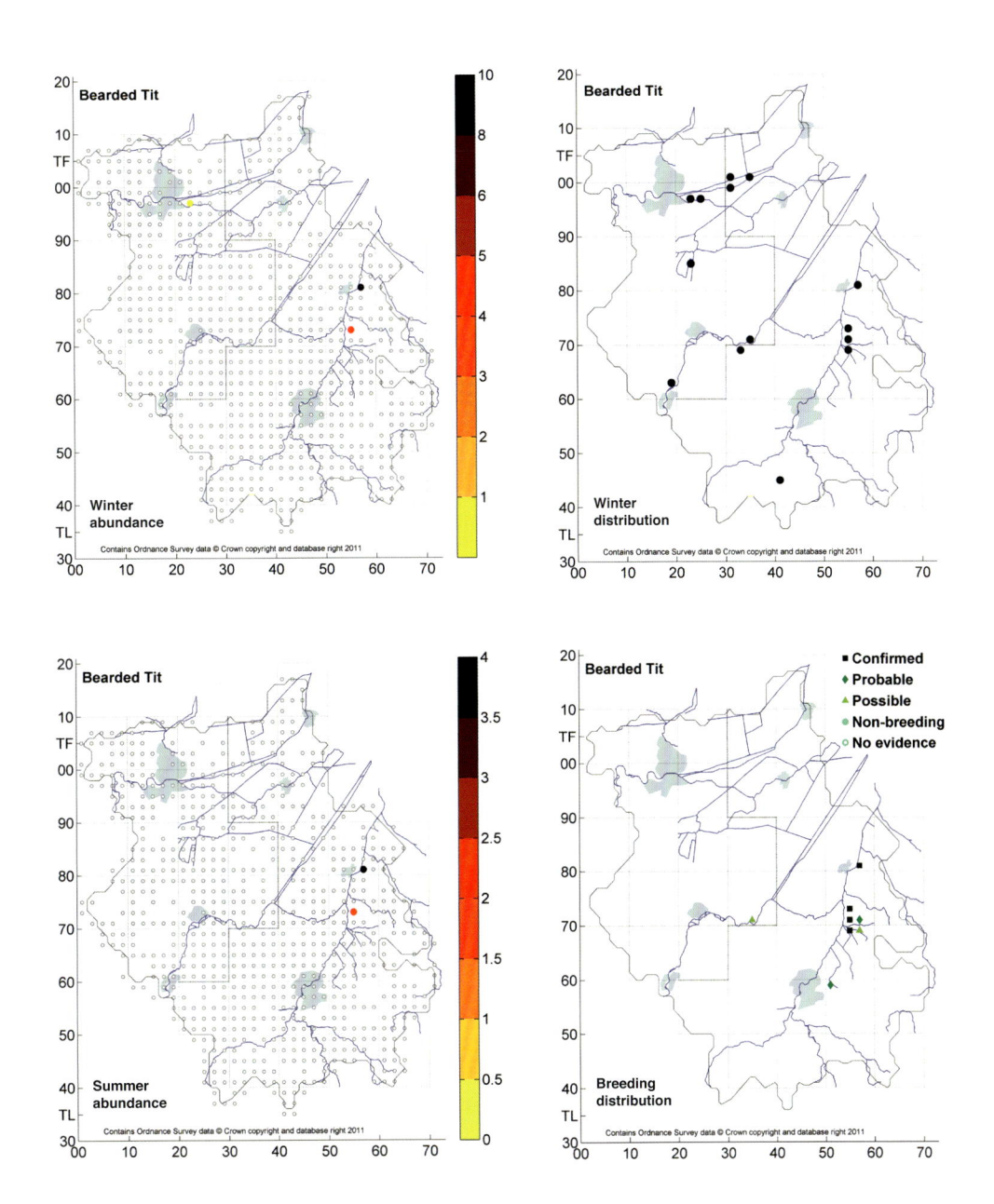

	Confirmed	Probable	Possible	Non-breeding	No evidence	Total summer (% county)	Total winter (% county)
Total tetrads	4	2	2	0	0	8 (1%)	14 (1%)

SKYLARK *Alauda arvensis*
Red List. Common, but much declined, resident; very common passage migrant and winter visitor

Breeding population estimate: 10,000-20,000 pairs
Wintering population estimate: 25,000-40,000 individuals

In the breeding season Skylarks occur widely throughout the county, avoiding urban areas and with some absences in the fens. The tetrads with the greatest recorded abundance in the breeding season are found scattered across the county with no clear pattern of distribution, although they are less frequent in the northern fens. In the winter Skylarks similarly occur widely across the county. The tetrads with greatest abundance in winter exhibit a clumped distribution with concentrations along the River Great Ouse (Old West River) and in the area of the Great Fen Project. Some gaps in mapped occurrence in winter may relate to reduced coverage; however, in the southern third of the county many absences are real.

The current breeding distribution is similar to that found at the time of the previous two county atlases. The current winter abundance appears similar to that recorded by the Wintering Atlas of 1981–84 (Lack, 1986).

The long-term (1970–2010) trend for the breeding population of Skylarks in England is a decline of 63% (Baillie et al., 2012), the 15-year (1995–2010) trend for England and Eastern England is a decline of 24% in both cases (Risely et al., 2012). The Skylark declined rapidly from the mid-1970s until the mid-1980s, when the decline slowed but still continues. There is good evidence that agricultural intensification is the most likely cause of this decline. In particular, the change in arable cropping from spring to autumn sowing of cereals has led to both reduced chick productivity and reduced over-winter survival. Autumn sowing of cereals results in taller and thicker crops earlier in the breeding season and this reduces the number of breeding attempts in a season. Autumn sowing of cereals also eliminates the presence of winter stubbles, a useful source of food (Baillie et al., 2012).

Ringing studies and observations of visible migration indicate that in the winter the local breeding population is augmented by visitors from further north within the UK and from Scandinavia. In hard conditions both UK-bred and foreign visitors will move west and south (Wernham et al., 2002).

Peak winter counts (>300) were recorded in the Great Fen Project area, Farcet Fen, the Fenstanton/Fen Drayton area, north of Cottenham and south of Melbourn.

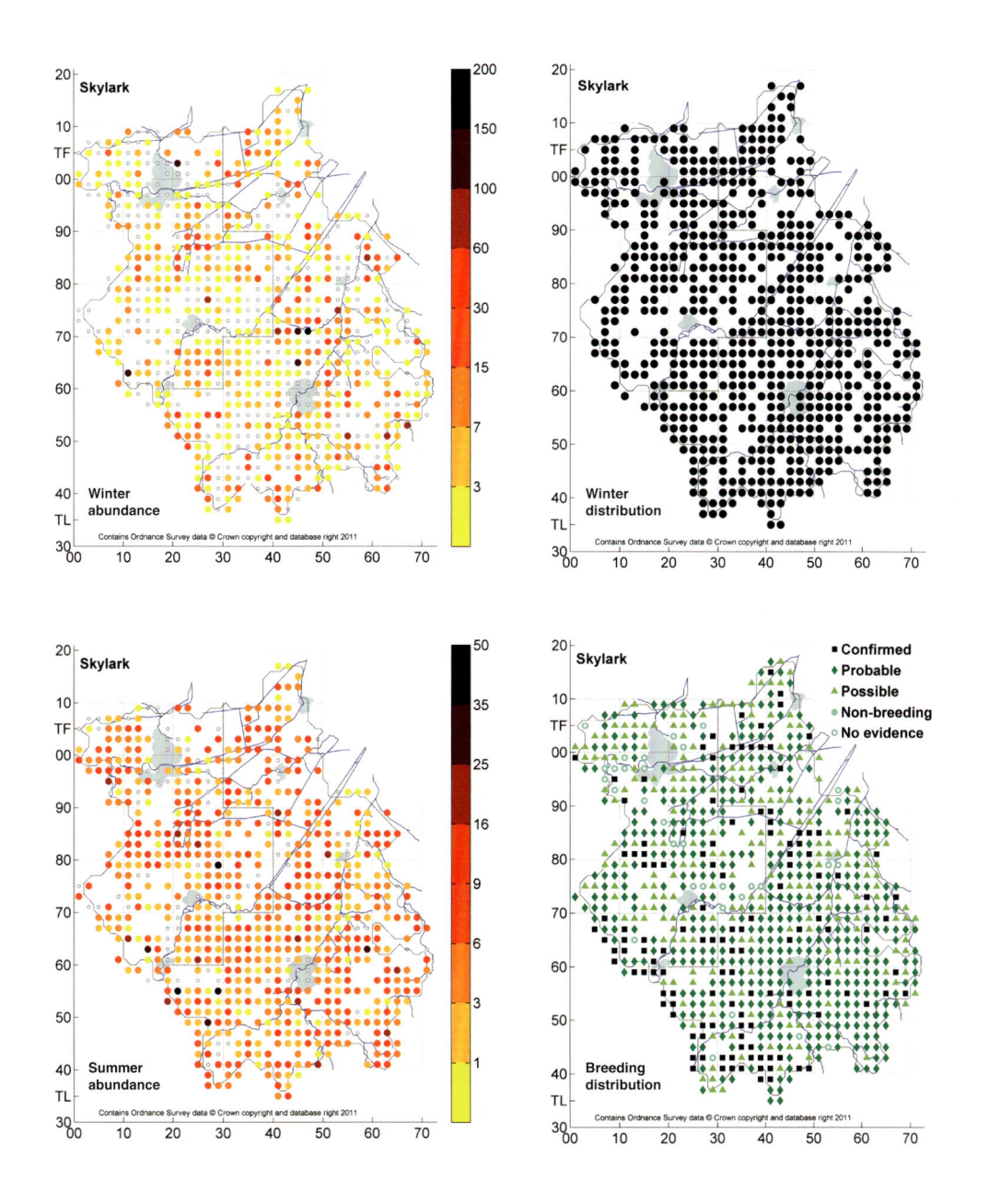

	Confirmed	Probable	Possible	Non-breeding	No evidence	Total summer (% county)	Total winter (% county)
Total tetrads	134	441	233	0	32	840 (87%)	661 (68%)

SAND MARTIN *Riparia riparia*
Amber List. Fairly common, but declined, migratory breeder and passage migrant

Breeding population estimate: 750-2,000 pairs
Not a wintering species

Sand Martin populations have always been subject to wide fluctuations and it is always difficult to distinguish between occupied and inactive nest holes. The species is amber-listed due to its declining populations across Europe, but the overall UK and Ireland status is considered stable or even slightly increasing. The long-term trend is a 40% increase since 1970. Adult survival and wet-season conditions on their African wintering grounds significantly affect the numbers returning each year to breed and can cause wide swings among years.

In Cambridgeshire Sand Martins breed almost exclusively in man-made environments. These principally comprise old sand and gravel-pit workings (many of which are now small local reserves), brickworks and active quarry workings. Some small colonies are established in old drainage pipes and artificially constructed colonies have seen some success at Kingfishers Bridge and Dunkirk. Rather few, if any, birds now seem to nest in natural riverbank situations.

It is thus not surprising that Sand Martin colonies are concentrated in the northern half of the county, particularly along the Nene and Ouse gravel pit complexes. In fact, apart from the large colony at Everton (TL25F, actually just in Bedfordshire) and a few pairs on new workings at Stapleford, no Sand Martins breed south of Cambridge. In recent years variable but fairly stable colonies have been recorded at Block Fen (up to 150 pairs), Ely Beet Factory, King's Dyke/McCain Pits (up to 50 pairs), Maxey Pits (up to 50 pairs), Over/Ouse Fen (up to 100 pairs), Paxton (up to 300 pairs), Priors Fen/Tanholt Farm, Somersham/Earith/Colne Fen Pits (up to 200 pairs), and Sutton North Fen (up to 150 pairs). Small (10 pairs or fewer) riverside urban colonies occur in masonry along the rivers at Peterborough (Rivergate/Fengate), Hemingford Grey and at St. Ives Quay. These four-year totals, however, will represent maxima; colony size varies widely between years, and Sand Martins can be entirely absent from previously established colonies in some years. No attempt was made during the atlas period to carry out a formal census of Sand Martin colonies and a comprehensive single-year survey of known historical sites is overdue.

In the previous Cambs Atlas, there were 31 confirmed/probable tetrads and an additional 26 with presence noted; in the Hunts Atlas there were a further 31 confirmed, seven probable and 13 possible, making a county total of 108 tetrads (11%). The current atlas period had far fewer confirmed sites, and many more tetrads where presence of birds was simply noted. However, the total number of tetrads was only slightly larger than the previous totals.

What seems certain is that the total numbers breeding during the atlas period were significantly lower than the recent peak of 1,500 pairs at 13 colonies recorded in the 2000 CBC report (CBR 74).

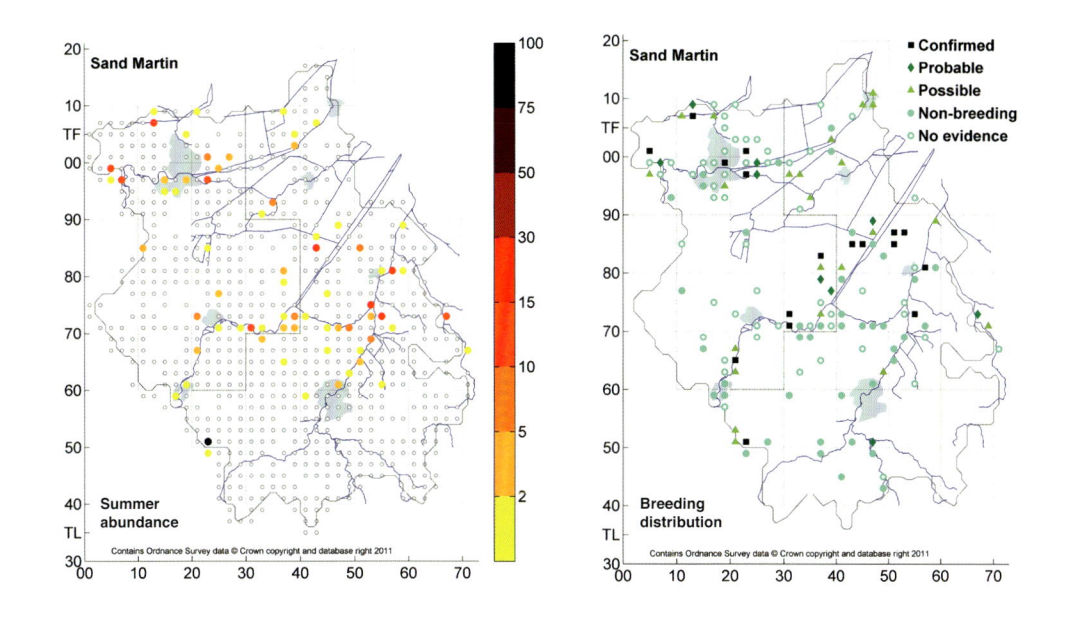

	Confirmed	Probable	Possible	Non-breeding	No evidence	Total summer (% county)
Total tetrads	18	9	23	41	54	145 (15%)

SWALLOW (Barn Swallow) *Hirundo rustica*
Amber List. Common, but declined, migratory breeder and passage migrant

Breeding population estimate: 7,000-10,000 pairs
Not a wintering species

Swallow is currently amber-listed due to a widespread decline in numbers across Europe. In the UK, however, there is recent evidence showing slight increases since the 1990s.

The BBS trends for the UK and England show long-term (1995–2010) increases of 35% and 37%, respectively. The Eastern England 15-year trend is an increase of 14% (Risely *et al.*, 2012).

In counties such as Cambridgeshire, the familiar pattern of a loss of mixed and livestock farming, reductions in grazed grassland, and arable intensification continue to make things difficult for Swallows, despite an increase in their population. Swallows remain very widely distributed throughout the county except in urban areas and in largely prairie arable tetrads lacking suitable buildings in which to breed. The number of tetrads with confirmed or probable breeding remains broadly similar to that of the previous atlases (previous total 714 tetrads (75%), total tetrads in which present 83%), but it seems likely that there will have been some changes in density as farmland changes and as modern, 'hygienic', less Swallow-friendly structures replace traditional farm buildings. Their preferred habitats, with significant elements of pasture and grazing livestock, are now limited to the north and west of the county, but their ability to utilise small areas of suitable habitat means that they continue to be a common, widespread breeding species throughout most of the county.

From July onwards, Swallows gather in substantial roosts, usually in reeds, sometimes comprising over 1,000 birds. Such roosts, particularly on the washlands and in the fens, often include Sand Martins and attract both species on migration from further north, as has been shown by ring-recoveries.

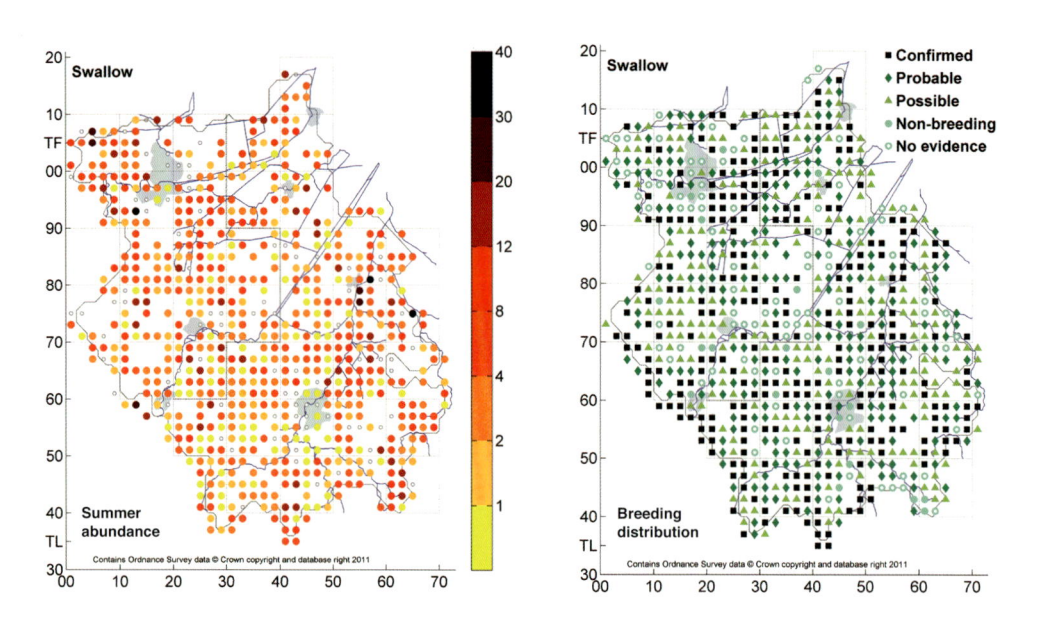

	Confirmed	Probable	Possible	Non-breeding	No evidence	Total summer (% county)
Total tetrads	281	229	232	21	91	854 (88%)

HOUSE MARTIN (Common House Martin) *Delichon urbicum*
Amber List. Common, but declined, migratory breeder and passage migrant

Breeding population estimate: 2,000-5,000 pairs
Not a wintering species

The House Martin has declined by 55% during the past 36 years of monitoring by the BTO. The national picture shows that this decline is particularly marked in Eastern England. The species was moved onto the Amber List in 2002. Accurate monitoring is always difficult as colonies and individual nest sites are constantly in flux – new ones appear as old ones are abandoned.

In Cambridgeshire, House Martins are a familiar and generally well-loved feature of towns and villages. In the previous atlases, there were 275 (Cambs Atlas) and 264 (Hunts Atlas) tetrads with this species present, most with probable or confirmed breeding. This amounts to 539 tetrads, 55% of the modern county. The current atlas recorded House Martins in 504 tetrads, indicating a similar distribution, but there will have been an inevitable reduction in population sizes. Fewer are seen in the fenland parts of the county, and the abundance also seems lower in the eastern half. The highest abundances recorded during TTVs were in an area to the south-east of Cambridge, around Huntingdon and to the west of Peterborough. This latter area is interesting, as the previous Hunts Atlas recorded very few here. Breeding is relatively easy to confirm with this suburban, obvious species, as reflected in the numbers of tetrads from which breeding was confirmed. Late summer brings highly visible passage movements, with large flocks often of over 500 birds gathering over wetlands and waterbodies.

The BBS trends for the UK show a long-term (1995–2010) small decrease of 2%. The England and Eastern England figures are more significant, with 14% and 30% decreases, respectively (Risely *et al.*, 2012). Little would seem to have changed in these largely man-made environments and the reasons for their decline are not understood; it is likely that the problems for House Martins lie in their poorly known wintering grounds.

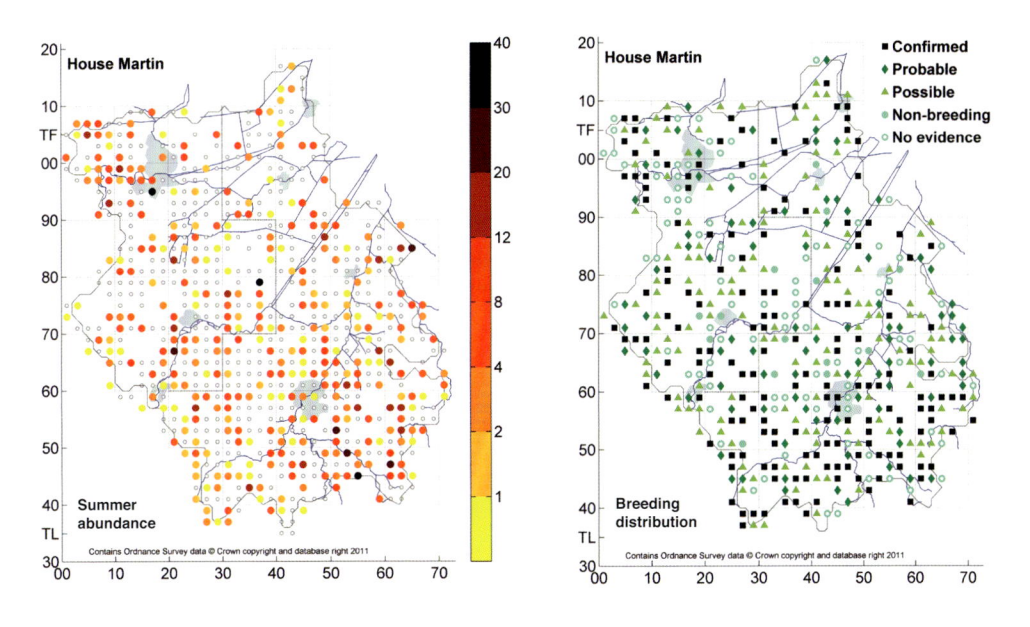

	Confirmed	Probable	Possible	Non-breeding	No evidence	Total summer (% county)
Total tetrads	167	89	142	15	91	504 (52%)

CETTI'S WARBLER *Cettia cetti*
Green List. Increasing resident breeder which is susceptible to harsh winters

Breeding population estimate: 30-70 singing males
Wintering population estimate: 60-200 individuals

Cetti's Warblers are far more often heard than seen. Their abrupt, loud, explosive song has become a regular feature of dense scrub in damp places in many parts of south-east England. Their habitat is often associated with reedbeds, but they are not usually found inside reed swamps. They arrived as a breeding species in the UK in the 1970s and spread quickly across south-east England. Cetti's Warblers bred at Wicken Fen in the early 1980s, but had disappeared from there by the 1988–92 Cambs Atlas. They returned after 2000.

Given their scarcity in the county, they were recorded infrequently during TTVs compared with the number of roving records. During the breeding season, Cetti's Warblers were recorded in 19 TTVs and 60 tetrads overall. Their headquarters in Cambridgeshire is undoubtedly Wicken Fen, where there is a notable concentration. They are found throughout the Ouse valley with some records in the Nene valley. Given their skulking habits and erratic song pattern throughout the year, they are probably under-recorded.

Cetti's Warblers were recorded as probable breeders in at least 26 tetrads but it is reasonable to assume that they were breeding in most of the 60 tetrads in which they were found. Cetti's Warblers are polygynous and all studies emphasise the difficulty of finding nests and females. Wicken Fen had at least ten male territories; this is the only county site where they are studied. Cambridgeshire probably holds between 30 and 70 male territories, accompanied by an unknown number of females. Over the last 20 years there has been a large expansion in range in England, although much suitable habitat remains unoccupied. Taylor & Marchant (2007) reported that the range and numbers of Cetti's Warblers in Norfolk increased by more than threefold during the preceding 20 years, with about one pair per occupied tetrad.

The population of Cetti's Warblers declines during hard winters, probably because they mainly feed on the ground. Their winter distribution is similar to that in the summer, unsurprising for a largely sedentary bird albeit one capable of long-distance dispersal movements, as shown by ring-recoveries. In winter, Cetti's Warblers were found on only six TTVs and in 23 tetrads overall. The difference between the summer and winter distribution seems more likely to reflect the behaviour of these unobtrusive birds as they sing less in winter, rather than any real difference in numbers and distribution. The winter population is thus likely to be similar to that in summer unless there is a hard winter.

Unless we have very severe winter weather in the next few years, we can expect Cetti's Warblers to become more widespread and numerous in the county.

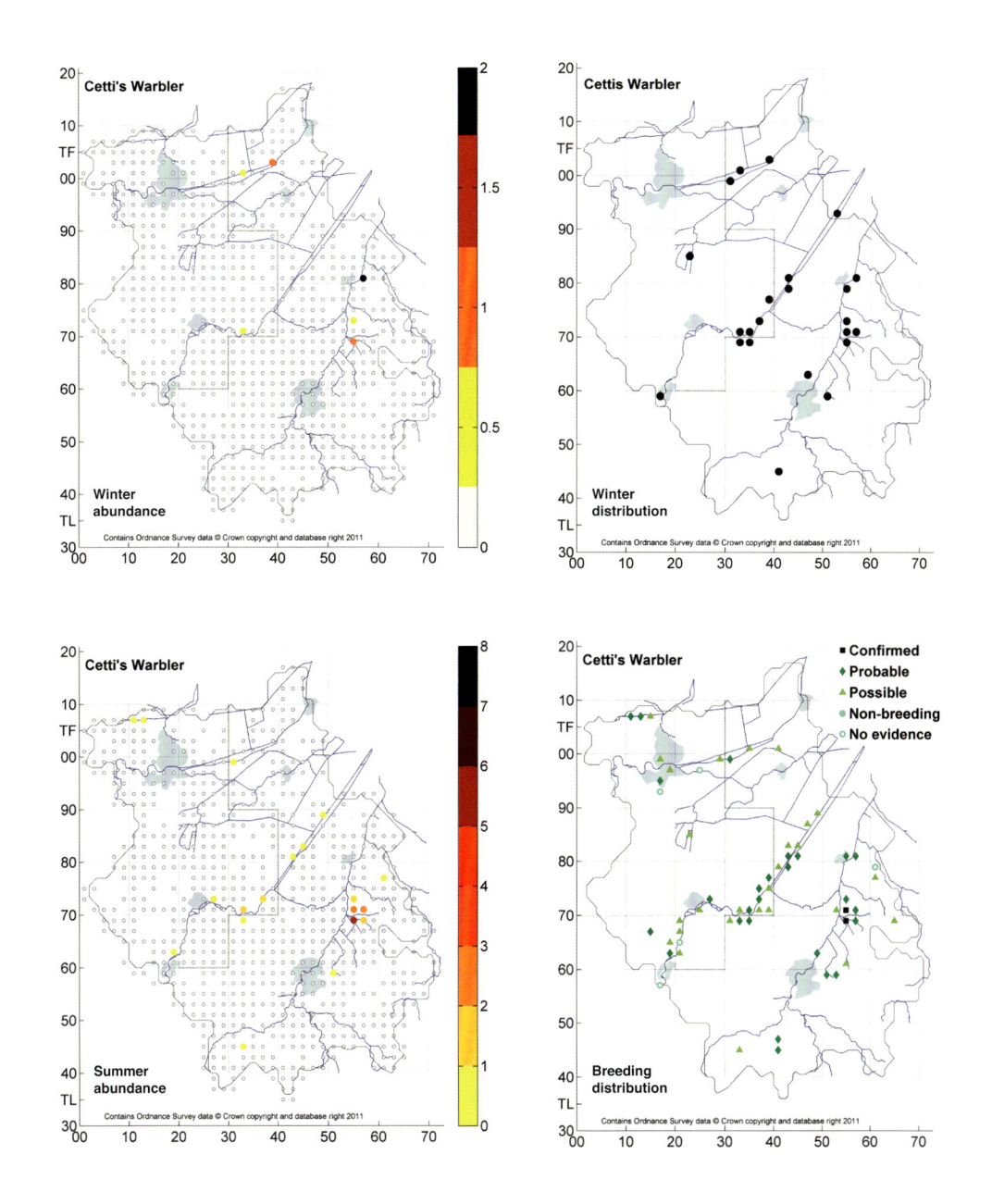

	Confirmed	Probable	Possible	Non-breeding	No evidence	Total summer (% county)	Total winter (% county)
Total tetrads	2	26	27	0	5	60 (6%)	23 (2%)

LONG-TAILED TIT *Aegithalos caudatus*
Green List. **Widespread and common resident**

Breeding population estimate: 2,000-4,000 pairs
Wintering population estimate: 5,000-10,000 individuals

Long-tailed Tits occur across the county, but there is a notable dearth in the core fenland areas where hedges, woodland and scrub are scarce habitats. As they relate to a relatively sedentary species, the four maps are quite consistent in terms of distribution. It is fairly easy to find proof of breeding, particularly the sight of fledged young moving with their parents in noisy family parties. Therefore, the areas where the species is relatively abundant are also the areas with confirmed breeding in the majority of tetrads visited. Due to the very early breeding of this species (eggs being laid in March) and to post-breeding flock formation, which begins to occur in mid-summer, the timing of the TTV visits will not accurately reflect breeding and wintering numbers. It is probably best to look at areas of high density represented on both the winter and summer TTV maps to identify the most important areas for this species – ringing data show us that it is unlikely that they move very far between seasons. Interpreting the maps in this way suggests that the areas west of Peterborough, mid-Huntingdonshire, south of Cambridge and around our more natural river courses have more Long-tailed Tits than pure fenland, urban centres, and higher land between river valleys where the species is relatively sparse.

This distribution has changed very little since the previous two county atlases, although there appears to have been a slight increase in the occupancy of the fens. This is probably related to a steady increase in population density, with BBS data showing a consistent rise both nationally and locally: from 14% of Cambridgeshire BBS squares to 42% and from six individuals per 10 squares to 15 in the period 1995–2010 (Risely *et al.*, 2012).

The highest summer TTV counts came in July when this species moves around in family parties, and families begin to join up to create larger flocks. Therefore 54 in two hours in TL26Z at the end of July 2009 does not necessarily represent a high density of Long-tailed Tits in that area, rather that the observer came across a few families during that particular hour; this number could represent the adults and young of just five successful pairs, and would be equivalent to a TTV count of 10 in April. Only April TTV counts can really give an indication of the density of breeding birds, and the highest one-hour counts made in that month were of nine, in TL35F, TL45K and TL28H. 'Fledged young' was used as a confirmed breeding code during May visits. The apparent variation in density shown by the summer TTV map thus should be treated with caution. In the winter, numbers decline over time through natural attrition, but flock sizes may increase until late winter, when pairs start to form and move into breeding territories; this can begin in February (nest-building was recorded on some February visits, classified as the atlas winter period). Therefore, timed counts and site maxima are again of limited value, but it is likely that the TTV map for winter gives a better representation of the variation in density across the county. Peak winter counts were of 55 (roving record) in TL35L and 51 (two-hour TTV) from TL28A.

In the winter period, Long-tailed Tits were recorded in 668 tetrads (69%), and 50 10 km squares, being unrecorded from one peripheral 10-km square.

Long-tailed Tit

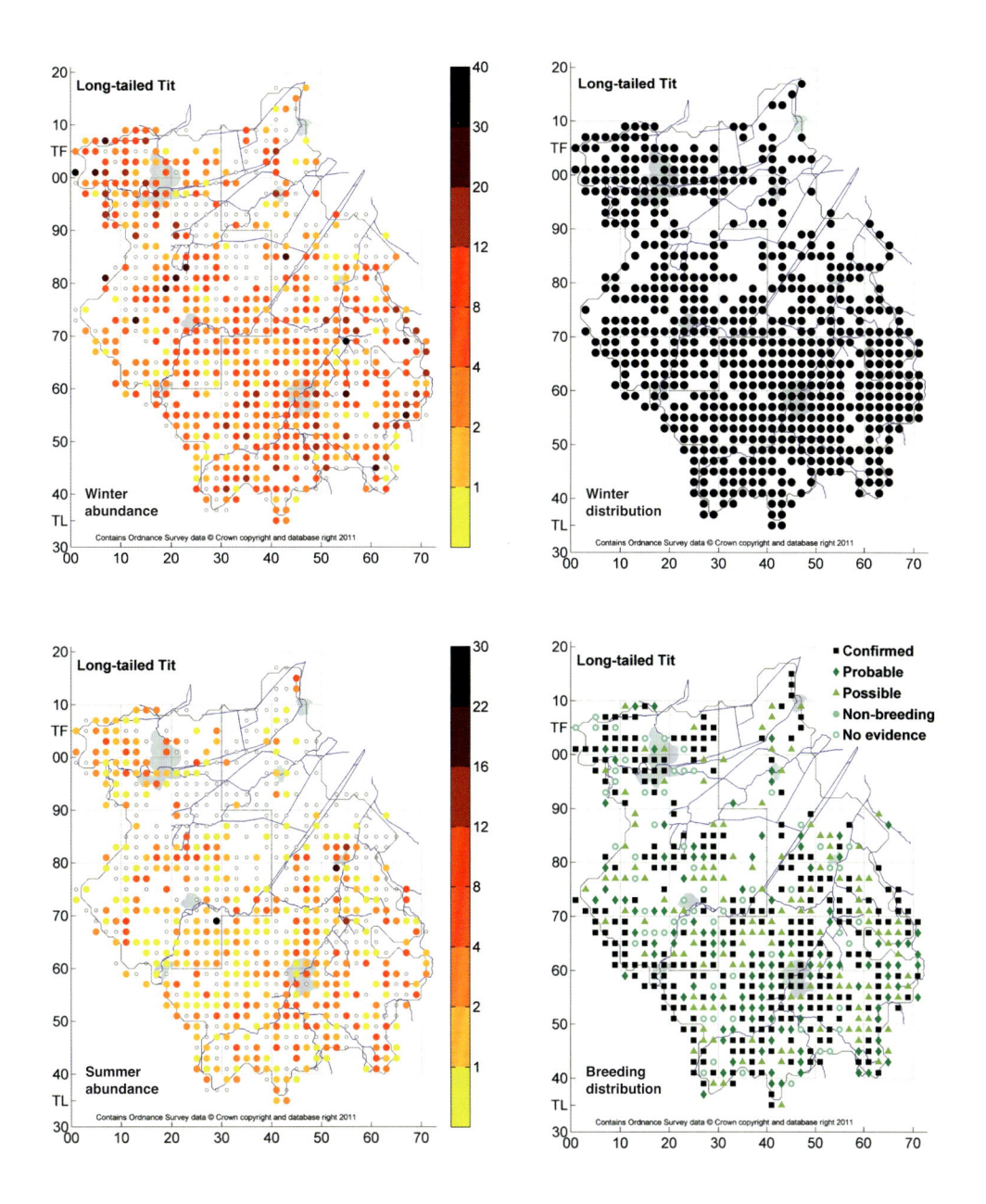

Winter abundance

Winter distribution

Summer abundance

Breeding distribution

	Confirmed	Probable	Possible	Non-breeding	No evidence	Total summer (% county)	Total winter (% county)
Total tetrads	292	113	137	0	61	603 (62%)	668 (69%)

CHIFFCHAFF (Common Chiffchaff) *Phylloscopus collybita*
Green List. Common migratory breeder and passage migrant; regularly overwinters

Breeding population estimate: 4,000-8,000 pairs
Wintering population estimate: 25-100 individuals

Invariably the first migrant warbler of spring, always present by late March, the far-carrying two-note song of the Chiffchaff is easily recognised. Detection of this species in spring and summer is easy and any tetrad surveyed thoroughly is unlikely to miss them. Chiffchaffs need tall trees and often sing near the top of them. For nesting they require a well-developed ground layer, and can be found anywhere with tall trees in parks, gardens, heaths and hedgerows as well as woodlands.

Chiffchaffs are found throughout Cambridgeshire and are only consistently absent in fenland tetrads without any tall trees. They are present in most tetrads in the west and south of the county. There were notable concentrations in TTVs to the west of Peterborough, in the Huntingdonshire NNRs of Monks Wood, Woodwalton Fen and Holme Fen, in the Wicken/Chippenham area and in south-east Cambridgeshire. They were recorded in 70% of TTVs, and roving records supplemented most tetrads outside the fens. In the previous Cambs Atlas, the species was largely unrecorded in the northern half, and was patchier in southern Cambridgeshire compared to the recent records. Some of these differences are undoubtedly due to under-recording. For example, the species was apparently not present in Wicken Fen in 1988–92. In the previous Hunts Atlas, Chiffchaffs were found much more often around Peterborough, were slightly more common in the fens and were generally recorded less frequently than for this atlas.

The BBS population index suggests that the population of Chiffchaffs has doubled in Eastern England in the last 15 years (Risely *et al.*, 2012). Typical estimates from other atlases suggest 6–12 pairs per tetrad. Nearly 2,500 Chiffchaffs were counted in 550 TTVs, probably nearly all males. Overall it was present in 651 tetrads. Given that not all birds would be detected in a one-hour visit, and that additional tetrads held birds, the population is probably not fewer than 4,000 pairs and may extend to double that.

Chiffchaffs are one of the two predominantly migrant warblers to be found in winter in Cambridgeshire. As with Blackcaps, small populations of Chiffchaffs have been recorded in winter in the UK for many years. Most of our Chiffchaffs spend the winter in the western Mediterranean, to the north of the Sahara. Chiffchaffs do not generally come to bird tables in winter and away from well-watched sites are thus harder to detect than Blackcaps, which are often found in gardens. Generally Chiffchaffs are silent in winter, making detection even more difficult. The winter population of this species is likely to be significantly under-recorded.

In winter Chiffchaffs were found in only six TTVs and a total of 45 tetrads over four years. Apart from one remarkable concentration in the Ouse valley, most records are of single birds. The records are less concentrated than Blackcaps in the urban areas and are often along river valleys. It is not known whether the same sites are used every winter by Chiffchaffs, although some sewage works regularly have overwintering birds.

A reasonable estimate suggests that no fewer than 20 individuals and perhaps as many as 100 may spend the winter in the county.

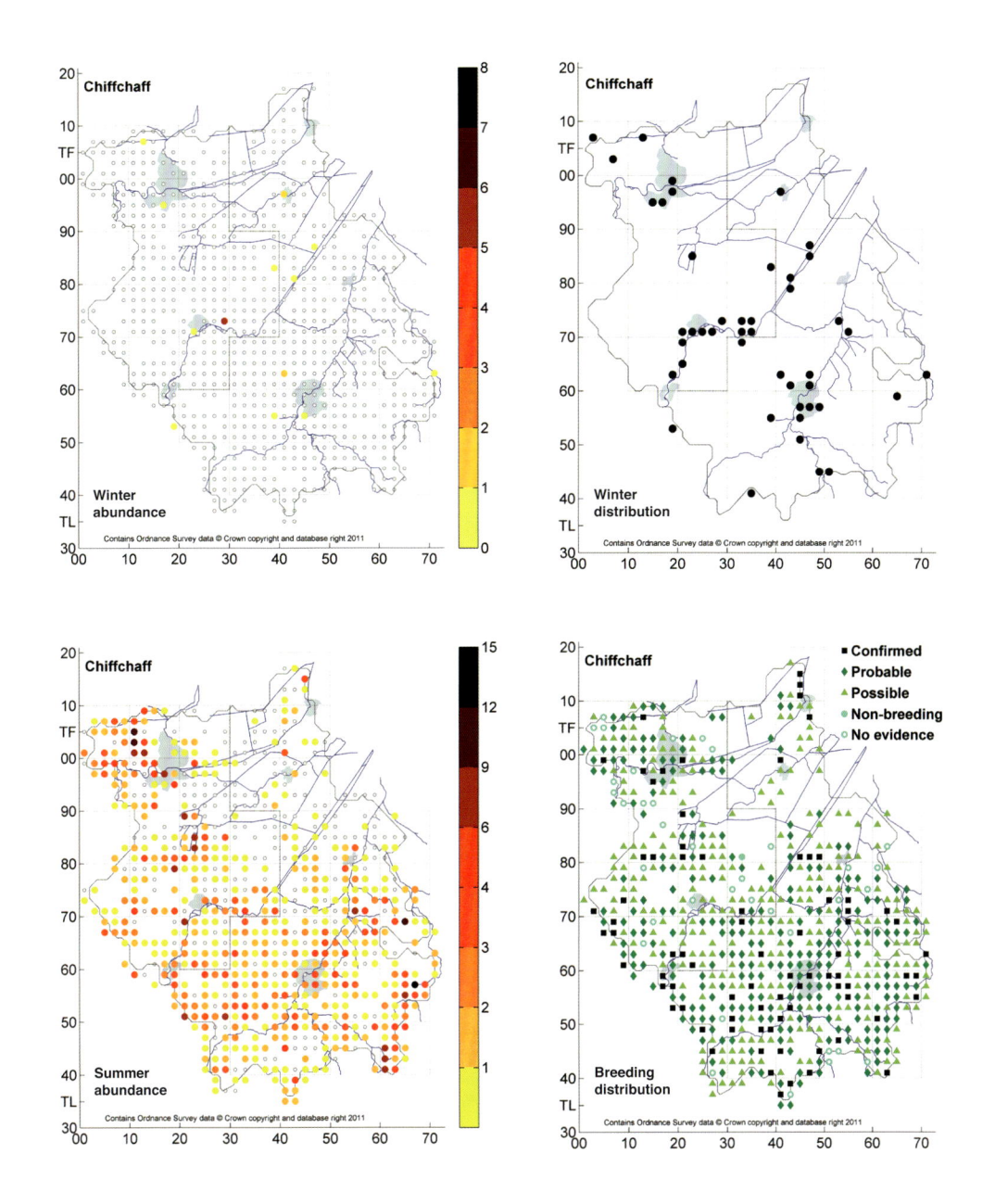

	Confirmed	Probable	Possible	Non-breeding	No evidence	Total summer (% county)	Total winter (% county)
Total tetrads	79	253	282	1	36	651 (67%)	45 (5%)

WILLOW WARBLER *Phylloscopus trochilus*
Amber List. **Common but declined migratory breeder and passage migrant**

Breeding population estimate: 1,500-3,000 pairs
Not a wintering species

The arrival of Willow Warblers from the beginning of April is an early sign of spring; their beautiful far-carrying cascading song is unmistakable. Birches and willows around open water are favoured habitats, along with open, less-mature deciduous woodlands and young copses. They are less restricted to woodland than their close relative, the Chiffchaff. Their abundance in England has declined markedly over the last 20 years (Eaton et al., 2012). Outside the agricultural fenland areas, Willow Warblers are found throughout Cambridgeshire, although their distribution is patchier than might be expected. There has been some contraction of range south of a line from Godmanchester to Wicken compared to the previous Cambs Atlas. Comparison with the Hunts Atlas suggests that Willow Warblers have declined markedly north of St. Neots although the distribution around Peterborough is similar. Good concentrations were found around Peterborough, in the NNRs of Monks Wood, Woodwalton Fen, Holme Fen and Wicken Fen, and in the St. Ives/Fen Drayton area. Although well distributed along the south-east edge of Cambridgeshire, they have been lost from many of the chalk areas. Given their distinctive song, Willow Warblers will be detected reliably, and thus this decline is probably genuine.

The BBS population index for Willow Warblers in Eastern England has fallen by 66% since 1995 (Risely et al., 2012). During the atlas, TTVs recorded Willow Warblers in about 320 tetrads, with a maximum of 23 birds in one tetrad. Adding roving records increased this to 431 tetrads. The Breeding Atlas (Gibbons et al., 1993) estimated 25 pairs of Willow Warblers per tetrad. Given the TTV records, this seems high for Cambridgeshire, while the Norfolk estimate of 4–6 pairs per tetrad (Taylor & Marchant, 2007) seems more reasonable. The minimum Cambridgeshire population probably exceeds 1,500 pairs, but is unlikely to exceed 3,000 pairs. Willow Warblers inhabit a transitional habitat, but habitat change has been much slower than their rate of decline; the reasons seem likely to centre on lower adult survival or reduced nesting success.

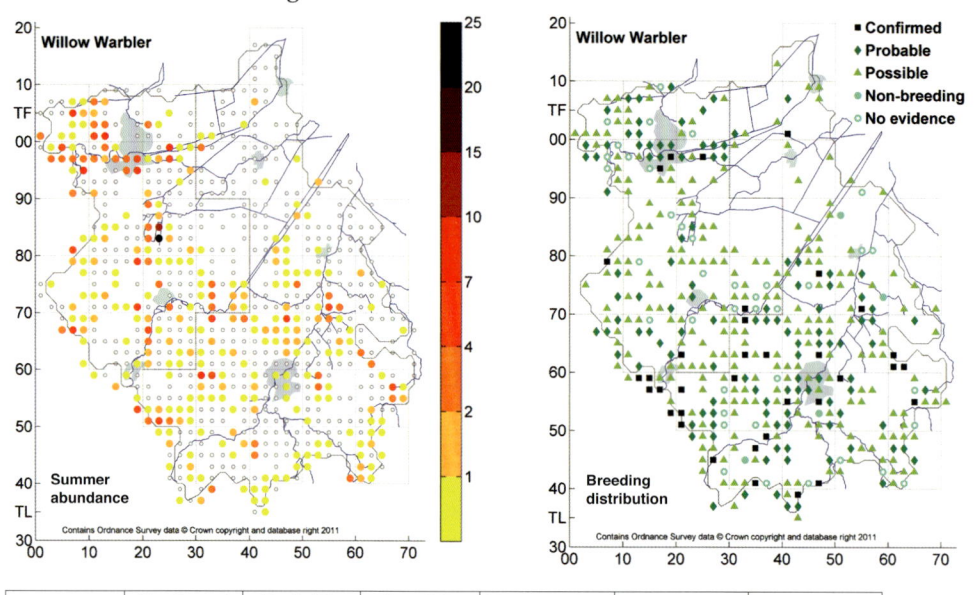

	Confirmed	Probable	Possible	Non-breeding	No evidence	Total summer (% county)
Total tetrads	35	115	238	4	39	431 (44%)

GARDEN WARBLER *Sylvia borin*
Green List. Fairly common migratory breeder and passage migrant

Breeding population estimate: 500-1,000 pairs
Not a wintering species

Garden Warblers generally arrive in May, usually the last of the common warblers. They advertise their presence with their beautiful song of rather deep notes, delivered at a brisk pace with long verses, sometimes likened to a rippling brook. Garden Warblers are primarily a woodland-edge species, needing dense scrub and shrub layers. They also nest in heathlands, large gardens, and in the tall scrub associated with old gravel workings and fens like Wicken and Woodwalton.

Garden Warblers have a wide but local distribution in Cambridgeshire, mostly outside the agricultural fenland area. This patchy distribution is mirrored in both the abundance and distribution maps, birds being absent from many tetrads where they might be expected. They sing well in May and are often heard through June, so detection on TTVs should be good. Their distribution is similar to the previous Cambs Atlas, but it is less widespread than in the Hunts Atlas, notably in TL07, 17 and 18. Garden Warblers are found principally in the west and central areas of Cambridgeshire and are very scarce in the fens. Particular concentrations were found at Castor Hanglands, Woodwalton Fen and Paxton Pits. Only 27 TTVs recorded more than one singing bird in the 172 TTVs where they were found. Roving records increased the number of tetrads in which they were present to 269.

The BBS population index suggests that Garden Warbler numbers may have fallen slightly since 1995 in Eastern England (Risely *et al.*, 2012). Some reports suggest that Garden Warblers and Blackcaps may compete for territories. If so, Garden Warblers may have suffered from the rampant increase in Blackcaps. Densities of 2–4 pairs per occupied tetrad are noted in other atlas studies. Hence, the county population of Garden Warblers is probably at least 500 pairs and perhaps as many as 1,000.

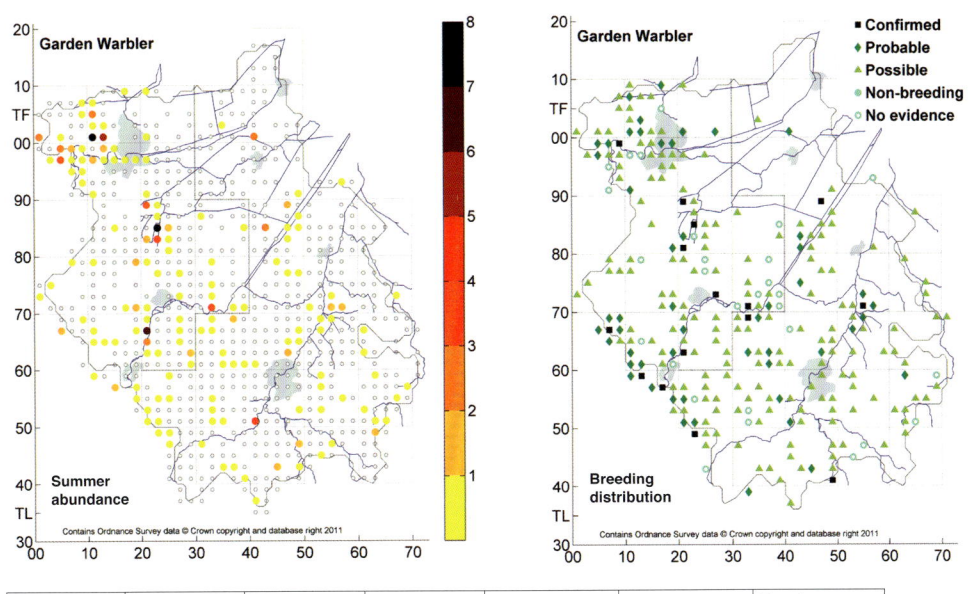

	Confirmed	Probable	Possible	Non-breeding	No evidence	Total summer (% county)
Total tetrads	15	51	175	0	28	269 (28%)

BLACKCAP (Eurasian Blackcap) *Sylvia atricapilla*
Green List. Very common migratory breeder, passage migrant and winter visitor

Breeding population estimate: 10,000-20,000 pairs
Wintering population estimate: 100-250 individuals

The Blackcap is widespread in Cambridgeshire. Blackcaps nest in tall scrub as well as in woodlands, parks and gardens with a thick understorey. Their loud, melodious and distinctive song makes detection easy from April to July.

In the breeding season, Blackcaps were recorded on TTVs and by roving records in 80% of all tetrads. Their distribution in the fens is patchy but, like Chiffchaffs, they can be found around the larger houses and farms and where there are isolated woodland fragments. The previous Cambs Atlas suggested that Blackcaps were very scarce in the fens, whether this was an effect of reduced coverage is uncertain. For example in TF40, Blackcaps were found in only two tetrads in the Cambs Atlas but in 14 tetrads this time. The Hunts Atlas reported that Blackcaps were scarce in the fens and west of Peterborough; the latter almost certainly due to under-recording.

Blackcaps have increased nationally over the past half-century and by 71% in the east of England since 1995 (Risely *et al.*, 2012). Whilst the number of tetrads with confirmed breeding was modest, it is highly likely that breeding was attempted in most tetrads in which they were recorded. Notably high concentrations of birds were found immediately west and south of Peterborough, in the Huntingdonshire NNRs of Monks Wood, Woodwalton Fen and Holme Fen and immediately east of Cambridge. Earlier atlases suggested an average of 8–12 pairs per occupied tetrad. The breeding population thus probably exceeds 10,000 pairs and may be as high as 20,000 pairs.

For many years, small numbers of Blackcaps have wintered in the UK. The Wintering Atlas (Lack, 1986) reported wintering Blackcaps all over England. Most birds are seen in gardens, especially after December. Evidence from birds ringed in winter indicates that the Blackcaps wintering in the UK breed in the Low Countries and Germany. They probably arrive here with the large westward autumn movements of Blackcaps from central Europe. Most Blackcaps breeding in the UK spend the winter around the western Mediterranean.

The pattern of winter Blackcap records follows closely the distribution of human population in the county, with records in 79 tetrads over four winters, although it was only found 12 times in TTVs. The chance of detecting the usually silent Blackcap in winter in woodland or scrub is low, but bird feeders and gardens provide excellent habitat for these birds. Thus most of the winter records were from urban areas with more than one-third of roving records in the cities of Peterborough and Cambridge. Whilst only one or two birds are usually observed on any occasion, ringing studies from a garden near Cambridge (Isted, 2011) showed that 30 different birds could pass through a garden in the winter, which must make the true population significantly more than can be estimated from structured counts such as used in the atlas. A minimum population is probably at least 150 birds each winter and may be many more.

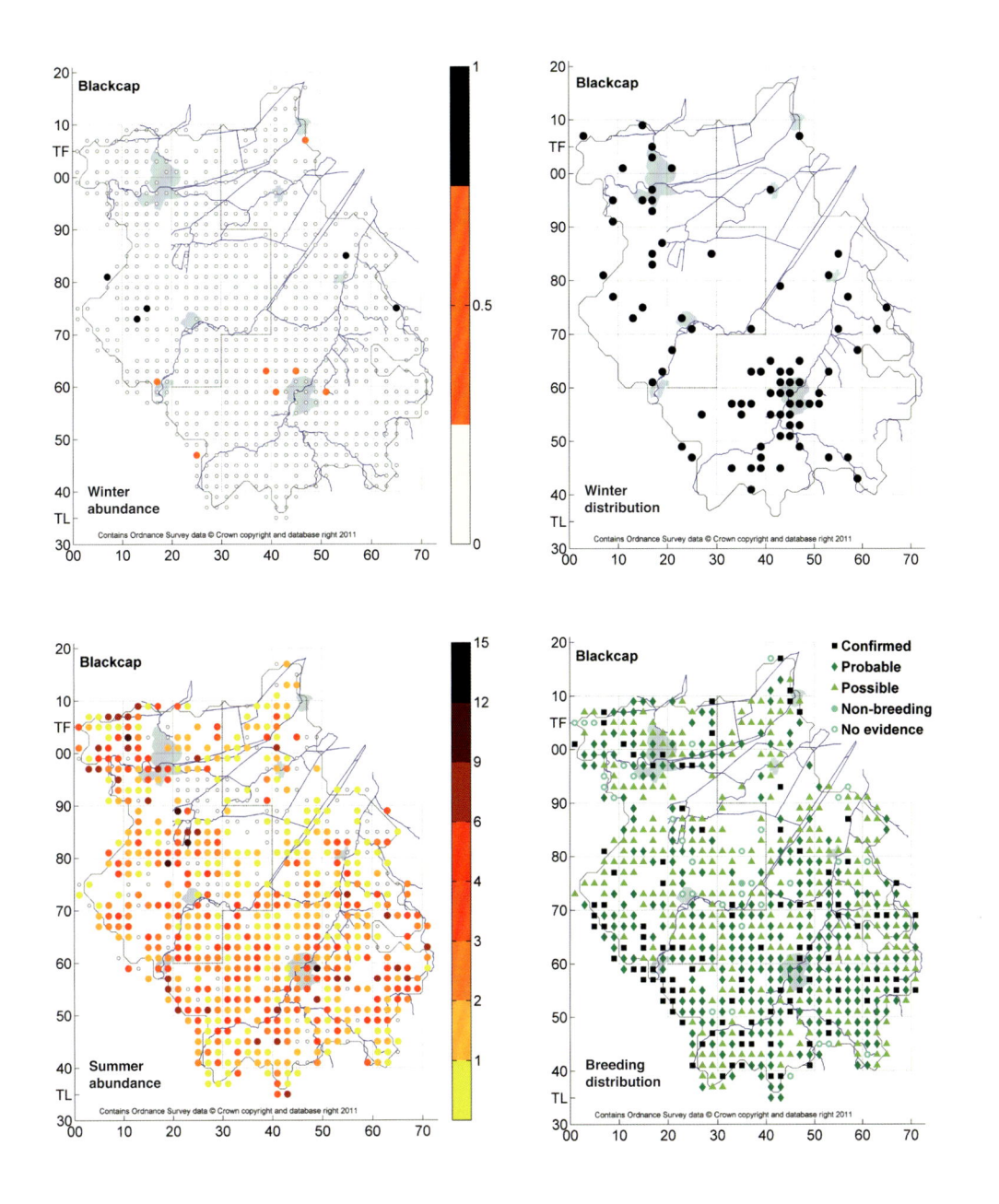

	Confirmed	Probable	Possible	Non-breeding	No evidence	Total summer (% county)	Total winter (% county)
Total tetrads	107	295	307	1	33	743 (77%)	79 (8%)

LESSER WHITETHROAT *Sylvia curruca*
Green List. Fairly common migratory breeder and passage migrant

Breeding population estimate: 1,000-2,000 pairs
Not a wintering species

The Lesser Whitethroat is an inconspicuous summer visitor. Its quiet song, a gentle rattle given from deep cover, is heard from late April to early June. Individuals sing over a short period; singing usually ceases once nest-building begins. The timing of TTV counts is thus critical for this species and they are likely to be under-recorded. The roving records support this: it was recorded in twice as many tetrads overall as in TTV counts alone.

Lesser Whitethroats favour thick hedges and dense scrub and avoid woodland and open farmland. They were recorded throughout agricultural areas in Cambridgeshire, although they were uncommon in the fens. In the west of the county the distribution is puzzling; it was not recorded in many tetrads in TL07, 17, and 18. A similar pattern was found in the previous Hunts Atlas. The distribution in the old Cambs Atlas was also similar to this atlas, although there are many more records in TL36, 46 and 56. Particular concentrations were recorded in TTVs around Haddenham, south of Huntingdon and to the west of Peterborough. It is probably present in almost all tetrads south of a line from Godmanchester to Wicken Fen but is much scarcer in the north-eastern part of our region, notably in TL39 and 49 and TF30, 40 and 41.

Confirmed breeding was uncommon (only 46 tetrads); unsurprising given the difficulty of detecting anything other than a singing male. In Norfolk, it is suggested that this species has increased in numbers since the 1980s (Taylor & Marchant, 2007). However, the BBS population index for Eastern England reports little change since 1995. In favourable habitat, they occur at a density of 2–4 pairs per occupied tetrad. As Lesser Whitethroats were recorded in 438 tetrads, the population is estimated to be between 1,000 and 2,000 pairs.

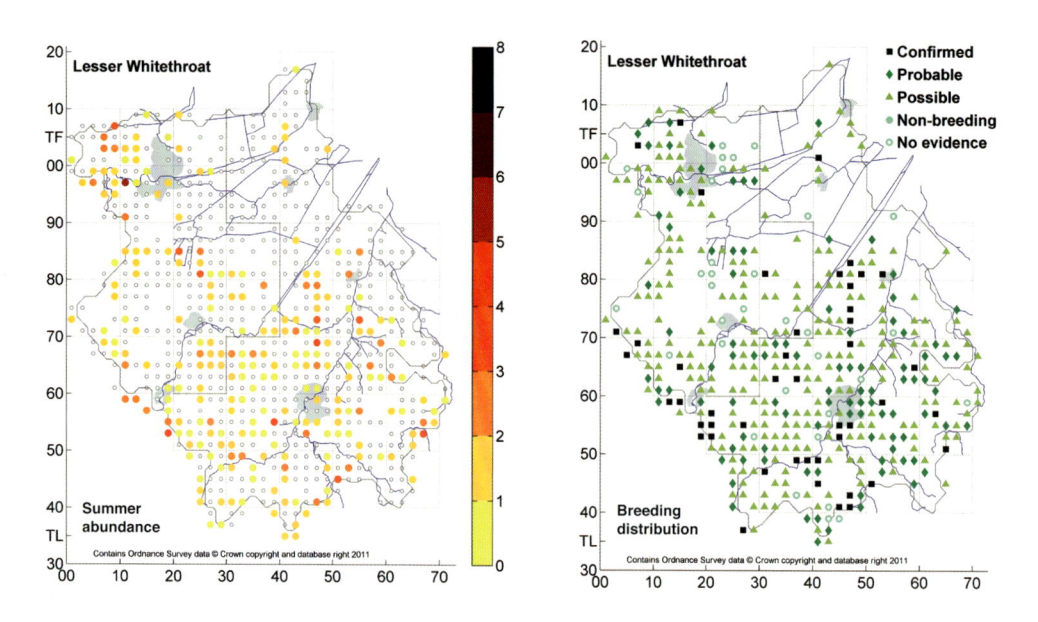

	Confirmed	Probable	Possible	Non-breeding	No evidence	Total summer (% county)
Total tetrads	46	98	260	0	34	438 (45%)

WHITETHROAT (Common Whitethroat) *Sylvia communis*
Amber List. Very common migratory breeder and passage migrant

Breeding population estimate: 9,000-12,000 pairs
Not a wintering species

Whitethroats are perhaps the most easily seen of all the warblers. They are found in relatively open landscapes and often sing from low cover (less than 1 m tall). They perform a distinctive song flight with their jerky, scratchy song, often from a bush. Thus detection is easy and thorough surveys of an area should provide accurate counts, since they have a long song period from April to July. Whilst traditionally using cover provided by hedgerows, Whitethroats will adopt any tall vegetation, such as that found around the ditches of fenland fields.

Whitethroat populations have fluctuated considerably over the last 50 years. Following a well-recorded population crash in 1969, the total number arriving in spring increased and then declined slightly; numbers have now substantially recovered to pre-1969 levels in southern England. The previous Cambs Atlas found Whitethroats throughout the southern two-thirds of old Cambridgeshire, and the Hunts Atlas found them widespread except for parts of the fens although, as with other species, the fenland part of the county had poor coverage.

Whitethroats were found in 87% of the 784 summer TTVs with almost three birds per hour recorded. Many of the gaps in records in TTVs were filled by roving records, to give a total of 86% of the tetrads in the county holding Whitethroats. Almost all tetrads without records were not surveyed fully. It is possible, therefore, that Whitethroats were present in every tetrad, except perhaps in a few urban ones, although they were recorded in all tetrads covering Cambridge and in all but three in Peterborough. BBS results for Eastern England suggest that Whitethroats have increased by about 25% in the past 15 years (Risely *et al.*, 2012). More than 6,000 were counted in TTVs, mostly singing males. In some tetrads more than 20 birds per hour were recorded, with notably high counts throughout the Ouse valley. Previous atlases suggested 8–12 pairs per occupied tetrad. The population may be as high as 12,000 pairs.

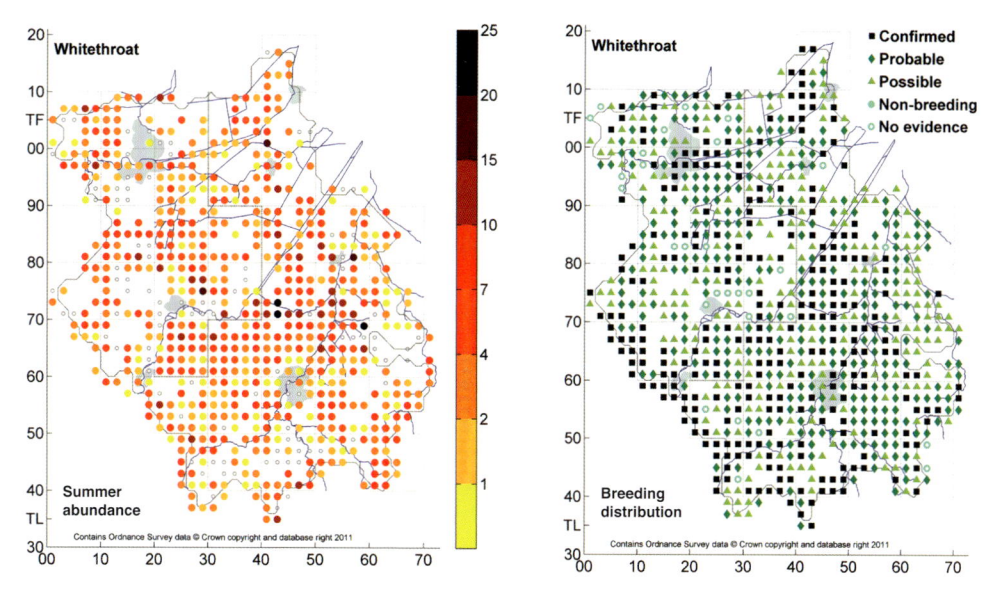

	Confirmed	Probable	Possible	Non-breeding	No evidence	Total summer (% county)
Total tetrads	271	307	229	0	29	836 (86%)

GRASSHOPPER WARBLER (Common Grasshopper Warbler)
Locustella naevia
Red List. Uncommon, declined migratory breeder and passage migrant

Breeding population estimate: 50-100 pairs
Not a wintering species

The Grasshopper Warbler is rarely seen and is usually detected by its monotonous reeling song. It sings vigorously after its arrival in mid-April and May, but becomes much quieter after territories are established. Its mouse-like behaviour, and tendency to sing most strongly at dusk and dawn, makes detection difficult unless it is specifically sought.

Grasshopper Warbler distribution in Cambridgeshire is very scattered and it is almost certainly under-recorded. While often found near the main rivers and drains, it can be found almost anywhere, given its preference for dense low vegetation, often in drier situations than favoured by Reed and Sedge Warblers. The overall distribution is similar to that found in the previous Hunts and Cambs atlases.

There were records of Grasshopper Warblers in 112 tetrads, but only 27 TTVs. Between one and five birds were recorded in TTVs per occupied tetrad. Breeding was confirmed in only four tetrads, emphasising the difficulty of detection other than by song. There were particular concentrations at Wicken Fen, Little Wilbraham Fen, the Ouse valley around Fen Drayton, Woodwalton Fen and around Peterborough.

At many sites it is an irregular visitor, perhaps because of habitat changes as, for example, when young plantations mature. Given the difficulty of detection, and year-to-year variability, population estimates are difficult. Other atlases estimate a population of about one pair per occupied tetrad. On this basis, the county population is at least 50 pairs, and possibly up to 100 pairs in most years. The species has declined nationally over the last 50 years for unknown reasons. The BBS 15-year trend is a decline of 59% (Risely *et al.*, 2012).

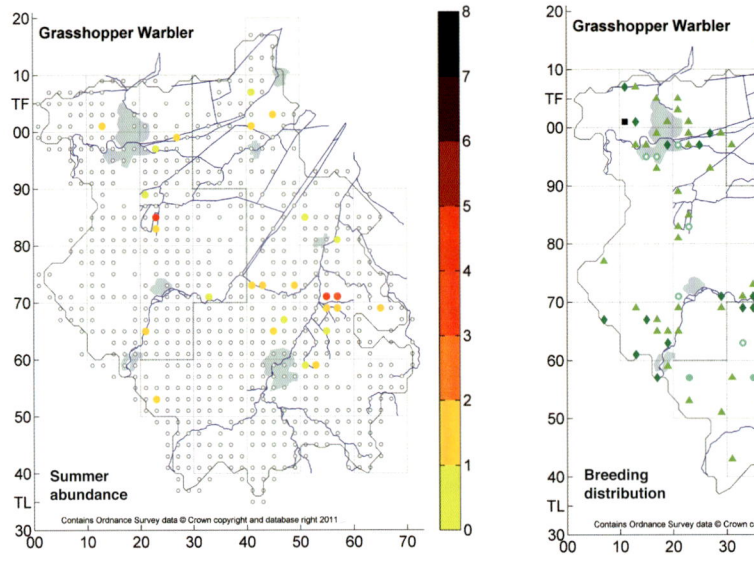

	Confirmed	Probable	Possible	Non-breeding	No evidence	Total summer (% county)
Total tetrads	4	26	68	6	8	112 (12%)

SEDGE WARBLER *Acrocephalus schoenobaenus*
Green List. **Very common migratory breeder and passage migrant**

Breeding population estimate: 3,000-5,000 pairs
Not a wintering species

Sedge Warblers loudly announce their arrival from mid-April onwards with their chattering song, often delivered from the tallest vegetation in an area, and with a brief song flight. Hence detection is easy, especially in any area with several noisy males. They sing for much of the summer although there is a gradual decline after territories are established.

Nationally, Cambridgeshire holds a significant proportion of the Reed and Sedge Warbler populations. The two species have a similar distribution in Cambridgeshire and can occur at high densities in suitable habitat. The current distribution of the Sedge Warbler is very similar to that found in the previous Hunts and Cambs atlases although the species is much scarcer in TL16 and 17 compared to the Hunts Atlas. Sedge Warblers are found along the river systems, in the large fens and reedbeds, along fenland ditches, and around old gravel pits. They favour nettles, willowherb and low scrub on the edges of reedbeds, as well as hedgerows and tall arable crops such as oilseed rape. Particular concentrations were found around the Cam and the Ouse from Ely to Wicken, along the Ouse Washes, and especially along the Nene Washes and to the south-east of Peterborough in TL28 and 29. In the fens and along the major rivers and dykes, there are probably few tetrads without a Sedge Warbler.

The BBS population index for Sedge Warblers in Eastern England since 1995 suggests a stable population (Risely *et al.*, 2012). Given the large variation in numbers among tetrads, population estimates are difficult: numbers in 326 TTVs varied from one to over 20 singing birds. Sedge Warblers were found in 351 tetrads. The previous Cambs Atlas suggested an average of around eight pairs per occupied tetrad, slightly higher than the Norfolk estimate (Taylor & Marchant, 2007). This would give a county population of about 3,000 pairs; this is probably a little low, and the population may be as large as 5,000 pairs.

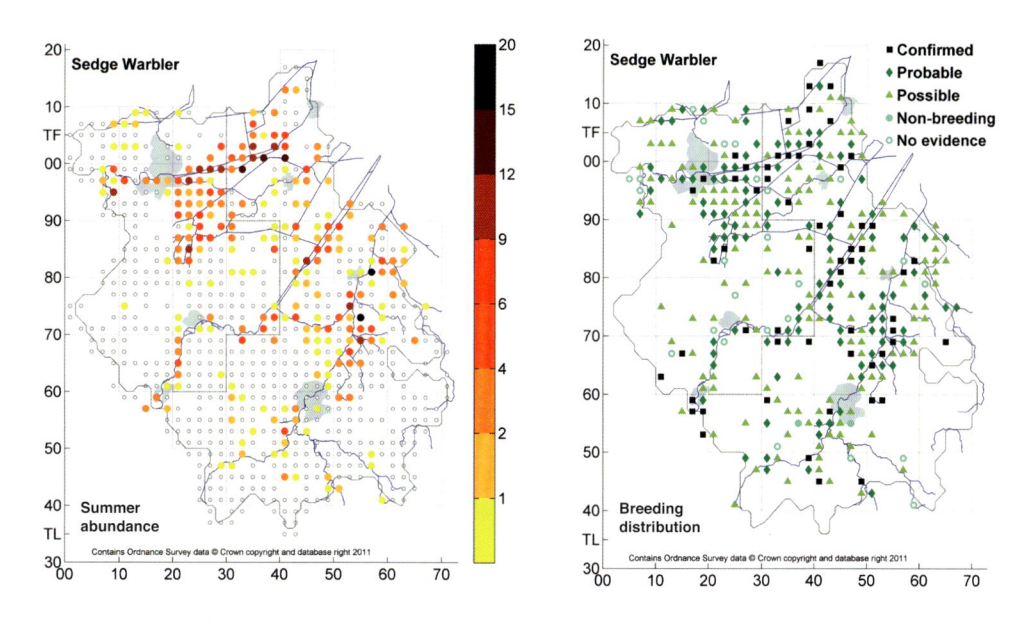

	Confirmed	Probable	Possible	Non-breeding	No evidence	Total summer (% county)
Total tetrads	61	112	151	2	25	351 (36%)

REED WARBLER (Eurasian Reed Warbler) *Acrocephalus scirpaceus*
Green List. Very common migratory breeder and passage migrant

Breeding population estimate: 5,000-10,000 pairs
Not a wintering species

This is the most common warbler in the fens. It has a close association with *Phragmites* which are found along dykes, ditches and rivers, as well as in the remaining ancient fens and around gravel pits and lakes. Most Reed Warblers arrive in the first half of May and early TTV spring counts may miss them. Their repetitive chatter, often from a hidden position, continues amongst reeds until late July. Thus overall detection in TTVs is likely to have been good, a feature emphasised when the abundance and distribution maps are compared.

In large areas of suitable habitat, they nest semi-colonially and can occur at high densities. Several tetrads recorded more than 30 singing birds with a maximum count of 40. When present in these large numbers, an accurate count by observation is difficult. Most ditches and dykes in the fens will contain a singing Reed Warbler. The Hunts Atlas found them in virtually every river valley tetrad. Reed Warblers appear more widespread in the fens than in the previous Cambs Atlas, but it is likely that this was due to poor coverage of fen areas in the earlier survey. The modern Cambridgeshire distribution mirrors closely the major waterways with notable concentrations at Wicken Fen, Ely, Woodwalton Fen and the Nene and Ouse Washes. Other than in the Nene, Ouse and Cam river systems, the species is absent from most of the west and south of the county, excepting a few small wetlands.

Confirmed and probable breeding occurred in most tetrads where recorded. According to the BBS population index, the species has maintained its numbers during the last 15 years in Eastern England (Risely *et al.*, 2012). Wicken Fen has a high concentration, estimated at 400–500 males. The uneven distribution, and large variation in density from tetrad to tetrad makes population estimates extremely uncertain. 2,200 were counted on TTVs, but many fenland tetrads had poor coverage. The Norfolk Atlas (Taylor & Marchant, 2007) and previous Cambs Atlas estimated 12–16 territorial males per occupied tetrad. Reed Warblers were present in 383 tetrads; thus a low population estimate would be 5,000 pairs and an upper estimate could be as high as 10,000. Cambridgeshire has around 8% of the UK population.

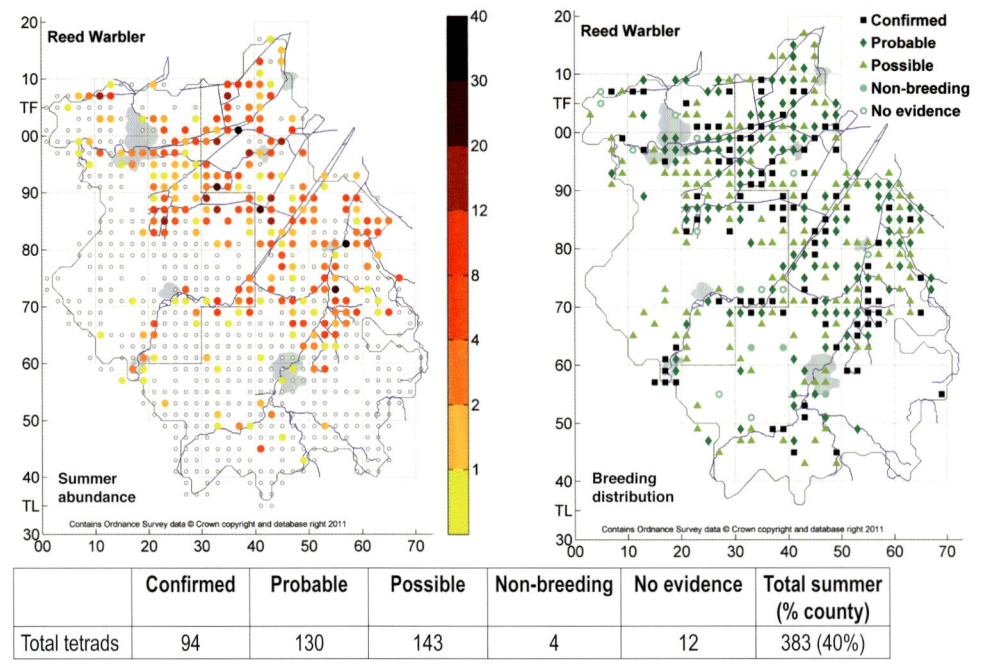

	Confirmed	Probable	Possible	Non-breeding	No evidence	Total summer (% county)
Total tetrads	94	130	143	4	12	383 (40%)

WAXWING (Bohemian Waxwing) *Bombycilla garrulus*
Green List. Scarce, almost annual, irruptive visitor

Not a breeding species
Wintering population estimate: 0–250 individuals

Only 24 records out of 178 were registered prior to the final winter of the atlas. This reflects the truly unpredictable and irruptive nature of the Waxwing. However, in the winter of 2010/11 the county was visited by good numbers. Recent invasions are in marked contrast to past patterns when this species was not only rare but also only recorded in small numbers. Their habit of stripping berries from trees means that they are frequently on the move, so whilst the distribution map is a fair reflection of their potential spread in an irruptive year, the TTV map, with only two entries, shows how infrequently they are detected whilst sampling random squares, even in a year when good numbers are present in the county.

Prior to the final winter, the only counts were of no more than seven birds. In stark contrast, the 2010/11 winter provided counts of up to 160 birds at some sites (CBR 85). That winter had Waxwings in 82 tetrads, and the popularity of this unpredictable visitor meant that some flocks were extremely well watched – especially when they settled in a suburban area with good feeding, which they are prone to do. Autumn food supplies in Scandinavia, other parts of northern Europe, and further north in the UK influence the numbers of Waxwings wintering in Cambridgeshire each year. 2010/11 was a good winter for this species throughout the east of England – large flocks arrived in the UK, and the weather and gradually declining supplies of food further north drove reasonable numbers to seek better feeding in the south and east by December. Flocks hung on until the spring, with several numbering over 50 at sites such as Gamlingay, Brampton and Huntingdon and groups of over 20 in other towns such as Cambridge and Cambourne. Some birds remained to the end of April.

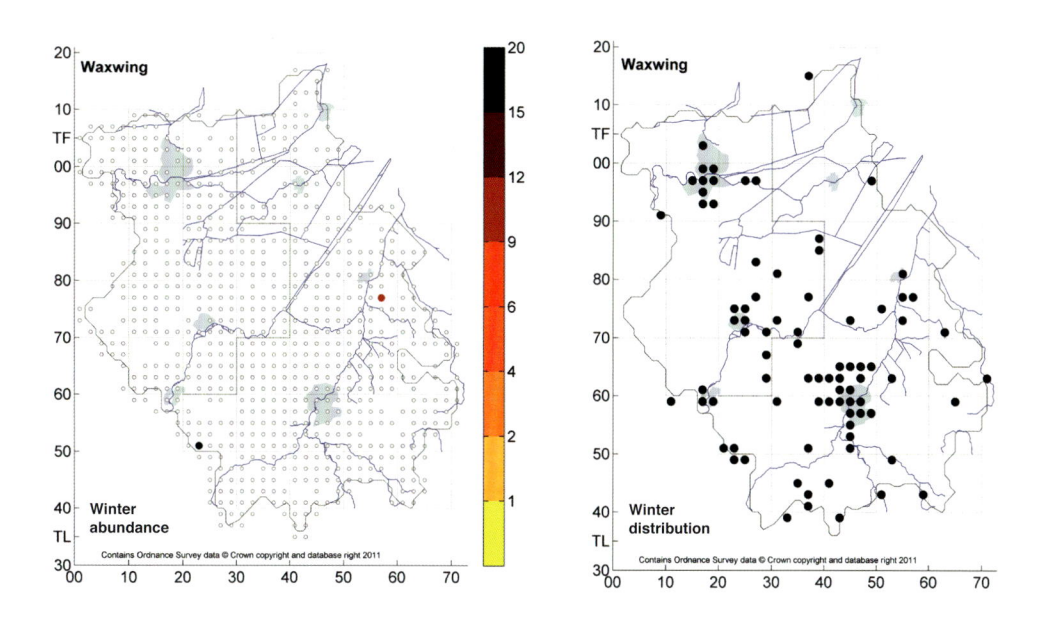

NUTHATCH (Eurasian Nuthatch) *Sitta europaea*
Green List. Fairly common but rather local resident

Breeding population estimate: 150-300 pairs
Wintering population estimate: 300-600 individuals

Nuthatches are woodland birds; they can adapt to parkland and well-wooded gardens but not to widely scattered trees in the way that Great-spotted Woodpeckers can, for example. They avoid open spaces, and require native broadleaved trees to supply large quantities of caterpillars for feeding their young and seeds for winter food; mature trees with suitable nesting holes are also important. It can take a long time to colonise suitable habitat, and they can become locally extinct in small isolated woods. The distribution maps show that they are restricted to the well-wooded parts of the county, particularly the north-west, south-west and south-east districts, but Monks Wood is the centre of a small area of dense population as well.

Although the distributions from the winter and summer TTVs look similar at the broad scale, close examination shows variation between seasons. This probably reflects chance encounters with a species that is not abundant within the sites where it occurs, rather than distribution changes between seasons. For example, TL17Q (Brampton Wood), provided a summer roving record, but no winter or TTV records. It is unlikely that the species deserted the wood in the winter, but rather that no recorders encountered it.

The low density of Nuthatches in many of our woods probably makes their detection harder, as territorial encounters (which can happen at any time of the year) are reduced in frequency. It is when they are proclaiming their territories, with loud and distinctive calls ringing through the trees, that they are most readily detected. They are easy to identify when seen, but in dense woodland may easily be overlooked.

Nuthatch distribution has possibly declined slightly since the previous Cambs Atlas, when there were more records around Cambridge and Newmarket. It was noted in that publication that a particularly systematic survey had been undertaken and it was considered that all but a handful of sites had been identified. At that time, Nuthatch was expanding its national range rapidly, having been present in just two 10 km squares in the 1968–72 Breeding Atlas (Sharrock, 1976). Compared with the previous Hunts Atlas, there have been losses and gains; the south-western area of TL06 and TL16 previously had more records, but Monks Wood had none – it spans four 10 km squares and all corners had plenty of Nuthatches in the current work. The expansion into Monks Wood probably reflects the ongoing eastward expansion.

Their range expansion also sees Nuthatches increasing rapidly in northern England and now Scotland. The expansion phase has passed through our area and it is likely that in Cambridgeshire, our woods are as densely populated as they will ever be. We have the least densely wooded county in the UK and it is not good Nuthatch country. The BBS shows an ongoing upward trend nationally, but there are not enough Cambridgeshire or Eastern England squares for a trend to be calculated (Risely *et al.*, 2012).

The highest summer counts were 12 at TL27 (Hinchingbrooke CP; no tetrad assigned), 10 from TL28A (Monks Wood) on a roving visit, and there were two TTVs with four: TL17Z (Monks Wood again) and TL25A (Gamlingay). In the winter, TTVs also peaked at four, this time in TF00M and TF00N, around Burghley Park and Stamford, while roving records peaked at 10 in both TL18 (Aversley Wood) and TL27 (Hinchingbrooke CP).

In the winter period, Nuthatches were recorded in 73 tetrads (8%) and 22 10 km squares (43%).

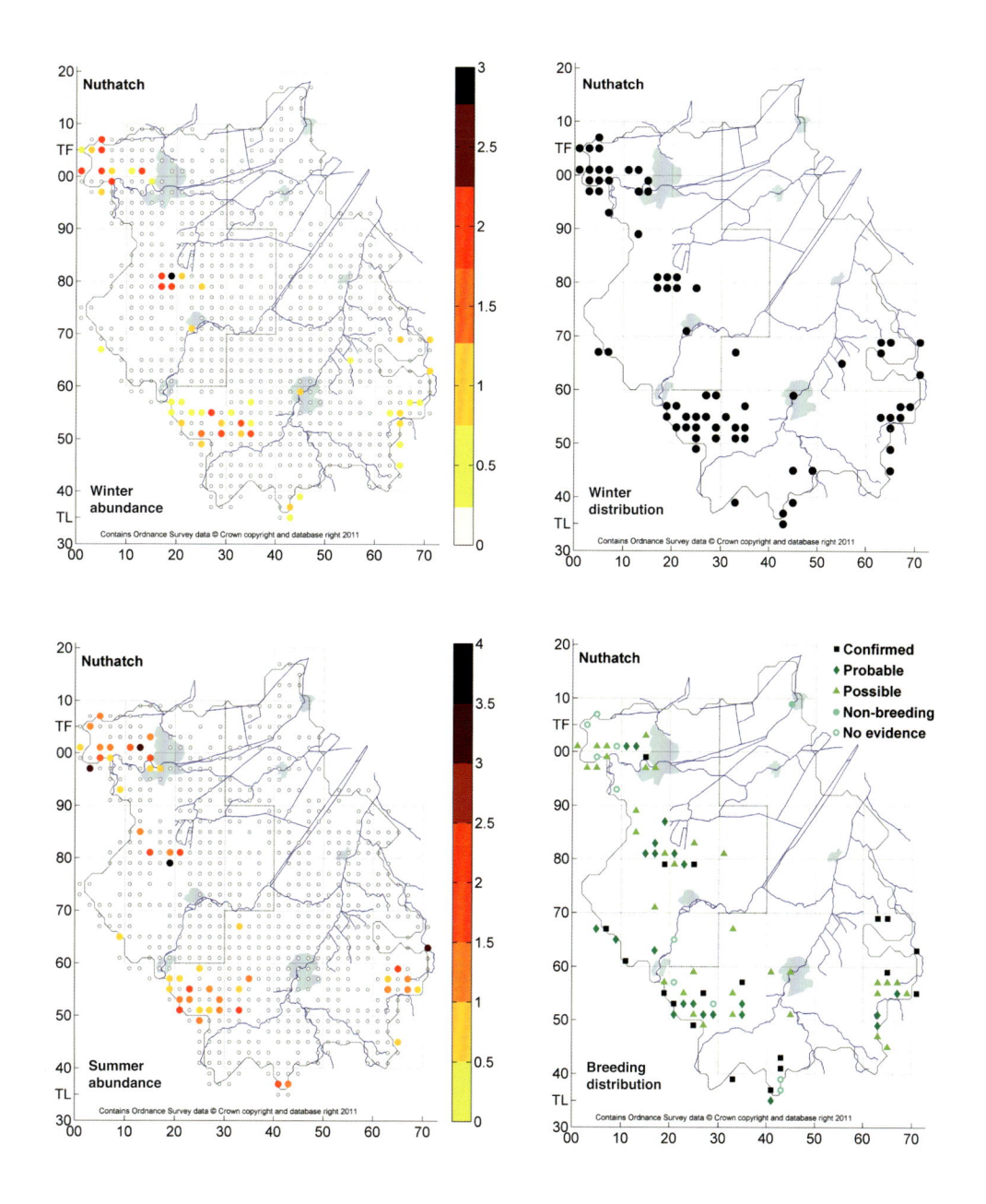

	Confirmed	Probable	Possible	Non-breeding	No evidence	Total summer (% county)	Total winter (% county)
Total tetrads	19	22	34	1	10	86 (9%)	73 (8%)

TREECREEPER (Eurasian Treecreeper) *Certhia familiaris*
Green List. **Fairly common resident away from fenland**

Breeding population estimate: 500-1,000 pairs
Wintering population estimate: 1,000-2,500 individuals

Trees are essential to Treecreepers, but they are less reliant on large areas of native woodland than Nuthatches; willow-lined riverbanks and areas with mixed broadleaved trees and conifers will also accommodate them. As a result this species has a larger range, occupying about three-quarters of the county when examined at 10 km resolution. Within this range, however, it is rather thinly distributed. Only two 10 km squares have more than 50% occupancy when examined at tetrad resolution – TL25 and TL35 in the south-west boulder clay woodland area. By contrast, the sparsest areas of the county are the fens, where virtually no records were obtained. There is evidence for a slightly wider distribution in the winter period, with 10% more 10 km squares occupied, despite a slightly smaller number of tetrads having records of this species. This suggests some winter dispersal behaviour, although ringing records suggest that the majority of individuals of this species are highly sedentary. Winter and summer maps show that the densest areas of Treecreeper populations remain the same: south-west Cambridgeshire, the area around Monks Wood and, to a lesser extent, the far south-east and north-west parts of the county. It is notable that in the less well-wooded chalk soils of south Cambridgeshire, Treecreepers follow the major river courses, presumably utilising trees lining the riverbanks and the abundant invertebrates associated with rivers.

Fewer than a quarter of occupied summer tetrads had the highest level of confirmed breeding, reflecting the difficulty of following this species in wooded habitats, and the rather unassuming way in which it behaves. Nonetheless, it is not particularly wary at the nest and can be observed returning with food given patient observation. It is notable that almost half the occupied tetrads in the previous Hunts Atlas had confirmed breeding, compared to the much lower proportion in the present work. This partly reflects the TTV approach not allowing time to confirm breeding, but also possibly a reduced observer density in wooded habitats on a roving basis.

Although there are no problems regarding identification (ignoring the extremely unlikely Short-toed Treecreeper), this species is quite unobtrusive. The main means of detecting its presence is through its subtle, rather high-pitched, calls, which some birdwatchers struggle to hear. It is therefore likely to have been missed on some visits and the maps may underestimate the true distribution. Certainly, more tetrads were recorded as occupied in the previous two atlases, but the overall pattern has not really changed. The decline in observed occupancy of the county is not matched by BBS data – nationally it has been remarkably stable over this period, but locally the number of Cambridgeshire BBS squares recording Treecreepers has increased.

The highest summer roving counts came from TL28A (Monks Wood) with 14, while a TTV count of seven came from TL25P (Croxton Park). In the winter, TL28A again had the highest counts, with 10 seen in Riddy Wood on a roving visit and eight on a TTV. Ten were also counted in Aversley Wood but not assigned to a particular tetrad in TL18.

In the winter period, Treecreepers were recorded in 169 tetrads (17%) and 41 10 km squares (80%).

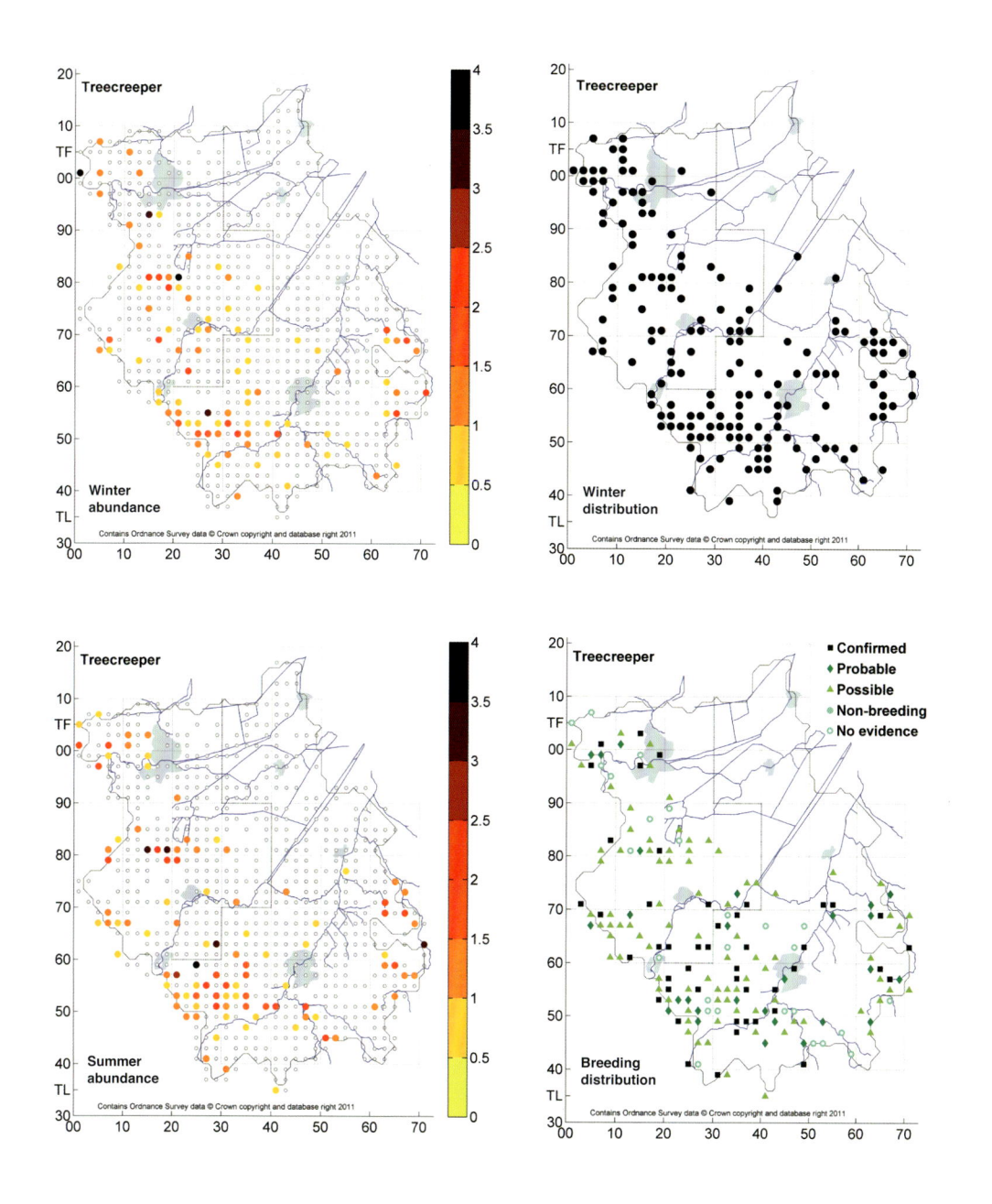

	Confirmed	Probable	Possible	Non-breeding	No evidence	Total summer (% county)	Total winter (% county)
Total tetrads	46	27	85	0	26	184 (19%)	169 (17%)

WREN (Winter Wren) *Troglodytes troglodytes*
Green List. **Widespread and abundant resident**

Breeding population estimate: 50,000-100,000 pairs
Wintering population estimate: 100,000-200,000 individuals

Wrens were recorded across the county, as we would expect for the most common bird in the UK (Musgrove *et al.*, 2013). The abundance maps show that Wrens are about three times more common in summer than winter. This may be a result of the detectability of non-singing birds. The two harsh winters during the atlas period may have affected populations, although this is not obvious from looking at the data; the harsher weather of the two latter winters did not seem to affect Wren distribution at the scale of these records. Ringing data also indicate that there was no significant impact on their numbers.

Most tetrads recorded Wrens, which is no surprise as this common species is so familiar and easy to identify, even for inexperienced observers. Confirmation of breeding was clearly not as straightforward as for some species; although most tetrads had a probable or confirmed breeding code, the former was registered more often. Again, this is most probably due to their strident song, and the fact that Wrens sing territorially against each other. They can be very secretive when nesting, so birds carrying food are not often seen, and nests are well hidden.

Ringing results show Wrens to be highly sedentary and there is no evidence of emigration or immigration into the county.

Wrens were recorded in 97% of TTVs in summer and 88% in winter. Maximum counts were 27 in summer and 14 in winter; the average encounter rate was 4.6 and 1.9 birds per hour, respectively.

The BBS 15-year trend (1995–2010) for the UK implies a 2% decline. For England the trend is similar at -1%, but for Eastern England the population trend is upwards, with a 6% increase between 1995 and 2010 (Risely *et al.*, 2012).

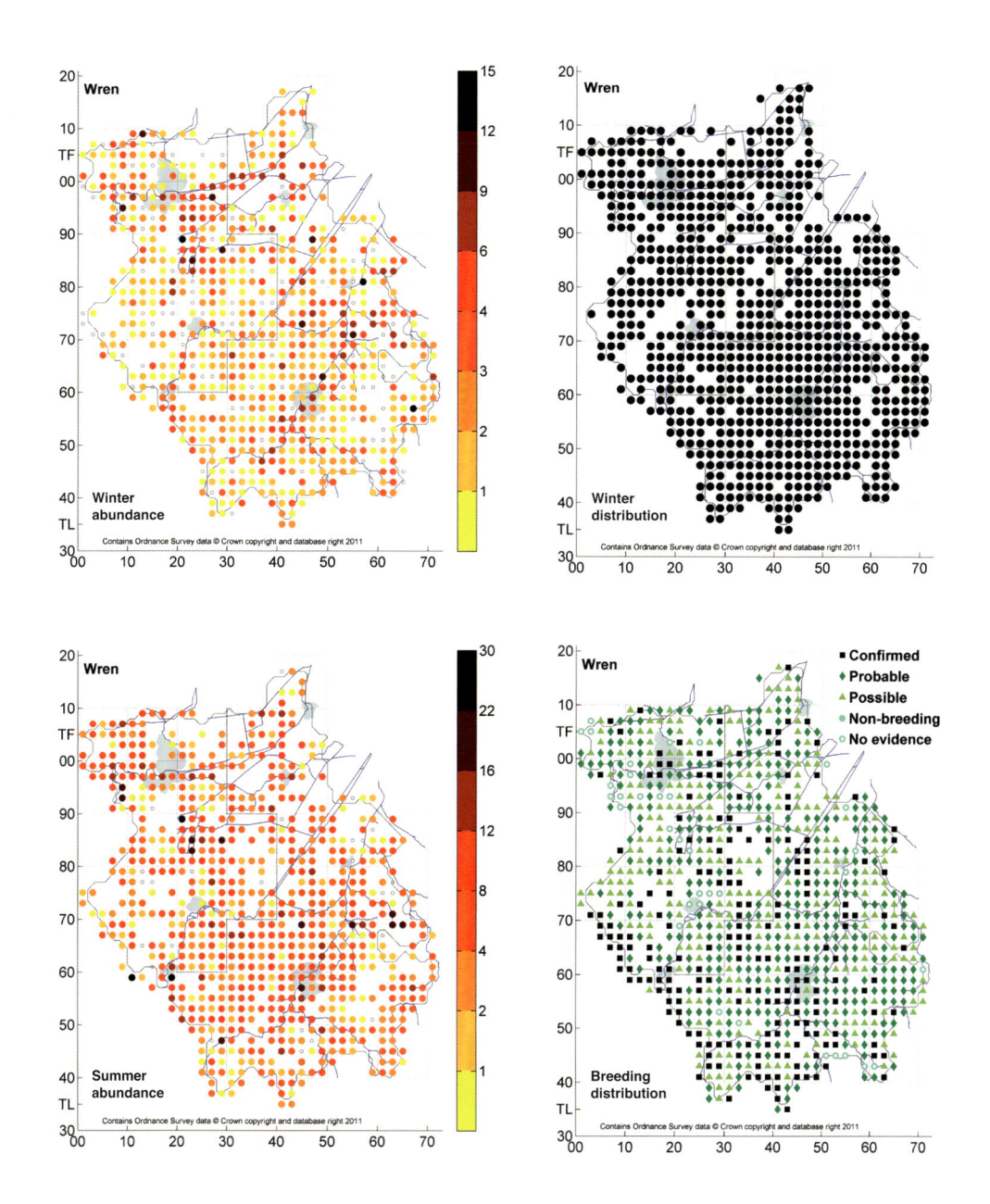

	Confirmed	Probable	Possible	Non-breeding	No evidence	Total summer (% county)	Total winter (% county)
Total tetrads	208	361	275	0	35	879 (91%)	799 (82%)

STARLING (Common Starling) *Sturnus vulgaris*
Red List. Very common, but declined resident; abundant winter visitor/passage migrant

Breeding population estimate: 15,000-25,000 pairs
Wintering population estimate: 50,000-100,000 individuals

Despite having declined in numbers, Starlings are still widespread and in some places numerous. Their distribution has changed little since the previous atlases. Found in at least 80% of tetrads in the county, they are far more numerous in winter, no doubt due to the boosting of our resident population with birds from northern Europe. The encounters per hour on TTVs reflect this, averaging seven in summer but 26 in winter. In the summer, 81% of TTVs recorded Starlings, but most counted fewer than 10 birds. Higher densities were in settlements and near a few key wetland sites. In winter, the distribution was similar, but numbers were higher with 3,000 on one TTV. When roving records are included, eight sites recorded over 1,000 on at least one occasion. Fen Drayton Lakes recorded the highest counts with several of at least 10,000; this site is well known for its winter roosts.

Breeding was confirmed in over 40% of tetrads. This is relatively straightforward for observers to establish; taking food into holes in houses or other buildings, noisy territorial behaviour, vocal nestlings and their gregarious habits when fledged mean that Starlings are obvious in the breeding season. The ease of telling young birds from parents means that visits in the second half of the summer usually confirmed successful breeding; many small villages or isolated buildings have healthy Starling populations. However, the fact that Starlings start to aggregate soon after breeding (they usually have only one brood) means that late-summer TTVs encountered sizeable flocks; if no attempt was made to exclude young birds from the counts, this could account for some of the large TTV counts in July. Starlings have distinctive roost gatherings – their swirling aerial displays are quite obvious; however, the TTV rules of completing counts an hour before dusk would preclude many roosts being recorded other than by roving.

The Cambridgeshire population is estimated to be 1.3% of the UK population during winter, but 2.2% in summer. This may imply that our summer populations are buoyant compared to some parts of the country, but perhaps we do not have as many winter migrants as some other regions.

The previous atlases recorded breeding evidence in 75% (Cambs Atlas) and over 90% (Hunts Atlas) of tetrads. The distribution is largely unchanged but no abundance measure was determined in either earlier work.

The BBS 15-year trend (1995–2010) for the UK implies a 50% decline. For England the trend is similar at -55%, while in Eastern England it is -41% (Risely *et al.*, 2012).

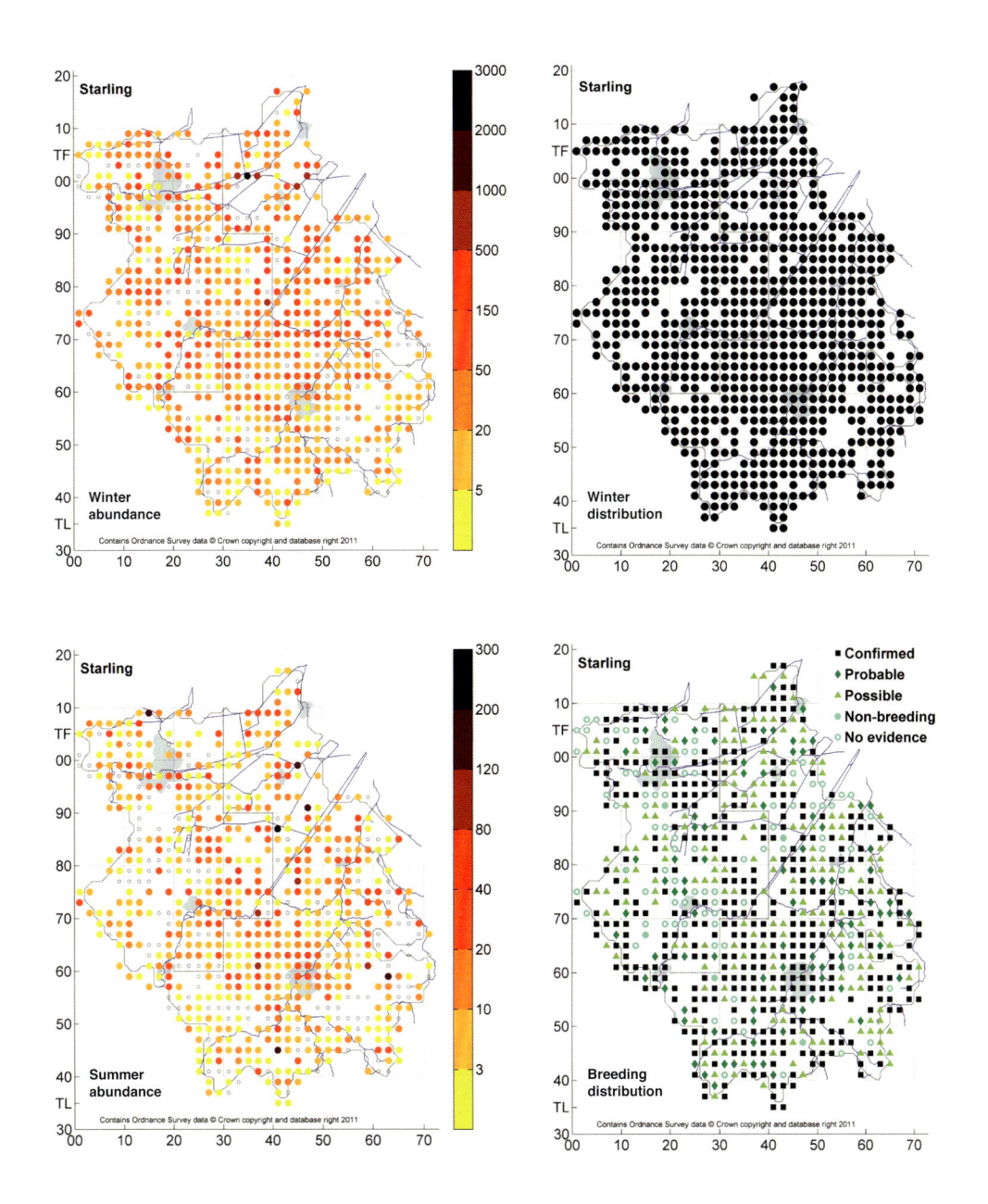

	Confirmed	Probable	Possible	Non-breeding	No evidence	Total summer (% county)	Total winter (% county)
Total tetrads	399	89	199	6	84	777 (80%)	804 (83%)

BLACKBIRD (Common Blackbird) *Turdus merula*
Green List. **Widespread and abundant resident, passage migrant and winter visitor**

Breeding population estimate: 50,000-100,000 pairs
Wintering population estimate: 100,000-300,000 individuals

The Blackbird is our most widespread thrush and is common in all habitats: rural, suburban and urban, farmland and woods, as well as on wetland sites wherever there is some cover. Brown & Grice (2005) reported that population densities vary among habitats, and a study by Mason (1998) in nearby north-east Essex suggested that the amount of open space in suburban areas was positively correlated with density. The abundance maps show that Blackbirds were found in nearly all tetrads surveyed for TTVs in winter and summer. As for the Wren and Robin, the familiarity and obtrusive nature of the Blackbird means that most atlas participants, no matter how inexperienced, would record accurately the presence and breeding activity of this species. Winter TTV counts were slightly higher than summer counts. This is to be expected as our resident population is bolstered by winter migrants, and locally by young birds from the previous breeding season, at least in the early part of winter.

Ringing results indicate the origin of these winter migrants to Cambridgeshire to be the near Continent – the Low Countries, Germany and Denmark – with some birds from Scandinavia.

The BBS 15-year trend (1995–2010) for the UK implies a 23% increase. For England the trend is similar at 21% and in Eastern England an increase of 8% (Risely *et al.*, 2012).

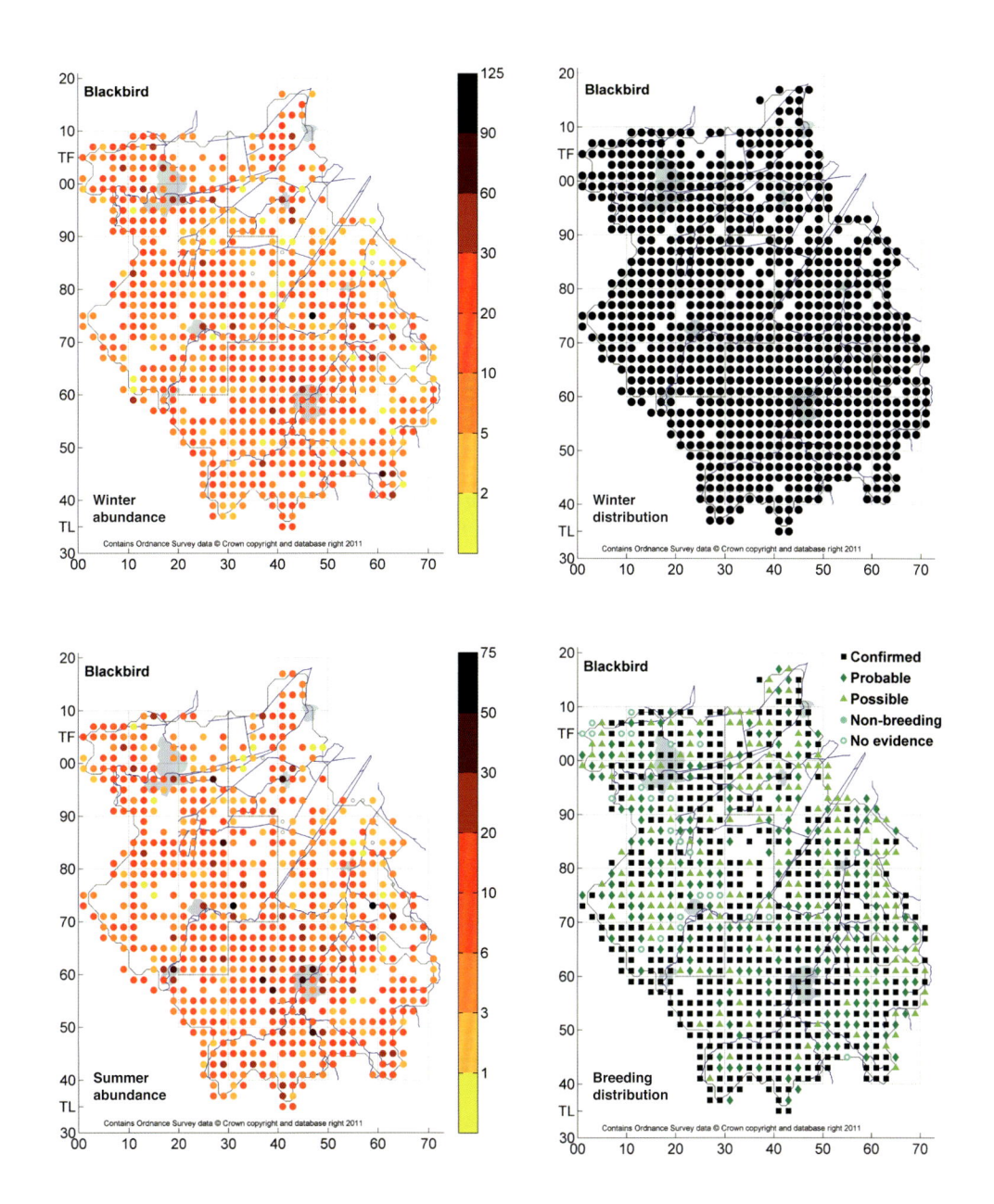

	Confirmed	Probable	Possible	Non-breeding	No evidence	Total summer (% county)	Total winter (% county)
Total tetrads	502	207	179	0	26	914 (94%)	899 (93%)

FIELDFARE *Turdus pilaris*
Red List. Abundant winter visitor and passage migrant, particularly in autumn

Not a breeding species
Wintering population estimate: 5,000-30,000 individuals

The Fieldfare is the more numerous of the two winter thrushes in our county, being four times as abundant as the Redwing. Recorded in many tetrads, few are seen in our large urban areas of Peterborough, Huntingdon and Cambridge as shown by the gaps in the TTV and distribution maps. The average count was of 29 birds per hour; many TTVs had counts of fewer than 50. The higher counts were concentrated in a belt across the centre of the county, and in the far north-east. This can be explained to some extent by the number of surviving orchards in these two areas. Orchards are favoured by Fieldfares – unharvested apples are high on their preferred food list. Whilst we may think of Fieldfares as birds of orchards, large hedges and other sites with abundant berries, this resource does not last all winter. They will move around the country to seek out new sources and later in the winter they often resort to feeding on both arable and grass fields. This accounts for their widespread distribution across the county. In total, Fieldfares were recorded from 829 tetrads, and from 88% of TTVs.

The second winter of the atlas period (2008/9), a mild one, was striking in that only two counts of over 300 birds were reported, the maximum being 365. The other three winters included many more counts of flocks of over 300 birds. The winter of 2007/8 had 15 counts over 300, peaking at 1,100 and 1,670; 2009/10 and 2010/11 both had seven counts of over 300 birds: peak counts in the former were 600 and 1,164 and in the final winter 573 and 700. The last two winters were far more severe. The mean flock sizes per winter (for records supplied with specific counts) were 56, 31, 43 and 45, representing just over 5% of the peak counts.

Ringing results show the origins of the Cambridgeshire birds to be mainly Fennoscandia, but interestingly some birds ringed in Cambridgeshire were found in subsequent winters in France, Italy, Portugal and Spain.

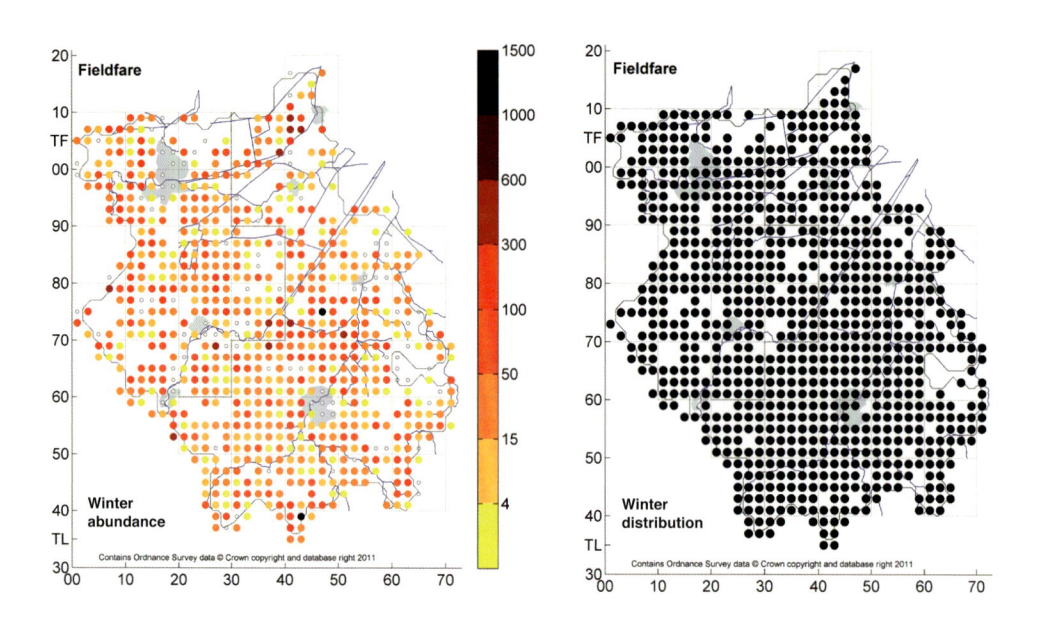

REDWING *Turdus iliacus*
Red List. Abundant winter visitor and passage migrant

Not a breeding species
Wintering population estimate: 2,500-20,000 individuals

Like their larger cousin the Fieldfare, Redwings visit our county during the winter. They arrive in mid-October and are widespread until the middle of December when, as the berry supply dwindles to exhaustion, they move on west and south before reappearing in good numbers in late February and March on their return migration. Feeding on berries and other fruit, Redwings tend to follow the availability of food supplies, both within the county and within their wider wintering area. Compared with Fieldfares, Redwings are found more in urban areas, and can be seen in mid-winter in parks and open spaces. Redwings are rarely found in such large flocks as Fieldfares, and their numbers did not seem to fluctuate as widely over the years of the atlas.

Over the four winters of the atlas, there were 18, 13, 16 and 16 counts of over 75 birds, respectively, with the top two flock counts in each winter being 385 and 268 (2007/8), 300 and 150 (2008/9), 300 and 200 (2009/10) and 250 and 192 (2010/11). The mean flock sizes per winter for those records with specific counts were 17, 15, 16 and 16, just over 5% of the peak counts.

Ringing results show the origins of most birds again to be Fennoscandia. There is some evidence of onward migration south, and birds ringed in England were found in subsequent winters in France, Italy, Portugal and Spain.

Redwings were recorded from 696 tetrads (72%) and on 75% of TTVs with an average encounter rate of seven birds per hour.

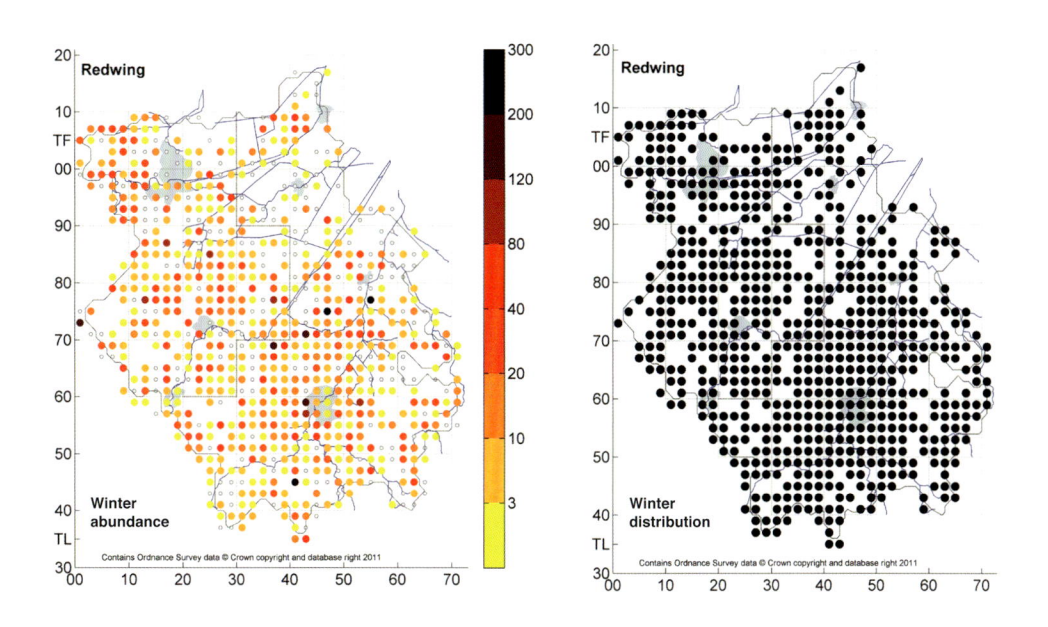

SONG THRUSH *Turdus philomelos*
Red List. Common but declined resident, winter visitor and passage migrant

Breeding population estimate: 10,000-15,000 pairs
Wintering population estimate: 30,000-50,000 individuals

The Song Thrush remains a widespread species, found in all habitats, much like the Blackbird, but at a much lower density; it has clearly undergone a significant decline in Cambridgeshire since the previous atlases, in contrast to the national population trend (Eaton *et al.*, 2012) which indicates a slight increase since the 1990s. Whilst still recorded in around 75–80% of summer and winter TTVs, on average only one or two birds per hour were encountered – a fraction of the number of Blackbirds. The main geographic areas where TTVs did not record Song Thrushes were parts of the northern and eastern fens where there are few hedges, settlements or woodlands. The other area clearly lacking this species is the west of Huntingdonshire. This is a more recent phenomenon; absence from the fens was clear in the previous atlases, but the western side of the county then had good numbers of this once-familiar thrush. The previous Cambs Atlas considered that this species was declining in numbers but not range, and had always been sparsely distributed in the eastern and northern part of the county. The Hunts Atlas recorded confirmed breeding throughout. In the present atlas the gaps in the western part of the county emphasise how much the Song Thrush has declined – there were numerous TTVs here with no Song Thrushes recorded. The maximum count on a TTV was 10 in summer and 13 in winter, and the winter maximum count from all record types is a little higher at 26; much lower figures than for the other thrushes.

In winter there is some immigration, although transient, of birds from north of the UK and the near Continent that may continue south.

The BBS 15-year trend (1995–2010) for the UK implies a 13% increase. For England the trend is similar at 15% but for Eastern England the long-term population trend is a small decline of 4% (Risely *et al.*, 2012).

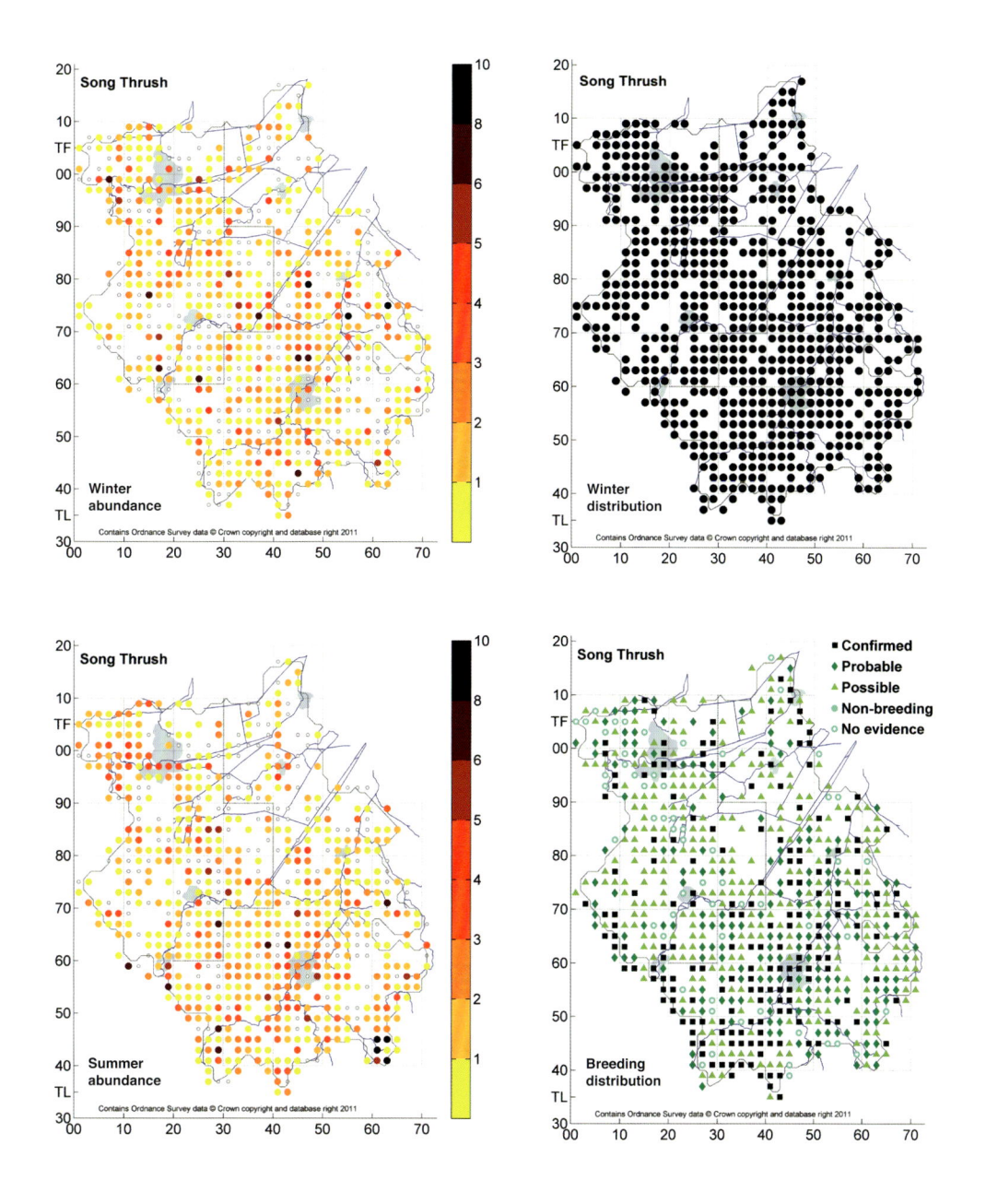

	Confirmed	Probable	Possible	Non-breeding	No evidence	Total summer (% county)	Total winter (% county)
Total tetrads	186	179	316	0	58	739 (76%)	688 (71%)

MISTLE THRUSH *Turdus viscivorus*
Amber List. Common and widespread resident; some passage migrants

Breeding population estimate: 1,000-2,000 pairs
Wintering population estimate: 2,000-5,000 individuals

Most Mistle Thrushes are found in the south of the county, or in the area west of Peterborough. Nationally, Mistle Thrush is an amber-listed species undergoing a significant long-term decline (Eaton *et al.*, 2012). This is also the case in Cambridgeshire. In comparison to the previous atlases when south and western Huntingdonshire apparently had strong populations, the Mistle Thrush has clearly been lost from some areas. Brown & Grice (2005) reported the decline to be greatest in eastern counties and the BTO trend shows a continual decline over the period between our atlases. The 15-year BBS trend (1995–2010) is a 28% decrease, for England is -35% and for Eastern England is -53% (Risely *et al.*, 2012).

Only around 50% of TTVs logged Mistle Thrushes, in both seasons. The loss of invertebrate-rich pastures is considered to be significant in East Anglia as studies have shown the decline to be driven by reduced adult survival (Siriwardena *et al.*, 1998).

Breeding was confirmed in 141 tetrads out of 556 where Mistle Thrush was recorded. Large TTV counts of between 12 and 28 (the peak summer count) were all recorded in the last week of July. As for the Starling, by this time of year the early-breeding Mistle Thrush can be found in post-breeding flocks, often feeding in arable fields. These counts may skew the population estimates. Only one winter count reached the same value; post-breeding flocks disperse with the onset of winter, and late winter will see highly territorial behaviour, defending food sources near potential breeding sites, and singing when the weather is mild. The sedentary nature of this species is reflected in a comparison of the winter and summer distribution maps. Ringing information suggests some short-distance movement within England but recoveries overseas are rare.

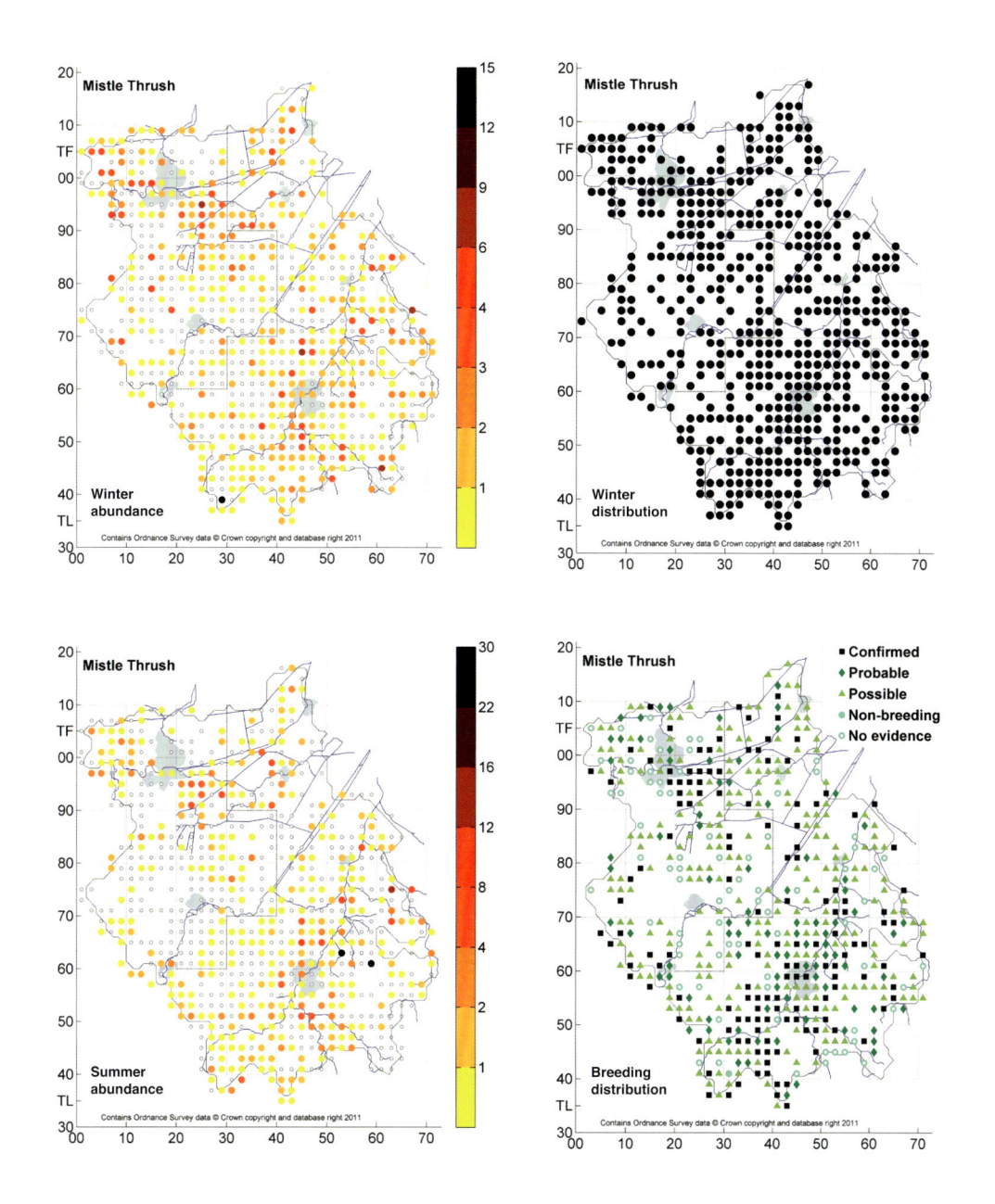

	Confirmed	Probable	Possible	Non-breeding	No evidence	Total summer (% county)	Total winter (% county)
Total tetrads	141	88	250	1	76	556 (57%)	563 (58%)

SPOTTED FLYCATCHER *Muscicapa striata*
Red List. Uncommon and greatly declined migratory breeder and passage migrant

Breeding population estimate: 100-200 pairs
Not a wintering species

The Spotted Flycatcher has undergone a significant population decline in recent years, possibly due to problems on migration, a decline in large flying invertebrates, or to habitat changes. The reasons for this decline are not fully understood. From being once a widespread and relatively common breeding bird in Cambridgeshire, it has become unusual. It was not widely recorded during the atlas, with records from only 10% of TTVs, and 22% of tetrads overall. However, this could include an element of observer bias: its song and call are high-pitched and not very strident; it arrives later in the summer than many migrants; and it is generally unobtrusive. Probably its most distinctive feature is its feeding flights – flycatching sallies out from a perch and back. Whilst Spotted Flycatchers have probably never been present in the open fens – preferring woodlands, parks, and mature wooded gardens – fenland towns such as Ely and Wisbech still hold populations, as they did in the previous Cambs Atlas. This appears to be in contrast to the bigger settlements of Huntingdon, Cambridge and Peterborough, where it was not recorded in most tetrads.

The decline in this species is quite apparent in the south and especially in the west of the county. Previously recorded in most tetrads in Huntingdonshire, it is now rarely encountered, but has a scattered distribution from St. Neots to Peterborough and in the wooded parkland to the west of that city. Southern Cambridgeshire still has widely distributed Spotted Flycatchers, although never abundant and much diminished compared to the previous Cambs Atlas, where confirmed breeding was recorded in 26% of old Cambridgeshire (as well as in over 70% of Huntingdonshire).

The BBS 15-year trend (1995–2010) for the UK implies a 50% decrease, for England the trend is similar at -55% (Risely *et al.*, 2012).

Two Cambridgeshire-ringed birds have been recovered in Morocco but information on wintering areas (thought to be West Africa) is sparse.

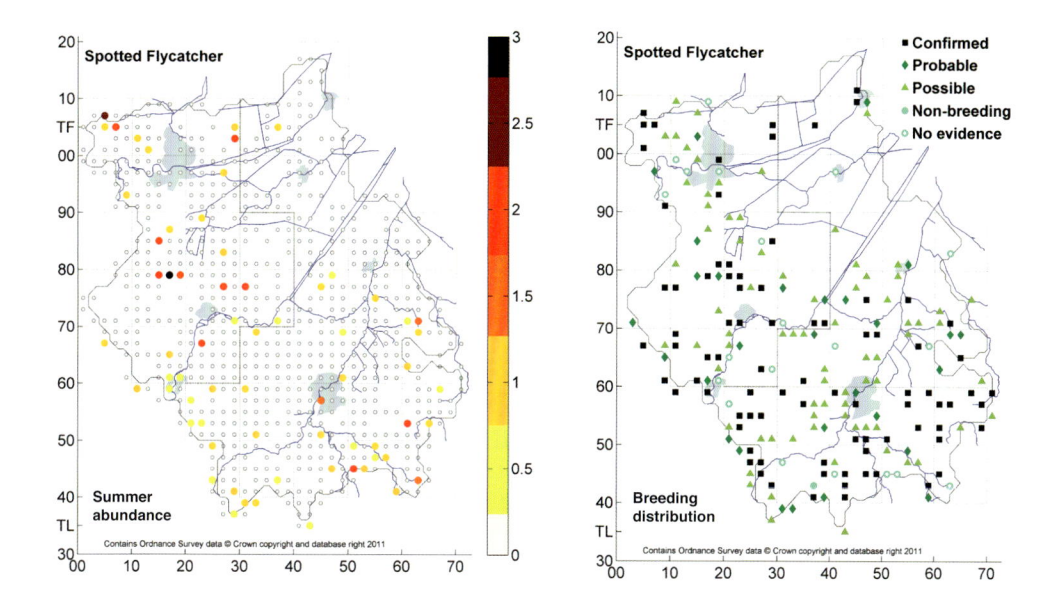

	Confirmed	Probable	Possible	Non-breeding	No evidence	Total summer (% county)
Total tetrads	85	29	76	1	20	211 (22%)

ROBIN (European Robin) *Erithacus rubecula*
Green List. Widespread and abundant resident; some passage migrants

Breeding population estimate: 40,000-60,000 pairs
Wintering population estimate: 100,000-150,000 individuals

We think of the familiar Robin as ubiquitous in Cambridgeshire; it is at home in rural, urban, suburban, farmland, woodland and even wetland habitats, although it is less common in the agricultural open spaces of the fens. Almost all TTVs logged Robin (96%); most of those which were blank are in the north-eastern parts of the county, where the limited settlements, few woods or hedges and wide-open agricultural vistas present a habitat not favoured by this species. This pattern was also evident in the previous Cambs Atlas. Even where Robins were found in the north-east of the county, their abundance was markedly lower than in the south-central regions. A lower abundance is also clear in the tetrads in the far west, although the reasons for this cannot be the same – this is a landscape with plenty of villages and hedges. Robin is a species for which it is easy to confirm breeding; distinctive youngsters, a familiar song maintained throughout the breeding season, and easy co-existence with humans all mean that breeding evidence is easy to gather.

Counts of over 20 birds were recorded in 19 tetrads, most on TTVs, with a maximum hourly count of 26 in summer and 25 in winter. The national BBS trend for Robin (1995–2010) shows a 10% increase; in England the trend is 16% and in Eastern England 24% (Risely *et al.*, 2012).

Robins that breed in the UK are generally sedentary, but some emigrate in winter to France or Iberia. In addition there is winter immigration of Robins to the UK mainly from northern and north-eastern Europe; some of these birds will continue further south.

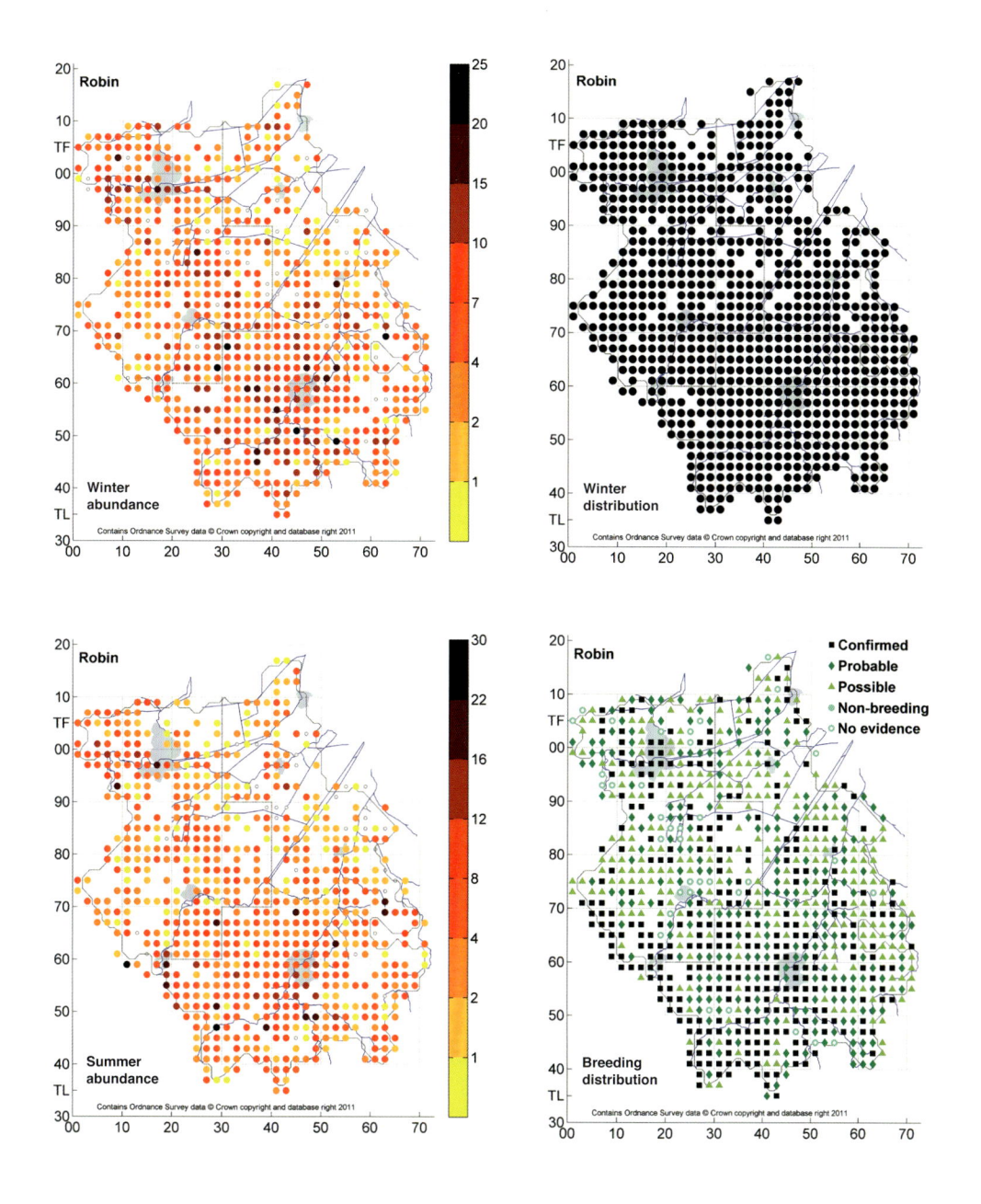

	Confirmed	Probable	Possible	Non-breeding	No evidence	Total summer (% county)	Total winter (% county)
Total tetrads	317	234	276	0	36	863 (89%)	856 (88%)

NIGHTINGALE (Common Nightingale) *Luscinia megarhynchos*
Amber List. Uncommon migratory breeder, most in west of county

Breeding population estimate: 100-200 singing males
Not a wintering species

The Nightingale has one of the most famous songs of all British birds, and this is undoubtedly the means by which most of the records of this species were obtained. It was recorded in 63 tetrads, representing 7% of the county. Rarely seen, the majority of birds will have been assigned as possible breeders on the basis of singing (34); probable breeders (22) mostly derive from multiple singing birds or repeat observations at the same spot. There were three tetrads with confirmed breeding. Unsurprisingly, most records were from gravel pits, although a few are still to be found in ancient woodlands, such as Monks Wood or Castor Hanglands. A very few singing birds were from isolated thickets or small woods; however, these were usually within a few tetrads of larger clusters of breeders. Perhaps these are birds still en route to nearby breeding grounds, or those unable to find a territory that opted for a nearby site. The map clearly shows the affinity of Nightingales for river valleys, especially the complex of pits along the Ouse. The larger wetland reserves away from the Ouse valley account for many of the other records, including Roswell Pits at Ely, Fowlmere, Woodwalton Fen and nearby Monks Wood. The largest populations, into double figures for singing males, were found at Castor Hanglands, Little Paxton Pits, Grafham Water and Marsh Lane gravel pits. The BTO national survey recorded a minimum total of 120 singing males for Cambridgeshire in 2012.

At 2–2.5% of the national total, Cambridgeshire holds a population just above average for the UK. The previous Cambs Atlas noted probable or confirmed breeding in 43 tetrads, and the Hunts Atlas in another 59, with birds present in an additional four and ten tetrads, respectively. Only about half this number of tetrads is occupied in the present atlas. Many of the losses are from the woodlands of the south and west, but also notably from some big wetland sites in the east, such as Wicken and Chippenham Fens. A possible explanation for this decline is the increase in deer numbers and the consequent loss of understorey.

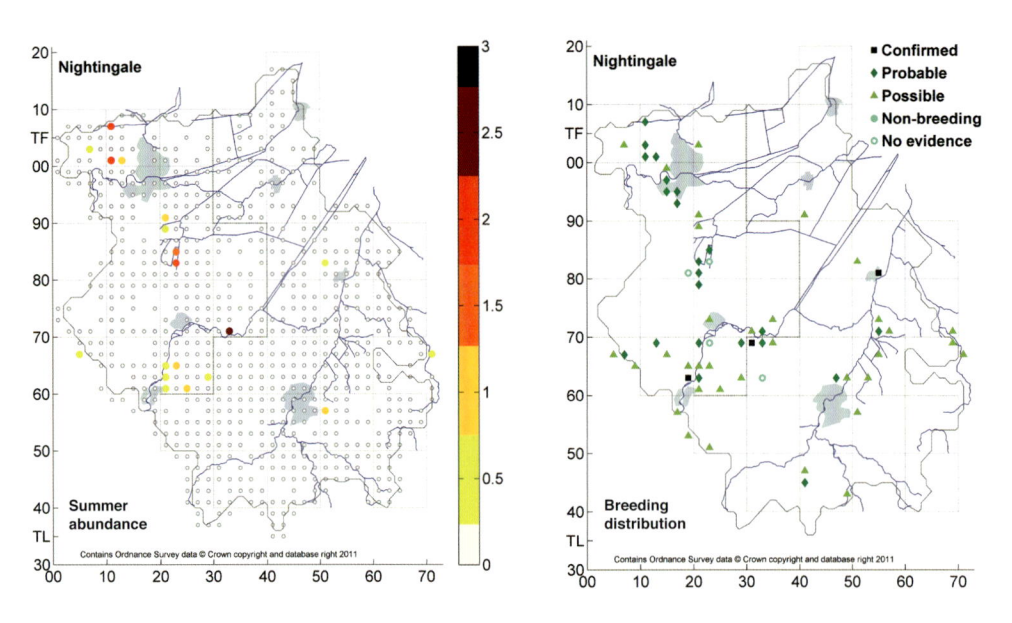

	Confirmed	Probable	Possible	Non-breeding	No evidence	Total summer (% county)
Total tetrads	3	22	34	0	4	63 (7%)

BLACK REDSTART *Phoenicurus ochruros*
Amber List. Scarce annual passage migrant, irregular migratory breeder, and winter visitor

Breeding population estimate: variable, 0-5 pairs
Wintering population estimate: 0-10 individuals

The status of the Black Redstart in Cambridgeshire has historically been erratic with some records of breeding, some passage birds and some winter visitors. Often periods of absence can be followed by a few records in the same year. During the period of the atlas more Black Redstarts were recorded in summer than winter. Most of the probable or confirmed breeders were in our larger settlements of Cambridge, Peterborough, Ely and Cambourne, but a minority were from villages. Some of the possible breeders could have been migrants, as several records were from April or late July. There was an even spread of records across the years, although slightly more were recorded in 2009.

The number of winter records is surprisingly low – only five were submitted, mostly in November. The wintering sites are surprisingly close to some of the summering areas. Neither of the previous atlases considered Black Redstart worthy of mapping, if it resided at all in the county. This species has colonised the UK during the last century and has spread further north in recent years. Only one TTV in each season recorded Black Redstarts, thus maps are not shown here as they provide little insight into the species' status.

The national status of Black Redstart shows a slight increase in the numbers of breeding birds (up to a maximum of 100 pairs) but the predicted expansion has not occurred (Brown & Grice, 2005). Passage birds and wintering birds are likely to be from the continental breeding population that winters in the western Mediterranean.

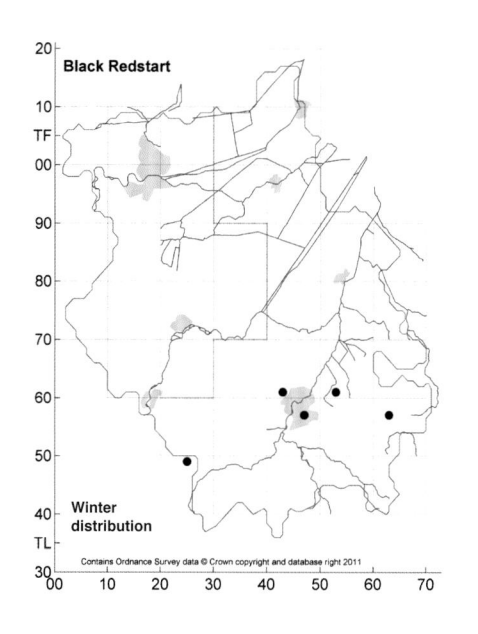

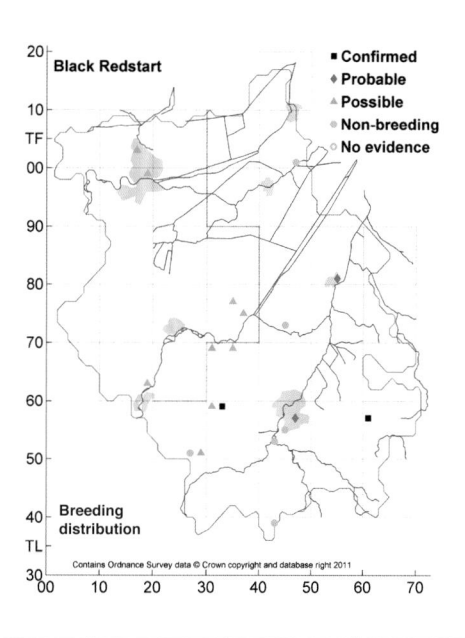

	Confirmed	Probable	Possible	Non-breeding	No evidence	Total summer (% county)	Total winter (% county)
Total tetrads	2	2	9	6	0	19 (2%)	5 (0.5%)

STONECHAT (Eurasian Stonechat) *Saxicola torquatus*
Green List. Uncommon winter visitor, passage migrant (mainly in the fens), and occasional breeder

Breeding population estimate: variable, 0-5 pairs
Wintering population estimate: 10-100 individuals

The Stonechat has historically been a winter visitor to Cambridgeshire, certainly in recent times, thus confirmed breeding at two sites in the county was a pleasant surprise for one or two keen observers. Two birds were observed together in late March in the south-west of the county, on the criteria of the atlas implying a probable breeder, but the exact habitat of these birds remains uncertain. Most surprising was that one pair with confirmed breeding was in a new settlement, albeit one with plenty of rough grassland, plantations and recently constructed lakes. To record Stonechat breeding less than a kilometre from Black Redstart was truly unusual for Cambridgeshire. Another pair, although recorded in three different tetrads and presumably quite mobile, was in a wet grassland/fen-creation area.

Records in winter came from 128 tetrads (13% of the county), biased towards river valleys, washes etc., but also with a scatter of records across the southernmost 10 km squares and the far west. Examining the number of records per winter provides a striking impression of the effects of weather. In the winter 2007/8 there were 127 records (93 tetrads), the following winter 61 (39 tetrads), then in the last two much harsher winters there were only 26 (17 tetrads) and 18 records (13 tetrads), respectively. This must reflect both harder wintering conditions in our area, and also harsher weather in the breeding grounds of these birds – hard winters have a tendency to foreshadow very late springs further north. A poor breeding season in the northern UK would have serious impacts on the number of wintering Stonechats in Cambridgeshire; it is unlikely that our birds come from much further afield than this.

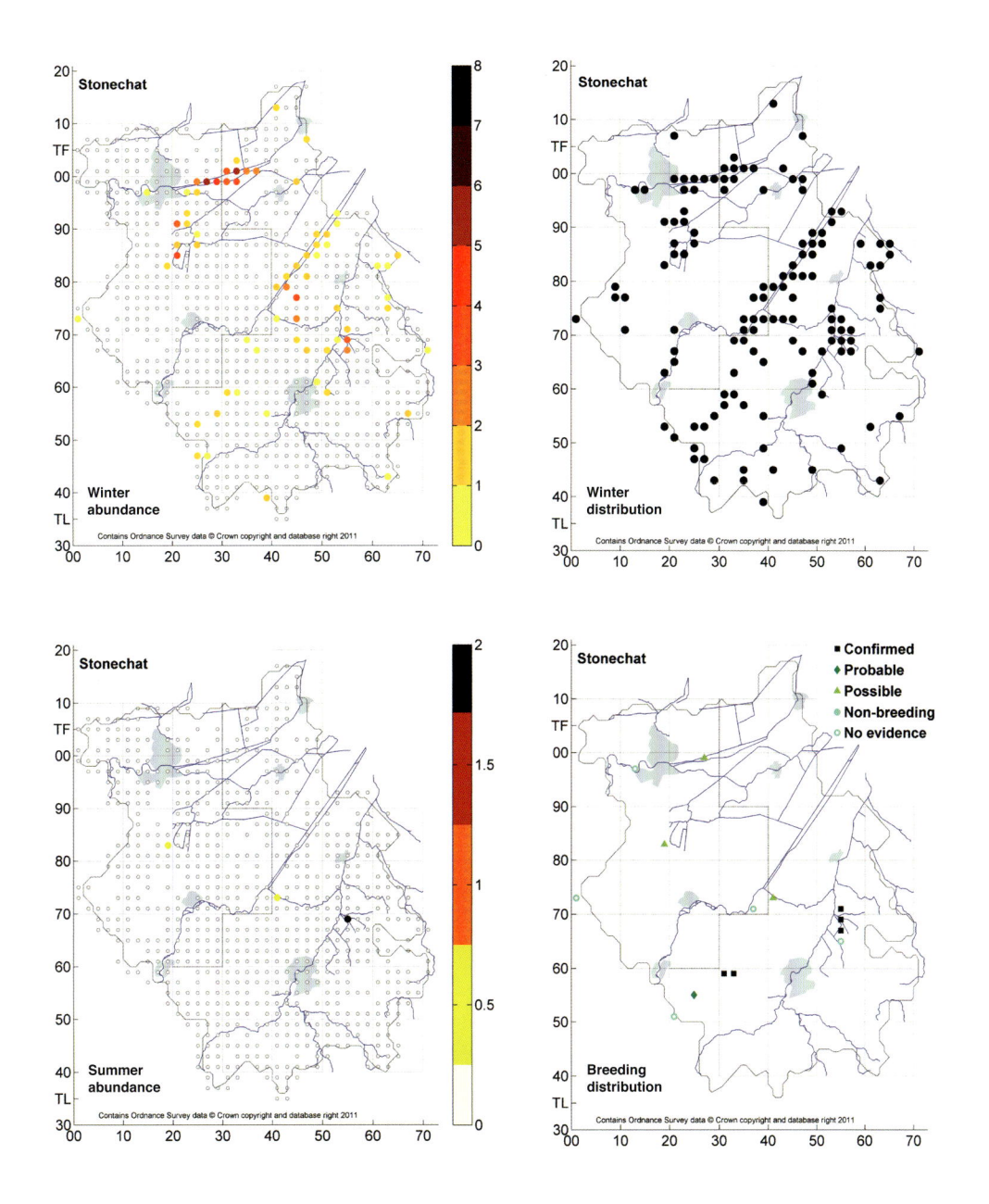

	Confirmed	Probable	Possible	Non-breeding	No evidence	Total summer (% county)	Total winter (% county)
Total tetrads	5	1	3	0	5	14 (1%)	128 (13%)

DUNNOCK *Prunella modularis*
Amber List. **Widespread and abundant resident; some evidence of passage migrants**

Breeding population estimate: 25,000-50,000 pairs
Wintering population estimate: 50,000-150,000 individuals

More unobtrusive than some of our smaller resident birds, Dunnocks were still widely recorded across the county, although like the Robin they are less abundant and less well distributed in the fens. It is harder to prove breeding success, as this species is quite secretive when breeding. This is borne out in the proportion of tetrads where breeding was confirmed. Singing birds are noticeable, but they become much quieter once breeding is underway. Virtually all probable breeders were categorised on the basis of territorial singing males.

Dunnocks are sedentary birds so numbers should remain fairly similar in summer and winter although winter mortality will have an effect. In urban and suburban habitats they continue to thrive but in semi-natural habitats their numbers have fallen; this may be linked to the rise in deer numbers and the resulting loss of understorey scrub – a favoured habitat.

Dunnocks were recorded in 89% of TTVs, but counts were never as high as for Robins or Wrens. The long-term BBS trends (1995–2010) for the UK, England and Eastern England are increases of 22%, 17% and 17%, respectively (Risely *et al.*, 2012).

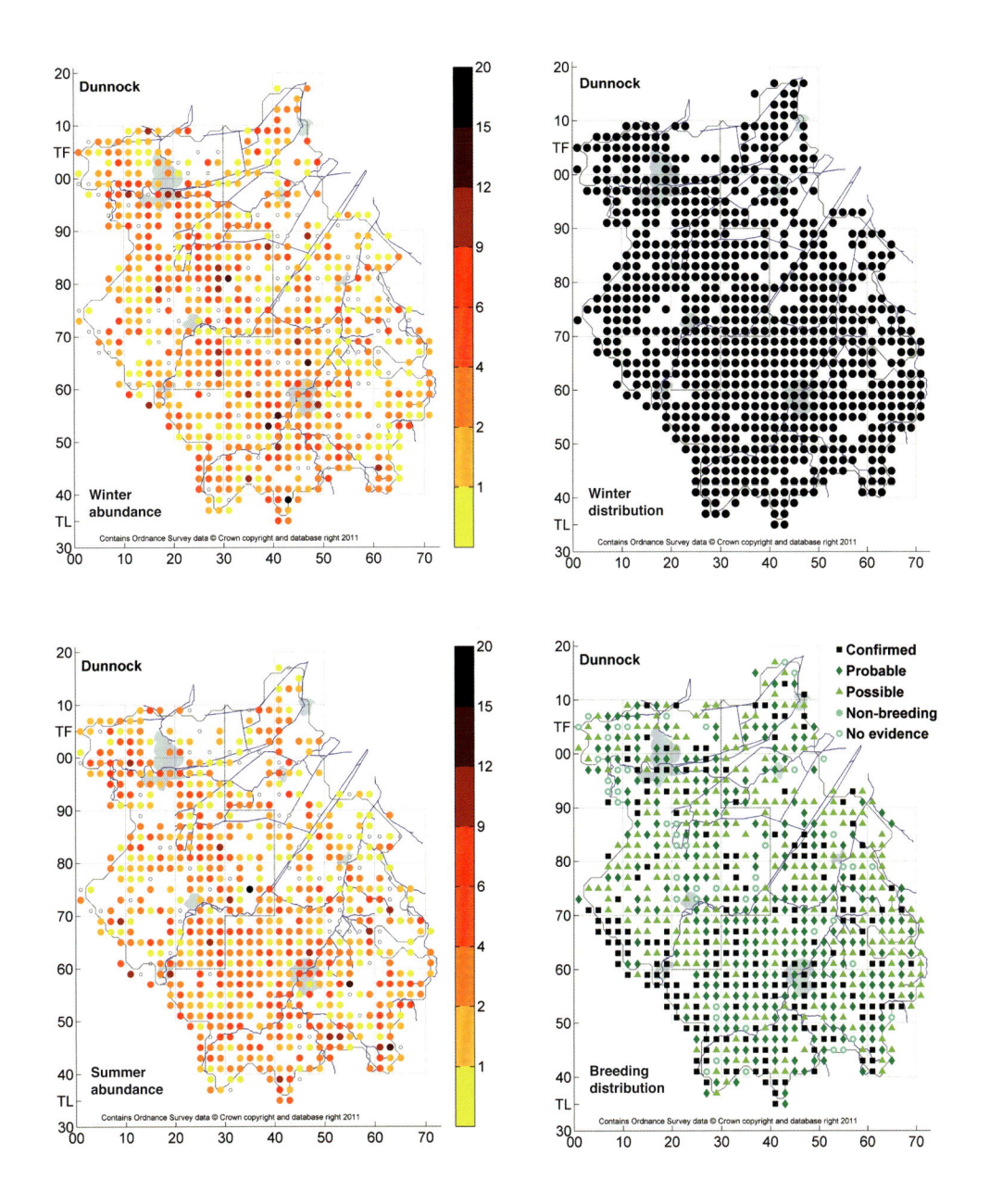

	Confirmed	Probable	Possible	Non-breeding	No evidence	Total summer (% county)	Total winter (% county)
Total tetrads	205	271	302	0	49	827 (85%)	795 (82%)

HOUSE SPARROW *Passer domesticus*
Red List. Abundant but declining resident

Breeding population estimate: 20,000-50,000 pairs
Wintering population estimate: 40,000-120,000 individuals

In the breeding season House Sparrows occur widely throughout the county with some absences in rural areas and in some of the northern parts of the Peterborough conurbation. The tetrads with the greatest abundance in the breeding season are found across a range of rural and urban tetrads with no clear pattern to account for this distribution. In the winter House Sparrows occur widely throughout the county with the gaps corresponding predominantly to areas with reduced coverage. Areas of highest abundance occur in both rural and urban locations. The patchy distribution of the House Sparrow is seen at the local scale as well as the tetrad level, with one street having a thriving population while the next street may have none at all.

The current breeding distribution in old Cambridgeshire is similar to that found at the time of the previous Cambs Atlas. The current breeding distribution in Huntingdonshire and Peterborough has a number of gaps compared with the previous Hunts Atlas. Areas where House Sparrows now appear to be absent in the breeding season include immediately south of Peterborough and to the west of Huntingdon. The current winter relative abundance appears similar to the findings of the Wintering Atlas (Lack, 1986).

The long-term (30-year) trend for the House Sparrow breeding population in England is a decline of 71% (Baillie *et al.*, 2012) and this is the reason for its red-listing. The 15-year (1995–2010) trends for England and Eastern England are declines of 14% and 34%, respectively (Risely *et al.*, 2012). These declines mask differences that have been noted between rural and urban areas – from the 1970s to 2000 the breeding populations in rural areas declined by 47% and those in urban and suburban areas declined by about 60% (Baillie *et al.*, 2012).

In rural areas agricultural intensification is thought to have reduced food availability and House Sparrow survival rates. Changes in breeding productivity may also have played a part. In urban areas it is thought that reduced breeding productivity is the most important driver of the decline (Baillie *et al.*, 2012).

Ringing studies indicate that House Sparrows undertake some local dispersive movements before birds settle to breed, but thereafter their movements are predominantly of less than 2 km. It is described as 'one of the most sedentary species of wild bird' by Wernham *et al.* (2002).

The tetrads with the greatest abundance in the breeding season were widely scattered throughout the county with some clusters of higher abundance notable in the northern fens. The peak winter count of 110 was in TL49H (near March).

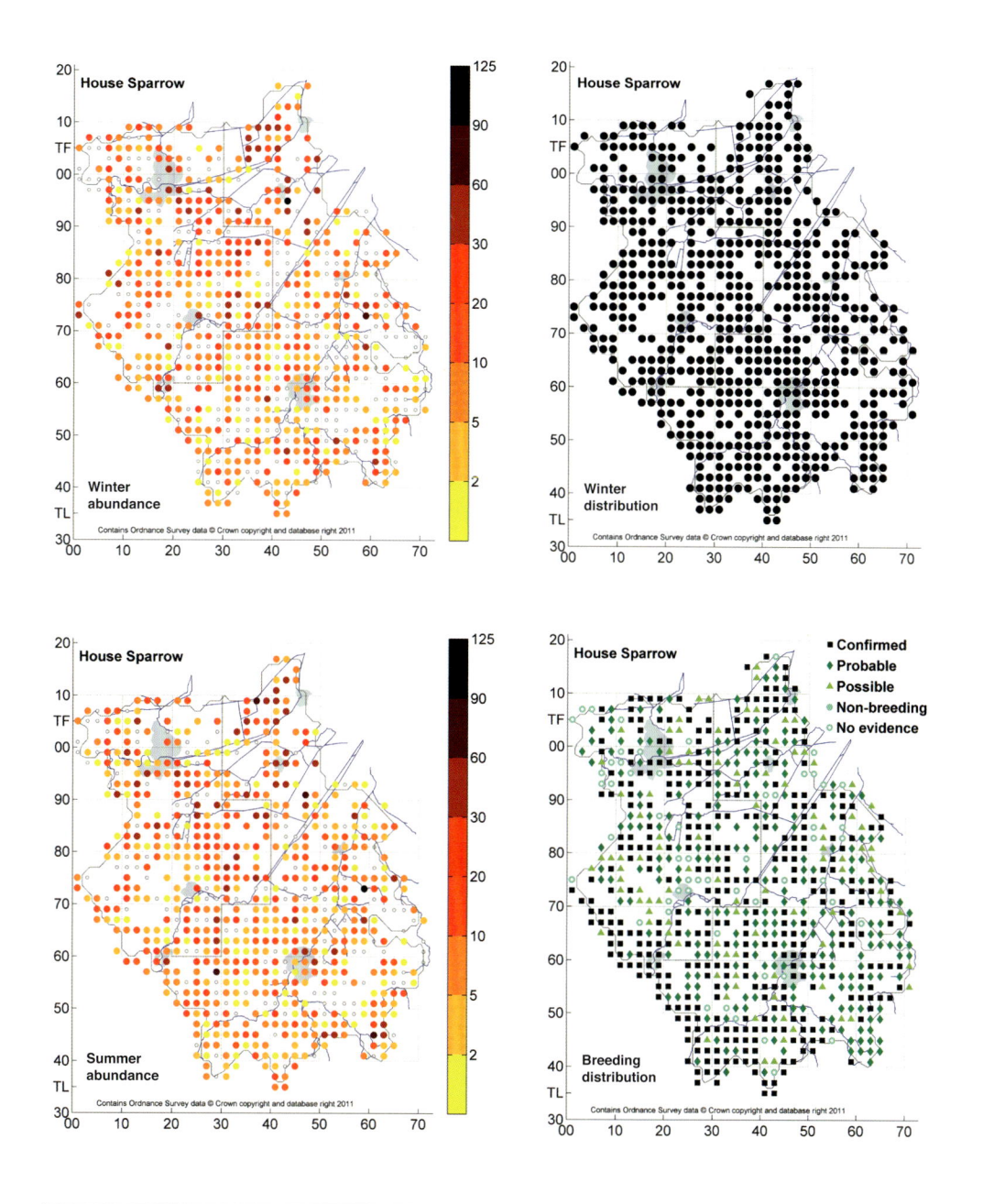

	Confirmed	Probable	Possible	Non-breeding	No evidence	Total summer (% county)	Total winter (% county)
Total tetrads	371	247	100	0	56	774 (80%)	662 (68%)

TREE SPARROW (Eurasian Tree Sparrow) *Passer montanus*
Red List. Uncommon resident and passage migrant (very local after a serious decline)

Breeding population estimate: 50-100 pairs
Wintering population estimate: 100-500 individuals

In the breeding season Tree Sparrows occur very locally in the fens around Wisbech, west of Upwell/Laddus Fen, Eldernell, Farcet Fen, Wimblington, Purls Bridge, Mepal, Witcham, Shippea Hill and east of Isleham. There is a small number of locations with confirmed breeding on higher land including near Helpston, to the west of Stilton, Catworth, Woodhurst, Somersham and Little Paxton Pits. There were some scattered occurrences in the south of the county but none was of confirmed breeding. The tetrads with greatest abundance in the breeding season are found in the fens.

In winter, small parties of Tree Sparrow can be found wherever flocks of winter finches and buntings congregate, particularly on wild-bird and game-cover strips. Ringing returns demonstrate that many of these Tree Sparrows are partial migrants from the north of the UK and this accounts for the numbers found in the south of the county where the species does not breed.

The current breeding distribution in old Cambridgeshire is much reduced from that found at the time of the 1988–92 Cambs Atlas with the loss of nearly all confirmed breeding tetrads in the south of the county and a significant reduction in the number of confirmed breeding locations in the fens. The current breeding distribution in Huntingdonshire and Peterborough is massively reduced from the time of the 1979-83 Hunts Atlas with only a handful of tetrads with confirmed breeding remaining compared to 181 tetrads in the earlier period. The current winter distribution is also much reduced compared to the findings of the 1981–84 Wintering Atlas (Lack, 1986) where they were found in all 10 km squares.

The long-term (30-year) trend for the Tree Sparrow breeding population in England is a decline of 96% (Baillie *et al.*, 2012). The 15-year (1995–2010) trend in England is a decline of 58% and it has become so scarce in Eastern England that a regional index cannot be calculated (Risely *et al.*, 2012). Tree Sparrow abundance declined dramatically in the UK between the late 1970s and the early 1990s, leading to many local extinctions, but there has been limited recovery since then (Baillie *et al.*, 2012). The reasons for this decline have been linked to agricultural intensification and it is considered that the loss of winter seed food, resulting in increased mortality outside the breeding season, is a significant factor (Baillie *et al.*, 2012).

The tetrads with the greatest abundance in the breeding season were in Farcet Fen and west of Upwell/Laddus Fen. The peak winter count of 180 was in TL19S (south-east of Peterborough).

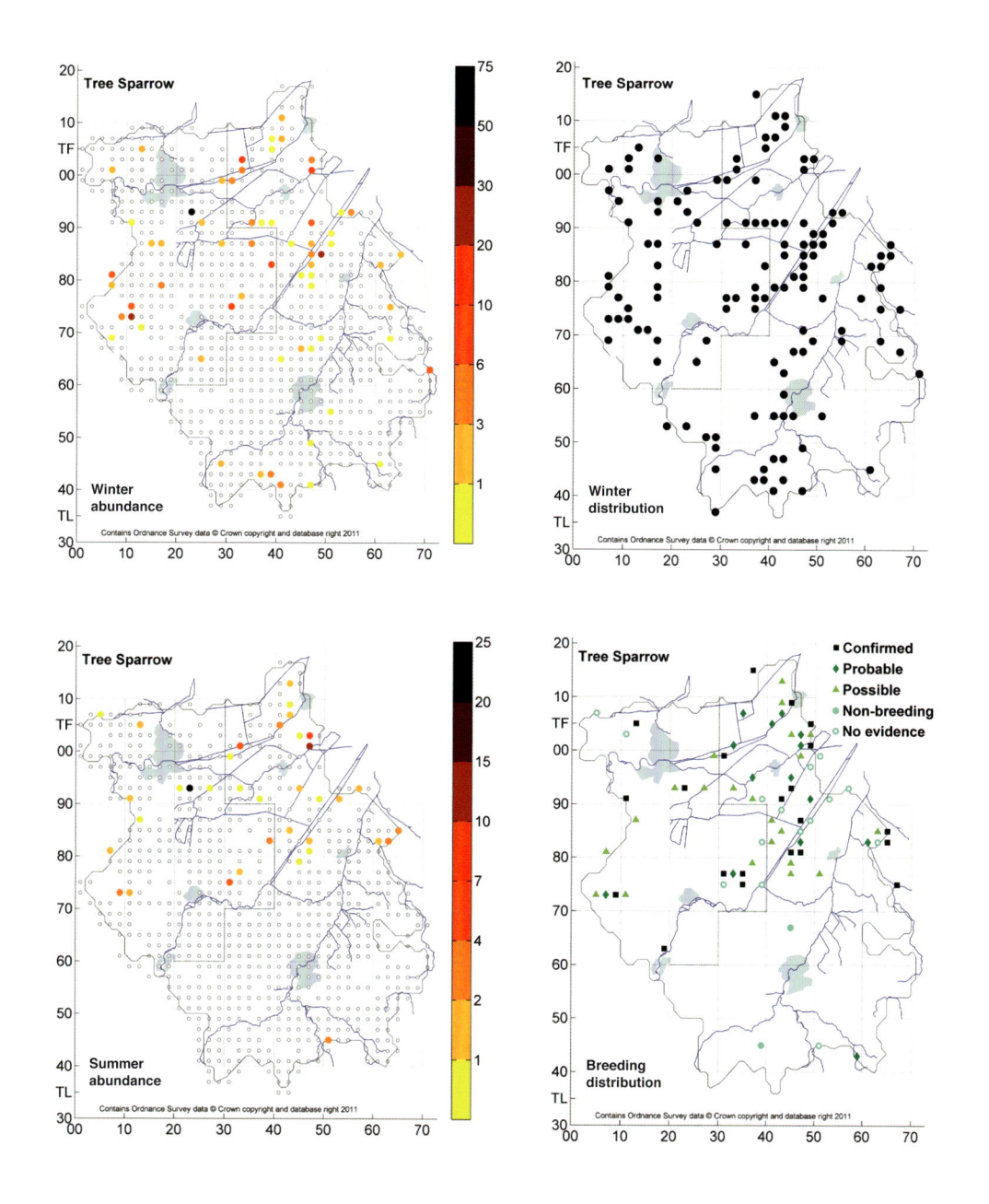

	Confirmed	Probable	Possible	Non-breeding	No evidence	Total summer (% county)	Total winter (% county)
Total tetrads	21	14	22	2	15	74 (8%)	127 (13%)

YELLOW WAGTAIL *Motacilla flava*
Red List. Fairly common, but declined, migratory breeder and passage migrant

Breeding population estimate: 1,000-1,500 pairs
Not a wintering species

The Yellow Wagtail race *flavissima* has a very restricted breeding range. Almost the entire population breeds in the UK, with the remainder found very locally along the near-Continent coast from northern France to southern Norway. The species, and this distinctive race, has been in steep decline since the 1970s, and was moved to the Red List in 2009. The formal long-term trend is -72% since 1970 and -50% since 1995 (Eaton *et al.*, 2012). Within the UK Yellow Wagtails are absent from Ireland, and from most of Scotland, Wales and the south-west. Cambridgeshire's fens, washes and farmland, which may hold some 10% of the British population, are thus of particular conservation importance. As a long-distance migrant, however, the underlying problems may well lie mainly elsewhere.

In Cambridgeshire Yellow Wagtail is nonetheless still a characteristic species of the Ouse and Nene Washes (each with some 20–50 pairs, and both supported by active conservation management), the county's wetland reserves, and wherever suitable meadowland and grazed pastures remain, particularly in the north of the county. The species is largely absent east of the A11 but is well, if patchily, distributed in the arable croplands along the western boundary greensands and increasingly on fenland farmland and on the drier chalk soils of southern Cambridgeshire. The CBC's 2002 Yellow Wagtail survey sought to investigate this trend of breeding deep within arable crops. The survey found that while a typical farmed fenland tetrad might hold up to 20 pairs, one on the chalk might only hold two or three. Cropping was critical, with most pairs found in peas and potatoes, fewer in cereals and beet, and none at all in oilseed rape. In the fens, birds were seen to feed extensively outside cereal crops on grass dyke banks and in other fallow areas and these additional feeding habitats, common in the fens but less so in more intensively farmed areas, seemed particularly important for breeding density.

Nonetheless the distribution of Yellow Wagtails has declined very substantially, both nationally and locally, since the previous Cambs Atlas. Confirmed or probable breeding was recorded this time in only 252 tetrads, compared to 364 in the earlier period.

Yellow Wagtail Summer abundance

Yellow Wagtail Breeding distribution

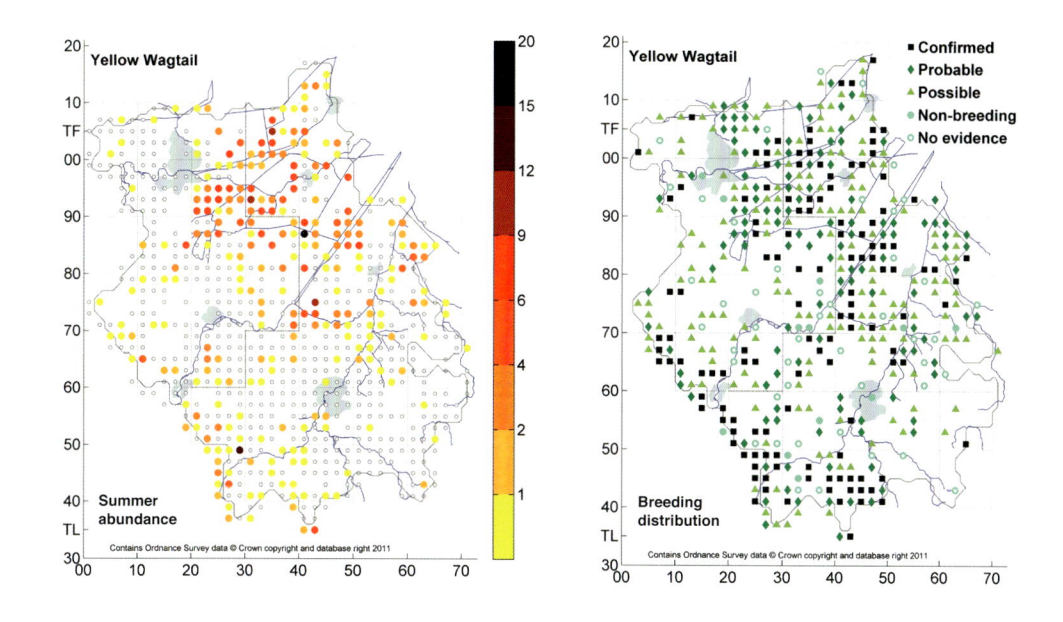

	Confirmed	Probable	Possible	Non-breeding	No evidence	Total summer (% county)
Total tetrads	128	124	172	12	46	482 (50%)

GREY WAGTAIL *Motacilla cinerea*
Amber List. **Uncommon/local resident and widespread winter visitor/passage migrant**

Breeding population estimate: 20-80 pairs
Wintering population estimate: 50-200 individuals

With their fondness for fast-flowing watercourses, Grey Wagtails are found at their highest densities in upland areas of the north and west of the UK wherever there are rocks, riffles and shingle banks, preferably with a riparian fringe of deciduous woodland. The two earlier national atlases showed the species to be scarce or absent over much of lowland eastern regions, where the sluggish nature of rivers and streams makes these largely unsuitable. Nonetheless Grey Wagtails are extremely adept at seeking out suitable breeding sites, often man-made, by weirs or mill-races, sluices at sewage works, gravel-pit and reservoir overflows and locks on canals, even in a county as flat as Cambridgeshire. Indeed it has frequently been suggested that pairs can most easily be pinpointed by careful examination of maps for this sort of feature. Breeding pairs are conspicuous and noisy, and are usually located quite easily. It is thus likely that breeding numbers were estimated with some confidence.

There is good evidence that Grey Wagtails steadily expanded their range eastwards during the 20th century, particularly exploiting man-made sites in these more marginal habitats, although severe winters inevitably caused setbacks. The first confirmed breeding in Cambridgeshire was in 1934 at Hildersham, and the upper reaches of the Cam and Rhee were soon to become their stronghold in the county; they remain such today. Bircham (1989) suggested that the population in the 1980s was only 1–3 pairs, but by the time of the previous county atlases there was confirmed/probable breeding in eight Huntingdonshire and 28 Cambridgeshire tetrads, with pairs also established at most suitable points along the upper Ouse from St. Neots to St. Ives. By that time some present-day traditional sites further to the east and north were also seeing regular breeding. This would suggest a minimum of 10–20 breeding pairs into the 1990s, with the same range of numbers reported in the CBRs of the early 2000s.

With limitations on suitable breeding sites as described above, the current atlas maps show little expansion of their range beyond the upper reaches of the main rivers (now including the Nene at Peterborough) and some established mill/sluice sites (such as Lode Mill). There has, however, probably been some increase in density, with additional pairs finding sufficient suitable territories on the smaller tributaries. Eaton *et al.* (2012) shows a 49% long-term decline for the UK since 1970, which has been particularly marked within the species' core upland range. Our small lowland population may be bucking the national trend.

In winter, Grey Wagtails can be found in a broader range of habitats, including among farm buildings, at sewage works, on cress-beds, and even in gardens and towns. In general, however, birds remain concentrated along the same stretches of river where they prefer to breed. Their presence is frequently betrayed by their characteristic loud flight calls. Birds are usually found singly or in pairs. It is likely that some 50–200 individuals winter in the county in most years. Local breeding birds are, no doubt, joined by partial migrants from the northern UK moving to winter in south-west England, Ireland, and across the Channel in France. Ring-recoveries have shown that some birds even make it to Iberia and North Africa, and that some continental birds (from Denmark, Belgium and Germany) are also involved in these winter movements.

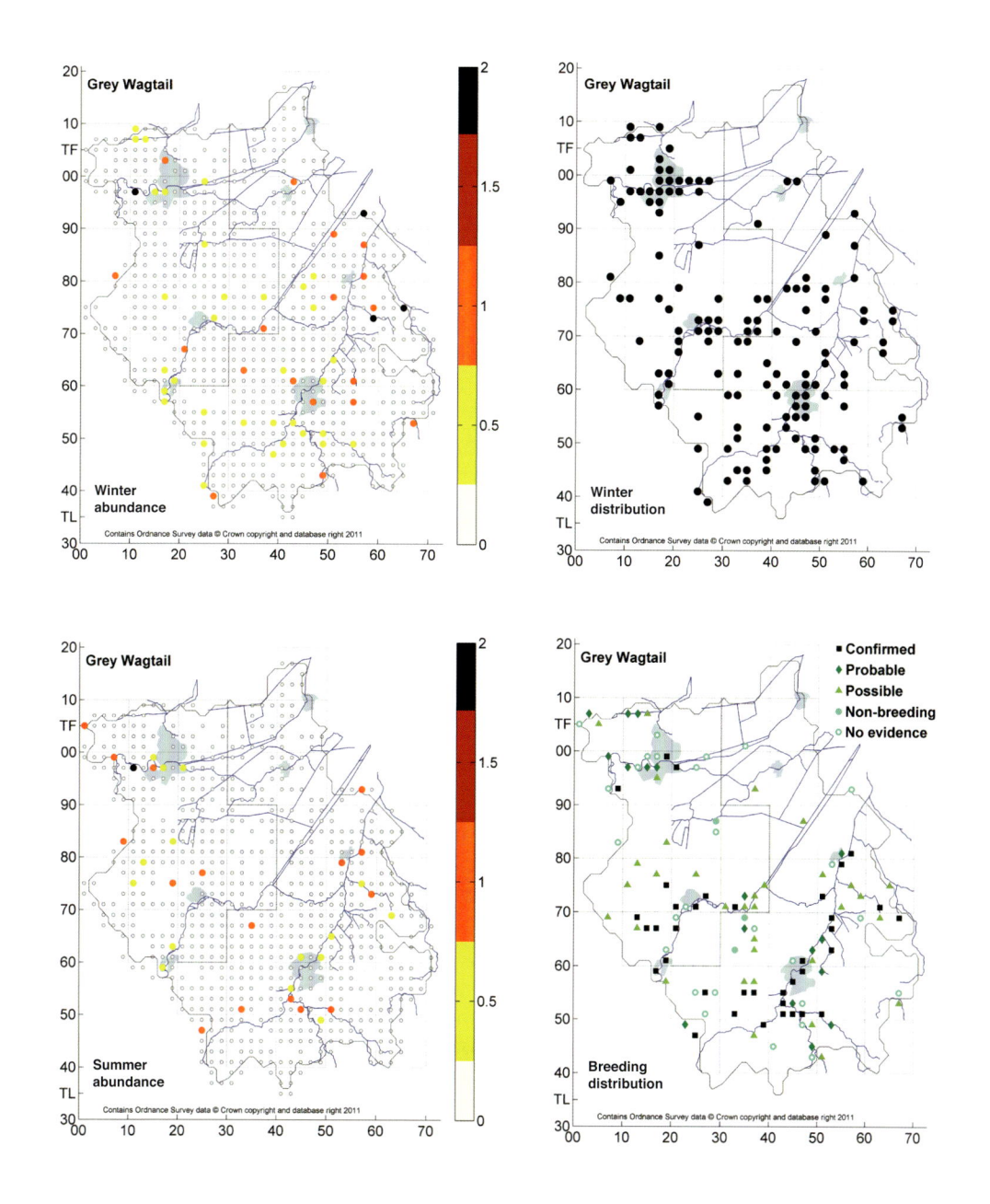

	Confirmed	Probable	Possible	Non-breeding	No evidence	Total summer (% county)	Total winter (% county)
Total tetrads	37	17	33	3	27	117 (12%)	139 (14%)

PIED WAGTAIL *Motacilla alba*
Green List. **Common and widespread resident, winter visitor and passage migrant**

Breeding population estimate: 2,500-5,000 pairs
Wintering population estimate: 5,000-20,000 individuals

As with the *flavissima* race of Yellow Wagtail, the UK and Ireland together hold almost the entire population of the familiar dark-backed race *yarrellii* Pied Wagtail. While at the species level Pied/White Wagtail is rated as of lowest conservation concern, this distinctive British race is amber-listed on the grounds that more than 20% of the European breeding population breeds here. In fact, apart from a few pairs on the adjacent continent, the true value must be closer to 100%. Pied Wagtails are widely distributed in the UK, but are significantly more abundant in the north and west. Recent BBS data show the species as stable or even slightly increasing nationally but in recent years there has been some evidence of a decline in Eastern England. Here there has been the familiar story of mixed farming being replaced by arable crops, more intensive use of chemicals, fewer livestock and tidier, more 'hygienic' farms – often with new buildings offering fewer nest sites – and the disappearance of small farm ponds and slurry pits in favour of deep reservoirs for crop irrigation schemes.

In Cambridgeshire, however, the species remains widespread, if patchily distributed, as an opportunistic breeder often in close proximity to man, particularly around farms and farm buildings, near pastures, and by roadways, fenland droves and tracks, in fact wherever there are nest sites, open space and a healthy insect population. Pairs can also be found in towns and gardens, often in unusual nesting circumstances – in vehicles or machinery, or in the old nests of other birds. Absences in the current atlas maps probably represent tetrads in thinly populated parts of the county lacking both accessible farm buildings and at least some water, although Pied Wagtails are less directly associated with waterways than the other wagtail species. The lack of records could just as easily represent patchy fieldworker coverage.

Ring-recoveries suggest that Pied Wagtails in southern regions of the UK are largely sedentary, whereas the population in the northern UK is largely migratory. There have been two recoveries of Cambridgeshire Pied Wagtails in Spain and Portugal.

The TTV counts suggest that the chances of encountering a Pied Wagtail increase significantly in winter, and that the population probably at least doubles. Mixed in with these northern birds, and also moving through to points further south, will be *alba* White Wagtails. It is now thought that the entire population of the nominate race from Greenland, Iceland and the Faeroes passes through the UK between August and November. Probably very few stay in this country for the winter, and as such will not be mapped during the atlas. Most of these *alba* birds will go unrecognised in autumn, but are more easily separable during their return passage in April, particularly at sites regularly watched by keen birders.

From July onwards, Pied Wagtails start to flock on sewage-farm filter beds and along watercourses and at other sites with a reliable food supply, and begin to roost communally. These roosts, sometimes of several hundred birds, tend to form in traditional sites but even these change unpredictably through the winter and can be suddenly abandoned. They can be in natural sites such as reedbeds and thickets – for example, at Wicken or Tubney Fens, Fen Drayton, the Ely Beet Factory, the Washes – or at urban sites, taking advantage perhaps of the security and warm microclimate provided by roof cover, sometimes with all-night illumination. A number of supermarkets and petrol stations are annual favourites and there have been regular gatherings in recent years at Queensgate in Peterborough and Addenbrookes Hospital in Cambridge and at university sites and science parks.

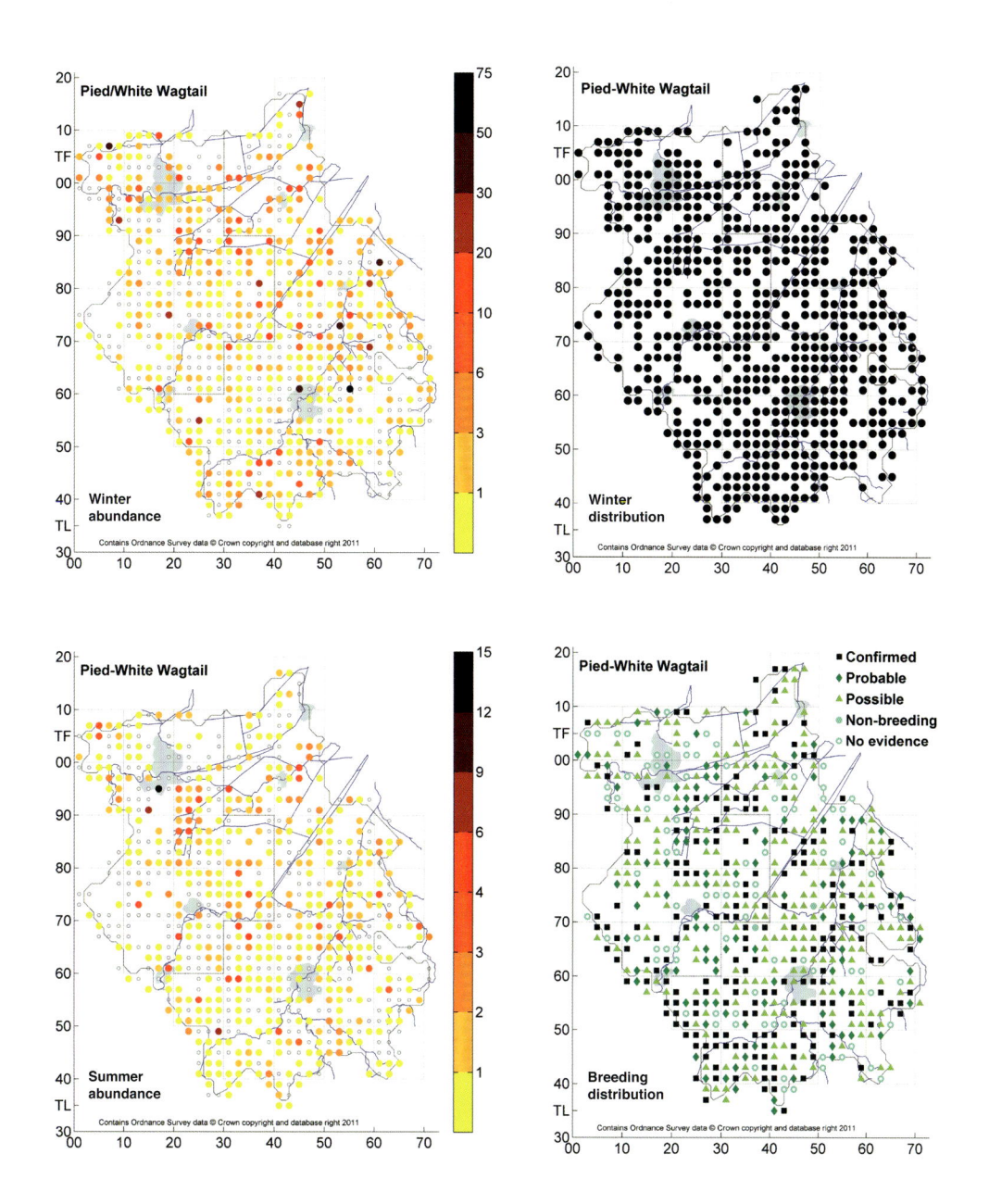

	Confirmed	Probable	Possible	Non-breeding	No evidence	Total summer (% county)	Total winter (% county)
Total tetrads	205	106	245	2	94	652 (67%)	639 (66%)

MEADOW PIPIT *Anthus pratensis*
Amber List. Common, somewhat local breeding species, winter visitor and passage migrant

Breeding population estimate: 400-1,000 pairs
Wintering population estimate: 2,500-5,000 individuals

The national picture for Meadow Pipit has been one of a steady downward decline of some 46% since the mid-1970s (Eaton *et al.*, 2012). Losses (mainly range contractions) have been particularly marked in lowland England. The situation in Cambridgeshire has perhaps been typical. While good populations persist in prime rough grassland and grazed habitats, particularly on the washlands, elsewhere breeding Meadow Pipits have been lost in more marginal situations. Pairs were found as confirmed or probable breeders in 237 tetrads in the previous Cambs Atlas; this was reduced to 111 in the present atlas. The county population must now be well below half the 1,000 pairs estimated for old Cambs in the previous atlas period.

The breeding map shows Meadow Pipits still commonly to be found along the lower reaches of the three main river systems, Ouse, Nene and Cam. The washlands still hold good numbers, particularly the Ouse Washes. Nowhere can the species be described as 'abundant' (unlike the previous Cambs Atlas) and breeding no longer occurs in every 10 km square. Losses in the south and east of the county have resulted from the usual factors – conversion of grazed pasture and grassland to arable, and the 'tidying-up' of rough marginal land. Some suitable areas remain on the chalk in the south with traditional sites, such as Newmarket Heath, and Fleam and Devil's Dykes, retaining small local populations.

From July onwards there is a vast emigration of Meadow Pipits from their strongholds in the uplands of the northern UK, where they occur at very high densities. Loose flocks of several hundred aggregate in favoured feeding areas on passage. Ring-recoveries suggest that most of these out-of-county birds continue south to wintering areas in south-west France and Iberia.

In winter Meadow Pipits appear to settle, and parties of birds, often quite small and probably comprising both resident and immigrant birds, can be found almost anywhere in Cambridgeshire where there is rough ground or winter stubble. Such winter groups give themselves away as they rise calling conspicuously when disturbed by a walker or a passing dog. Our winter population is possibly in the low thousands. Extreme weather affects the persistence of these wintering birds and they are likely to move south if conditions deteriorate.

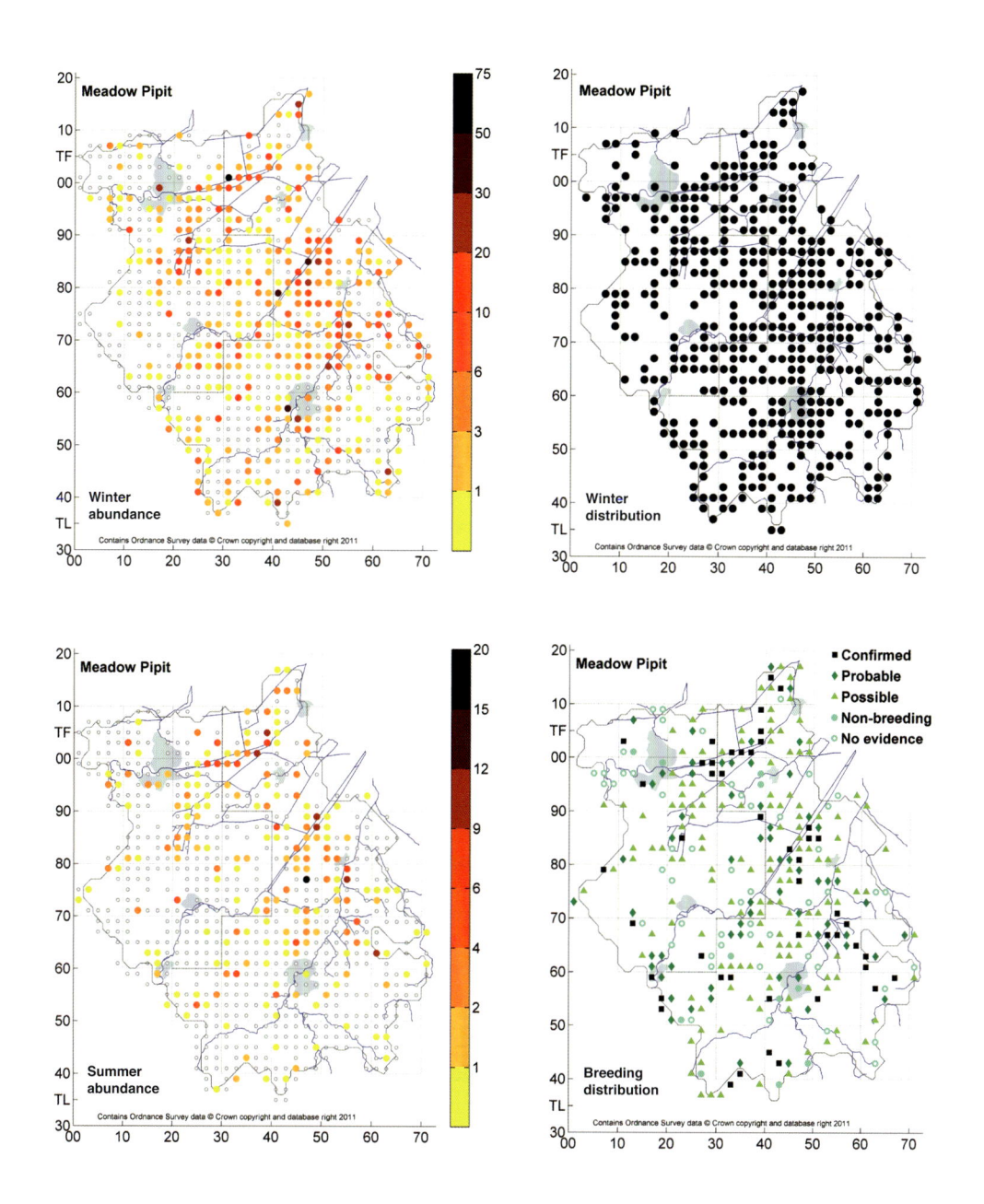

	Confirmed	Probable	Possible	Non-breeding	No evidence	Total summer (% county)	Total winter (% county)
Total tetrads	47	64	145	11	52	319 (33%)	464 (48%)

WATER PIPIT *Anthus spinoletta*
Amber List. Uncommon winter visitor and passage migrant, mainly on the Washes

Not a breeding species
Wintering population estimate: 5-25 individuals

This species was officially separated from the Rock Pipit in 1986. Both species are winter visitors and inevitably are found along river systems, particularly the Ouse and Nene Washes, at gravel pits and at Grafham Water and Ferry Meadows.

Historically Water Pipit was noted only as a subspecies of Rock Pipit and as such might well have been under-recorded. Nationally it remains a scarce visitor (Brown & Grice, 2005). Water Pipits breed in upland areas such as the Pyrenees, Massif Central, Jura, Alps, Appenines and Carpathians. Birds leave the breeding grounds and winter in the lowlands, some moving to the coasts. The fact that both local and national records have increased over time is more likely to be due to increased observer effort than to a particular change of habit in this species.

Since the maximum likely to be in England in any winter is 100 (BTO Birdfacts website) it is scarcely surprising that so few are recorded in Cambridgeshire. Low numbers are recorded each winter, through to March or early April; records during the atlas period were received from 12 tetrads. The distribution map shows birds almost exclusively associating with the main washlands of the Ouse, Nene and Cam.

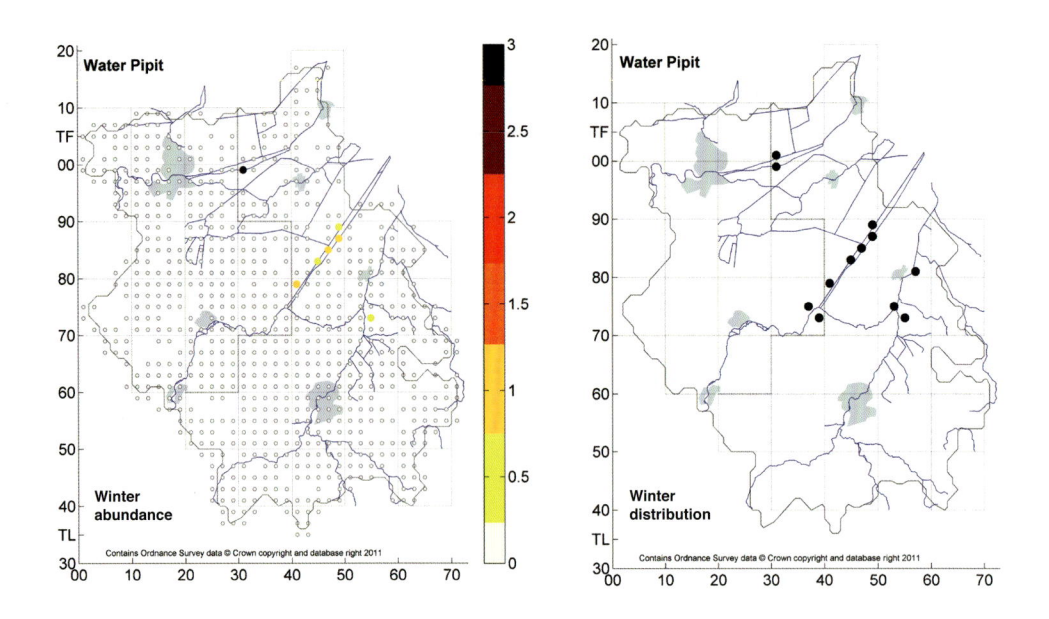

Rock Pipit (Eurasian Rock Pipit) *Anthus petrosus* is an even scarcer visitor, and was not regular enough to warrant mapping. Most records come from the autumn or spring migration seasons, rather than winter.

CHAFFINCH *Fringilla coelebs*
Green List. Abundant resident, winter visitor and passage migrant

Breeding population estimate: 30,000-60,000 pairs
Wintering population estimate: 75,000-150,000 individuals

In the past the Chaffinch has been described as the most widespread species in the county. In Cambridgeshire it is a common species in both rural and urban environments. The summer map shows that in the breeding season Chaffinches occur throughout the county and where there are gaps in the map this can be largely accounted for by tetrads with poor coverage. The map of abundance in the breeding season indicates that densities are lower in the fens, almost certainly related to the reduced occurrence of gardens, hedgerows, copses and woodland.

In the winter Chaffinches also occur throughout the county and again the gaps in distribution can be largely accounted for by tetrads with low numbers of visits. The areas of greatest abundance in the winter are shown to be either areas of higher land or at the fen edge.

The current breeding distribution in old Cambridgeshire is similar to that found in the previous Cambs Atlas in the south. In the northern half, Chaffinches appear to be more widespread now but this may be an artefact of better coverage in the latest atlas fieldwork period. The current breeding distribution in Huntingdonshire and Peterborough is similar to that recorded in the previous Hunts Atlas with similar local gaps, even where there was coverage, in the fens between Peterborough, Ramsey and Chatteris.

The current winter relative abundance appears similar to the findings in 1981–84 of the Wintering Atlas (Lack, 1986) suggesting little change over this period.

The long-term (30-year) trend for the Chaffinch breeding population in England shows an increase of 27% (Baillie *et al.*, 2012). The 15-year (1995–2010) trends in England and Eastern England are increases of 12% and 35%, respectively (Risely *et al.*, 2012). Chaffinch abundance increased in the 1970s and 1980s and stabilised during the 1990s. There has been a recent decline (since 2006) linked to the outbreak of the disease trichomonosis that began in 2005 (Baillie *et al.*, 2012).

Ringing studies indicate that local breeding birds are sedentary and that Chaffinches joining the resident birds in winter come from Fennoscandia (Wernham *et al.*, 2002). Birds passing through the county in autumn and spring have been shown to be moving to or from Ireland.

The tetrads with the greatest abundance in the breeding season were predominantly in the south and west of the county, as were the winter abundance records. The peak winter count of 250 occurred near Hatley St George in the south-west of the county. Other large counts were recorded in areas away from fenland arable.

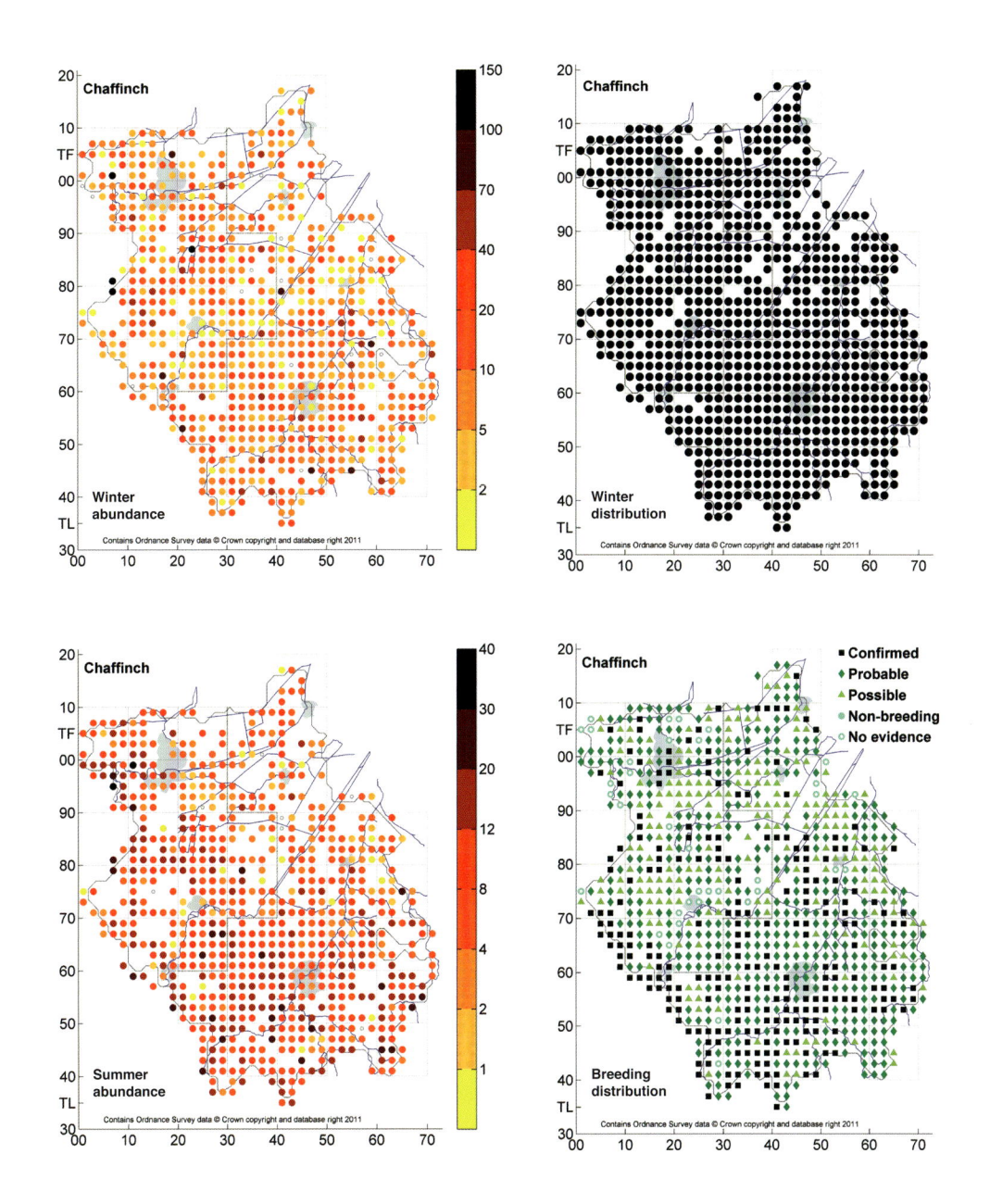

	Confirmed	Probable	Possible	Non-breeding	No evidence	Total summer (% county)	Total winter (% county)
Total tetrads	238	429	206	0	36	909 (94%)	881 (91%)

BRAMBLING *Fringilla montifringilla*
Green List. Fairly common winter visitor and passage migrant in variable numbers
Not a breeding species
Wintering population estimate: 50-500 individuals

Bramblings have always been winter visitors in variable numbers in Cambridgeshire. The winter map shows that they occur widely scattered across the county, being recorded in both the fens and higher land and showing no association at this scale with woodland. The locations with the highest abundance are similarly spread between the fens and higher land. Bramblings were observed into spring, most frequently as single birds, in a wide variety of locations across the county. No evidence of even possible breeding was recorded.

Ringing studies indicate that the birds that spend the winter in Eastern England originate from Fennoscandia. Birds that are wintering in the UK tend to stay for the winter, rather than moving on further south, but in subsequent years they may winter in continental Europe, as far east as northern Italy (Wernham et al., 2002).

The number of Bramblings wintering in the UK varies from year to year. In the current atlas period over half the county records came from the first winter (2007/8) and the lowest number of records from the winter 2009/10. There was a ninefold difference in the number of records between these winters. Over the atlas period, Bramblings were recorded in 111 tetrads (11%).

The peak winter count was of 124 on the Cambridgeshire-Norfolk-Suffolk border in TL68M but the majority of records were of single birds.

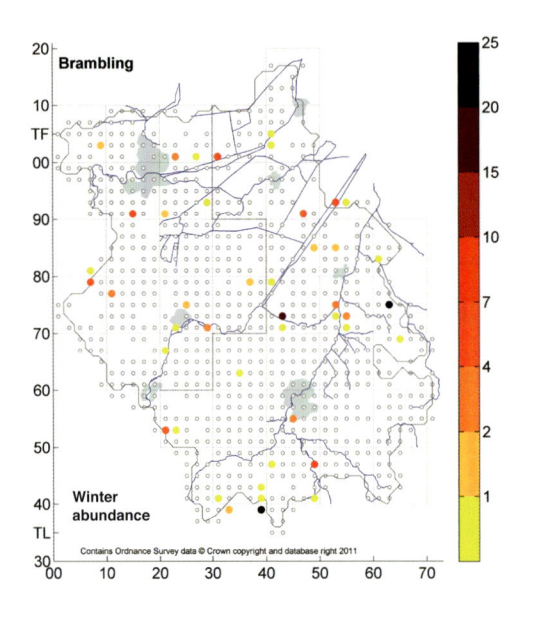

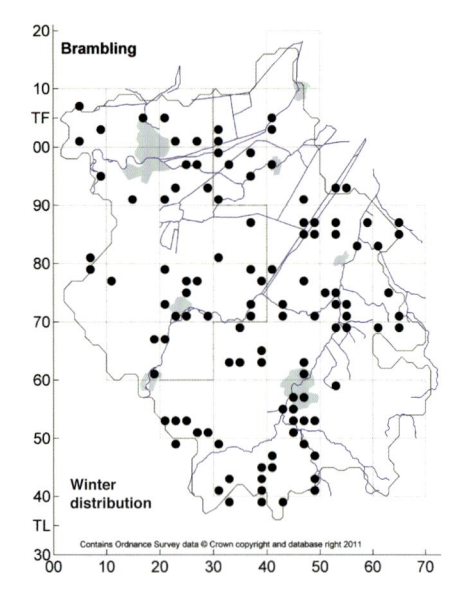

265

GREENFINCH (European Greenfinch) *Chloris chloris*
Green List. Abundant resident, passage migrant and probable winter visitor

Breeding population estimate: 5,000-20,000 pairs
Wintering population estimate: 10,000-50,000 individuals

Since county records began Greenfinches have always been widespread across Cambridgeshire, numbers can fluctuate from time to time but it is a species found in both rural and urban habitats. The summer map shows a slightly greater number of gaps than is the case for the Chaffinch, indicating some genuine absences rather than a result of reduced coverage. The map of relative abundance in the breeding season shows no clear trends; there are tetrads of both high and low abundance both in the fens and on higher ground. The current breeding distribution in old Cambridgeshire is similar to that found at the time of the 1988–92 Cambs Atlas. The current breeding distribution in Huntingdonshire and Peterborough is a little more patchy than that recorded at the time of the 1979–83 Hunts Atlas.

In the winter Greenfinches occur throughout the county, again with a slightly greater number of gaps than noted for the Chaffinch. There are localised patches of high abundance in winter in the southern and western parts of the fens, but winter abundance appears similar to the findings in 1981–84 of the Wintering Atlas (Lack, 1986) with a suggestion of reduced abundance in the south of the county.

The long-term (30-year) trend for the Greenfinch breeding population in England is a decline of 3% (Baillie *et al.*, 2012). The 15-year (1995–2010) trends in England and Eastern England show declines of 8% and an increase of 13%, respectively (Risely *et al.*, 2012). The planting of confier hedges such as *Leylandii* in gardens may have contributed to this increase by creating additional nesting sites. More recently there has been a sudden sharp fall in population due to the widespread and severe outbreak of trichomonosis that began in 2005 (Baillie *et al.*, 2012).

Ringing studies indicate that most Greenfinches in the UK are sedentary, moving less than 20 km, but that some (~10%) make extensive seasonal movements with females moving further than males. There are small numbers of winter visitors from continental Europe, mainly Norway (Wernham *et al.*, 2002). These movements are relatively irregular over the years, indicating that pressures on the breeding grounds (high populations and/or shortage of food) may trigger such movements.

The tetrads with the greatest abundance in the breeding season were grouped to the west, south and south-east of Peterborough and the peak winter counts (>100) occurred in locations in both fenland and the south-east, near Pymoor, south of Eldernell, Warboys, east of Wandlebury Country Park and south of Castle Camps.

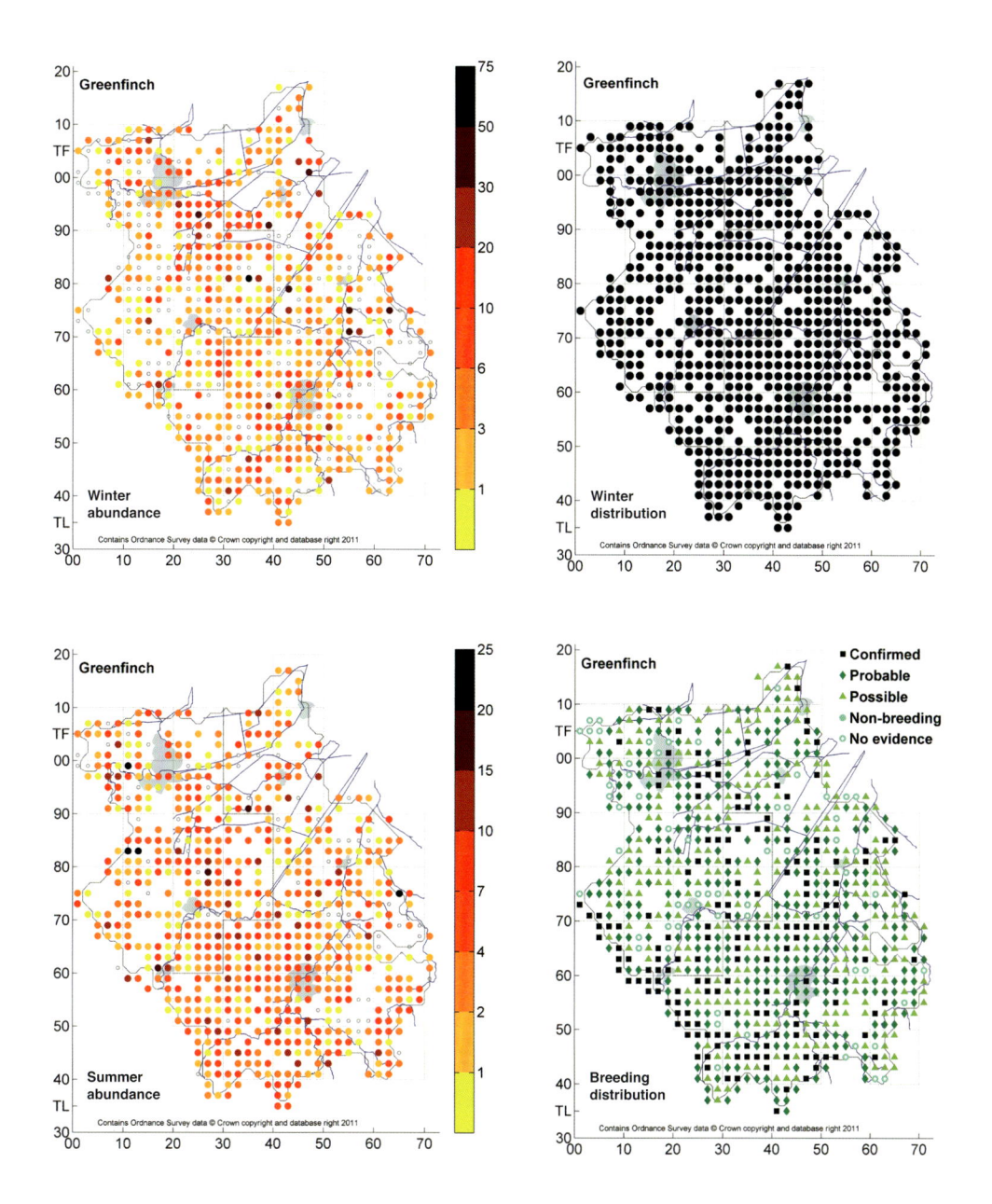

	Confirmed	Probable	Possible	Non-breeding	No evidence	Total summer (% county)	Total winter (% county)
Total tetrads	161	339	264	0	62	826 (85%)	743 (77%)

GOLDFINCH (European Goldfinch) *Carduelis carduelis*
Green List. Widespread and common summer visitor/resident and passage migrant

Breeding population estimate: 5,000-20,000 pairs
Wintering population estimate: 10,000-50,000 individuals

Goldfinches, always a common bird in the county, are almost certainly recorded more frequently now due to their liking for niger seed provided for them in many gardens. The summer map shows that they occur throughout the county but with a slightly sparser distribution than the Chaffinch. The map of abundance in the breeding season shows no clear trends with tetrads of high and low numbers both in the fens and on the higher ground. The current breeding distribution in old Cambridgeshire is similar in extent, but with fewer gaps, to that found in the previous Cambs Atlas indicating a slight increase in distribution even after accounting for coverage. In Huntingdonshire and Peterborough the distribution is similar to that recorded in the previous Hunts Atlas.

In the winter Goldfinches occur throughout the county, again with a slightly greater number of gaps than noted for the Chaffinch. The areas of higher relative abundance tend to occur along the western and southern parts of the fens. Winter abundance appears similar to the findings in 1981–84 of the Wintering Atlas (Lack, 1986). The 10 km scale at which the comparison can be made does not make it possible to identify evidence of the recently observed tendency of Goldfinches to feed on niger seed in gardens.

Although Goldfinch abundance was observed to have decreased from the mid-1970s until the mid-1980s the long-term (30-year) trend for the Goldfinch breeding population in England suggests an increase of 55% (Baillie *et al.*, 2012). The 15-year (1995–2010) trends in England and Eastern England are increases of 82% and 43%, respectively (Risely *et al.*, 2012). Goldfinch population changes have been explained by changes in annual survival rates; from the mid-1970s until the mid-1980s agricultural intensification would have reduced the availability of weed seeds, whereas in the more recent period artificial feeding is suggested as the reason for their greater survival rate (Baillie *et al.*, 2012).

Ringing studies indicate that a significant proportion of our breeding Goldfinches move to western France and Iberia for the winter, with females tending to winter further south. There is also some evidence for birds from further north in Europe passing through the eastern UK en route to wintering grounds further south (Wernham *et al.*, 2002). It would be interesting to know whether the proportion of British-breeding Goldfinches moving south has reduced as a result of the increasing use of seed feeders in gardens in winter.

The tetrads with the greatest abundance in the breeding season were widely scattered throughout the county with no particular pattern evident. The peak winter counts (>150) occurred in the Earith to Bluntisham area, Shippea Hill and Chittering.

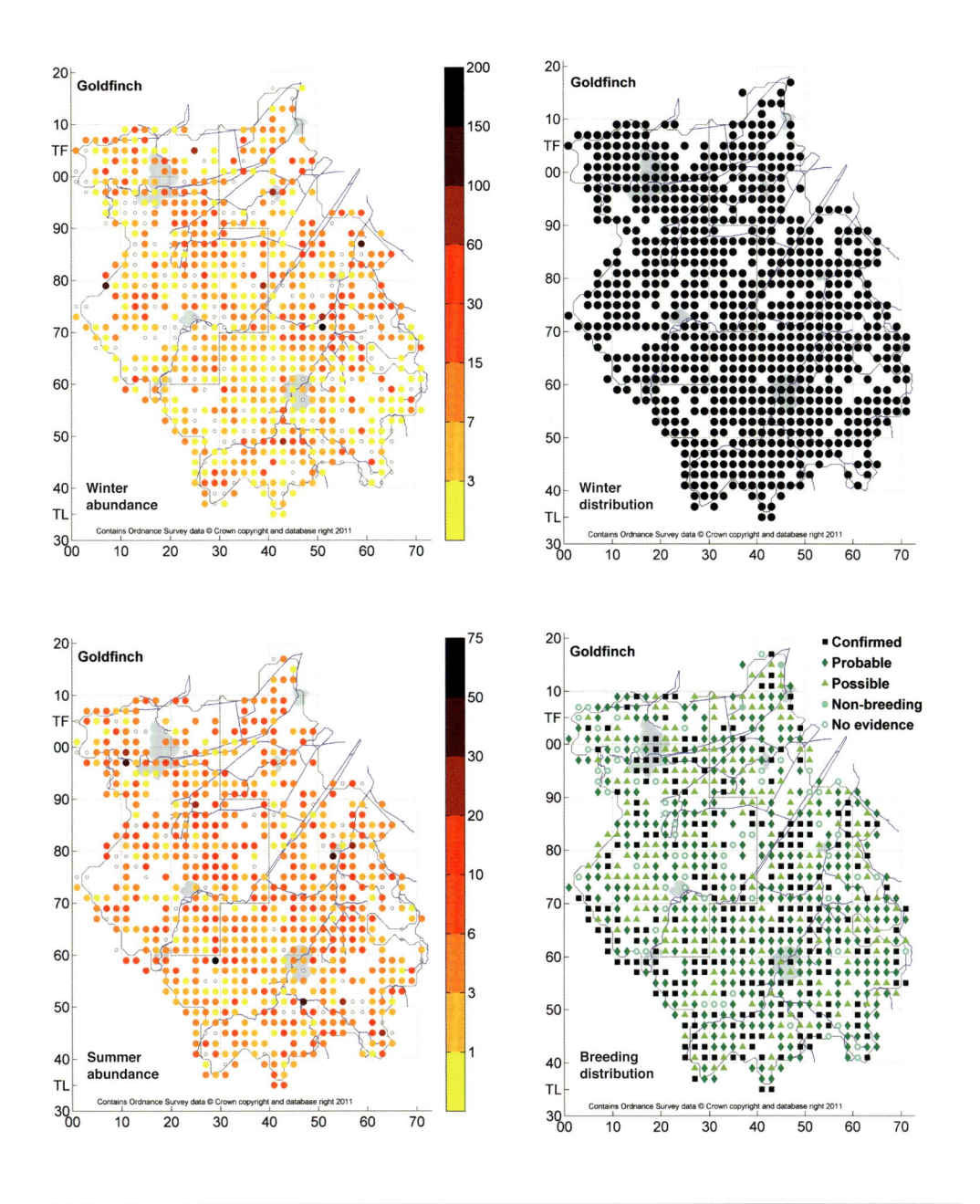

	Confirmed	Probable	Possible	Non-breeding	No evidence	Total summer (% county)	Total winter (% county)
Total tetrads	234	346	212	2	64	858 (89%)	781 (81%)

SISKIN (Eurasian Siskin) *Carduelis spinus*
Green List. **Fairly common winter visitor and passage migrant; occasionally summers**

Breeding population estimate: 0-10 pairs
Wintering population estimate: 250-1,500 individuals

While Siskins can be found in a number of locations in winter they are still an unusual bird in summer and although there are some breeding records, these are sporadic. The atlas project shows that Siskins occur in scattered locations across the higher ground in the breeding season and on the southern and western edge of the fens. The majority of these observations relate to non-breeding birds in late March or April. There were two records of confirmed breeding (recently fledged young) at Bedford Purlieus and Gamlingay. Four records of probable breeding occurred at Monks Wood, Gamsey Wood, south of Stetchworth, and at Bassingbourn. This represents a change relative to the 1988–92 Cambs Atlas and the 1979–83 Hunts Atlas when there were no breeding records.

The winter map shows that Siskins occur in widely scattered locations across the higher ground of the west and south of the county with other clusters of records in the Great Fen Project area, the Wicken Fen area and along the Ouse Washes. Siskins are most abundant in the winter along the river valleys and in the areas of natural or restored fenland where they are strongly associated with alder and birch. In winter Siskins appear to be both more widespread and more abundant when compared to the findings in 1981–84 of the Wintering Atlas (Lack, 1986).

A long-term trend for the Siskin breeding population in England is not available due to its historic scarcity (Baillie *et al.*, 2012). The 15-year (1995–2010) trend in England shows an increase of 50% but with large fluctuations from year to year, possibly the result of influxes from the Continent (Baillie *et al.*, 2012). A 15-year trend in Eastern England is not available again due to the scarcity of Siskins in the breeding season (Risely *et al.*, 2012). The 1988–91 Breeding Atlas (Gibbons *et al.*, 1993) identified a considerable expansion of the breeding range into southern regions of the UK.

Ringing studies indicate that the birds which are seen in winter and early spring in the county are a combination of birds from further north in the UK, wintering birds from the Continent and birds from the Continent passing through on passage (Wernham *et al.*, 2002).

The peak winter counts (>50) occurred at Ferry Meadows Country Park, Bainton Pits, Woodwalton Fen, north-west of Godmanchester, Fordham and Chippenham Fen.

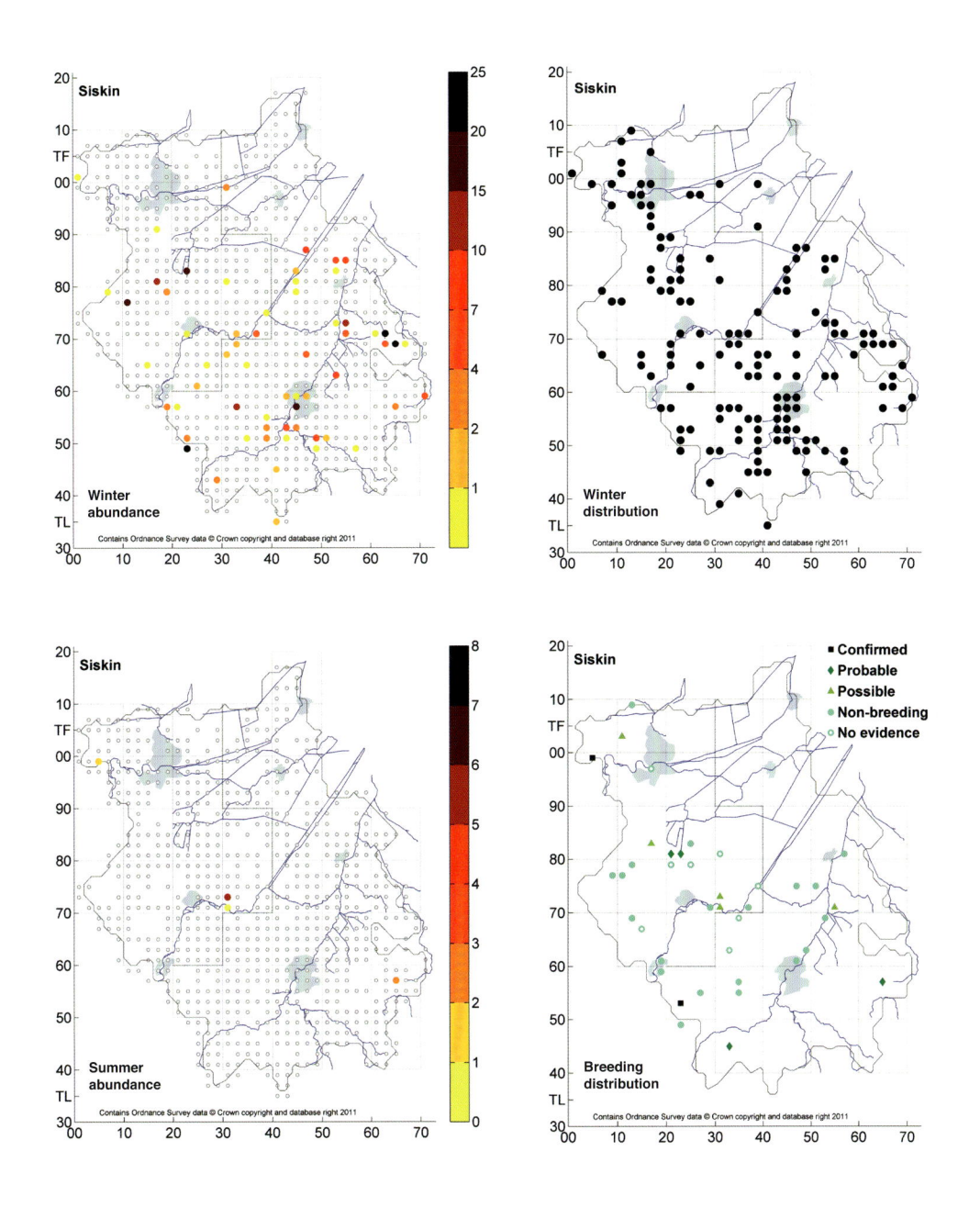

	Confirmed	Probable	Possible	Non-breeding	No evidence	Total summer (% county)	Total winter (% county)
Total tetrads	2	4	5	20	8	39 (4%)	147 (15%)

LINNET (Common Linnet) *Carduelis cannabina*
Red List. Very common, but declined, resident/partial migratory breeder and passage migrant

Breeding population estimate: 5,000-10,000 pairs
Wintering population estimate: 10,000-25,000 individuals

Linnets, once such a common sight in the countryside have been in decline in Cambridgeshire for some time. Unlike other finches they have not adapted to artificial feeding in gardens. The breeding-season map shows that Linnets still occur widely across the county although with some gaps in their distribution. The zero counts on a proportion of TTVs indicate that Linnets are more scarce than other small finches. Breeding distribution in old Cambridgeshire is similar to that found in the previous Cambs Atlas; in Huntingdonshire and Peterborough it is a little more patchy in the southern part than that recorded by the previous Hunts Atlas.

In winter Linnets are less widely distributed than in the breeding season, with the tetrads of highest abundance occurring in the fens, but the current winter relative abundance appears similar to the findings in 1981–84 of the Wintering Atlas (Lack, 1986).

The long-term (30-year) trend for the Linnet breeding population in England shows a decline of 76% (Baillie *et al.*, 2012) and this is the reason for its red-listing. The medium-term 15-year (1995–2010) trends in England and Eastern England continue to show declines of 27% and 30%, respectively (Risely *et al.*, 2012). Linnet abundance fell rapidly in the UK between the mid-1970s and mid-1980s with the decline being less severe since then, possibly linked to the increasing area of oilseed rape. During the period of most rapid decline, the cause was found to be an increase in nest-failure rate at the egg stage (Baillie *et al.*, 2012).

Ringing studies indicate that the Linnet is a partial migrant with some birds remaining in the UK for the winter while others migrate to western France and Spain. Some birds from Scandinavia also pass though Eastern England or visit for the winter (Wernham *et al.*, 2002).

The tetrads with the greatest abundance in the breeding season were in the fens. The peak winter counts (>250) occurred at the Nene Washes, east of Isleham, north of Cottenham, Knapwell (RSPB Grange Farm), south of Melbourn and south of Chrishall Grange.

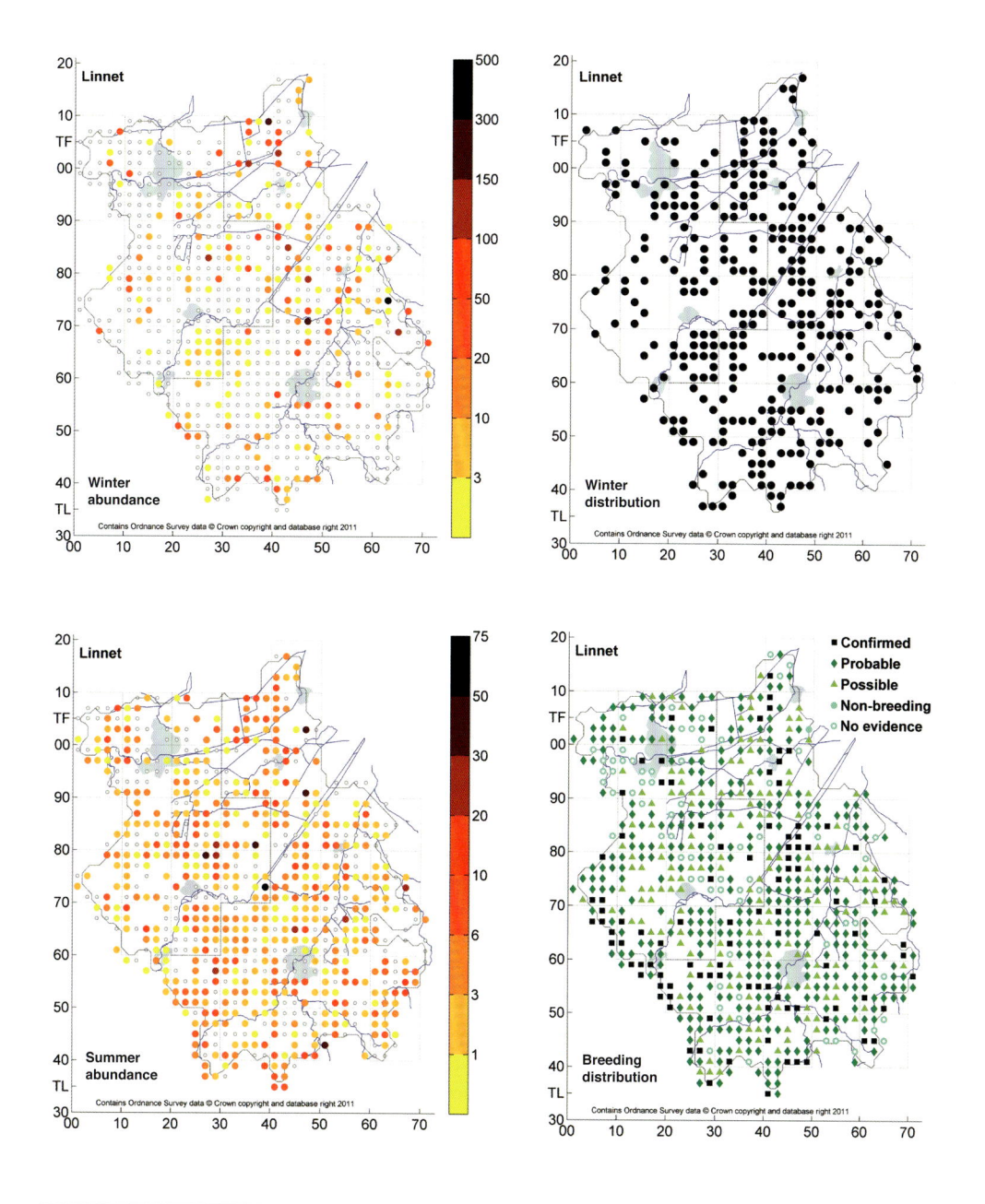

	Confirmed	Probable	Possible	Non-breeding	No evidence	Total summer (% county)	Total winter (% county)
Total tetrads	100	362	168	1	70	701 (72%)	325 (34%)

LESSER REDPOLL *Carduelis cabaret*
Red List. Uncommon passage migrant and winter visitor

Breeding population estimate: 0-1 pairs, last confirmed 2002
Wintering population estimate: 250-1,500 individuals

From being a common species in the late 1960s and early 1970s, the Lesser Redpoll has become more of a visitor in the county although numbers fluctuate from year to year. The summer map shows that in the early spring very small numbers of Lesser Redpoll may occur in a number of locations in the southern half of the county, probably lingering on after wintering or moving through on passage. Only at Monks Wood were Lesser Redpoll noted in May 2009 as probable breeders. This is a considerable reduction from what had been recorded in the previous Cambs and Hunts atlases. In old Cambridgeshire at that time there was confirmed/probable breeding in 121 tetrads and in Huntingdonshire and Peterborough there was confirmed/probable breeding in 154 tetrads.

In winter Lesser Redpolls occur more widely across the higher land in the south and the west of the county but are rare in the fens other than Wicken Fen and the Great Fen Project area. These wintering sites are associated with birch or alder along the river valleys. Lesser Redpolls are increasingly observed in gardens, coming to niger seed feeders.

The national long-term (30-year) trend for the Lesser Redpoll breeding population shows a decline of 89% (Baillie et al., 2012); this is the reason for its red-listing. The 15-year (1995–2010) trend in England shows a decline of 10%. An index for Eastern England cannot be calculated due to insufficient data (Risely et al., 2012). The reason for these declines is unknown.

Ringing studies indicate that Lesser Redpolls visiting the county for the winter come from further north in the UK and that a proportion of these birds move through to winter in France and the Low Countries (Wernham et al., 2002).

The fluctuating nature of their occurence is shown by analysing the four atlas years separately: the winters of 2007/08 and 2010/11 had approximately 50% more records than the other two winters in the atlas period.

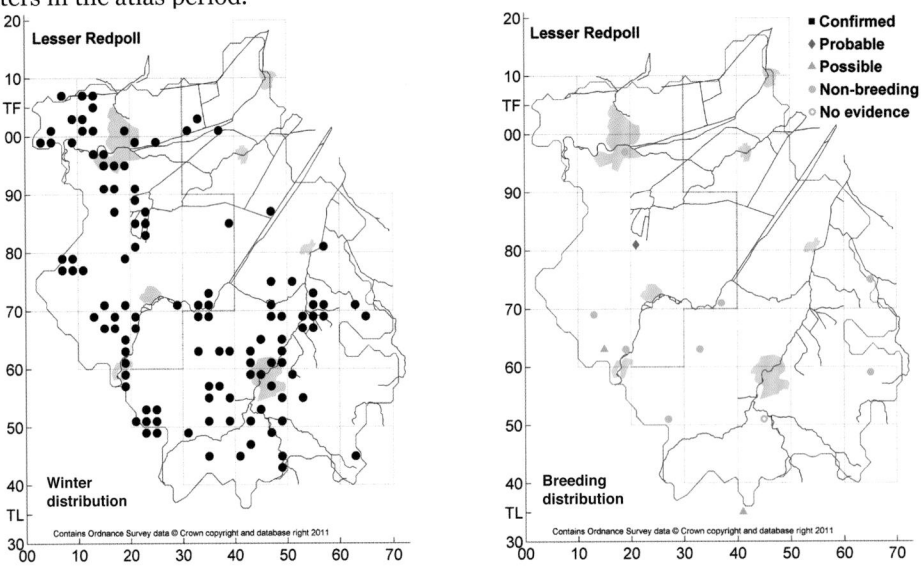

	Confirmed	Probable	Possible	Non-breeding	No evidence	Total summer (% county)	Total winter (% county)
Total tetrads	0	1	2	8	1	12 (1%)	116 (12%)

COMMON CROSSBILL (Red Crossbill) *Loxia curvirostra*
Green List. Scarce annual irruptive visitor; has bred after influxes

Breeding population estimate: 0-1 pairs, last confirmed 1988
Wintering population estimate: up to 100 individuals

Although Common Crossbills breed in the Norfolk and Suffolk brecklands, records in Cambridgeshire are limited in the main to dispersing birds or winter visitors. The summer map shows that in spring and summer Common Crossbills occur at locations scattered across the higher land of the county with most of the very small number of records in the fens coming from the 'island' of higher ground at Ely. The vast majority of these records are from June or July, well past the breeding season for this species, and are highly likely to relate to wandering post-breeding individuals or flocks seeking out suitable cone-bearing conifers.

Many Crossbill records in the county come from the autumn, a period not represented in the atlas. Numbers are lower in winter than in the breeding-season. There were only five early or mid-winter records from four sites, each involving single-digit numbers of birds. Whether this pattern reflects true scarcity or is due to recording bias, is unclear. This irruptive speces is well known to move to new areas as a result of food shortage or population expansion, and may remain to breed for one or two seasons before disappearing again. Late-summer influxes across the county do seem to be increasing in frequency, and hence Crossbills may feature in the county avifauna more regularly in the future. Just over half the atlas records came from a single year (2008) with the majority of the possible breeding records also coming from this year.

There was no evidence of breeding in old Cambridgeshire in the previous Cambs Atlas and none from Huntingdonshire and Peterborough in the previous Hunts Atlas.

The tetrad with the greatest abundance in the spring and summer was in the Monks Wood area.

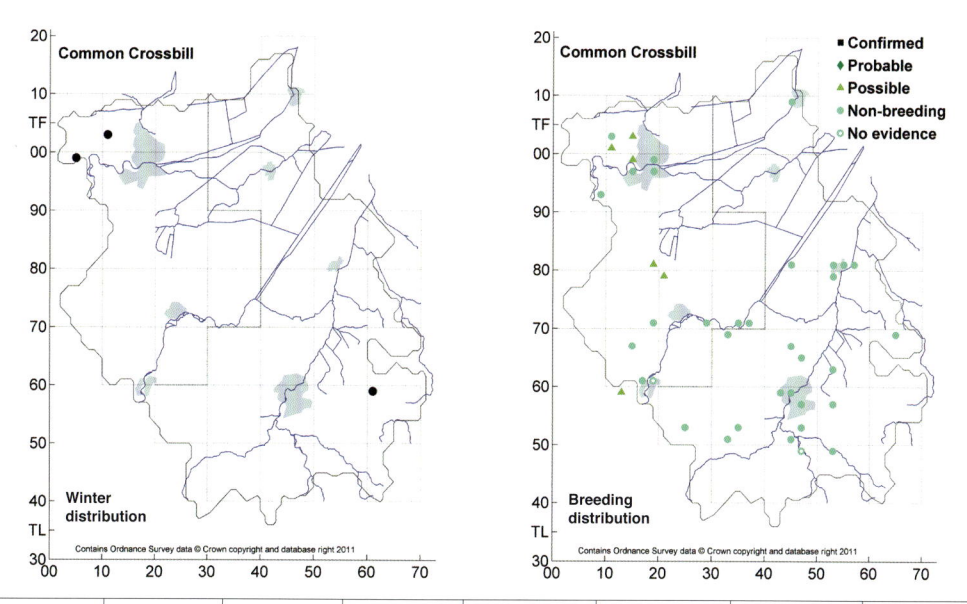

	Confirmed	Probable	Possible	Non-breeding	No evidence	Total summer (% county)	Total winter (% county)
Total tetrads	0	0	6	32	2	40 (4%)	3 (0.3%)

BULLFINCH (Eurasian Bullfinch) *Pyrrhula pyrrhula*
Amber List. Common, but declined, resident; scarce autumn immigrant

Breeding population estimate: 1,000-3,000 pairs
Wintering population estimate: 2,000-7,000 individuals

Bullfinches have been in decline in Cambridgeshire and the once common sight in the countryside of small family parties is now less observed. The atlas results suggest that in the breeding season Bullfinches occur across the higher land of the west and south of the county, with a much more localised occurrence in the fens. There are localised groups of tetrads with higher abundance in the breeding season in the area around Sutton and Mepal, north-east of Huntingdon, Fen Drayton and Caxton. Some of the areas traditionally associated with orchards, such as around Wisbech, Earith, north of Cambridge and Melbourn/Meldreth, did not appear to hold a particularly high abundance of Bullfinches. Bullfinches can be extremely secretive in the breeding season, which could contribute to under-recording. Breeding is also not readily proved, hence the low number of confirmed breeding tetrads. The breeding distribution in old Cambridgeshire is similar to that found in the previous Cambs Atlas while in Huntingdonshire and Peterborough it is similar in the north but much reduced in the south, particularly around Huntingdon, compared with the previous Hunts Atlas.

In winter Bullfinches are found more widely across the higher land of the west and south of the county but they remain thinly scattered across the fens. Areas of high winter abundance in the west of the county, at Wicken Fen, and around Cambridge, are not reflected in the breeding-season records. Winter abundance appears similar to the findings in 1981–84 of the Wintering Atlas (Lack, 1986).

The population decline is reflected in the long-term (30-year) trend for Bullfinches in England of -45% (Baillie *et al.*, 2012); this is the reason for its amber-listing. The 15-year (1995–2010) trends in England and Eastern England are an increase of 2% and a decrease of 8%, respectively (Risely *et al.*, 2012). The pattern of change was an initial steep decline in the 1970s, a shallower decline in the 1980s, and a period of relative stability since then (Baillie *et al.*, 2012). The mechanism underlying the decline remains unclear but is thought to be related to the loss of food resources and nesting cover associated with agricultural intensification and changes in woodland (Baillie *et al.*, 2012).

Ringing studies indicate that locally breeding birds are non-migratory and the rare observations of the continental race in the UK indicate that resident birds are joined by a small number of winter visitors (Wernham *et al.*, 2002).

The peak winter count (27) occurred at Knapwell (RSPB Grange Farm).

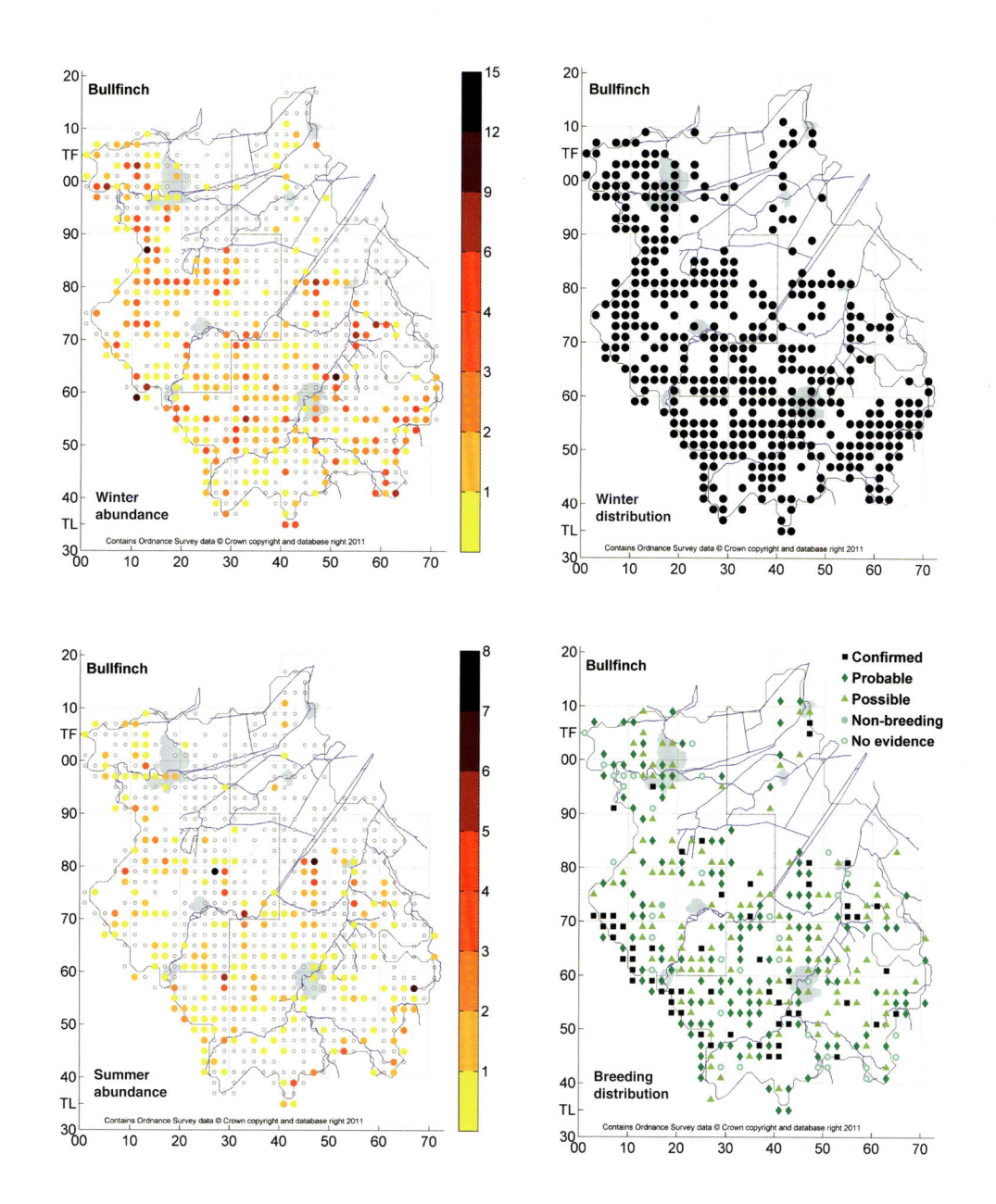

	Confirmed	Probable	Possible	Non-breeding	No evidence	Total summer (% county)	Total winter (% county)
Total tetrads	58	148	124	1	34	365 (38%)	432 (45%)

HAWFINCH *Coccothraustes coccothraustes*
Red List. **Breeding last confirmed in 2000, but an elusive species. Current status unclear; may still be resident in very small numbers**

Breeding population estimate: 0-3 pairs, last confirmed 2000
Wintering population estimate: 1-10 individuals

Hawfinches are notoriously difficult to find and for this reason their status in Cambridgeshire has always been a little uncertain. The summer records with possible breeding status (single birds in suitable nesting habitat) were at Castor Hanglands, Upton Wood and Benwick. The current breeding distribution in old Cambridgeshire is similar to that found in the previous Cambs Atlas, which also had no probable or confirmed evidence of breeding. In Huntingdonshire and Peterborough the Hunts Atlas recorded one tetrad with probable breeding and two tetrads with possible breeding, all in the St. Neots area. There were no records from the north-west of Hunts in that Atlas, in contrast to Clark (2008) who implied that Hawfinches bred in the north-west of the county in the 1970s and 1980s.

In winter there were 15 Hawfinch records of up to six birds in eight tetrads, plus another tetrad just outside the county. The highest counts came from Southorpe in the north-west with a maximum of two birds at all other locations. The current winter distribution appears to be more widespread compared to that found in 1981–84 during the Wintering Atlas (Lack, 1986).

The Hawfinch is red-listed due to its 74% breeding population decline over the period 1984–2004. Its main strongholds remain in south-east Wales, the New Forest and Kent (Holling *et al.*, 2012).

Ringing studies indicate that British breeding birds are largely sedentary and that there are irregular occurrences of winter visitors from northern Europe (Wernham *et al.*, 2002).

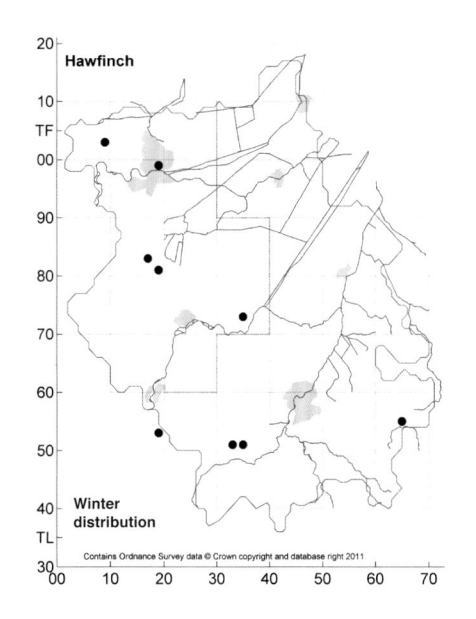

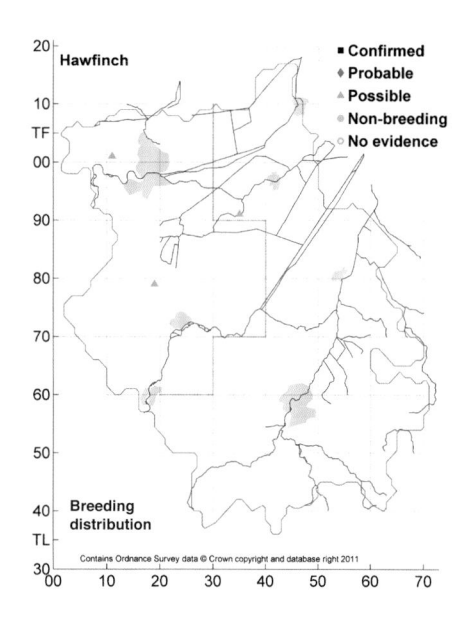

	Confirmed	Probable	Possible	Non-breeding	No evidence	Total summer (% county)	Total winter (% county)
Total tetrads	0	0	3	0	0	3 (0.3%)	9 (1%)

YELLOWHAMMER *Emberiza citrinella*
Red List. Common, but declined, resident and passage migrant

Breeding population estimate: 5,000-10,000 pairs
Wintering population estimate: 10,000-25,000 individuals

Once a common bird of arable farmland and the countryside, Yellowhammers have declined noticeably in recent years. The breeding-season map shows that Yellowhammers occur throughout the county but are more sparsely distributed in the fens. They are also absent from urban areas. The tetrads with greatest abundance in the breeding season are found in the south-east clay hills and the western clay plateau, possibly due to a greater density of hedgerows. The breeding distribution in old Cambridgeshire is similar to that in the previous Cambs Atlas while distribution in Huntingdonshire and Peterborough appears a little more patchy, with a larger number of tetrads with no breeding-season records, compared to that recorded in the previous Hunts Atlas.

In winter Yellowhammers show a similar but more patchy distribution. This reflects the fact that they flock in winter to exploit localised food supplies. The current winter relative abundance appears similar to the findings in 1981–84 of the Wintering Atlas (Lack, 1986).

Population levels have shown a significant decrease as is indicated by the long-term (30-year) trend for the Yellowhammer breeding population in England – a decline of 57% (Baillie *et al.*, 2012). The 15-year (1995–2010) trends in England and Eastern England are declines of 23% and 20%, respectively (Risely *et al.*, 2012). Yellowhammer abundance began to decline on farmland in the mid-1980s and that downward trend continues. A decline in annual survival has been proposed as the underlying reason for this decrease. A shortage of food in winter resulting from changes in farming practices is considered to be the most likely reason for this change in survival (Baillie *et al.*, 2012).

Ringing studies indicate that the breeding population is largely sedentary with few movements greater than 25 km and no evidence for large-scale passage through the county or supplementation of wintering populations by visitors from the continent (Wernham *et al.*, 2002).

The tetrads with the greatest abundance in the breeding season are found in the south-east clay hills and the western clay plateau. The peak winter counts (>200) occurred at Knapwell (RSPB Grange Farm), Melbourn and to the east of Royston.

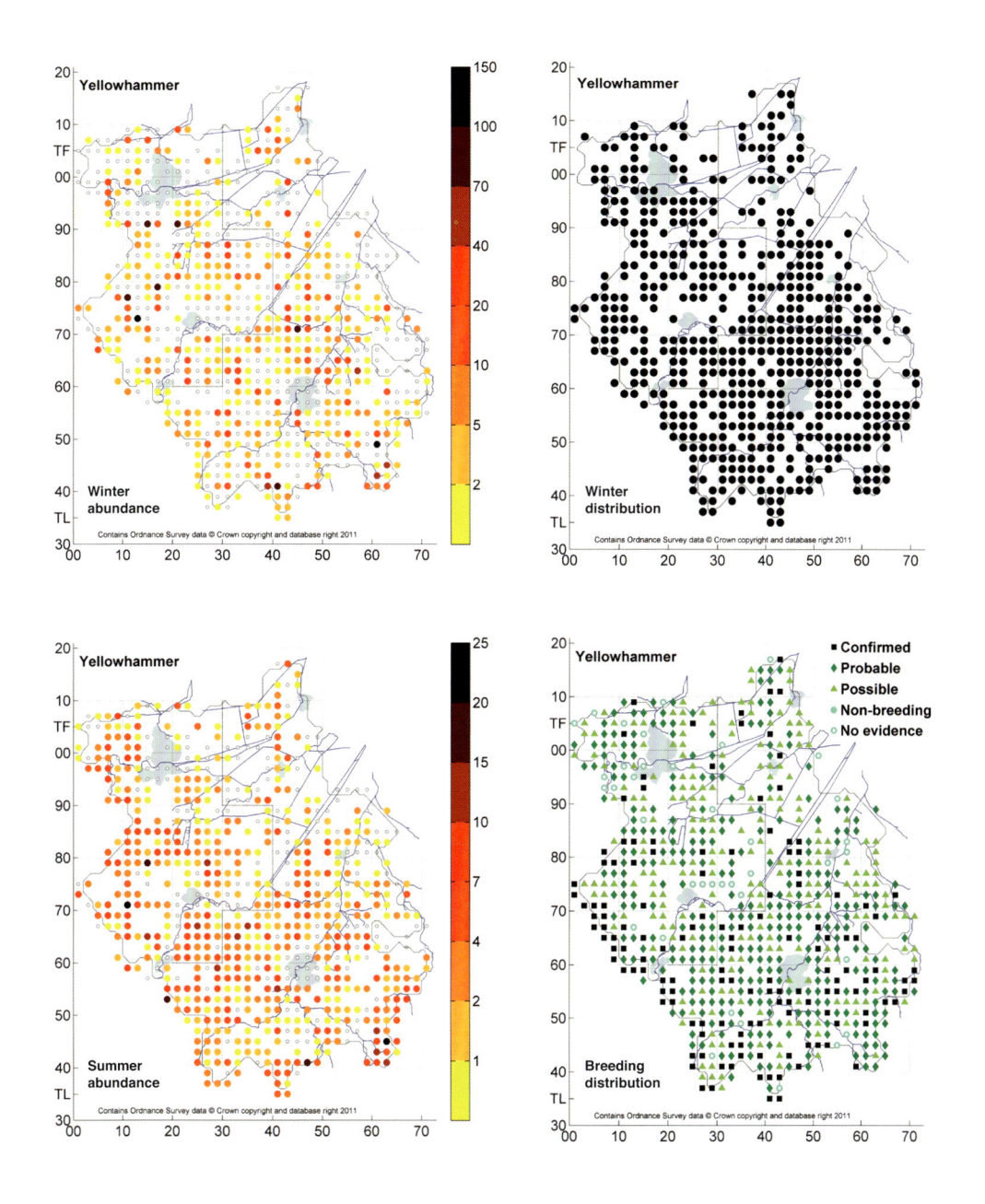

	Confirmed	Probable	Possible	Non-breeding	No evidence	Total summer (% county)	Total winter (% county)
Total tetrads	140	313	235	0	38	726 (75%)	563 (58%)

REED BUNTING (Common Reed Bunting) *Emberiza schoeniclus*
Amber List. Locally common, but declined, resident and passage migrant

Breeding population estimate: 3,000-10,000 pairs
Wintering population estimate: 6,000-25,000 individuals

Reed Buntings ought to thrive in a county with so much wetland and ditch and dyke systems. This is reflected in the breeding-season distribution map showing that Reed Buntings occur widely across the county, other than on higher ground underlain by limestone in the north-west and chalk in the south-east where their preferred wetland habitat is scarce. The tetrads with greatest abundance in the breeding season are found across the fens and in the main river valleys, with clusters of high abundance around the Nene Washes, the Great Fen Project area, the Ouse Washes and Wicken Fen. On lower ground and in valleys where wetlands are absent, Reed Buntings will breed in oilseed rape. There is no evidence of any decline in distribution from either of the previous two local atlases.

The winter distribution map shows that Reed Buntings have a similar distribution to that of summer, and with similar areas of high abundance. The current winter abundance appears similar to the findings in 1981–84 of the Wintering Atlas (Lack, 1986).

As with other buntings, population levels have fallen over the long term. The 30-year trend for the Reed Bunting in England suggests a decline of 20% (Baillie *et al.*, 2012), however, the 15-year (1995–2010) trends in England and Eastern England are increases of 28% in both areas (Risely *et al.*, 2012). There was a rapid decline in the 1970s, probably associated with agricultural intensification, then a period of stability, followed by a more recent increase which may be related to feeding in winter at game cover and at feeders.

Ringing studies indicate that UK Reed Buntings remain in the country for the winter and are joined by a small number of birds from Scandinavia (Wernham *et al.*, 2002). At a finer scale some birds from Eastern England, including birds ringed in the breeding season in the fens, move south or south-west within England in the winter.

The peak winter counts occurred at Burnt Fen, Shippea Hill, Kingfishers Bridge, Colne Fen gravel pits, Spaldwick, Fowlmere and Melbourn.

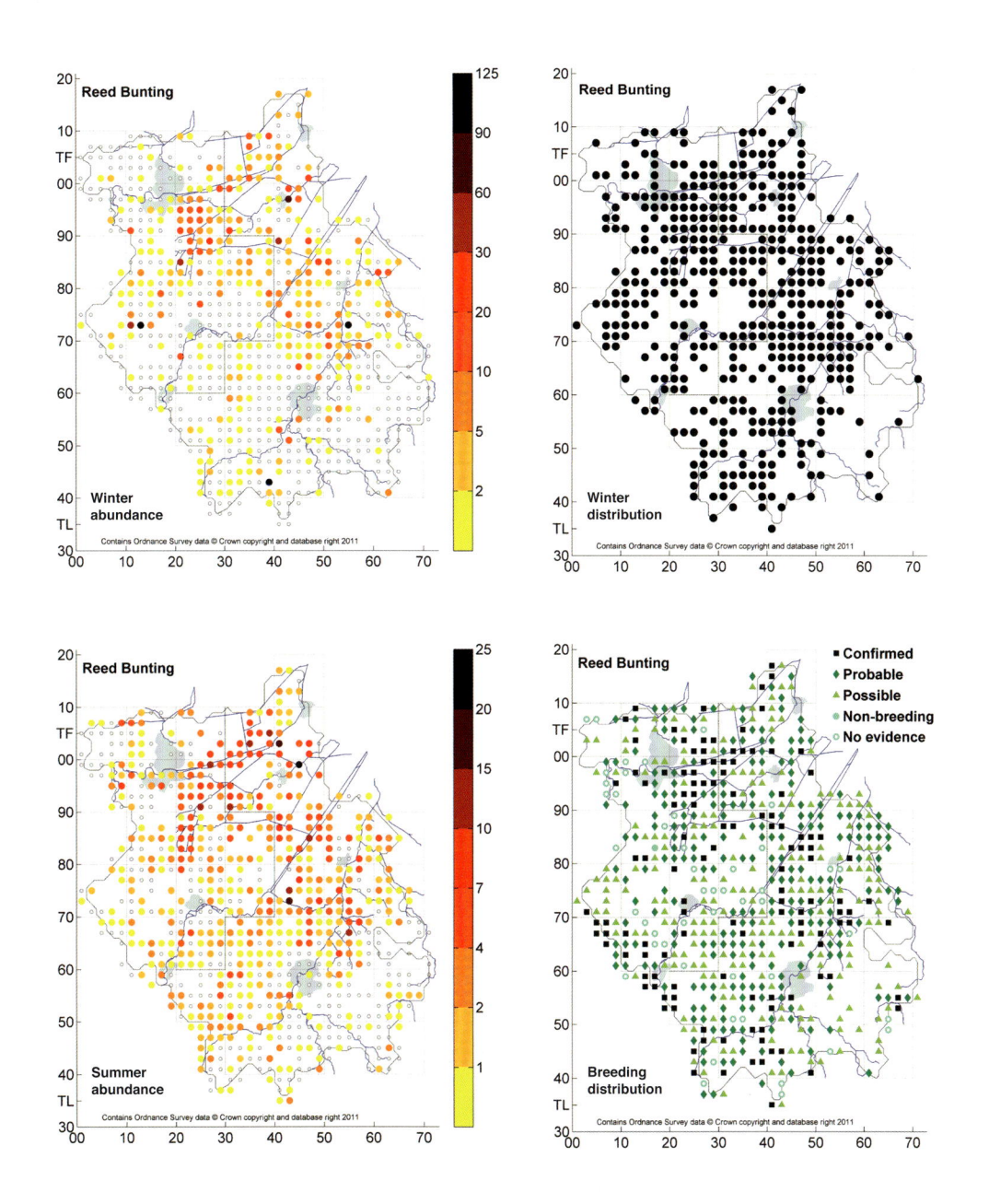

	Confirmed	Probable	Possible	Non-breeding	No evidence	Total summer (% county)	Total winter (% county)
Total tetrads	128	248	220	1	47	644 (66%)	468 (48%)

CORN BUNTING *Emberiza calandra*
Red List. Fairly common, but greatly declined, local resident

Breeding population estimate: 1,000-1,500 pairs
Wintering population estimate: 2,000-4,000 individuals

Corn Buntings, often considered to be associated with barley-growing, are undoubtedly less common than in the 1970s. The maps show that in the breeding season Corn Buntings occur throughout the fens and in the south of the county but are absent from the north-west and mid-west. This distribution possibly results from an avoidance of areas where, because of poor soils, there has historically been a higher density of woodland and small pasture fields. The tetrads with greatest abundance in the breeding season are found in the Great Fen Project area, the Ouse Washes, south and east of Earith, and in the extreme south of the county. The current breeding distribution in old Cambridgeshire is similar to that found in the previous Cambs Atlas. The current breeding distribution in Huntingdonshire and Peterborough shows some signs of a reduction in distribution relative to the previous Hunts Atlas in the south, and to the east of St. Neots, and an increase in distribution south-east of Peterborough.

The winter distribution map shows that Corn Buntings have a similar distribution to that of the summer. The current winter abundance appears to have increased in the fens compared to the findings of the Wintering Atlas (Lack, 1986) but such comparison may be subjective given that it is made between the current tetrad-based atlas and a 10-km square approach.

The size of the population decline is demonstrated in the long-term (30-year) trend for the breeding population in England – a decline of 87% (Baillie *et al.*, 2012). The 15-year (1995–2010) trends in England and Eastern England show continuing declines of 31% and 22%, respectively (Risely *et al.*, 2012). Changes in farming practices that have led to reduced invertebrate abundance for feeding chicks, reduced seed availability over the winter, and the loss of second broods to earlier harvested crops have been identified as potential causes of their decline.

Ringing studies indicate that Corn Buntings are largely sedentary, showing some short-distance dispersal away from breeding areas in winter; there is no evidence of continental birds wintering in England (Wernham *et al.*, 2002).

Peak winter counts (>100) occurred in the Great Fen Project area, north of Shippea Hill, north of Cottenham, at Whittlesford and at Melbourn.

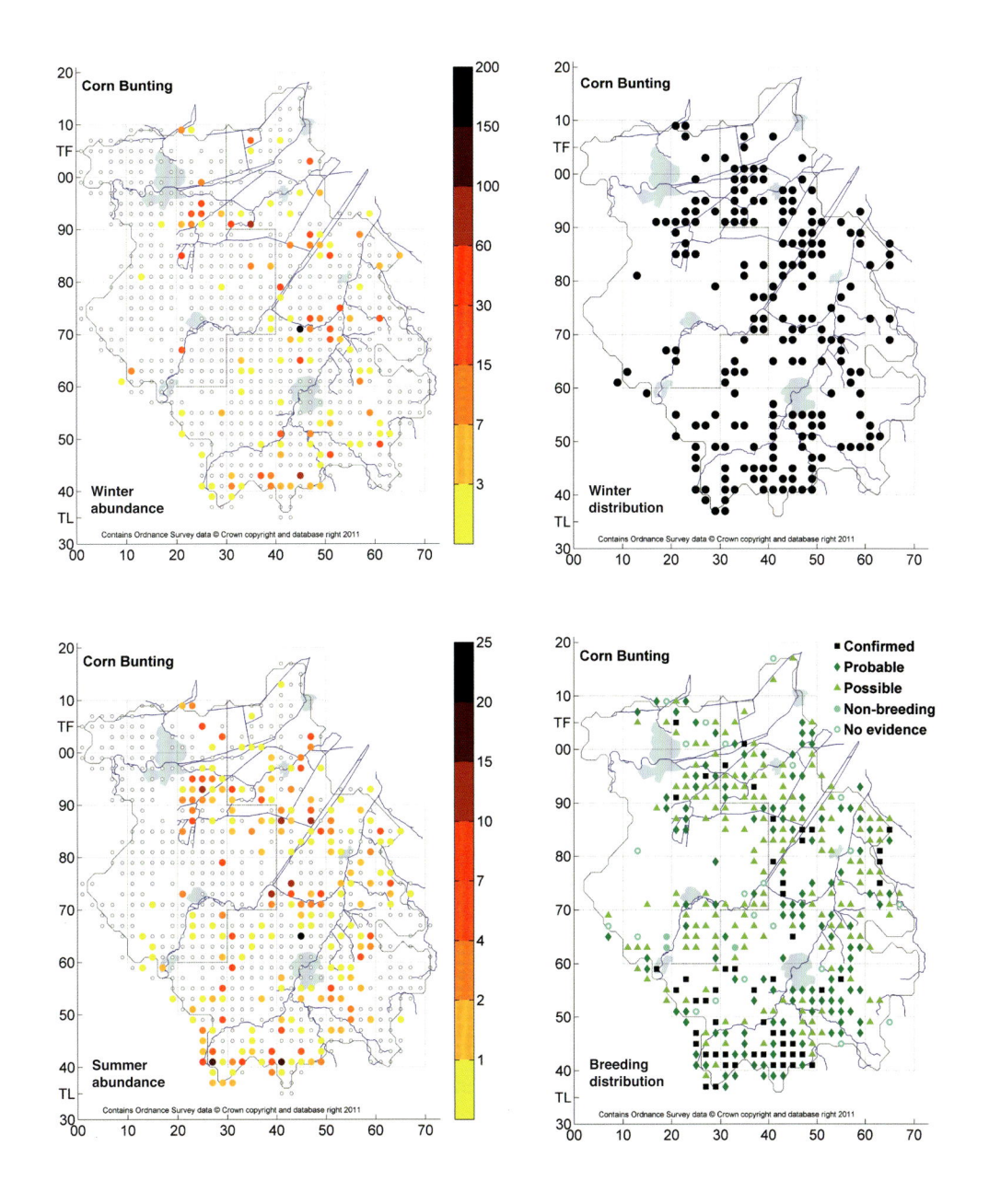

	Confirmed	Probable	Possible	Non-breeding	No evidence	Total summer (% county)	Total winter (% county)
Total tetrads	54	136	172	3	22	387 (40%)	202 (21%)

References

ADEBAR (in preparation). *Atlas Deutscher Brutvogelarten*. [German Breeding Bird Atlas]. Unpublished preliminary version of maps and species accounts.

Bacon, L., Herkenrath, P. & Radford, D.J. (2007). Cambridgeshire Bird Club Breeding Owl Survey 2004-2006. *Cambridgeshire Bird Report* **81**, 160–167.

Baillie, S.R., Marchant, J.H., Leech, D.I., Renwick, A.R., Eglington, S.M., Joys, A.C., Noble, D.G., Barimore, C., Conway, G.J., Downie, I.S., Risely, K. & Robinson, R.A. (2012). *BirdTrends 2011*. BTO Research Report **609**. British Trust for Ornithology, Thetford.

Baker, H., Stroud, D.A., Aebischer, N.J., Cranswick, P.A., Gregory, R.D., McSorley, C.A., Noble, D.G. & Rehfisch, M.M. (2006). Population estimates of birds of Great Britain and the United Kingdom. *British Birds* **99**, 25–44.

Bircham, P.M.M. (1989). *The Birds of Cambridgeshire*. Cambridge University Press.

Bircham, P.M.M., Rathmell, J.C.A. & Jordan, W.J. (1994). *An Atlas of the Breeding Birds of Cambridgeshire*. Cambridge Bird Club. **(Cambs Atlas 1994)**

Brown, A. & Grice, P. (2005). *Birds in England*. T. & A.D. Poyser, London.

BTO (2013). Online Ringing Report: Recoveries – Buzzard.

Cadbury, J.C. & Rooney, M.S. (1982). Survey of breeding wildfowl and waders of wet grasslands in Cambridgeshire in 1980 and 1982. *Cambridge Bird Report* **56**, 28–34. Cambridge Bird Club.

Charman, E.C., Smith, K.W., Gruar, D.J., Dodd, S. & Grice, P.V. (2010). Characteristics of woods used recently and historically by Lesser Spotted Woodpeckers *Dendrocopos minor* in England. *Ibis* **152**, 543–555.

Clark, J.S. (1996). *The Birds of Huntingdonshire and Peterborough*. Hilton, Cambridgeshire.

Clark, J.S. (Ed.) (2000). *The Birds of Cambridgeshire: Checklist 2000*. Cambridge Bird Club.

Clark, J.S. (2008). Species which no longer breed in the county. *Cambridgeshire Bird Report* **82**, 167–182.

Clements, R. (2000). Range expansion of the Common Buzzard in Britain. *British Birds* **93**, 242–248.

Cramp, S. (ed) (1985). *The Birds of Europe, the Middle East and North Africa. The Birds of the Western Palearctic. Volume IV (Terns to Woodpeckers)*. Oxford University Press, Oxford.

Easy, G.M.S. (1996). The Rook *Corvus frugilegus* in Cambridgeshire. *Nature in Cambridgeshire* **38**, 55–61.

Eaton, M.A., Brown, A.F., Noble, D.G., Musgrove, A.J., Hearn, R.D., Aebischer, N.J., Gibbons, D.W., Evans, A. & Gregory, R.D. (2009). Birds of Conservation Concern 3: the population status of birds in the United Kingdom, Channel Islands and the Isle of Man. *British Birds* **102**, 296–341.

Eaton, M.A., Cuthbert, R., Dunn, E., Grice, P.V., Hall, C., Hayhow, D.B., Hearn, R.D., Holt, C.A., Knipe, A., Marchant, J.H., Mavor, R., Moran, N.J., Mukhida, F., Musgrove, A.J., Noble, D.G., Oppel, S., Risely, K., Stroud, D.A., Toms, M. & Wotton, S. (2012). *The State of the UK's Birds 2012*. RSPB, BTO, WWT, CCW, NE, NIEA, SNH and JNCC, Sandy, Bedfordshire.

Gibbons, D.W., Reid, J.B. & Chapman, R.A. (1993). *The New Atlas of Breeding Birds in Britain and Ireland 1988–1991*. T. & A.D. Poyser, London.

Gillings, S. & Fuller, R.J. (2009). How many European Golden Plovers *Pluvialis apricaria* and Northern Lapwings *Vanellus vanellus* winter in Great Britain? Results from a large-scale survey in 2006/07. *Wader Study Group Bulletin* **116**, 21–28.

Hagemeijer, W.J.M. & Blair, M.J. (1997). *The EBCC Atlas of European Breeding Birds*. T. & A.D. Poyser, London.

Holling, M. & the Rare Breeding Birds Panel (2012). Rare Breeding Birds in the United Kingdom, 2010. *British Birds* **105**, 352–416.

Holloway, S. (1996). T*he Historical Atlas of Breeding Birds in Britain and Ireland 1875–1900*. T. & A.D. Poyser, London.

Holt, C., Austin, G., Calbrade, N., Mellan, H., Hearn, R., Stroud, D.A., Wotton, S. & Musgrove, A.J. (2012). *Waterbirds in the UK 2010/11 - The Wetland Bird Survey*. BTO/RSPB/JNCC, Thetford.

Isted, R. (2011). Blackcaps wintering in a suburban garden. *Cambridgeshire Bird Report* **84**, 151–153.

Jarman, R. (2012). The disappearance of three species of woodland breeding birds in Cambridgeshire. *Cambridgeshire Bird Report* **85**, 163–167.

Lack, P. (1986). *The Atlas of Wintering Birds in Britain and Ireland*. T. & A.D. Poyser, London.

Limentani, J., Elliott, G. & Everett, M. (1988). *The Breeding Birds of Huntingdonshire and Peterborough 1979–83*. Elliott and Everett Enterprises. **(Hunts Atlas 1988)**

Mason, C.F. (1998). Habitats of the Song Thrush *Turdus philomelos* in a largely arable landscape. *Journal of the Zoological Society of London* **244**, 89–93.

Mitchell, C., Hearn, R.D. & Stroud, D.A. (2012). The merging populations of Greylag Geese breeding in Britain. *British Birds* **105**, 498–505.

Musgrove, A.J., Aebischer, N.J, Eaton, M.A, Hearn, R.O, Newson, S.E, Noble, D.G, Parsons, M.A, Risely, K. & Stroud, D.A. (2013). Population estimates of birds in Great Britain and the United Kingdom. *British Birds* **106**, 64–100.

Musgrove, A.J., Austin, G.E., Hearn, R.D., Holt, C.A., Stroud, D.A. & Wotton, S.R. (2011). Overwinter population estimates of British waterbirds. *British Birds* **104**, 364–397.

Newson, S.E., Evans, K.L., Noble, D.G., Greenwood, J.J.D. & Gaston, K.J. (2008). Use of distance sampling to improve estimates of national population sizes for common and widespread breeding birds in the UK. *Journal of Applied Ecology* **45**, 1,330–1,338.

Nisbet, I.C.T. & Vine, A.E. (1955). Regular inland breeding of Shelducks in the fens. *British Birds* **48**, 362–363.

Parkin, D.T. & Knox, A.G. (2010). *The Status of Birds in Britain and Ireland*. Christopher Helm, London.

Parslow, J. (1973). *The Breeding Birds of Britain and Ireland: Historical Survey*. T. & A.D. Poyser, London.

Pettifor, R.A. (1984). Habitat utilisation and the prey taken by Kestrels in arable fenland. *Bird Study* **31**, 213–216.

Prince, P.A. & Clarke, R. (1993). The Hobby's breeding range in Britain: what factors have allowed it to expand? *British Wildlife* **4**, 341–346.

Rebecca, G.W. (2011). Spatial and habitat-related influences on the breeding performance of Merlins in Britain. *British Birds* **104**, 202–216.

Risely, K., Massimino, D., Johnston, A., Newson, S.E., Eaton, M.A., Musgrove, A.J., Noble, D.G., Procter, D. & Baillie, S.R. (2012). *The Breeding Bird Survey 2011*. BTO Research Report **624**. British Trust for Ornithology, Thetford.

Sharrock, J.T.R. (1976). The Atlas of Breeding Birds in Britain and Ireland. T. & A.D. Poyser, Berkhamstead.

Siriwardena, G.M., Baillie, S.R. & Wilson, J.D. (1998). Variation in the survival rates of British passerines with respect to their population on farmland. *Bird Study* **45**, 276–292.

Smith, K.W. & Charman, E.C. (2012). The ecology and conservation of the Lesser Spotted Woodpecker. *British Birds* **105**, 294–307.

Taylor, M. & Marchant, J.H. (2007). *The Norfolk Bird Atlas: Summer and Winter Distributions 1999–2007*. BTO Books, Thetford.

Wernham, C., Toms, M., Marchant, J.H, Clark, J., Siriwardena, G.M & Baillie, S.R (2002). *The Migration Atlas*. T. & A.D. Poyser, London.

APPENDIX

All species recorded in Cambridgeshire during the four summer and winter seasons (2007–2011) of the atlas. TTV % tetrads: the percentage of tetrads where the species was recorded on timed visits, combined for both visits within a season; birds/hour: the average count on timed visits per hour of surveying; roving tetrads: the number of tetrads in which the species was recorded for all records during the atlas. Species with more than five records in either season are featured in the preceding species accounts. Note that some winter visitors appear in the summer list, as they were encountered in low numbers in April or even May prior to northward migration. Species (races in italics) on the County List are given first, followed by species considered to be escapes.

2013 CBC code	Species name	Winter TTV % tetrads	Winter birds/hour	Winter roving tetrads	Summer TTV % tetrads	Summer birds/hour	Summer roving tetrads
1	Mute Swan	37	2	366	31	1.1	332
2	Bewick's Swan	3.7	1.4	89			3
3	Whooper Swan	5.2	2.3	105	0.28	<0.01	14
4	Bean Goose			2			
5	*Taiga Bean Goose*			5			
	Tundra Bean Goose			8			
6	Pink-footed Goose	0.65	0.04	25			3
7	White-fronted Goose			8			2
8	*Greenland White-fronted Goose*			1			
	European White-fronted Goose			10			
10	Greylag Goose	15	2.4	182	23	1.7	257
12	Canada Goose	14	2	178	21	1.1	235
14	Barnacle Goose	0.65	<0.01	23	0.55	<0.01	17
15	Brent Goose			5			3
	Dark-bellied Brent Goose			7			
18	Egyptian Goose	1.7	0.01	26	0.55	<0.01	27
20	Shelduck	3.7	0.1	54	5.3	0.1	101
21	Mandarin Duck	1	0.01	18	0.28	<0.01	18
22	Wigeon	11	14	134	2.2	0.04	50
24	Gadwall	11	1.3	140	8.2	0.26	107
26	Teal	14	2.7	178	3	0.12	64
27	Green-winged Teal						2
28	Mallard	57	6.7	570	67	3.4	678
30	Pintail	3	1.3	51	0.28	<0.01	15
31	Garganey			2	1.1	<0.01	34
32	Blue-winged Teal						4
33	Shoveler	6.6	0.57	98	5.4	0.22	77
34	Red-crested Pochard	0.26	<0.01	19	0.41	<0.01	13
36	Pochard	8.9	1.3	115	2.5	0.04	55
39	Ferruginous Duck			1			2
40	Tufted Duck	18	3.3	195	18	0.66	212
41	Scaup	0.39	<0.01	24			6
47	Long-tailed Duck			4			
48	Common Scoter			7			4
51	Velvet Scoter			1			
54	Goldeneye	3.6	0.11	54	0.28	<0.01	18
56	Smew	0.52	<0.01	20			
57	Red-breasted Merganser	0.26	<0.01	4			2

2013 CBC code	Species name	Winter TTV % tetrads	Winter birds/hour	Winter roving tetrads	Summer TTV % tetrads	Summer birds/hour	Summer roving tetrads
58	Goosander	1.7	0.02	47			3
59	Ruddy Duck	0.39	<0.01	14	0.41	<0.01	6
64	Red-legged Partridge	55	2.7	564	65	1.1	677
65	Grey Partridge	14	0.3	212	18	0.16	296
66	Quail				1.1	<0.01	67
67	Pheasant	83	2.7	792	89	2.3	843
73	Great Northern Diver			2			2
77	Fulmar						4
93	Gannet						2
94	Cormorant	25	0.51	273	18	0.23	231
97	Shag			3			2
100	Bittern	0.26	<0.01	49	0.55	<0.01	21
103	Night-heron						2
105	Squacco Heron						2
106	Cattle Egret			4			7
108	Little Egret	5.8	0.04	128	6.5	0.08	113
109	Great White Egret	0.26	<0.01	11			10
110	Grey Heron	36	0.33	396	30	0.29	389
116	Spoonbill						5
118	Little Grebe	13	0.13	169	9.3	0.11	130
119	Great Crested Grebe	13	0.23	139	15	0.26	188
120	Red-necked Grebe			2			
121	Slavonian Grebe			1			
122	Black-necked Grebe	0.39	<0.01	6	0.28	<0.01	13
123	Honey-buzzard						2
125	Red Kite	8.4	0.07	132	9.7	0.06	205
129	Marsh Harrier	3.5	0.02	66	10	0.07	203
130	Hen Harrier	1.6	<0.01	90			21
132	Montagu's Harrier						13
133	Goshawk	0.26	<0.01	2			4
134	Sparrowhawk	37	0.18	464	26	0.11	421
135	Buzzard	46	0.34	565	44	0.32	616
136	Rough-legged Buzzard			4			
139	Osprey						25
141	Kestrel	75	0.59	765	65	0.44	735
143	Red-footed Falcon						11
145	Merlin	3.1	0.01	83	0.28	<0.01	15
146	Hobby				10	0.04	298
149	Peregrine	3.5	0.01	75	0.28	<0.01	22
150	Water Rail	4.3	0.02	84	0.97	<0.01	38
151	Spotted Crake						3
155	Corncrake				0.28	<0.01	3
156	Moorhen	60	2.3	571	64	1.2	631
159	Coot	26	5.6	266	31	1.7	331
161	Crane			9	0.41	<0.01	27
166	Oystercatcher	1.6	0.01	36	6.5	0.06	131
167	Black-winged Stilt						2
168	Avocet			1	1.4	0.02	33
169	Stone-curlew	0.26	<0.01	1	0.28	<0.01	9
174	Little Ringed Plover				1.9	0.02	71
175	Ringed Plover	0.26	<0.01	8	0.69	<0.01	32

2013 CBC code	Species name	Winter TTV % tetrads	Winter birds/hour	Winter roving tetrads	Summer TTV % tetrads	Summer birds/hour	Summer roving tetrads
183	Dotterel						7
184	American Golden Plover			1			
186	Golden Plover	18	13	249	0.55	0.11	57
187	Grey Plover			7			23
190	Lapwing	35	21	436	33	1.5	422
192	Knot						3
193	Sanderling			1			16
197	Little Stint			5			4
198	Temminck's Stint						10
205	Curlew Sandpiper						5
207	Purple Sandpiper			1			
208	Dunlin	0.9	0.01	29	0.28	<0.01	38
210	Buff-breasted Sandpiper						2
211	Ruff	1.4	0.05	29			15
212	Jack Snipe	0.9	<0.01	34			5
213	Snipe	16	0.24	213	3.9	0.11	84
218	Woodcock	7.6	0.04	150			17
219	Black-tailed Godwit	1.7	0.41	33	1.5	0.06	50
222	Bar-tailed Godwit			1			17
226	Whimbrel				0.69	<0.01	55
228	Curlew	0.65	<0.01	45	0.97	<0.01	67
231	Common Sandpiper	0.26	<0.01	5	1.8	<0.01	62
233	Green Sandpiper	3.1	0.01	70	0.55	<0.01	73
236	Spotted Redshank			2	0.28	<0.01	13
238	Greenshank			3	0.28	<0.01	49
241	Wood Sandpiper				0.28	<0.01	18
242	Redshank	4.7	0.12	71	6.2	0.23	86
244	Turnstone	0.26	<0.01	6			23
254	Kittiwake						5
257	Black-headed Gull	76	19	742	34	1.7	390
258	Little Gull			2			6
262	Mediterranean Gull	0.26	<0.01	5			18
265	Common Gull	42	2.8	514	2.9	0.21	80
266	Ring-billed Gull	0.26	<0.01	1			
267	Lesser Black-backed Gull	26	1.3	331	18	0.69	262
269	Herring Gull	21	1.3	249	7.1	0.2	126
271	Yellow-legged Gull	0.26	<0.01	27	0.28	<0.01	8
272	Caspian Gull			13			
274	Iceland Gull			6			6
277	Glaucous Gull			9			3
278	Great Black-backed Gull	5.8	0.1	121	0.83	0.01	34
282	Little Tern						6
285	Whiskered Tern						6
286	Black Tern						32
287	White-winged Black Tern						2
289	Sandwich Tern						13
293	Common Tern				16	0.27	209
295	Arctic Tern						29
307	Feral Pigeon	26	1.8	272	26	1.1	306
308	Stock Dove	57	2.3	607	71	1.4	753
309	Woodpigeon	100	120	925	100	30	933

2013 CBC code	Species name	Winter TTV % tetrads	Winter birds/hour	Winter roving tetrads	Summer TTV % tetrads	Summer birds/hour	Summer roving tetrads
310	Collared Dove	76	5.1	719	82	4	783
311	Turtle Dove				21	0.14	345
314	Ring-necked Parakeet			1	0.28	<0.01	4
316	Cuckoo				21	0.13	270
319	Barn Owl	7.8	0.03	262	10	0.05	427
323	Little Owl	6.8	0.03	120	10	0.06	220
324	Tawny Owl	1.8	<0.01	140	2.6	0.01	182
325	Long-eared Owl	0.26	<0.01	10	0.41	<0.01	32
326	Short-eared Owl	1	0.01	45	0.28	<0.01	29
334	Swift				56	2	608
339	Kingfisher	11	0.05	168	9	0.05	183
345	Wryneck						2
346	Green Woodpecker	62	0.46	591	72	0.68	670
348	Great Spotted Woodpecker	58	0.43	584	51	0.4	538
349	Lesser Spotted Woodpecker	0.65	<0.01	14	0.55	<0.01	22
354	Golden Oriole						3
360	Great Grey Shrike			2			2
365	Magpie	91	2.3	828	85	1.6	783
366	Jay	40	0.36	416	30	0.19	340
368	Jackdaw	83	13	782	84	5.6	800
370	Rook	80	26	749	71	9.7	692
371	Carrion Crow	96	6.4	890	97	4.3	904
373	Raven	0.26	<0.01	4			7
374	Goldcrest	29	0.25	337	19	0.14	243
375	Firecrest	0.26	<0.01	6	0.28	<0.01	20
377	Blue Tit	98	5.7	869	95	4	845
378	Great Tit	95	3.7	841	93	2.8	839
381	Coal Tit	17	0.14	227	15	0.13	230
382	Willow Tit	0.26	<0.01	2	0.28	<0.01	2
383	Marsh Tit	9.8	0.09	106	8.4	0.07	105
384	Bearded Tit	0.39	<0.01	14	0.28	<0.01	8
392	Woodlark			2			
393	Skylark	67	4.1	661	88	4.1	840
395	Sand Martin				9.5	0.44	145
399	Swallow				88	3.1	854
400	House Martin				46	1.4	504
401	Red-rumped Swallow						2
403	Cetti's Warbler	0.78	<0.01	23	2.6	0.02	60
404	Long-tailed Tit	71	2.7	668	60	1.1	603
416	Wood Warbler				0.28	<0.01	9
417	Chiffchaff	1.7	0.01	45	70	1.1	651
421	Willow Warbler				41	0.52	431
422	Blackcap	1.6	<0.01	79	81	1.7	743
423	Garden Warbler				22	0.17	269
425	Lesser Whitethroat				33	0.25	438
429	Whitethroat				87	2.8	836
438	Grasshopper Warbler				3.7	0.03	112
446	Icterine Warbler						2
449	Sedge Warbler				32	0.71	351
453	Reed Warbler				35	1	383

2013 CBC code	Species name	Winter TTV % tetrads	Winter birds/hour	Winter roving tetrads	Summer TTV % tetrads	Summer birds/hour	Summer roving tetrads
457	Waxwing	0.26	0.02	82			8
460	Nuthatch	6.7	0.05	73	6.8	0.05	86
461	Treecreeper	12	0.08	169	14	0.09	184
463	Wren	88	1.9	799	97	4.6	879
467	Starling	87	26	804	81	7.4	777
478	Ring Ouzel			3	0.41	<0.01	33
479	Blackbird	100	10	899	99	7.7	914
485	Fieldfare	88	29	829	2.9	0.31	101
486	Song Thrush	73	0.94	688	79	1.2	739
488	Redwing	75	7.3	696	0.55	<0.01	11
489	Mistle Thrush	56	0.64	563	49	0.51	556
493	Spotted Flycatcher				9.1	0.05	211
494	Robin	96	4.2	856	96	3.7	863
502	Nightingale				2.6	0.02	63
507	Pied Flycatcher						2
508	Black Redstart	0.26	<0.01	5	0.28	<0.01	19
509	Redstart				0.41	<0.01	22
513	Whinchat				0.41	<0.01	36
515	Stonechat	8.9	0.09	128	0.41	<0.01	14
517	Wheatear				4.8	0.03	178
523	Dunnock	89	2.1	795	89	2.2	827
525	House Sparrow	70	6.5	662	81	7	774
527	Tree Sparrow	8.3	0.27	127	5	0.10	74
529	Yellow Wagtail				36	0.51	482
533	Grey Wagtail	7.1	0.03	139	4.4	0.02	117
534	Pied Wagtail	65	1.2	639	60	0.58	652
535	*White Wagtail (alba)*			2			12
540	Tree Pipit				0.28	<0.01	7
542	Meadow Pipit	47	1.4	464	27	0.43	319
544	Rock Pipit			1			4
546	Water Pipit	0.9	<0.01	12			8
548	Chaffinch	98	9.2	881	99	7	909
550	Brambling	5.7	0.11	111			25
551	Greenfinch	80	3	743	91	3	826
554	Goldfinch	85	5.5	781	91	3.4	858
555	Siskin	7.9	0.24	147	0.55	<0.01	39
556	Linnet	28	3.3	325	70	2.1	701
557	Twite	0.26	<0.01	4			
558	Lesser Redpoll	4.8	0.09	116	0.41	<0.01	12
559	Mealy Redpoll			3			
563	Common Crossbill			3	0.28	<0.01	40
567	Common Rosefinch						3
569	Bullfinch	43	0.64	432	30	0.29	365
571	Hawfinch	0.26	<0.01	9			3
573	Snow Bunting			3			
574	Lapland Bunting	0.26	<0.01	3			
588	Yellowhammer	54	2.6	563	76	1.9	726
598	Reed Bunting	42	1.4	468	64	1.3	644
601	Corn Bunting	14	0.78	202	28	0.52	387

2013 CBC code	Species name	Winter TTV % tetrads	Winter birds/hour	Winter roving tetrads	Summer TTV % tetrads	Summer birds/hour	Summer roving tetrads
Escapes							
	Black Swan	0.52	<0.01	12	0.55	<0.01	10
	Ross's Goose			7			2
	Snow Goose			1			
	Lesser White-fronted Goose	0.26	<0.01	1			
	Greylag Goose (domestic)	0.26	<0.01	14	0.55	0.01	23
	Red-breasted Goose			3			
	Bar-headed Goose	0.26	<0.01	6	0.28	<0.01	6
	Ruddy Shelduck			1			3
	Muscovy Duck	0.52	0.03	9	0.41	0.02	5
	Wood Duck	0.26	<0.01	5	0.28	<0.01	4
	Mallard (domestic)	1.6	0.14	56	2.5	0.09	55
	Rosy-billed Pochard	0.26	<0.01	1			
	Hooded Merganser						2
	Golden Pheasant				0.28	<0.01	2
	Reeves's Pheasant				0.28	<0.01	2
	Helmeted Guineafowl			1	0.41	0.01	5
	Indian Peafowl	0.39	<0.01	4	1.1	<0.01	17
	Northern Bobwhite						2
	Harris's Hawk			1			
	Eastern Rosella	0.26	<0.01	1			
	Zebra Finch						2